Ecclesia: The Long Journey to Tomorrow

Ecclesia: The Long Journey to Tomorrow

Ecclesia a Long Journey to Tomorrow

Deslee Campbell

Published by Deslee Campbell, 2024.

While every precaution has been taken in the preparation of this book, the publisher assumes no responsibility for errors or omissions, or for damages resulting from the use of the information contained herein.

ECCLESIA A LONG JOURNEY TO TOMORROW

First edition. June 3, 2024.

ISBN: 979-8227988089

Written by Deslee Campbell.

Table of Contents

Prologue

Ecclesia: The Long Journey to Tomorrow

This book, Ecclesia: The Long Journey to Tomorrow, is the second of two well-researched, up-to-the minute books in the mini-series Synagogue and Church, by mother-and-son duo Rev. Justin Campbell and Dr Deslee Campbell.

This, the second volume is about Ecclesia, the personification of the Church who is pictured on the front cover. This volume will explain how Christianity (i.e., the Church) here called by the Greek term Ecclesia, travelled and progressed through the turbulent centuries in the post-Constantinian era, having separated from her spiritual mother, Synagoga, to become more numerous and the more politically powerful through the centuries, down to today.

Ecclesia: The Long Journey to Tomorrow is a handbook, written for Bible College students, for 'the Christian in the pew', for school and college students of religious education, studies in religion and/or church history, for 'gap-year' students and interns with missions and Christian NGOs and for undergraduate students of theology and especially for the supporters of the Jewish roots of Christianity. Both pastors and students will find much of interest in its pages and in its plans, photographs and drawings.

This book will present such readers with recent discoveries, discussion and analysis in a manner that can benefit

churchgoers as well as help students and clergy. Ecclesia: The Long Journey to Tomorrow will consider topics such as: 'how Christian tradition and teaching began with Jesus and St Paul', 'Roman persecution over three centuries', 'Celtic Christianity',

'the Reformation', 'Ecclesia in America, Australia and Britain', 'the Missionary Movement', 'the 20th Century' and finally, the future, which is now covered with fog because of the pandemic.

Jewish-Christian interactions and the contribution of women to Ecclesia over its history will form important elements.

Ecclesia: The Long Journey to Tomorrow is more a book of history and ecclesiology than of theology. Where the chronological sequence is known, it is followed. Coverage of topics will be uneven as this book is an overview and a basis for further investigation of topics of interest, aided by its extensive bibliography. Such a short book will select the most relevant episodes in the vast history of Ecclesia beginning with Jesus' earthly lifespan and the Apostolic period. This volume will show the reader how the great personalities and political events of the Judeo-Christian world have come together to create the colourful tapestry of the Christian world in the 21st century.

Many people have assisted us in the production of this mini-series. Our first thanks must go to our wonder photographer, Mr Ian Finnin, for a task so willingly and professionally completed. Secondly, we are indebted to numerous academics and others for great and freely given assistance for one or both volumes of the Series Synagoga and Ecclesia : to Israeli Professors Boaz Zissu; Eilat Mazar and Asher Ovadiah; to Drs Meridel and Jay Rawlings; to Father Juan Maria Solana and Professor Marcela Zapata-Moza of the Magdala Project. Assistance was also given from North America: from Professor Lawrence Welborn in the U.S.A. and Professor John Kloppenborg in Canada and in Australia, kind assistance was provided by Emeritus Professor Alanna Nobbs, Rev. Dr John Dixon, Rev. Robert Evans, Rev. Dr John Reid and Mrs Glenda Valais. We thank them all most sincerely.

We also thank family members: Michael, David, Beth, Marnie and Heidi Campbell for their patience and help in 100 important ways without which the work could not have been completed.

Rev. Justin Campbell and Dr. Deslee Campbell

Chapter 1
Introduction

This work is the second of two volumes in the series Synagogue and Church. It concerns the sweep of Christian history over more than three thousand years, two millennia of that being the era of the Church; Ecclesia's era. Volume 1, Synagoga's Heritage: Tabernacle, Temple, Synagogue and Church has brought the reader up to the earliest days of the earthly life of Jesus of Nazareth and the origins of the Church in Old Testament (or the days of Temple Judaism) that is, the days before Rabbinic Judaism developed after the destruction of Jerusalem and the Temple in 70 CE. So that this volume can stand alone if necessary there is some overlap between the two volumes, although this volume moves the narrative forward, up to the 21st century. It will explain how the multi-denominational, international church of today has emerged and, lastly, will consider its future.

Plates 1.1 and 1.2.

Ecclesia and *Synagoga* of Strasbourg.

The cover of this book, 'Ecclesia: the Long Journey to Tomorrow', shows an image from the façade of a famous French landmark, the Cathedral at Metz. She is Ecclesia, the Church. Although the term Ecclesia Kyriou in the Old Testament first meant 'congregation of the Lord' (that is, the Jewish people) believers in Jesus could, and did, legitimately apply the term to themselves (Deut. 23:21; I Chron. 21:8;

Hurtardo, 1999, 54f). In Greek, ekklēsia, meant the gathered population of a Greek city-state or a mass assembly, much as the Greek loan-word synagoga meant in Judaism (Ferguson, 1996, 130f; James 5:14 and 2:2). Both words would, however, soon become terms for the building in which each group met.

Jesus, James and Paul chose to use the word ekklesia/ecclesia and altogether it was used 114 times in the New Testament,

but with various meanings, as in Eph. 1:23 (His body and the fullness of Him who fills all in all); Eph. 3:10-11 (God' Eternal Purpose); Eph 5:23 (His body); Eph 5:29-30 (His holy and loved one) (Frost and Hirsch, 2009, 169ff). The term has overtones of massed assembly, unity of purpose and social similarities. It was also used for community meetings (Frost and Hirsch, 2009, 31). Jesus, however, used the word with a special connotation, which it still has: a corporate or group entity that meets together in his name (Mat. 18:20). Driscoll and Breshears, 2008, 28) define it as:

"a community of regenerated believers who confess Jesus Christ as Lord. In obedience to Scripture they organise under qualified leadership, gather regularly for preaching and worship, observe the biblical sacraments of baptism and communion, are unified by the Spirit, are disciplined for holiness, and scatter to fulfil the great commandment and the great commission for God's glory and their joy."

In the Middle Ages this concept was often made concrete via a female personification of the Church. Usually, as at Strasbourg Cathedral, the stone icon of Ecclesia is one of a pair. There, on the opposite side of the Great West Door stands a representation of Judaism (Synagoga): the one in Plate 1.2. The Strasbourg Ecclesia (in Plate 1.1) is presented as a queen with a crown, a cloak, a banner and a chalice, which are her usual attributes. [1]

As at Strasbourg, an image of Ecclesia is usually depicted in Europe on the exterior of the western wall of cathedrals. Her bearing is regal with face uplifted her cross-shaped banner of represents warfare or victory and her chalice represents the Mass, Holy Communion or Eucharist.

Plate 1.3.
Synagoga **of Paris. Photo: D. Campbell, 2005.**

Similar examples of this iconography can still be seen throughout Europe: as in Strasbourg (c.1239) (Plate 1.1); Paris (11631345); Bamberg (13th century); Metz (Plate 1.4a) and Reims (1275). These cathedrals provide settings for dramatic monumental sculptures of these two female personifications: Ecclesia and Synagoga. Images of the pair also survive in cathedrals and minsters in England: in Rochester, Lincoln, Winchester, Salisbury, London and York.

Virtually invariably Ecclesia is balanced with, but contrasted with Synagoga. At Strasbourg, Synagoga has a broken staff and no crown. She is downcast, poorly clad and blindfolded (in Plate 1.2). At Notre Dame, Paris (in Plate 1.3), Synagoga appears to be blind, her staff is broken, her head is not uplifted and the tablets of the Ten Commandments she holds are slipping.[2] She is not crowned but wears a 'Jew hat' (a 'badge' of dishonour, worn by men in Appendix Plate 2.1).

There were other Medieval presentations of these two. For example stained-glass windows of the pair can also be seen in cathedrals at Freiburg, Chartres, Marburg, Châlon and the

Basilica of St Denis, Paris. In the early-14th-century stained-glass window in Freiburg Cathedral, a victorious Queen,

Ecclesia, carries her banner and chalice proudly and rides a war-horse in the spirit of the Crusades but blindfolded Synagoga barely manages to ride her donkey (Seiferth, 1970, 28). Synagoga's crown falls, her banner has broken and she is depicted wearing the yellow dress of a Jewess. Her attributes include a goat's head, which represents the Jewish sacrificial system. Whatever attributes she wears or carries she is often beautiful in her sorrow.

As in Plate 1.4a Ecclesia is always depicted standing strongly and triumphantly compared with her opposite number (as in Plate 1.4b) because Medieval Christians believed that the Church was triumphing over all other religions, including Judaism, which had the nearest claim to primacy being based upon the Old Testament of the Bible. The majestic cathedrals in the Latin/Roman Catholic world are evidence of the authority of Ecclesia. Christians who only know Europe have western perceptions and interpretations of religious art, although now European cathedrals are more 'tourist attractions' than 'houses of worship'. Originally these beautiful medieval European cathedrals announced the victory and splendour of European Christianity with its headquarters in Rome. This institution overshadowed the memory of Eastern Christianity, which was wealthier and more numerous at that time.

Hagia Sophia (Holy Wisdom), first built by the Byzantine Emperor Justinian in the 6th century, is the supreme example of the glory of Eastern Christianity. [4] By the 15th century (well after the Muslim conquest of virtually the whole of the Byzantine Empire, including the capital, Constantinople, now Istanbul), Hagia Sophia became a mosque and four minarets were built (Plate 1.5).

Now this amazing building is a museum and a tourist attraction and nearby Hagia Irene is used as a concert hall,

Plate 1.4a and 1.4b.
Ecclesia and *Synagoga* at Metz Cathedral, France.[3][3]

although recently Muslim worship has recommenced in Hagia Sophia, although its popularity with tourists and its moneymaking potential are still potent influences upon its future.

Plate 1.5.
Hagia Sophia, Istanbul, with added minarets.
Photograph: D. Campbell, 2008.

This volume is about Ecclesia, but Synagoga is vitally important because Christianity grew out of Judaism so that Old Testament Judaism was Ecclesia's spiritual mother. [5] Some readers may be shocked by this, but then some Christians are shocked to hear that Jesus was a Jew, who never went to church in his life and that neither Peter nor his wife had ever eaten non-kosher food because his mother-in-law kept a kosher kitchen (Acts 10:14).

This volume often refers back to Jews and Judaism in relation to the church. As will become clear, Synagoga has remained an important background figure in the life of Ecclesia until today. Each reader is encouraged to read Volume 1 of the Synagogue and Church series. Its title is Synagoga's Heritage: Tabernacle, Temple, Synagogue and Church.

This volume, 'Ecclesia,' picks up the narrative of the church's journey into the future. Issues which are considered across both volumes include: 'who or what is the church?', 'where did she come from?', 'how and where did she develop?', 'what was the ongoing relationship between Ecclesia with Synagoga', 'how can their sculptured personifications be interpreted', 'is the church correctly portrayed by these iconic images?', 'Ecclesia during two millennia', 'how is the Church going' and 'what of her future?' This is not a book of theology but of history, ecclesiology and a little missiology. Coverage of topics will, of necessity, be uneven as this book is an overview, a handbook and a basis for further investigation of topics of interest, aided by its useful bibliography, which includes many online sources. This work features more women than is usual in church history texts but men's stories can often be told through the lenses of their significant others.

<u>Readership</u>

'Ecclesia' is written for Bible College students, for 'the Christian in the pew', for senior school students, for college students of religious studies or church history, for 'gap-year'

students and interns with missions and for undergraduate students of theology. Pastors, students and the growing roll of devotees of the Jewish roots of Christianity will find much of interest within the pages of both volumes with their helpful plans, photographs and drawings and their easy reading style. There is an emphasis upon the people who contributed and not just 'the great ones': some

forgotten Christians will feature. Both volumes will present readers with recent discoveries, discussion and

analysis to benefit churchgoers as well as help students and clergy.

<u>Sources</u>

Documentary sources have been used as much as possible. Reputable scholarship that has stood the test of time but is readily accessible in college and seminary libraries has been used, where appropriate. Bible references are within the main body of text, as the convention requires. The Oxford Dictionary of the Christian Church (ODCC) is the standard for dating biographies and major events.

<u>Method</u>

This volume begins by recapping some material in Volume 1: Jesus, Paul and the Early Church. Each one of these chapters, however, even each section, would warrant whole tomes, perhaps whole libraries, for itself. It is impossible in a work of this length to more than highlight the highlights. Here the layout is user-friendly and the extensive bibliography,

including on-line sources, will lead Bible students in new directions. 'Ecclesia' may, at times, make uncomfortable

reading because it will challenge assumptions and even some scholarship from the 20th century, and earlier. Ecclesia's

history is constantly being rewritten: its archaeology, especially, is a fertile area for research. Through the ages, Ecclesia has included all sorts of folk but all have advanced the work of the Kingdom in life, even those who somehow 'fell from grace', as in the case of Dr Paul Yongi Choo, whose unfortunate story is noted but whose impact upon South Korea has been vast.

<u>Geographic Parameters</u>

This volume will concentrate on the Western Church, even though the earliest (Judaeo-Christian) church began in the East and divergence between East and West was not clear-cut until the Great Schism between them in 1045. Furthermore, all of the earliest growth of the church and most of the great early theologians were of the Greek-speaking East. The Early Church was birthed in the East: Europe was 'the mission-field' but a field that was unified by the Latin language.

<u>A note about art</u>

Paintings, sculptures and drawings informed the masses in an age before literacy was common, communicating both Bible stories and doctrines. Unlike Volume 1, this work deals with a period in which literacy was increasingly common and art was used more for decoration than educating and catechising the faithful. Therefore the printed word, the Book, became central to Ecclesia.

In the Eastern churches, however, icons (images) played an entirely different role, being windows by which the individual could enter into the world of the depicted saint, provided the identity of the saint was either written or identifiable by their usual and well-known attributes.

<u>Conclusions</u>

Christianity is coming full circle to value its heritage and learn from the past: to learn from the early saints, the early bishops and the martyrs. The desert mothers and fathers and the Celtic monastics of Britain are attracting renewed interest along with the pioneer missionaries and modern-day saints and martyrs (Waddell, 1998; Swan, 2001). Her heritage includes Ecclesia's roots in the Pentateuch/Torah, in the prophets' visions of shalom, justice and community and the Holy Spirit's work in the Book of Acts.

This book notes the Jesus Movement, the modern era, the worldwide spread of the gospel, new life in Christ and the hope for renewal (Ringma, 'Phronésis' 14.1, online, and 2, 2007, 70). It offers insights into how elements of the past helped spread Christianity into a worldwide faith and how successful elements and practices being embraced in the 21st century might assist more people and congregations today.

<u>Questions</u>: At the end of each chapter there will be questions for personal reflection and/or for group discussions.

For this chapter the question is: Do you expect that the theme of Judaism in relation to Christianity (which is obviously so important to Volume I, "Synagoga's Heritage: Tabernacle, Temple, Synagogue and Church") will be important in this volume? Why and/or why not?

Chapter 2
Jesus, Paul and the First Century Church

<u>2.1. Jesus</u>

The story of Ecclesia begins with Jesus of Nazareth, his life, his work, his death and his resurrection. Each of these elements is essential to the birth of the Church and the early Christians preached these four elements. Central to every sermon was "*Christ* (Messiah, Anointed One) *and him crucified*" (I Cor. 2:2). He was crucified just outside the walls of Jerusalem as they existed at that time: perhaps here on this hill, (Plate 2.1) or perhaps at the Church of the Holy Sepulchre (Plate 5.3), which is now within the Old City, but not originally.

Plate 2.1
'Place of a skull', Jerusalem.
Photograph: D. Campbell, 1988.

In Matthew 16:18 and 18:17 Jesus introduced the concept of his Ecclesia. Numerous biblical passages indicated its character.

It was to be inaugurated by baptism (Mat. 28:19) and characterized by love (Jn.15:12). It was to be communal (Mat. 18:20; Acts 2:44); universal

(Mat 28:19; Acts 1:7); centered around Jesus (Mat. 28:20); fruitful (Jn. 15:16) and everlasting (Mat. 28:20).

Saul of Tarsus, who was, at first, an angry opponent of Ecclesia, became the Apostle Paul, the giant of the early mission, largely because of the dying witness of the first martyr, the deacon Stephen (Acts 6). Through his death, Stephen's final witness to Jesus indirectly changed the known world, by changing Saul. He, as a Christian called Paul, undertook many wide-ranging missionary journeys around Asia Minor and the Mediterranean World, taking the gospel of Jesus as far afield as Rome and perhaps even to Spain. He was accompanied by a variety of companions, including Luke the physician, who wrote the Acts of the Apostles and the third gospel. Paul had great success but he suffered great hardships over decades and was eventually martyred.

While Paul was journeying, other apostles were also travelling in various directions and into different areas to preach. John (the son of Zebedee and Salome) apparently went to Ephesus; Peter (at first a business-partner of Zebedee) travelled throughout Israel (Acts 9:32) and in Asia. John-Mark accompanied Paul on the first journey to Cyprus and Asia before returning there with his relative, Barnabas, (Acts 15:39) and eventually travelling in Africa where he, too, was martyred (Eusebius, E.H., II. 16). Thomas Didymus is believed to have evangelised the Parthians and travelled to India where he was martyred and buried at Mylapore, near Madras ('Thomas, St., Apostle', in ODCC).

While Jesus' brother, James, was administering the home-base in Jerusalem as *"world head of Christianity"* (Barnett, 1999, 314),

his other brothers, Joseph/Joses, Simon and Jude, and their

believing wives, also travelled widely (I Cor. 9:5) (Epiphanius, On Weights and Measures 15). Except for James, who remained in Jerusalem to lead the church there, the early apostles, including Peter, were itinerant missionaries deliberately travelling on mission. Meanwhile others evangelized wherever they happened to be. Unnamed or lesser-known Christians were also busy travelling: for example Tychicus took various of Paul's epistles to Ephesus, Colossae and to Philemon (Col. 4:7-9; Eph. 6:21f) and Epaphroditus took his 'Epistle to the Philippians' to Philippi, returning with a gift during Paul's first imprisonment (Phil. 4:18) and

Silvanus took Peter's first epistle throughout Asia Minor (Turkey) (I Pet. 1:1; 5:12) presumably from Rome.

Prior to Paul's conversion (in about 34 CE) churches had already been founded in Syrian Antioch and as far away as Libya, Rome and Damascus (Acts 2:10). Ananias and/or the Judas of Acts 9:10-19 were members of the church in Damascus, although they don't seem to have known each other so perhaps there were two or more congregations there.

Material from the Pauline Epistles can be utilized to clarify the narrative of Acts but full scholarly consensus has not been reached on the sequence of events in Paul's journeys. The paraphrasing of Acts is not the writing of history, as Chris Forbes has noted (Forbes, in Harding and Nobbs [eds], 2017, 10) but the following is good background material for students and may illuminate some interesting connections.

2.2. Paul's First Journey (c.46-47CE)

The Church in Syrian Antioch (which is now in Turkey) sent Paul and Joseph Barnabas on mission. First they sailed to

Cyprus, accompanied by John-Mark. They crossed the island

from Selucia to Salamis and Paphos and then sailed to Asia Minor (Turkey) landing in the area of Pamphilia where John-Mark left them. They moved due North to Antioch in Pisidia

and then progressed in an Easterly direction to found

churches in Iconium, Lystra and Derbe. They returned through those cities to Perga and then Attalia on the coast (Acts 14:25) and sailed to Selucia, the port of Syrian Antioch, to report to the sending-church.

Plate 2.2.
View from the 5th century BCE Parthenon, Athens.
Photograph: D. Campbell, 1969.

<u>2.3. Paul's Second Journey (c.49-52CE)</u>

For Paul's extensive second missionary journey he was accompanied by Silas. They visited these same cities, via Tarsus and Pisidian Antioch. In Lystra they were jointed by Timothy (Acts 19:22) who, later on, was left in Ephesus to oversee the church during a doctrinal crisis (I Tim. 1:3).

At Troas Luke joined their team. Paul then responded to a Divine call to Macedonia where he landed in the port of Neapolis

(Plate 2.3.). By following the ancient Via Egnatia, Paul's party moved on to Philippi, Amphipolis, Thessalonica and Berea, founding churches in each city. From Macedonia they entered Greece, visiting Athens, Corinth and its port city, Cenchreae, where churches were founded. They returned by ship across the Aegean Sea, to Ephesus and then Caesarea Maritima. Paul completed his second missionary journey by taking a quick trip back to Jerusalem and then to Syrian Antioch.

Plate 2.3.
Neapolis from the ancient Via Egnatia. Public domain.

2.4. Paul's Third Journey (c.54-60 CE)

For Paul's third missionary journey he was accompanied by Luke, Timothy, Erastus, Sopater, Aristarchus, Secundus, Gaius, Tychicus and Trophimus (Acts 20:4). They began in Syrian Antioch (v. 23) and went overland to Paul's home-town, Tarsus, and then on to his previously established churches (Derbe, Lystra, Iconium and Pisidian Antioch).

While Paul was travelling to Jerusalem and then inland in Asia Minor, the eloquent Alexandrian Jew, Apollos, arrived in the coastal town of Ephesus. Although he accurately knew the way of Jesus, Apollos did not know of Christian baptism,

although he knew of the immersion taught by John-the-Baptist (v. 25). Therefore Paul's fellow tentmakers, Priscilla and Aquila, took him aside and instructed him. As a result, when he went on to Achaia/Greece he powerfully witnessed to the Jews there that Jesus was the Messiah (18:18-28).

Apollos had probably departed (v. 27) before Paul returned, but news of his remarkable ministry reached Luke and Paul.

Paul stayed for three months in Ephesus with Priscilla and Aquila but, because of opposition from the synagogue, he

withdrew from it and hired the lecture-hall of Tyrannus for two years (Acts 19:9-10).

Timothy and Erastus were sent forward from Ephesus to Macedonia while Paul remained in Asia. Meanwhile, Demetrius, a silversmith in

Ephesus, promoted a riot in support of the cult of the goddess Diana of the Ephesians, which endangered Paul's companions, Gaius and Aristarchus. Paul was therefore forced to leave Ephesus and the riot was quelled (Acts 19:29-20:4). Paul went to Macedonia to visit his church-plants in Thessalonica and Berea, and he also spent three months in Corinth (Acts 20:1-3).

Paul returned to Macedonia, revisiting Neapolis, Philippi, Amphipolis, Appolonia and Berea. Having strengthened his Macedonian and Greek churches Paul returned by sea much the same way that he came, but his companions sailed directly across the Aegean Sea to Asia (Acts 20:4), rejoining Paul in Troas (v.13). After sailing from Assos, Paul, Timothy and Luke hopped south from one port city to another. Together they sailed south to Mitylene, Trogyllium and Miletus, where, because of Paul's haste to reach Jerusalem by Pentecost (20:16), he had asked the leading Ephesian Christians to meet him (20:18-35). The party sailed on to the islands of Cos and Rhodes and changed ship at Patara for Tyre (in modern Lebanon). They then spent a day in Ptolemais and stayed many days in Caesarea with Philip the evangelist and his four daughters (21:7-14). (These women, who had the gift of prophesy and later lived in Ephesus, would be important in passing details of Jesus' teachings on to Papias, Bishop of Hierapolis in Turkey) (Eusebius, H.E, III. 39.9). Paul ignored prophetic warnings and went up to Jerusalem and stayed in the home of Mnason, an early believer (15-16). After forty months away Paul had brought donations for the poor of Jerusalem but there is no record of how, or even if, they were received. This was Paul's final visit to the elders in Jerusalem (Bible History Online, 'Paul's Third Missionary Journey').

In Jerusalem, Paul was arrested under Antonius Felix, the corrupt Roman procurator, and imprisoned for two years (58 and 59 CE) (Barnett, 1999, 341). When the next governor, Porcius Festus, arrived, and it seemed that Paul would be handed over to the Jewish judges, he, being a Roman citizen, appealed to be tried in Rome.

Shortly afterwards the Bishop of Jerusalem, James, sometimes called 'the Just', was killed. According to Josephus (Antiquities of the Jews XX. 9.1) he was tried by a council of Jewish judges and stoned to death, so Paul's departure had been timely but Christian tradition has preserved a different account of James' death (Eusebius, H.E., II.I.1; II.22.4ff; 23.4-17, citing Hegesippus). By appealing to Caesar Paul lived about seven more years and was enabled (at government expense) to minister in Rome.

<u>2.5. Paul's Fourth Journey (c.60-63 CE)</u>

Following Paul's imprisonment in Caesarea, and under guard, Paul had been taken by ship towards Rome accompanied by Luke and Aristarchus, but the ship was wrecked on the island of Malta. The crew and passengers, who all survived, were given hospitality in Malta for three months before sailing on to Rome where Paul spent two years under house arrest.

During his imprisonment Paul obtained the time to write the 'prison epistles' (Ephesians, Philippians, Colossians and to his friend,

Philemon). The narrative of Acts ceases at this point but Paul may have been released and have travelled to Greece and/or Asia. He may have been rearrested in Corinth and have undergone multiple legal hearings prior to being beheaded in c.67. He may even have gone to Spain: a much-debated

possibility. During his imprisonment in Rome, Paul fulfilled the Lord's word that he would testify also in Rome (Acts 23:11).

During his second imprisonment Paul was in chains but was able to write to Titus and twice to Timothy, although the

authorship of the Pastoral Epistles is much contested.

[For a conservative evangelical opinion see 'Timothy and Titus: Epistles to: iv Authenticity', in NBD.] Paul's presence in Rome, the great capital of the empire, and the journeys that his key followers undertook from there enabled the gospel to be spread widely [for example Crescens went to Galatia or Gaul/France and Titus to Dalmatia (II Tim 4:10)].

<u>2.6. Leadership in Pauline Churches</u>

Whenever mature people with leadership experience or potential were among the early converts Paul took particular notice and/or utilised them in their fledgling congregations. Such people were often wealthy. Examples include the proconsul of Cyrrus, Sergius Paulus (Acts13:4-12); Crispus, the ruler of the synagogue in Corinth whom Paul, himself, baptised (Acts 18:5-8); Lydia, a businesswoman who dealt in expensive purple cloth in Philippi (Acts 16:14) and Dionysius the Areopagite, in Athens (Acts

17:34) ('Dionysius the Areopagite', in ODCC). Paul encouraged wealthier men and women with large houses to invite believers to meet in their homes, offering hospitality. Examples of people who did this include Stephanus in Corinth (I Cor.1:16) and Lydia from Thyatira (Acts 16:40; Rev. 2:18ff). Phoebe, who was called a diakonos (female deacon, minister or servant) was an affluent patroness who ran a house-church at Cenchreae, near Corinth (Rom. 16:1f); as Nympha also did in Laodicea or Colosse (Col. 4:15). Prisca and Aquila opened their home for house-churches in Rome (Rom. 16:5), in Corinth (I Cor.16:19) and in probably also in Ephesus (II Tim. 4:19).

Perhaps the Apphia of Phil. 2:1 was a single woman who helped Philemon run the house-church in Colossae but she may have been Philemon's wife, as John Chrysostom

supposed (Alexander, eds, 1973/1983, 625): or she may have been Philemon's mother, or his sister (Mowczko, 'Apphia of Colossae', online). Quient is persuaded that she was the hostess and a prominent woman leader (Quient, Priscilla Papers 31.2, 2017, 12).

A house-church met in the home of John-Mark's mother, Mary, in Jerusalem (Acts 12:13ff). She was sufficiently wealthy to have a large house with a courtyard and a maid (a slave-woman named Rhoda).

Rhoda knew Peter so well that she joyfully recognized his voice. She was probably a Christian, not just a slave woman (Barnett, 1999, 198). Finegan (1992, 233) proposes that the 'upper room' of the last supper may have been in Mary's house, but Barnett proposes a separate 'upper room community' (Barnett, 1999, 198).

Mary's son, Johannes-Marcus (John-Mark), had been given a good education and probably spoke Greek, Aramaic and perhaps some Latin. In Rome he became Peter's scribe and/or translator and later recorded all that he had heard from Peter (1 Cor. 9:5) which is now know as 'The Gospel According to St Mark' (Scott, JETS 18, 1975, 217-227).[6] Most scholars believe that this gospel and extra sources were used as source material by the writers of the other synoptic gospel (that is, Luke and Matthew). Although Ecclesia met in homes including for prayer (Acts 2:42; 12:12) and for 'the breaking of bread' (2:46) they also continued to attend synagogues, as was their custom, and met daily in the Temple courts (2:46), notably in Solomon's Colonnade where they preached, taught and even performed miracles (3:11).

Paul appointed leaders for his early Galatian churches (Acts 14:23) but he did not do so in every church-plant, for example in Ephesus the Holy Spirit had led the people in their own choice of episkopoi (overseers or bishops) (20:28) (Guthrie,

1990. 35). Paul recognised Timothy's grounding in the Hebrew Scriptures and his potential and, despite his timidity and youth,

Paul sent him on numerous errands to visit churches (to Thessalonica, to Macedonia with Erastus and to Corinth). Timothy accompanied Paul to Jerusalem with the donations for the poor and he was left to oversee matters of concern in Ephesus, notably false doctrines (I Tim. 1:3), an appointment confirmed by prophesy (I Tim. 1:18; 4:14). At the end of his life, Paul sent to Ephesus for Timothy (II Tim. 4:9; 4:21) but whether he arrived in Rome in time is unknown. Because Nero spent two years away from Rome (in 66-68 CE.) and had a backlog of judicial matters to attend to upon his return the historian E. M. Blaiklock opines that Paul was executed in 67 CE after a trial by the city prefect (Blaiklock, 1962, 51). Nero suicided in 68 CE.

2.7. The Jews Early in the First Century

For Jews throughout the Roman Empire the first half of the first century was a period of relative peace and progress as both Julius Caesar (45-44 BCE) and Augustus (27 BCE-14 CE) permitted Jewish religious practices including sending their 'first fruits' to Jerusalem, receiving the grain allowance without having to break the Sabbath and the right to earn citizenship (we note that St Paul was born a citizen). Two contemporaries, Josephus in Judea and Philo of Alexandria in the Diaspora, provide excellent evidence.

Christianity was so closely associated with Judaism in the early period that the disdain with which either was viewed also fell upon the other. Thus Christians were apparently expelled from Rome as Jews by Claudius I (41-54 CE) (Acts 18.2) (Suetonius, Life of Claudius XXV.4, in Bettenson, Documents of the Christian Church, II, [DCC] 1968, Section I.b.).

Christians followed the Jewish custom of burying their dead, rather than cremation. In the land of Israel that meant burial in a cave, necropolis or a rock-hewn tomb, such as behind

Absolom's pillar in the Kidron Valley and the Garden Tomb off Nablus Road in Jerusalem (Plate 2.4).

In Rome, it meant that both Jews and Christians were buried in the now famous catacombs outside the city walls: but they differentiated their graves in inscriptions, icons and locations.

Catacombs were carved into the volcanic tufa wherever it was found (such as in Rome and Naples) because tunneling was easy but the soil became hard and eventually stable when exposed to the air.

Plate 2.4.
The Garden Tomb. Photo: Justin Campbell, 2019.

From over the four to five centuries of usage only 534 Jewsih names have survived on inscriptions in Roman catacombs: but, from total burials there, it is estimated that 40,000 Jews lived in Rome. They attended at least twelve different synagogues which used Hebrew, Greek or, in one case, only the Latin language. From the spelling errors in Greek inscriptions it has been deduced that literate Jews were unable to pay for higher education (Lendering, online). Many, the oldest burials, appear to have been of freed slaves taken to Rome by Pompey in 63 BCE.

The Judaism practised in Rome was of an archaic variety in that men could still marry their brother's widow; they still slaughtered the Passover lamb in the traditional way and refused to change.

There is no mention of a 'rabbi' in any Roman inscription: so perhaps prayer was more prominent than teaching. According to Lendering (online), they had no 'rabbis' in the catacomb period but were led by elders, scribes, presidents, governors and an *archigerousiarch* and had no female elders (a matter contested in Brooten, 1982). The chief synagogue official was an '*archisynagogus*' (ruler of the synagogue) who was assisted by the 'hyperetes' (who looked after the buildings) while the '*archigerosiarch*' led the community.

A most interesting but undated Roman inscription is of a woman, Beturia Paulina, who converted to Judaism at the age of 70, took the name Sara and lived to be 86. She was described as 'the mother of the synagogues of Campus and Volumi(i)us.' Perhaps this was an honourifc title because of her age but it may have indicated an actual leadership role, as Brooten argues (Brooten, 1982, 57ff, 68 and Silver, BHD April 17, 2019).

There were synagogues throughout the Jewish Diaspora including at Ostia near Rome and, as the New Testament confirms, in Greece, Africa and Asia Minor.

Plate 2.5.
Panel of Triumphal Procession, Arch of Titus,
Rome. Photograph: D. Campbell, 2010.

2. 8. Jews of the Roman Empire Later in the First Century CE

Before the Roman invasion of Judea in 70 CE the province had been directly ruled from Rome and life for the Judean Jews was difficult and fraught with danger. The situation for Jews changed dramatically after the first rebellion in Palestine, which resulted in Vespasian's invasion and the battles to subdue each Jewish town from the North (from 66 CE) down to the South (by 73 CE). The progress of this military campaign is recorded in detail by Josephus in War of the Jews. Afterwards, Rome and many other cities were flooded with Jewish slaves, probably sold at discount prices because there were so many of them. The, now much damaged, Triumphal Arch of Titus in Rome (c.81-85 CE) was built by Domitian, to honor his deceased brother, Titus, and is currently undergoing restoration. Undoubtedly one panel depicts the treasures that were looted from the Temple before it was burned (Plate 2.6) but whether the twenty-one male figures were soldiers or slaves is debated. Plate 2.5 depicts Titus in a quadriga being crowned by the goddess Niki (winged Victory) to indicate his deification in death (BAR Staff, 'Jewish Captives in the Imperial city', BHD 28/1/2013). The quadriga has passed through a triumphal arch accompanied by the genius of the Roman Senate (wearing a toga) and the genius of the Roman people (with bare chest) and the horses are being led by the goddess Roma.

On the curved ceiling above, an eagle is carrying the deified Titus to heaven (his apotheosis).

After the Roman army had destroyed Jerusalem, no stone of the actual Temple remained upon another as Jesus had foretold, although its foundation platform is extant. Herod the Great's extensive beautifications had lasted less than a century.

During the reign of Vespasian (which began during the first war against the Jews) Jews and Christians of the House of David were killed. Apparently the Emperor knew that a new king would come from David's royal line (but he did not learn that the King had already come). This policy of annihilation was continued by Vespasian's sons, Titus and Domitian, and their successor, Trajan, so that the Davidic line was almost extinguished. Eusebius noted that Domitian interviewed St Jude's two grandsons, James and Zoker, in Rome, but permitted them to return home to their farms as they were poor and seemed no threat to him. They returned to the Jerusalem church with the status of confessors and leaders (Eusebius, H.E. III. 19-20; Barnett, 1999, 33).

Plate 2.6.
Panel of Israel's ruin, Arch of Titus, Rome.
Photograph: D. Campbell, 2010.

Six decades after the 'great destruction', the status of Jews throughout the Empire and the fortunes of those within the Land suffered a second time, when Bar Kochba led an ill-fated second revolt against Rome. After both wars, many once thriving Jewish towns, such as Gamla, were never rebuilt and Jerusalem lay in ruins.

Questions:

(1) What personal qualities made Paul a successful missionary?

(2) What principles did Paul follow in promoting leaders to his church-plants?

Chapter 3
Persecution and Peace

Once Bishop James, St Peter and St Paul had given their lives as martyrs the main leaders of Ecclesia were gone, but believers were scattered from Britain to India. As Eusebius commented, error began to enter the church once that generation who had seen and heard Jesus in person had been martyred or had died, prior to which time the church (he said) had been a 'virgin' (Eusebius, H.E. III. 32). [By the 4th century 'virginity' suggested 'pure' or 'pristine' and was elevated above marriage, but male Jews had, from the beginning, been taught to *be fruitful and multiply*" (Gen. 1:28, A.V.)].

It has long been thought that St John wrote the fourth gospel against Gnosticism, so some heresies must date from the first century, moreover Bishop Ireneaus of Lyon (Against Heresies) (c.130-c.200) claimed that all heresies stemmed from Simon Magus. He was a hypocritical convert and magician whom Saints Peter and Philip met in Samaria (Acts 8: 9-24). Another major divergent or unorthodox teaching was Arianism, taught in Alexandria by Arius (c.250 – c.336 CE). The Germanic tribes were soon to exchange paganism for Arian Christianity.

In the Roman Empire Judaism was a legal religion (religio licita) and earliest Christianity had been protected under Roman law as a sect within Judaism, provided that the Jewish tax (the fiscus judaicus) was paid. But once Gentiles predominated, especially in Rome, it became obvious that Christianity was not Jewish but a religio illicita (illegal religion) and thus without legal protection. This was the basis of imperial persecution of 'the way', which began with the Emperor Nero (54-68 AD) and continued, intermittently, for 249 years. During this time peace and security were precarious commodities for Christians of all varieties and shades.

Persecutions depended upon imperial decision and the preferences of local officials, who were often brutal and bloodthirsty, devising ingenious ways to torture and kill (with snakes, scorpions, drowning, flaying, pulling teeth and fingernails, roasting alive, cutting off breasts and so on). Local mobs also engaged in intermittent violence and revenge killings. Rome's official position tended to be that Christianity offended the Roman gods, weakened the divine protection of the Empire and that Christianity was a *superstitio* (Aldridge, online, Section 2, f/n. 38).

There is considerable scholarly contests about which emperor did what, when and to whom, as though exonerating one or more emperors will undermine the total picture: but there can be no doubt that whole groups of people and named and unknown individuals died for their faith in the Early Christian Period. Such deaths occurred during the reigns of the following emperors of the post-Crucifixion era: Nero (54-68), Domitian (81-96) (although Wilson, Mark, 'Alternative Facts', BHD 24/7/2017, citing Jones, 1992, claimed that Domitian's persecution is 'fake news') and Trajan (98-117). An abundant and extant collection of letters sent between the Emperor Trajan and his friend Pliny, a governor in Asia Minor, has survived and they have become famous as evidence for persecution (Pliny to Trajan XCVI and Trajan's, Epistle to Pliny XCVII, Bettenson, DCC, 1968, 3-6). Through this two-way correspondence it can be learnt that obstinately adhering to the name of Jesus was a capital offence. Trajan's reign, which commenced in the late-1st-century CE, established the basis for later persecutions: continued adherence to the name 'Christian' warranted the death penalty (Letters: Pliny to Trajan, Book 10b, 96).

The list of persecuting emperors continues with Marcus Aurelius (151-180),

Lucius Verus (161-169), Commodus (180-192), Scapula (Stevenson (ed.), 1965, 179). Septimus Severus (193-211) and his son Caracalla (211-217), Elagabalus (218-222), Alexander

Severus (222-235), Maximinus Thrax (235-238), Decius (249-251), Valerian (253-260), Aurelian (270-275) are included (Lactantius, On the Deaths of the Persecutors, II). Those associated with Diocletian (284-286) included Maximian Herculius (286-305 and 307-308) and his son and part co-ruler, Maxentius (306-312) and Maximian Galerius (305-311). Of this long list, the most important are Trajan, Decius and Diocletian. During the short Decian persecution (249-251 CE) a rigorous test was applied to separate the faithful from ex-Christians, the lapsed and polytheists. Real

Christians refused to curse Christ, taste the sacrificial meat, pour libations of wine, burn incense to the emperor's image, invoke the gods and sign certificates of loyalty (proofs of compliance, which protected from further harassment).

The persecution by Diocletian was, however, the worst. It has long been called 'the Great Persecution'. First it targeted copies of Scripture and churches, then bishops, clergy and office holders and then all Christians. In theory, without leaders the church would falter and decline. Diocletian had begun as a good, capable emperor, who reorganised the military and the imperial government. He dividing the empire into East and West, with an augustus in charge of each, supported by a caesar. Diocletian and his son-in-law, Galerius, ruled in the East with Maximian Herculius and Constantius in the West. When he became old, however, after nearly twenty years as Emperor, Diocletian yielded to pressure from Galerius, his junior colleague (Bruce, 1958/62, 185; Boer, 1976, 102ff). Because Galerius was victorious over the Persians in 296, his power increased. The evidence indicates that many Christians were martyed even before the first of Diocletian's official edicts was promulgated against buildings and Bibles in 303, although these Christians may have been killed by Galerius or perhaps by Maximian Herculius.

Galerius and Constantine were each greatly influenced by their mothers. Galerius's mother was a devotee of the Eastern

goddess Cybele who urged her son to persecute Christians, which he did (Frend, 1967, 362) and which he urged Diocletian to do also (Lactantius, 36.4-5; Eusebius, H.E. 9.5). In contrast, Constantine's mother, Helena, was a Christian (or perhaps a proselyte) so Constantine (like his late father) quietly declined to follow Diocletian's policy of persecution (Bruce, 1958/52, 186). In 305 both Diocletian and Maximian Herculius abdicated, which was most unusual, but there were always considerable changes of personnel as soldiers often depart this life while in office, for which reason, for example, Constantius had been replaced by his son, Constantine I (307-337 CE).

Just before his death in 311 Galerius had issued an 'edict of toleration' but his nephew, the Caesar Maximin Daia, briefly reinstituted both persecution and the pagan priesthood, before later issuing another 'edict of toleration'. Daia was defeated by Licinius (Constantine I's brother-in-law) in 313, and there is controversy over whether Licinius did or didn't persecute (Aldridge, online, f/notes 226-238). Constantine and Maxentius (the son of Maximian) were left to battle each other for control of Rome. Constantine was victorious in the Battle of Milvian Bridge (312) after seeing a cross and a message in the sky *In hoc signo vinces* ("*in this sign conquer*") (Boer, 1976, 105). Constantine and Licinius promulgated the Edict of Milan (312), by which complete religious toleration was established (Bettenson, DCC, 1968, 22). Although Constantine established peace by issuing this Edict of Toleration in 312 Christianity was not made the official religion of the Empire until Theodosius I did so in 381 with the decree 'cunctos populos' (Quora, online).

Meanwhile Constantine, not yet a baptised Christian, called and presided over a church council at Nicaea in 325. Its

Plate 3.1.
Coin of Constantine 1. Public domain.

outcomes have endured in the West (but less so in the East) and it has proved to be the most important of all ecumenical councils for Christianity as it established basic Trinitarian doctrine. It also set a precedent for imperial control of councils, giving the state power over a council's orders, in punishing bishops who dissented.

Nicaea was very significant for Jewish-Christians relations and demonstrated how far apart they had already become. The historian Eusebius, who attended, recorded that the Council voted for the date of Easter to be separated from the date of the Jewish Passover because all Jews carried the blame for Jesus' death, having "*impiously defiled their hands with enormous sin*" (Eusebius, Life of Constantine, III.18).

The Emperor Constantine is blamed by both Jews and Christians for the decisions reached at Nicaea but he was a very new Christian (if that) and although he arrived wearing purple and gold he was an emperor, not a bishop.

He only had observer-status and did not vote. Because Constantine wanted unity within the Church he accepted what the bishops almost unanimously agreed to and he lent the force of the law to those ends. Being the figurehead, he has borne the acrimony ever since.

Plate 3.2.
St Eusebius of Caesarea, bishop and historian.
Photograph: J. Campbell, 2019.

<u>Questions:</u>

(1) How many different reasons did Roman Emperors from Nero to Constantine have for persecuting Christians?

(2) How many different reasons did Constantine have for not persecuting Christians?

Chapter 4
Egypt and Byzantium

<u>.1. The Eastern Church: Egypt and North Africa</u>

Christianity reached Egypt very early and spread down the Nile River, across North Africa and flourished. Simon of Cyrene who carried Jesus' cross (and his sons, Rufus and Alexander), the Ethiopian eunuch and Apollos were all Africans and there were Egyptian Jews and Libyan Jews from Cyrene in Jerusalem for Pentecost and they heard Peter preach (Acts 2:10). After Stephen was stoned to death, the Hellenistic-Jews were scattered and they evangelised other Jews wherever they went. Some believers from the Island of Cyprus and from Cyrene (in North Africa) went across to Antioch in Asia and evangelised gentiles there (Acts 11:20). John-Mark and his relative, Barnabas, travelled to Antioch (Acts 12:25) and back to Cyprus (Acts 15:39) to preach. The historian Eusebius places Mark in Alexandria in 43 CE and local tradition places him in Cyrene in about 66 CE and in Alexandria for his martyrdom in 68 (Oden, 2007, 18; 158; 40 Map 4). In this way the gospel was penetrating throughout the Eastern Mediterranean world.

<u>.2. The Desert Fathers and Mothers</u>

Egyptian Christianity is best known for monasticism but from pre-Christian times monasteries of celibate male and female Jews or devotees of the Egyptian god Serapis existed in Egypt (as is noted in Volume 1 of this series: Synagoga's Heritage).

Called Therapeutae, they had given away their property to follow asceticism, living solitary lives of contemplation and study, in separate, small houses in the desert but gathering

together on the seventh day for a shared meal ('Therapeutae', in ODCC). Christian monasticism, which began in Egypt, must have been influenced by these numerous, earlier ascetics. St Anthony's 'rule' (c. 250-347) also adopted the eremitic lifestyle. Anthony's 'rule', like theirs, was strict, but a little different.

Because it was safer, communal monasticism developed after some decades. This was safer and more suitable for women: but the best-known ascetic, Mary of Egypt, lived entirely alone in the wilderness near the Jordan River for many years, virtually naked. Near the end of her life she met Father Zosimas, from whom she received the sacrament for the first and only time; and to whom she entrusted her testimony ('The Life of Our Holy Mother Saint Mary of Egypt', online).

.3. African Christians Were Both Heterodox and Orthodox

Gnosticism was *"the knowledge falsely so called"* (Eusebius, H.E. III.32). It was regarded as flawed and heretical. It had begun to emerge in the 1st century but this accelerated after the Apostolic period and Gnosticism was one of the greatest threats to Orthodoxy. From about 117 to c.300, Gnosticism was strong in Egypt where Gnostic teachers were active: Valentinus, Basilides, Heracleon, Carpocrates and his son Epiphanes, Apelles, Julius and Cassianus. Many hidden Gnostic writings, once thought to have been suppressed into oblivion, were discovered, in Nag Hammadi, Egypt, in the 20th century. Gnosticism, which had developed from Greek dualism and Jewish influences, could not accept the delinquent Creator as described in the O.T. and it developed a convoluted system of demiurges and other cosmic powers to explain the accidental creation of humanity. Nor could they accept that God could adopt material form, because that, too, was evil (Tomkins, 2003, 28).

There was a great melting pot of ideas as 'theology' was being formed in the early centuries of Christianity and each group though their own insights were correct.

In Egypt certain views that came to be regarded as heresies flourished: those of Apion of Alexandria, Marcion, Montanism, Celsus, Novation, Sabellianism, Manachaeism, Neo-platonists (including Plotinus and his disciple Porphyry) and, importantly, Arianism (named for Arius, an Alexandrian presbyter who was born in Cyrenaica,

North Africa, c.260) (Oden, 2007, 160-167). Arius taught 'pluralistic Trinitarianism', that the son was not eternal but created and not God by nature, but whose dignity was bestowed upon him because of his foreseen righteousness.

Of the great early African writers and scholars, whose extant work were inherited by the Latin Church, two came to be considered heretics, but were never-the-less very influential in the short-tern. They were Tertullian (d.225) and Origen (c.185-253/54).

Tertullian, born in Cartghage, was the first Christian theologian to write in Latin, not Greek, so that he greatly influenced the Western church, despite later being a Montanist (Tertullian, Quintus Septimus Florens, in ODCC). Tertullian was a prolific writer and promoted his opinions forcefully. He was married, but was conflicted about marital sex, and he was almost obsessively preoccupied with women, for example their clothing, jewelry, make up, behaviour, roles and celibacy. In his opinion women were to be sidelined and silenced which greatly contributed to the reduced status and role of women in the Western Church compared with that of the East (Torjesen, 1995, 172).

Origen, the son of a martyr, was born in Egypt, probably in Alexandria, but spent years teaching in Palestine. He was an ascetic, a great and original thinker, a prolific writer and a staunch opponent of the heretical teachings of Celsus. Origen was widely followed for more than a century before his work fell under suspicion.

The two main disputed Origenist doctrines were: the "pre-existence of the soul" and the "restoration of all things" (Universalism) which were thought to minimize or deny the Incarnation and disparage the body in favour of the spirit (in the Greek manner). By the Late-4thcentury doubts about Origen's orthodoxy were expressed and then controversy raged, so that most of his work has been lost to posterity. In 250, during the Decian Persecution, Origen had been tortured and eventually had died because of it (Origen, in ODCC).

Orthodox Egyptian leaders. These included: Clement, Bishop of Alexandria (c.150-c.217/222);

Dionysius, Bishop of Alexandria (c.190-c.260); Cyprian, Bishop of Carthage (c.200); Victor, Pope of Rome from 189 to 198; the historian Lactantius (c.240-c.320) and Augustine, Bishop of Hippo (354430). One remarkable African woman, Perpetua, wrote (or rather, commenced) a written record of her own martyrdom, and that of her companions, Felicitas, Saturus, Revocatus, Saturninus and Secundulus (Rader, in Wilson-Kastner et al., 1981, 1). The work may have been completed by Tertullian (Oden, 2007, 164). These women and men won their crowns of martyrdom in 202/203 with wild beasts in the arena. The above is a long list of names from Africa, which indicates that there were many Christians and much intellectual debate, able teaching and rigorous support of heterodoxy and orthodoxy alive in North Africa. If one considers the number of martyrs killed there (as discussed in Chapter 22 of Volume 1, Synagoga's Heritage) and the frequency of persecution, a vigorous confessing church is revealed. These are the forerunners of today's Copts, who are now also experiencing persecution.

Justin Martyr. Justin was born in the Holy Land. He studied Stoic and Platonic philosophy before his conversion in about 132 CE and was the first Christian philosopher to harmonise

Christianity with Greek philosophy, namely neo-Platonism

"and laid the basis for a theology of history" (Britannica, 'Saint Justin Martyr', online). He understood that the transcendent and unchangeable God was the central goal of all philosophical thought and that traces of truth could be found in the great works of pagan philosophy (Britannica, 'Saint Justin Martyr', online). An authentic record of his martyrdom, based upon court reports, survives (Justin Martyr, St., in ODCC).

<u>4.4. St Athanasius and St John Chrysostom</u>

Relations between one bishop and another, and between bishops and their Christian rulers, were not always sweetness and light. The careers of two of the most famous

prelates of the Eastern Church, St Athanasius (296-373) and St John Chrysostom (c.347-407) will demonstrate this.

<u>4.5. St Athanasius (296/7-373 CE)</u>

Athanasius attended the Council of Nicaea of 325 CE as his bishop's assistant and always staunchly upheld Nicaean teachings about Christ as homoousios (of one substance) with God. Even while he was a deacon, Athanasius was the great champion against the African heretic Arius (c.250-c.336) and Arianism ('Athanasius, St', in ODCC) (see 4.3 above).

When Athanasius became Bishop of Alexandria, in Egypt, he incurred the enmity of the Emperor Constantine I, who exiled him in 336 for his strict orthodoxy and his refusal to compromise with Arianism. On the emperor's death he returned to his see but Constantine's son, Constantius, opposed him (having himself adopted Arianism) so Chrysostom fled to Rome where the Western Emperor, Constans, supported him ('Athanasius, St', in ODCC).

When Constans died, the Arian, Constantius, became sole emperor (of East and West) and the Orthodox (proto-Catholics) were persecuted. Numerous bishops, such as Athanasius of Alexandria,

Hilary of Poitiers, Pope Liberius and others, were exiled until Constantius died in 361 CE. Athanasius returned to Alexandria in secret but the next Eastern Emperor, Flavius Claudius Julianus (called 'Julian the Apostate' because he rejected Christianity) again exiled him in 362. There was also a fourth exile in 365-6 ('Athanasius, St', in ODCC).

For Ecclesia, one positive outcome of Julian's promotion of paganism was that, when they faced a common foe (an outright pagan emperor) the semi-Arians, who had believed in homoiousios ('of like substance') merged with Nicaean orthodoxy, who believed that the Father and Son were of 'one substance' (homoousios) (Wand, 1961, 173). The Arians were left isolated, although they also opposed Julian.

Athanasius was an able writer and theologian, having written his famous De Incarnatione in his early adulthood (c.318). He directed the Council of Alexandria in 362. He was a friend of the Egyptian monk St Pachomius and the Egyptian monk and bishop, St Serapion of Thmuis, in the Nile Delta. As noted in 5.8 below, Athanasius wrote a biography of the founder of eremitic monasticism, St Anthony, which helped introduce monasticism to the West ('Serapion, St'. in ODCC). Athanasius, a hero of Eastern Orthodoxy, lived about 77 years.

4.6. St John Chrysostom (347-c.402 or 407 CE)

John Chrysostom of Syrian Antioch was about 50 years younger than Athanasius. He had followed St Pachomius' monastic rule with such austerity that his health deteriorated.

He was ordained a deacon in 381, a priest in 386 and was consecrated patriarch of Constantinople in 398, although against his will. He immediately began to impose clerical disciplines, which the clergy disliked.

For example, he opposed accommodating subintroductae (dedicated virgins who lived in 'spiritual marriage' with celibate men), which had long been forbidden (by the Council

of Nicaea in 325 CE) although the practice persisted and was

popular (Wand, 1961, 212).[7] His outstanding abilities were: prodigious writing; the literal interpretation of scripture (as distinct from the Alexandrian preference for allegorical interpretation); its practical application and the eloquence of his preaching. 'Chrysostom', meant 'Golden Mouth' (Wand, 1961, 212). Chrysostom used his preaching skills against the Jews because he really believed that they had killed Christ (for which there was no atonement) and because members of his own congregation were attending Jewish festivals/feasts (Tomkins, 2003, 56f; Wilken, 1983, 79f). He used extremely derogatory expletives against Jews and against the headstrong and pleasure-loving Empress Eudoxia whom he called both 'Jezebel' and, later, 'Herodias' (the mother who demanded John the Baptist's head on a platter) (Boer, 1976, 154ff; Wand, 1961, 213). The Empress Eudoxia (wife of the weak Eastern Emperor, Arcadius) combined with Theophilus of Alexandria to condemn Chrysostom. Now this Theophilus had been Chrysostom's rival for the see of Constantinople but had failed to become Archbishop/Patriarch so the ultimate humiliation for him was being forced to consecrate Chrysostom (Wand, 1961, 212). The Eastern Emperor, Arcadius, under pressure from his wife, then deposed and banished Chrysostom. From 404 to 415 the Pope, who constantly supported Chrysostom, had broken off relations with the other Eastern Patriarchs, because they sided with the Emperor Arcadius, against Chrysostom. This break between East and West was a portent of the final schism. The Emperor Arcadius banished Chrysostom, first to Antioch, then to Armenia and finally the patriarch died because of a hard 'forced march' when he was about 60.

<u>4.7. Nestorius (died c.451 CE)</u>

Nestorius was a Syrian monk in Antioch. Because of his fame as a preacher, he was not elected but appointed

.Patriarch of Constantinople by the Emperor Theodosius II, in 428 CE.

He very soon became the centre of a violent controversy over his Christology and the term *theotokos* (God-bearer) a title being used for the Virgin Mary. Nestorius, who opposed the term, held that the nature of Christ was a 'conjunction' of the two natures (God and man) rather than a 'union' and, in 430, he was condemned and deposed by Pope Celestine (422-432) ('Nestorianism', in ODCC).

The Emperor called a church council in Ephesus in 431-432, which confirmed the title Theotokos upon the Virgin, which both reflected and enhanced her emerging cult. In 431, the Council confirmed the deposition of Nestorius, who was sent back to his monastery. In 436 he was exiled to Upper Egypt ('Nestorianism', in ODCC).

<u>4.8. The Nestorian Church in the East</u>

In c.457, shortly after the death of Nestorius (one time Patriarch of Constantinople) a large Nestorian school was set up by Barsumas, at Nisibis. In 540-52 Mar Aba I helped organise the Nestorian church. Abraham of Kaskar (491-586) put monasticism on a firm footing and Mar Babai the Great (569-628) defined Nestorian principles in his Book of Union (meaning union of the God-man). Nestorians developed its own patriarchate and a diocesan system parallel to orthodoxy throughout the East, with its centre in Persia/Iran, where they enjoyed royal support in the late 5th century. Nestorian missionaries travelled to Arabia, India, China, Mongolia and everywhere along the trade routes, establishing churches (Jenkins, 2008, 62-67; 255-56). They introduced an alphabet and literacy wherever they went: to Monguls, Turks, Uigurs and Manchurians who "derived their alphabets from Syriac, the language of the Nestorians" (Pierman, in Winter and Hawthorne (eds), 1981/1999, 261).

Timothy (d. 823) was Nestorian Patriarch or catholicos from c.780 and was their most able leader.

Plate 4.1.
Reproduction: Nestorian icon.
Photo: Prof. Gary Lee Todd. Creative Commons Share Alike.

He appointed bishops to such remote regions as Tibet, Arabia and Yemen, presiding over nineteen metropolitans and eighty-five Nestorian bishops and "*Perhaps a quarter of the world's Christians looked to Timothy as both spiritual and political head*" (Jenkins, 2008, 6 and 10f).

In China (as in Plate 4.1)[8] Nestorian gravestones feature a cross emerging from a lotus blossom (the latter a symbol of Buddhist enlightenment) (Jenkins, 2008, 15). Nestorian Christians, now called 'the Assyrian Church of the East', do not claim 'Nestorianism' but regard Nestorius as a saint ('Assyrian Christians', in ODCC ; Murre-van den Berg, online) and say that his teachings have been oversimplified (Jenkins, 2008, x).

<u>4.9. Conclusion</u>

The Eastern Mediterranean was a hive of Christian activity in the first few centuries with a rapid spread and many colourful but dedicated leaders. Identifying doctrinal orthodoxy and then ensuring that it was accepted posed serious problems after the Apostolic Age had passed.

Early tensions between the church and the state had quickly developed into persecution and such tension continued under 'Christian' emperors, although with less bloodshed.

<u>Questions:</u>

(1) Why did Nestorianism become popular in the East?

(2) Read the pieces on John Chrysostom here and in the following chapter. Did he deserve his fate?

Chapter 5

Women and Men of the Fourth-Century Church

.4. The Great Persecution

The 4th century was a most remarkable period for Ecclesia which began with the most terrible of the persecutions: that of Emperor Diocletian, called 'the Great Persecution'. As noted in Chapter 3, above, he first targeted copies of Scriptures, then churches, then bishops, clergy and office holders and then all Christians. In theory, without leaders the church would falter and decline and a whole generation of leaders was mown down when bishops and clergy were lost.

The centuries of persecution opened the way for quite young people to rise to the top, which was, in a way, its own breath of fresh air but the wisdom of the generation that knew those who had been taught by the disciples of apostles was prematurely lost. In Chapter 22 of Volume I, Synagoga's Heritage, Tabernacle, Temple, Synagogue, Church, many bishops who died in the Great Persecution are named. At that time being elected Pope was a death sentence. Many other such Christian leaders had died in previous persecutions, for example, the martyr St Polycarp, who had sat at the feet of St John, and St Ignatius, whose tradition was directly from St Peter, and, of course, St Peter himself, St Paul and other apostles.

The Constantinian Peace followed the Great Persecution, bringing its own mix of vice and virtue to Ecclesia but she was like a bud opening and blossoming, although the various heretical groups were alive and thriving too.

Plate 5.1.
Manger Square, Bethlehem. Photograph: D. Campbell, 1988.

.5. Peace

Many of the female and male martyrs and confessors over the centuries had been sexually abused or died protecting their virginity so that virginity took on some of the sanctity of sainthood, as extant memorials that feature the words *"virgin martyr"* demonstrate. After the Peace, one could no longer die as a martyr but one could sacrifice marriage and parent-hood by taking a vow of celibacy, joining Mary, Jesus and even (according to Jerome) Joseph. It was a given that Christians should emulate Jesus, but chastity and modesty had long been the chief virtues of the Roman woman; woven into the fabric of their self-identity.[9]

.6. Christian Women

Our Book 1, Synagogas' Heritage has already noted two famous women of the 4th century church but their contributions will be revisited below. They are Helena, the mother of Constantine I, and the much-travelled nun, Egeria, both of whose lives promoted pilgrimage to holy sites in the Land and elsewhere.

The saints travelled widely for study, pilgrimage and evangelism, which witness to the universal nature of the church and the close ties between its Latin and Greek spheres. Indeed it was only at the end of this century (in 395) that the empire was divided under two emperors, Honorius (395-423) and Arcadius (395-408) (the sons of Theodosius the Great [378-395]). Until then there was one Roman Empire and one orthodox church.

Plate 5.2.
Plaque of Thekla. Public domain.

Every Christian woman in those days walked to some extent in the footsteps of St Thecla/Thekla, the virgin disciple of St Paul, who dressed as a man, became an evangelist and is known from the, oncepopular, Acts of Paul and Thecla. There may be some fact behind her fascinating but mysterious story but, if so, St Paul gave no hint of her in his canonical epistles. What matters is that everyone believed in her, for example the scholarly bishop, Gregory of Nazianzus, spent time at her shrine (Gregory, Oration IV. 69, Against Julian) and eulogia bearing her image were widely dispersed in the East. On these she is usually depicted bound and standing between two lionesses (one of which died defending her) (as in the plaque for a building, in Plate 5.2) (Cohick and Hughes, 2017, 4, 5, 6, 14, 20, 22, citing Acts of Paul and Thecla).

Augusta Helena was an exemplary Christian woman of the 4th century. Her mission in The Land was to identify holy sites and to build churches upon them; only two of which have survived. In the process she is said to have discovered the True Cross of the Crucifixion, which gave her added fame and sanctity, and which is why she is invariably depicted holding a Cross (as in the example in Plate 5.3).

Plate 5.3. Helena, Constantine and the True Cross in St Onuphrios' Church Göreme, Turkey. Photo: D. Campbell, 2007.

The church of Christ's Nativity, in Bethlehem, is the best preserved of Helena's churches; retaining many original features, although there is much uncertainty about which of the 'Constantinian' churches Helena 'built' or only 'decorated' (Wilkinson, 1991, 167). The Church of the Holy Nativity basically follows Helena's original layout and some of its columns are original, as is the mosaic flooring (which can be viewed through trapdoors in the modern wooden flooring). Manger Square (Plate 5.1) was originally a colonnaded courtyard from which the church was entered. In the 6th century the church was enlarged by the Emperor Justinian with the addition of fourteen new columns, internally (Bagatti, 1971/2004, 177, fig. 49; 183. Finegan, 1992, 32-35).

The Church of the Holy Nativity is now in an area under the control of the Palestinian Authority and is a centre for Arabic-speaking Christianity.

Plate 5.4.
Catholicon of the Church of the Holy Sepulchre. Photograph: Justin Campbell, 2019.

While Macarius was Bishop of Jerusalem (c.313-c.334) the historian, Eusebius, was his Metropolitan Bishop in Caesarea and the Church of the Holy Sepulcher was being built in Jerusalem under directions from Constantine I. In 335, when the church was consecrated with great ceremony in the presence of the Emperor a local lad, Cyril, had been ordained deacon. Cyril went on to become Bishop of Jerusalem in c.350 CE and his episcopacy spanned 36 years, although he spent a total of 15 years in exile (357359; 360-362; 367-378). The liturgical cycle, which the pilgrim Egeria described a decade after Cyril's death, is attributed to him ('Macarius, St' in, ODCC) and the process of baptism was described in his own writings (St Cyril's Procatechesis and Mystagogical Catecheses, I-III).

5.4. Olympias and St John Chrysostom

St John Chrysostom (347-407 CE) has been considered in Chapter 4 but he also belongs in this chapter and indeed knew many of the personalities to be considered below: for example, Jerome spent two years in Constantinople being taught by John Chrysostom. While Chrysostom was Patriarch of Constantinople he owed much to the financial help of an extremely wealthy aristocratic widow,

Olympias/Olympiada, (c.362-409).[10]

Olympias' origins are disputed. She may have been an orphan, raised by her Christian uncle, Procopius. Because of her enormous wealth she was probably the daughter of Theodosia and Seleucus the excount, Seleucus, who was a pagan, in which case her paternal grandfather would have been the Praetorian prefect, consul and senator, Ablabius (Palladius, Lausiac History, Chapter LVL. 1; New Advent, 'Letters to Olympias', online). Theodosia (St Olympias' mother or governess, was the daughter or sister of St Nonna's brother, St Amfilohije/ Amphilochius of Konya/Iconium, who tutored Nonna's sons as children (New Advent, St Gregory of Nazianzus, online). These details fit Olymias' life well but perhaps her wealth also came from her husband of 21 days, as, at a young age Olympias, had been very briefly married to Nebridius, treasurer to Emperor Theodosius the Great, who was obviously a man of status and wealth (Eternal Word Television Network, 'St Olympias, Widow - 368-410', online).

In her widowhood, Olympias was taught by Melania the Elder, who, in turn, had been taught by Marcella in Rome (Palladius, The Lausiac History, LVI.1).[11]

Olympias, as the abbess of the monastery she established beside the Great Church of Hagia Sophia in Constantinople

(Plates 1.5 and 7.4) ,[12] knew many bishops of the East, such as Amphilochius of Iconium, who was related to Theodosia

(Oympias's mother or governess) and their friend, St Basil the Great. Procopius, Olympias's uncle, was a friend of Gregory Nazianzus (New Advent, 'Letters to Olympias', online) and Gregory of Nyssa dedicated his Commentary on the Song of Songs to her. Olympias readily gave hospitality, for example, to such bishops as Gregory of Nyssa, his brother Peter of Sebaste, Onesimus of Pontum and Epiphanius of Cyprus (Elizabeth A. Clark, 1979, 127-42, citing an anonymous 'Life of Olympias'). Olympias donated to the poor, to charitable institutions and to monasteries. Patriarch Nectarius (381-397) ordained her a deaconess of the Great Church, where her fellow deaconesses were Pentadia, Proklia and Salbina ('Holy Woman Olympias [Olympiada] the Deaconess of Constantinople', by the Orthodox Church of America, online).

Although Olympias had often helped Theophilus of Alexandria he turned against her, undermining her holy reputation because she maintained her affection for his arch-rival, Chrysostom (as noted above). Olympias was not only a supporter of Chrysostom, she was his companion, who

organised his food to make sure that he was well nourished and that he did not fast to excess as his health was poor, due (as noted above) to excessive asceticism.

When Chrysostom was to be banished, Olympias was so devoted to him that *"it was necessary to tear her from his feet by violence"* and she sent him money and medications during his exile. Because she refused to acknowledge the bishop who

usurped Chrysostom's position (Arsacius) she, also, was banned from the city (Eternal Word Television Network, 'St Olympias, Widow - 368-410', online). She and Chrysostom's most loyal supporters were accused of attempting to burn

down Hagia Sophia (Iconandlight, 'St Olympias', online). The next bishop (Atticus) exiled or imprisoned Olympias in

Nicomedia in 405, with her fifty nuns, although there was no evidence against her (Elizabeth A. Clark, 1979, 107-57; Torjesen, 1995, 109, f/ns. 28; 29, citing Murphy, 'Melania the Younger...', Traditio 5 [1947] 59-77). Because she contended for truth the people of Constantinople classed her as 'a confessor' (Palladius, The Lausiac History, LVI. 2). Olympia's final years in exile were called *"a lingering martyrdom"* as she suffered from depression and bouts of bad health (New Advent, 'Letters to Olympias', online). Chrysostom often wrote to her from his exile to console her and 17 of his letters are extant. He had depended upon her money but she was emotionally depended upon him and often wrote, begging him for letters, while he admonished her for not taking his spiritual guidance to heart sufficiently. Her condition was obviously more serious than Chrysostom understood as she was only 41 or 42 at her death in 409/410 (New Advent, 'Letters to Olympias', online).

For all his charisma, Chrysostom spent little time in his see and much in exile, where (as noted in

Chapter 4) he died from his privations in 407 (The Orthodox Church in America, 'Holy Woman Olympias [Olympiada] the Deaconess of Constantinople', online).

5.5. Anthousa, Marcella, Monica, the Macrinas, Nonna, the Melanias and Paula the Elder

Seven Christian families are particularly significant during this century, each one led by a matriarchal figure.

Their contributions have been downplayed by the church in favour of those whom they mentored, taught and cared for, and who became bishops, priests, abbots and, occasionally, nuns. These matriarchs were learned in the ways of God, lovers of the Scriptures and, whether in widowhood, or unwed, had chosen to be consecrated in celibacy. Their families were all interconnected by friendship and/or birth.

Because most of their offspring chose celibacy they rarely intermarried, although they were Christians and from the

right social class (when most were not).

As listed above, the main matriarchs (not in chronological order) are:

(1) Anthousa (2) Marcella (3) Monica (4) Macrina the Elder and Macrina the Younger (5) Nonna (6) Melania the Elder and Melania the Younger (with her husand, Pinian) (7) Paula the Elder and then her daughter, Julia Eustochium.

5.6. The Seven Families Consisted of:

(1) Anthusa, her husband, Secundus, and son, John (Chrysostom). Chrysostom's aunt was the deaconess, Sabaniana (Palladius, The Lausiac History, LIV and XLI.4).

(2) Marcella, her extensive circle of spiritual children and her Brown Shirt Society.

(3) Monica, her husband Patricius, their daughter, Perpetua, and sons, Augustine and Navigius, and Augustine's son, Adeodatus.

(4) Macrina the Elder, her son Basil the Elder, his wife Emmilia, and the ten grandchildren. They were Macrina the Younger,

three bishops (Basil, Gregory and Peter) and a hermit-monk, St Naucratius, as well as five other siblings (one of whom died young).

(5) St Nonna/Nona and her husband, Bishop Gregory of Nazianzus the Elder, and their three children St Gregory of Nazianzus, St Gorgonia (who had five children and some grandchildren) and St Caesarius, the physician. Nonna's brother, Amfilohije, was the father of both Bishop Amphilochius of Konya and Theodosia, the mother (or the governess) of St Olympias (ICONANDLIGHT, 'Saint Nonna, Mother of Saint Gregory the Theologian', online). (The former option would make Nonna the great-aunt of St Olympias).

(6) Melania the Elder, the mother of two children (including Publicola) and mother-in-law of Caeonia Albina (Palladius, The Lausiac History, LIV.1). Her granddaughter was Melania the Younger whose husband was Pinian. Melania's cousin or cousin-in-law was Paulinus of Nola, near Naples (d.431) some of whose correspondence with Melania, Ambrose, Jerome, Augustine and Martin of Tours (316-397) has survived. Melania the Elder was the aunt of Avita, who was the wife of Apronianus, and the mother of Eunomia (Palladius, The Lausiac History, LIV.1). Melania was also a spiritual mother to Evagrius of Pontus.

(7) Paula was the mother of five children: St Blaesilla, Paulina, St Julia Eustochium, Rufina and one son, who was named Toxotius after his father. Paula was the grandmother of little Paula and a boy, St Eustochius, the children of Toxotius and his wife, Laeta. St Pammachius was Paula's son-in-law (a former senator who had been married to Paulina before becoming a widower) (Palladius, The Lausiac History LXII). In Bethlehem, Paula was a mother-figure to Jerome and probably to his brother and fellow monk, Paulinian.

.7. Family 1 – led by Anthousa

St Anthousa (c.330-c.373 CE)

St Anthousa is honoured in the Orthodox tradition as the mother of a great saint. She was married to Secundus, an official of the Imperial Army in Syria.

At the age of 20, when she was left a widow with a son, John, she chose not to remarry and dedicated herself to John's upbringing.

She, herself, was well educated and was anxious about educating John in Antioch, a rough and large city, so she chose to home-school him, especially in the Scriptures. As John was clearly an able student Anthousa later sent him to the great scholars of the age: the pagan orator, Libanus, in Antioch, and then he studied theology under Diodore of Tarsus. John felt responsible for his devoted and devout mother and thus was unable to follow his own calling to the monastic life so he lived with his mother under a monastic rule. St Anthousa, who sowed her life into her son, has been largely forgotten, but John, called Chrysostom, became a renowned preacher and Patriarch of Constantinople and a Doctor of the Church ('Chrysostom, John, St.', in ODCC).

.8. Family 2 – led by Marcella

St Marcella (325-410 CE)

Marcella's parents are unknown but they had a palatial home on the outskirts of Rome where they hosted some

notable house-guests in the 340s. These included Peter of Alexandria and Patriarch St Athanasius of Alexandria (296-373), who gave her a copy of his Life of St Anthony (the founder of Egyptian monasticism), which she treasured. When she became a young widow, after less than a year of marriage, Marcella naturally looked to the life that Anthony exemplified and turned her home into a monastery, behaving like a pauper in plain sight (which was a scandal for a woman of such high rank) (Cohick and Hughes, 2017, 194ff).

As an independent, aristocratic, educated, wealthy woman Marcella could mix in the highest circles. She had worn silk garments but she chose humility and poverty in order to serve the poor: she and her followers donned simple brown robes and were called the Brown Shirt Society (Tucker, 2016, 9).

Many Christians, including Jerome for three years, Paula, her daughters Eustochium and Blaesilla, and Melania the Elder,

came under her sway. Those who lived in her house also

included Marcella's spiritual daughter, Principia, to whom Jerome's Letter 127 is addressed. Once Jerome was no longer available, having left Rome for the Holy Land, the Pope (Anastasius I) and many others consulted Marcella for sage advice and Scriptural interpretations. Her relative, Paulinus of Nola said of her, "*what a woman she is, if one can call so virile a Christian a woman*" (Ephesians. 29: 5-6).

Marcella's contribution to the 'Origenist controversy' was to collect witness statements about the damage that Origen's theories had caused to Christians and, according to Jerome, she virtually singlehandedly dismantled their errors (Cohick and Hughes, 2017, 197). At the age of 85, Marcella was assaulted by the Gothic invaders of Rome under Alaric in 410 and died the next day ('Marcella, St', in ODCC).

<u>5.9. Family 3 – led by Monica/Monnica, mother of St Augustine, grandmother of Adeodatus.</u>

St Monica (c.331-387 CE)

St Monica, a Berber from Africa, was the widow of Patricius, a pagan man of high status who was baptised in old age (Religionfacts, 'St Augustine of Hippo', online). Married life in Tagaste (Algeria) had been particularly difficult to endure as Patricius was short-tempered but as a Christian Monica learnt patience, long-suffering, wisdom and devotion in the school of life. There were three children: Augustine (354-430), his brother, Navigius and one sister, Perpetua. Monica laboured in prayer and fasting for many years, while Augustine was living a dissolute life searching for the truth in various philosophies and sects (such as Manicheanism[13] and Neo-Platonism). Augustine lived with an unnamed woman who was of a lower social class and by whom, as a nineteen year old, he had a son,

Adeodatus.

Augustine briefly taught in Rome (in 383-84) and then took a position as professor of rhetoric at the imperial court of Milan. [14] Bishop

Ambrose of Milan (c.340-397) was famed as a rhetorician, which interested Augustine sufficiently to attend his church as *"a careless and scornful looker-on"* (Mirus, online, citing Augustine's Confessions, Bk. 5). When Monica arrived in Milan she was delighted with Bishop Ambrose's preaching and loved him as an angel of God. As Ambrose was often unable to meet them Augustine found Simplicianus, an old rhetorician who had taught Ambrose (Mirus, online, citing Augustine's Confessions, Book 6). Augustine longed to surrender to God but was held prisoner by his lusts and ambitions (Religionfacts, 'Augustine of Hippo', online).

St Monica gave Augustine the news that she had arranged a marriage for him to a suitable girl who was still too young to marry and she persuaded the reluctant Augustine to send away his son's mother, the woman whom he had loved for fifteen years. For solace, Augustine immediately took another concubine for two years (Bonner, 2002, 38; Cohick and Hughes, 2017, 180). *"Celibacy seemed to me a painful course,"* he wrote (Mirus, online, citing Augustine's Confessions, Book 6). He advised his mother that he was no longer a Manichee, though not yet a Christian and then he discovered NeoPlatonism; which he embraced for a time.

When the Empress Justina, the Arian mother of the child-emperor, Valentinian II, began persecuting Bishop Ambrose of Milan and his church Monica became a prayer warrior in his defence. It was then, to comfort the congregation, who feared for the bishop's life, that harmonious singing of psalms and hymns, as practised in the Eastern Churches, was introduced in Milan (and from there into the West) (Mirus, online, citing Augustine's Confessions, Book 9).

After much soul-searching and anguish, when Augustine was 33, he surrendered to God. Augustine then organised a retreat in remote Cassiciacum for eighteen weeks of rest, recreation and discussion.

He gathered together his brother, Navigius, and his fourteen year old son, Adeodatus, his long-time friends, Alypius and Nebridius, and other ascetic young men, with Monica taking care of them as 'house mother' and providing wise theologian input and counsel. *"Longevity of relationship with God and stalwart faith qualify Monica as an indispensable authority in the philosophical search for wisdom"* (Cohick and Hughes, 2017, 181).

Once back in Milan, at Easter 387, Augustine resigned from his position and prepared for baptism. He and his son, Adeodatus, were baptised by Bishop Ambrose, along with his friend, Alypius (Religionfacts, 'Augustine of Hippo', online). The family began began their return to Africa but, at the age of 55/56, Monica, having lived to see Augustine baptised, died of a fever at the Port of Ostia as they were about to sail home. A short sentence about her burial is notable as it indicates that a funerary Eucharist was held: *"the Sacrifice of our ransom was offered for her, when now the corpse was by the grave side"* (Mirus, online, citing Augustine's Confessions, Book 9).

When Adeodatus, a brilliant young man of about nineteen, died in c.391, Augustine turned his home into a monastery, sold his inheritance and was ordained presbyter. [15] He was nominated by Valerius, Bishop of Hippo Regius, as his successor in 395 and consecrated bishop in 396. Augustine died in 430 during the Vandal siege after decades as a busy bishop and productive apologist against Donatism, Pelagianism and Manicheanism. His Confessions is perhaps the first, certainly the most complete, autobiography of his era (Religionfacts, 'Augustine of Hippo', online).

<u>5.10. Family 4 – led by Macrina the Elder, then her daughter-in-law Emmilia and then Macrina the Younger</u>
St Macrina the Elder (c. 270-340 CE)
The paternal grandmother of the family was Macrina the Elder, who began as a disciple of St Gregory the

Wonderworker/Thaumaturgus (c.213-c.270), who was himself a disciple of, and an apologist for, Origen ('Gregory Thaumaturgus, St', in ODCC). With her husband, who was an advocate and rhetorician, Macrina escaped persecution for three years, surviving in exile in Pontus, suffering hunger, deprivation and loss of property ('Macrina the Elder', in ODS). Afterwards, and when their financial situation improved, they became generous supporters of churches and monasteries. Their son Basil the Elder married Emmilia, whose father was a martyr (Cohick and Hughes, 2017, 163, f/n 13; New Advent, 'Basil the Elder', online). Nine of their ten children survived, three of whom became bishops (for which St

Emmilia is honoured in the Eastern church) and a further two also became saints.

<u>5.11. St Macrina the Younger (c.327-379 CE)</u>

Macrina the Younger was the oldest of St Emmilia's ten children. When Macrina's father, Basil the Elder, died, Macrina the Younger took over the mothering role, including of their mother, "*whom she led into the ascetic life*" (Cohick and Hughes, 2017,166). St Emmilia seems not to have coped well with widowhood and the tragic death in a fishing accident of her son, the hermit-monk, St Naucratius. Macrina the Younger became both mother and teacher so that her youngest brother, Peter, was entirely home-schooled by her, especially in the Biblical Wisdom literature, (Laing, 2017, 140-145). His consecration to the See of Sebaste was a credit to Macrina's Christian learning and knowledge of the Scriptures. Another of Macrina's brothers, Gregory, said of her: "[*she was*] *Peter's father, teacher, guardian, mother and advisor of every good*" (Cohick and Hughes, 2017, 163).

Three of St Macrina's brothers became bishops: St Basil of Caesarea, St Gregory of Nyssa and St Peter of Sebaste. The first two are remembered as 'Cappadocian Fathers'. The illustrious St Basil the Great was closest to his friend, St Gregory the Younger, Bishop of Nazianzus, who was the third of the 'Fathers' and who formed part of their group. St Basil's brother, St Gregory Nyssa, who became Bishop of Nyssa, seems to have been closer to their sister, Macrina, and was her great admirer. It was this brother, Gregory (c.330-c.395), who wrote Macrina's Life (Vita Macrinae Junioris) praising her scholarship and her character, and in De Anima ac Resurrectione he praised her competence as a theologian ('Macrina, St.', in ODCC).

On the family's property at Annisa, in Pontus, St Macrina had established and directed a flourishing ascetic community which lived under her rule and which, for a time, included two of her brothers, Basil and Peter (Cohick and Hughes, 2017, 163; Laing, 2017, 141, 144, 147). The monastic Rule of St

Basil and his Liturgy, which (much altered) is occasionally used in the East today, may owe much to St Macrina who influenced her siblings and the local community at the family estate in Pontus, for good (McManners, OIHC, 1990, 133; Cohick and Hughes, 2017, 163).

<u>5.12. Family 5 – led by Nonna/Nona and her husband, Gregory</u>

St Nonna was raised by Christian parents (Philotatos and Gorgonia) but they had arranged a marriage for her to Gregory, who was a pagan devotee of Hypsistos. Nonna devoted years of prayers, fastings and tears before God for his conversion and he became Bishop Gregory of Nazianzus, the Elder. Nonna trained her three children in the Scriptures and

Christian devotion. They were St Gregory, who later assisted his father as Bishop of Nazianzus, St Gorgonia and St

Caesarius, the physician. St Gorgonia married Alypius, whom she persuaded to be baptised (Cox [ed.], 2005, 278).

They had five children.[16] Their daughters were Alypiani, Eugenia and Nonna and their two sons becane monks. St Nonna's nephew or brother was St Amphilochius of Konya/Iconium who was Basil the Great's friend and was the brother of Theodosia, who (as above) was the mother or the governess of St Olympias ('Saint Nonna Mother of Saint Gregory', online).

Gregory the Elder was converted through a dream in which he was singing *"I was glad when they said unto me, let us go into the house of the Lord"* (Ps. 122:1). Because Bishop St Leontius of nearby Caesarea was passing through Nazianzus on his way to the First Ecumenical Council at Nicea (325 CE) Nonna presented her husband to him for baptism. Gregory became a devout and learned Christian and when he became Bishop of Nazianzus his wife, Nonna, was ordained deaconess at the same time.[17]

Nonna and Gregory buried their younger son, St Caesarius, in 368 and their daughter, St Gorgonia, in 369/70. Gorgonia was only 38 years old and left her five children, some still young. Nonna's 100-yearold husband died in 374 and a few months later St Nonna died in church while at prayer.

The family of Nonna's parents, Philotatos and Gorgonia, included numerous saints: St Nonna and her husband (St Gregory Nazianzus The Elder), her brother (?) (St Amphilochius of Konya), Nonna's daughter, St Gorgonia and the sons (Ss Caesarius and Gregory Nazianzus the Younger) [18] and Gregory's cousin and successor (St Eulalius of Nazianzus[19]). St Gorgonia's children also produced children. If St Theodosia was a blood-relative, so was her daughter, St Olympias. Gregory Nazianzus the

Younger's cousin, Bishop Eulalius of Nazianzus, translated some of his writings, a task that was completed by Gregory's great-nephew Nichobulos (McGuckin, 2001, xi; 241).

5.13. Family 6 - led by Melania the Elder, then Melania the Younger and her husband.

St Melania the Elder (c.345-c.410/417 CE)

This Melania had no biographer and was largely overlooked because of her role in the 'Origenist controversy' so her Vita has to be pieced together from extant letters and a few references. Not only did Rufinus of Aquileia, who favoured Origen, live in or near her monastery, but she, herself, read Origen's works (three million lines of them) and directed her life by them (Palladius, Lausiac History, LV.3; Cohick and Hughes, 2017, 206f). Perhaps the taint of Origenism marred her reputation although her biblical knowledge was legendary, as was her knowledge of theology and of early Christian texts. Melania's pagan Spanish parents were Marcellinus, of consular rank, and Caeonia Albina. At the age of fourteen Melania married Valerius Maximus Basilius, Proconsul of Achaea and prefect of Rome from 361 to 363 (Murphy, 'Melania the Elder...', Traditio 5, 1947, 64).

By the age of twenty-two she had lost her husband and two of her three sons and had moved to Rome where she became a Christian. After ten years Melania left her surviving teenage son, Valerius Publicola, in the care of a guardian and, influenced by St Jerome, she sold property to fund a move with her servants to Egypt where she lived for six months visiting monks and hermits (Cohick and Hughes, 2017, 204f; f/n. 59). Melania is regarded as a 'desert mother' as, when persecution broke out in Egypt after the death of St

Athanasius, in 375, many monks were banished from Egypt by the Arian emperor, Valens (because they were staunch supporters of the Council of Nicaea) and Melania followed them into exile in Palestine. Palladius met some of them who verified the following story: Melania donned slaves' clothing

to secretly minister to the needs of the imprisoned monks and was caught and imprisoned for it but her high rank turned her fortunes around (Catholic online, 'Saint Melania the Elder,

online). Rufinus of Aquileia, an ex-consul, came to Egypt to escort Melania to Jerusalem where she built monasteries on the Mount of Olives for men and women. Evagrius of Pontus was Melania's protégée and the source of some information about her. Fellow Spaniard, and a relative,

Paulinus of Nola, told his friend, Sulpicius Severus, that Melania had given him a fragment of the true cross, which she had received from Bishop John of Jerusalem (385-417) (Letters of St. Paulinus of Nola, Walsh [trans.], 1967, 2.125-33).

When Paulinus of Nola planned to visit the Holy Land with Melania and Rufinus, Jerome discouraged the idea saying, *"it is just as easy to reach the portals of heaven from Britain as from Jerusalem"* (Ep, 58.3). Jerome was sour because he was under Bishop John's ban from entering both important churches: the Holy Sepulchre in Jerusalem and the Holy Nativity in Bethlehem. Jerome's negative attitude and the antagonism between Rufinus and Jerome over Origenism (Cohick and Hughes, 2017, 135) caused Jerome to redact his complementary opinion of Melania. Previously Jerome had called her 'a new Thecla' but later she was *"black in name and black in nature"* (Murphy, Traditio 5, 1947, 59; Catholic online, 'Saint Melania the Elder', online).

In Jerusalem, Melania the Elder carefully shepherded her finances to maintain her monasteries and devoted herself to good works. In 397, she and Rufinus returned to Italy where Melania met her niece, Avita, and her pagan husband Apronianus, whom Melania instructed in the faith. When he converted Melania persuaded them and their daughter, Eunomia, to live a life of celibacy (Palladius, Lausiac History, LVC. 1).

In 408, Melania fled to Sicily ahead of the Goths with a group of refugees that included Melania the Younger, her husband, Pinian, her mother, Caeonia Albina, and Publicola's son. In Sicily, Melania instructed her grandson in the faith but this reference is brief and his activities are largely unrecorded (Palladius, Lausiac History, LIV. 6.1). According to Augustine of Hippo, his father, Valerius Publicola had died in Africa in 406 (E. A. Clark, in Fitzgerald and C. Cavadini [ed.], 1999).

Rufinus died on Sicily in 412 and the others went to Egypt where they lived for seven years on the family estate in Thagaste. Two years after returning to Jerusalem Melania the Elder also died. She had been deeply involved in the theological debates that were raging in the 4th century, not only about Origen's theories but also about Pelagianism. The author of The Lausiac History, Palladius of Helenopolis, was another bishop who was her friend and admirer. He is a source for her life; along with various letters and Gerontius's Vita Sanctae Melania Junioris (Life of St Melania the Younger) Greek and Latin versions of which have survived (Barnes, 2010, 249).

5.14. Melania the Younger (c.383/5-c.439 CE)

As noted, Valerius Publicola and Caeonia Albina were Melania the Younger's parents. At fourteen Melania married Valerius Pinianus (Pinian) who was seventeen. Seven years later Pinian reluctantly agreed that they would live celibate, dedicated lives together as she had almost died in childbirth and neither of her babies had survived (Cohick and Hughes, 2017, 209, f/n. 81). Melania had said, *"if God had wished us to have children, He would not have taken away my children untimely"* (Palladius, Lausiac History, LV.3). Pinian and Melania were each extremely wealthy but, despite great opposition, they quickly sold assets and properties to fund monasteries. In c.408, they fled from Rome to Egypt, via Sicily, with others, as noted above. Rufinus of Aquileia died in Sicily (as noted) but the others reached Africa (Cohick and Hughes, 2017, 209ff).

Historian Peter Brown notes a culture-clash between the many Roman wealthy, aristocratic Christian refugees from Alaric's invasion of Rome and the provincial Christianity of Africa (Brown, 2012, 291301). This is illustrated in Melania's and Pinian's lives in that the local congregation of Thagaste, where they owned property, clamoured for St Augustine of Hippo to ordain Pinian so that he (and his wealth) would remain there. His wife, Melania, intervened and refused, so instead they founded two monasteries at Thagaste, promised that if Pinian was ever to seek ordination it would be at Hippo and departed; leaving *"Augustine to sort out the mess"* (Cohick and Hughes, 2017, 212).

In 417 the young couple journeyed to Bethlehem to join St Jerome. In 418 they met with the English monk, Pelagius, and wrote to Augustine of Hippo in positive terms about his views but Augustine did not approve, and said so (Cohick and Hughes, 2017, 214).

Pinian died in 431 and Melania founded another monastery on the Mount of Olives and continued her generosity to monks, churches and the poor. In 437, she travelled to Constantinople to visit her pagan uncle and experienced his death-bed conversion. She prayed for the Empress Aelia Eudocia's injured ankle to be healed. Upon Melania's return to Jerusalem, the empress visited the Holy Land and Melania led her on a pilgrimage to the biblical sites. Melania the Younger died in 439, aged 55.

5.15. Family 7 – Led by Paula and then Julia Eustochium

St Paula (347-404 CE)

Paula's Spanish parents, Blaesilla and Rogatus, were of noble Roman descent and settled in Rome. There Paula married Toxotius, a senator, but, at the age of 32, she was left a wealthy widow and the mother of five children (Cohick and Hughes, 2017, 198, f/n. 28; Jerome's Lettter 108 records Paula's early

life and Letter 127 is a Life of Marcella). Paula was grief-stricken but the widow Marcella helped her to find a purpose and hope, greatly influencing her towards the ascetic life.

When Paula and her children lived in Marcella's communal home for religious women in her villa outside Rome Paula met St Jerome. He had arrived in c.385, with Bishops Epiphanius of Salamis (on Cyprus) and Paulinus of Antioch. Jerome then lived with Marcella for three years. Paula arranged marriages for three of her four daughters (Blaesilla, Paula and Rufina) but Eustochium (d.419) was determined to embrace celibacy from the start, although two others did so in widowhood (St Blaesilla, who died in c.384, and Rufina, who died in c.386). Another daughter, Paulina, married Pammachius (c.340-410), a wealthy senator who was Marcella's cousin and a schoolmate of Jerome, but when Paulina died Pammachius became a monk (Cohick and Hughes, 2017, 198). Like Marcella, he was killed in the Gothic invasion of Rome, in 410 CE.

Paula's only daughter-in-law, Laeta, was the mother of little Paula, who was dedicated to virginity at birth, and perhaps of a son, St Eustochius, about whom little is known. It was this Paula, Paula the Younger, who closed St Jerome's eyes in 426, the last of three generations of women who had financed his monastery, cared for him with devotion and assisted his work of translation.

5.16. Jerome or Hieronimus (d. 426 CE)

Jerome had had a dissolute youth, arrived in Rome after his conversion and extensive travels in Gaul and Asia, including the two years he spent in Constantinople with John Chrysostom (noted above). In Rome he managed to gain entry into aristocratic society (perhaps through his school-friend, Pammachius) and became closely associated with Marcella's group of brown-clad women, so much so that he was accused of sexual impropriety with Paula. When his protector and

friend, Pope Damasus, died Jerome was charged with clerical misconduct by the ecclesiastical court, found guilty and exiled from Rome. He defended himself by publishing copies of letters written by him to both Paula and Marcella, to prove that their contacts had been on a high spiritual plane. Thus at least one side of these relationships is known to posterity (Cohick and Hughes, 2017, 199; 192).

Plates 5.5, 5.6 and 5.7.

Ss Paula, Jerome, and Eustochium, door of St Catherine's Bethlehem. Photographs: D. Campbell, 1988 and J. Campbell, 2019.

Paula's daughter, St Blaesilla, had also become a disciple of Jerome before her tragic death from excessive asceticism in 384. When exiled, Jerome planned to live in the Holy Land

and persuaded Paula and her daughter, Julia Eustochium, to follow him. In 385 Jerome waited for Paula and Eustochium

on the island of Cyprus with Epiphanius of Salamis. Together Jerome, Paula and Eustochium visited Paulinus of Antioch in Syria before going up to Jerusalem where they stayed with Melania the Elder and Rufinus. They then toured the Holy Land and visited Egypt, where they stayed with the ascetic monks.

Of all the holy sites Paula was most moved by those in the Church of the Holy Sepulchre and that of the Holy Nativity, in Bethlehem. Her devotions were extreme. In the former she kissed and licked the holy places and in the latter she entered into the events so fully that she could hear King Herod's little victims crying. In the grotto of the Nativity she prophesised about Bethlehem's importance to redemptive history. Thus, she considered Bethlehem to be the right place to live (Cohick and Hughes, 2017, 162-68; 199f, citing Jerome, Epistle 108.20.1-7).

In 386, Jerome wrote in the women's names, pleading with Marcella to come too, saying *"we adjure you to give back to us the Marcella whom we love"* (Letter 46, Paula and Eustochium to Marcella). Marcella was already 66 years old and declined, staying in her home until her violent death. Eleven of

Jerome's letters to Marcella are extant (Mommaerts and Kelly, in Drinkwater and Elton (eds), 1992,

120f).

In Rome, Marcella had been a mother to them all but in Bethlehem, where Paula and Jerome lived in the separate monasteries which Paula's fortune had founded, she took such care of Jerome that she even fed him chicken soup when he was ill. Paula could not be his wife but she was the next best thing: his advisor and motherly companion. He, in turn, was devoted to Paula and he was with her as she died. Jerome, Paula and Eustochium are buried close to each other beneath the Church of the Holy Nativity.

Paula and Eustochium had sailed away leaving family members who included Toxotius, a boy of about five, crying for her on the wharf: perhaps a lesson to them in how not to parent one's child; but it was considered a virtue to prove one's devotion by putting Christ first and that was how

Jerome presented it (Cohick and Hughes, 2017, 199). (Similarly, the martyr, Perpetua, when deprived of her nursinginfant before her martyrdom, had seen the renunciation of her child and the rejection of her father's pleas as mere challenges on her path towards God [Rader, in Wilson-Kastner et al., 1981, 4f]). Later, in Rome, Paula the Elder's son, Toxotius, and his wife, Laeta had a baby, also called Paula. Jerome wrote, urging them to permit Paula the Elder to raise and educate the child in the convent from the age of four. He and Paula wanted to play 'mothers and fathers' but St Julia Eustochium, who took over as abbess when St Paula died, educated the child from the age of seven or eight. In her turn, Paula the Younger became abbess. St Eustochium was a scholar and a financial manager as she paid off her mother's debts and had put the monastic community on a sound footing before she died in 419 (Swan, 2000, 141).

Jerome is elevated as a Doctor of the Church and was considered a great theologian and translator of the Greek Bible into Latin (the Vulgate)[20] but he had had a troubled youth (sexually), and was ambitious, manipulative and short tempered. He was emotionally and financially dependent upon his women friends (both Marcella and Paula who were strong and stable characters). Like Origen, Jerome held

extreme views of sexual renunciation, arguing that marriage was a necessary evil and *"only for those who cannot attain to the spiritually elite"* (Cohick and Hughes, 2017, 198, citing Jerome, Epistle 22). Controversy had raged in Rome when Paula's daughter, Blaesilla, died at age twenty because of excessive fasting. Many wanted to stone the monk(s) who had directed her, but Paula supported Jerome (Cohick and Hughes, 2017,

198f). He was central to numerous doctrinal controversies and argued with St Augustine of Hippo and others about marriage but his views were in keeping with his temperament.

<u>5. 17. The Origenist Controversy (393-397 and 398-401 CE)</u>

As previously noted, the teachings of Origen, the famed philosopher-theologian and a Doctor of the Church, came into question long after his death. He had been tortured in the Decian persecution and had consequently died, in 253/54, aged 69 ('Origen', in ODCC).

The young Origen had been so successful in Alexandra and abroad, in both Christian and pagan philosophy, that his bishop had become suspicious and, in 231, Origen had been defrocked and banished to the Holy Land. There, the bishops of Jerusalem and Caesarea had welcomed him and he set up his school at Caesarea where St Pamphilus the Martyr had established the library that the historian Eusebius (c.260-340) would soon utilise (Castellano, 2009 I.1, online). Eusebius wrote an Apology for Origen, which was suspect because Eusebius, himself, was already considered to be semiArian. In Caesarea, Origen wrote his best works: his Commentary on St John and his Commentary on Song of Songs.

As noted above, the two main disputed Origenist doctrines were: the *"pre-existence of the soul"* and the *"restoration of all things"* (Universalism). These were seen as minimising or denying the Incarnation and disparaging the body in favour of the spirit. Late in the 4th century Bishop Epiphanius of Salamis expressed doubts about Origen's orthodoxy and from then on controversy raged about his divergent beliefs, especially his Universalism.

In 393, Epiphanius of Salamis, who had been a monk in Palestine, was invited by Bishop John of Jerusalem to preach a sermon in the Church of the Anastasis (Resurrection).

He denounced Origenism but was offended because Bishop John did not support him. In 394 Epiphanius ordained

Jerome's brother, the monk Paulinian, in Bethlehem, and Bishop John was angry that his canonical jurisdiction had been violated. The two patched things up by letter and in so doing Epiphanius provided seven doctrinal issues that were corrupting monks in the East, including *"the devil will return to his former dignity and rise again to the kingdom of heaven."* (Castellano, I.1, online).

Naturally the bishops mentioned in this chapter were in the thick of the controversy, as was Melania the Elder because of her own attachment to Origenism and her very close association with Rufinus of Aquileia, who lived in the monastery she had built on the Mount of Olives. Back in Rome, her friend

Marcella became involved, because of her vigorous pursuit of orthodoxy. Jerome, who had previously praised Melania the Elder, turned against her; although he, Paula and Melania the Elder had all been taught by Marcella and all must have previously been friends.

These two ordained monks, Jerome and Rufinus, who were indeed old friends, became embroiled in controversy because each had translated Origen's work and both were therefore thought by others to condone Origen's views. Each tried to establish that the other was the more Origenist, and therefore more of a heretic. They bitterly opposed each other's opinions. The Vulgate was Jerome's greatest achievement but Rufinus attacked his right to use the Jews' Hebrew text to translate the Greek Septuagint (Old Testament) into Latin: and to have a heretic (a Jew) help him do it!! He behaved as if he thought that the Greek Septuagint (LXX) was the God-given original, rather than having been, itself, a translation made by Jews from previously known text in Hebrew.

The upshot of the conflict was that Bishop John of Jerusalem appealed to Rome, and Theophilus of Alexandria mediated peace. John, Jerome and Rufinus were reconciled in 397

(Castellano, I.2, online). A year later, however, Rufinus (unwisely) translated Eusebius' Defense of Origen and two works by Origen himself and stated that Jerome had smoothed over difficult parts of Origen to make them acceptable to Latin readers. Now Jerome was branded as dishonest as well as an Origenist. Jerome responded by producing a new translation in which he pointed to where Rufinus had softened Origen's text. The two corresponded. Jerome wrote a conciliatory letter but it was never delivered. Jerome's moderate position was rather uncharacteristic of him but matters were taken over by Theophilus of Alexandria (no longer a peace-maker) who successfully petitioned Pope Anastasius I to ban Origen's writings from monasteries, because of the damage being done by them in Egypt. Theophilus was heavy handed against the Egyptian monasteries and so was called to Constantinople, by Emperor Arcadius and John Chrysostom (Patriarch 395-404), to apologise. Theophilus then sought revenge against Chrysostom and successfully colluded with the empress Eudoxia to have him exiled. What began as a doctrinal controversy would take both Chrysostom and his supporter, St Olympias, to early graves. Meanwhile, in Rome, Marcella's relative and Jerome's friend, the monk St Pammachius (c.340-410) (who was also Paula's son-in-law) were gathering witnesses to testify about the heresies of Origen before Pope Anastasius I (Castellano, I.3.2, online).

Rufinus wrote in a subservient tone to the Pope saying that he was merely a translator and declaring his orthodoxy and his appreciation of Papal authority. The Pope condemned Origenism but handed Rufinus's case back to his bishop, John of Jerusalem. At the same time that Marcella was leading an anti-Origenist campaign, her friend, Melania the Elder, was still allied with Rufinus, who, despite his protestations, was not entirely free of doctrinal suspicion.

5.18. Pelagius, Pelagianism and Semi-Pelagianism

Pelagius was a lay-monk from Britain or Ireland who went to Rome teaching against the idea of original sin. He also held that human choice comes before divine grace in the conversion process, that the person was solely responsible for their own moral choices, that the Law and the Gospel permit entrance to heaven and that all do not die because of Adam, nor will all rise because of Christ's resurrection ('Pelagius', in ODCC). This view was contrary to the teachings of St Augustine of Hippo, who was virtually a predestinarian.

Pelagius had success from 400 CE in Rome where he met the British lawyer, Celestius/Coelestius. After the sack of Rome in 410 they went together to Carthage where African bishops, including St Augustine, opposed them. Celestius then went to Ephesus and Pelagius went to Palestine. Pelagius was supported by the infamous Nestorius, who had been appointed Patriarch of Constantinople by the emperor Theodosius II in 428 (until Nestorius was deposed by the Council of Ephesus in 431). Pelagius was attacked by Augustine, Jerome and Paulinus of Milan before being opposed or excommunicated by two Popes and eventually condemned by two Synods and five Councils. (He was exiled to his monastery in Upper Egypt). Imperial edicts were issued against both Pelagius and Celestius after the Council of Carthage (417) although eighteen bishops were deposed for being reluctant or unwilling to subscribe (Bettenson (ed.), DCC, llll, 83). Pelagianism continued in Southern Gaul and parts of Britain, disappearing in the 6th century ('Pelagius', in ODCC). Semi-Pelagianism was half-way between Pelagianism and the extreme predestination position of Augustus of Hippo, who taught the 'irresistible grace' of God and 'infallible perseverance'. Semi-Pelagianism held that the initial step towards conversion was taken by the person, after which God's grace was extended. This was the general consensus in Gaul for 200 years ('Semi-Pelagianism', in ODCC).

5.20. Eustathios, Cross-dressing and the Council of Gangra

Virginity was extolled in 4th century. In Armenia, under the influence of Eustathios of Sebaste, marriage was considered loathsome, married women were considered unfit for Heaven and were despised, while others refused

to engage in liturgies performed by married priests and established their own assemblies. Some married women repudiated their husbands and then fell into adultery and women began to cut their hair, dress as men and even wear monks' clothing (Patricia Cox Miller, 2005, 150f).

The bishops of Asia Minor were so concerned about all of this that they gathered at Gangra in c.345 and published twenty canons, many of which condemned these practices and attitudes, and anathematised any who followed them (Gangra, Council of, in ODCC).

5.21 Conclusions

Many Christians moved to and fro in the whole Mediterranean world, which was one large fish-pond in which educated, aristocratic and/or wealthy women played vital but oft-overlooked roles. Many of the great theologians of the period (even desert monks) depended upon these women for financial and/or moral support and spiritual guidance.

Their finances and their monasteries were dotted all over the Holy Land and Asia Minor. They seemed to love adopting monks and becoming very close to them, mothering them and

travelling about with them. They greatly enjoyed lavishing their fortunes on the unfortunate and embraced privations,

including not taking a bath and not sleeping in beds (for example, Melania the Elder, Palladius, The Lausiac History, LV.2, online). All of this was contrary to social norms and their pagan relatives' opinions. Their donations changed the

Christian landscape: they enabled monasticism to flourish as vocations were possible only if a monastery could feed everyone. They raised the status of Christianity and they

provided space and leisure for scholarly work. These families' wealth had been accumulated in the 3rd century while pagan ancestors had held high imperial offices, a situation which could not be so readily repeated with the increasing Christianisation of the empire, nor would money ever flow so readily from Rome after its sacking in 410 CE. The glorydays of monasticism in the Hoy Land lasted only one century.

Aristocratic women were more influential when devoted to celibacy, than they would otherwise have been (E. Clark, Patristic Studies 18, 1989, 173). Averil Cameron called them *"desexed women"* (Cameron (ed.), 1990, 196/16) and their vow of sexual renunciation enabled them to mix freely with men as well as women. Certainly the desert mothers' wisdom would not have been memorised and copied for centuries if they had been stock-standard wives and mothers. Of them, Amma Syncletica and Amma Theodora are the most famous (Swan, 2000, 43-56; 64ff).

The 4th century was the main period in which the nature of Christ (i.e., Christology) was being hammered out. It was a century of intense scholarly debate and therefore of intense clarification of Christian doctrine, while at the same time heresies were multiplying and boundaries were being rigidly erected and enforced. Origenism, which had previously been influential, was declared to be heretical by three patriarchs and two emperors in c.400 CE (Castellano [2009, 2013], online I. 2-3 and I.3.3).

Questions:

(1) Which of the matriarchs 1-7 do you think made the greatest contribution to Ecclesia? Why? Why were the foremost Christian women widows?

(2) Was their contribution greater as patrons of important males, as theologians and intellectuals or

as family matriarchs: wives, mothers and grandmothers to their immediate family?

Chapter 6
Diversity: The Jews. The Eastern Churches

<u>6.1. Fourth to Sixth Century Changes in the Byzantine Church</u>

As St Paula's acts of devotion in Jerusalem c.385/6 demonstrate, the cults of relics and holy sites had developed quickly after the Constantinian peace and also the cult of saints (such as martyrs and confessors). Marian devotion elevated Mary above all other women and was enhanced in 432 when the Council of Ephesus accorded her the title Theotokos (Godbearer/Mother of God) although she was clearly important earlier and paintings of her in the Roman Catacomb of St Priscilla may, perhaps, be dated from 150 CE.

The Marian cult was advanced by the Empress Pulcheria (c.420) and by the Emperor Justin (c.565) and his wife, Sophia (Holum, 1982, 142, f/n.; 143; 227). Pulcheria built three churches to house the Virgin Mary's relics (Hodegoi, Chalkoprateia and Blachernai). A high point of the Marian cult was Mary's elevation as the guardian of Constantinople and the use of her cloak and girdle as palladia to ward off the Avar attacks on the city between 619 and 629 (Cameron, JTS, N.S. 29.1, 1978, 79, 89; Whittow, 1996, 239).

During these centuries, in Rome, Mary began to be depicted with orb and sceptre as a queen and/or Queen of Heaven [for example Santa Maria Maggiore, Santa Maria Antiqua, Santa Maria in Trastevere and San Lorenzo fuori-le-mura and a 6th century chapel in the amphitheatre of Durrës (Dyrrachium) in Albania].

A cycle of Marian feasts and their liturgies developed in the Holy Land in the 6th century and her increasing prominence accounts for the importance of such Marian sites in Jerusalem

as the Dormition Abbey on Mt Zion and the Tomb of the Virgin in the Kidron Valley. Many in the East, however, denied her the title theotokos, while perhaps accepting Christotokos.

Religious affairs became official business as Constantine I and subsequent Christian emperors became increasingly involved. They were called philochristos basileus (Christ-loving emperor) (Cameron, 1978, 99f). These factors operated within the Byzantine Empire while Christology was being clarified and contributed to the further separation of Christianity from Judaism (especially as Judaism shunned such practices of extreme devotion as mentioned above). Matters concerning Jews and Judaism were more significant under Christian emperors than they had ever been but the tensions were considerable. In general, the more Christianised a region became the more hostile the State was towards Jewish inhabitants and their institutions (Linder, 1987, 87).

<u>6.2. Jews in the East Before the Muslim Conquest of the Levant</u>

Just as Julius Caesar and Augustus had legislated to preserved Jewish rights and Judaism, later Emperors began to dismantle those rights while enhancing the legal position of Christianity. This began in 321 CE, when Constantine I made Sunday a day of rest from work and then, in 325 CE, made Christianity an official religion. This progressed haphazardly from then on until Christianity triumphed under Theodosius II. Laws could be made and repealed but change largely moved downhill for Jews especially if Jewish privileges impacted Christians directly, such as in the case of Jewish slaveownership. From 527 to 565, the Emperor Justinian's laws protected apostate Jews, while tempting

Jews to convert, with inducements, but many means were used to encourage conversion to

Christianity (Linder, 1987, 80).

A few earlier legal indications will be provided:

(a) Jews and Christians may not intermarry (Theodosian Code 3.7.2; Justinian Code 1.9.2).

(b) Christian conversion to Judaism was forbidden. (Theodosian Code 16.8.7; Justinian Code 1.7.1). Those who performed their circumcisions were to be executed: the same punishment as for castration (Linder, 1987, 81).

Conversion of Jews to Christianity were not unknown but forced conversions also occurred *"in many communities throughout the empire, when local religious enthusiasm fanned by clergymen erupted into violence against non-Christians*" (Maas, 2000/2003, 201 quoting Severus of Minorca, Letter on the Conversion of the Jews 3.6-7; 6.1-4; 13.1-14; 24.1.10; 30.1-2, Bradbury, trans., 1996, 83, 85, 93, 95, 117, 119, 123).

Meanwhile, outside of the Empire, the Jews of Mesopotamia flourished, and those in Persia, although considered 'inferior', were treated as "*people of the Book*" and fared tolerably well (Maas, 2000/2003, 192). Once the Levant was overrun by Muslim armies in the mid-7th-century many Jews came under the control of different Islamic powers, the last of which were the Ottoman Turks. This remained the status quo until 1917; as Volume 1 of this series details (Justin Campbell and Deslee Campbell, Synagoga's Heritage: Tabernacle, Temple, Synagogue and Church, 2019/ 2020).

6.3. Christian-Jewish Relations in the Middle Byzantine Period

In the Greek speaking East, as the Byzantine Empire began to wane and shrink in size there were fewer Jews under

Christian rule but a certain panic set in. Forced baptism of both Jews and polytheists was decreed by the Emperor Heraclius in the 630s (although intermittently enforced) and then by Leo III in 721-2, by Basil in c.873-4 and by Romanos I (919-44). During much of the period under review and prior to

the crusades Byzantium's Jews experienced "spasms of intolerance", with "two and a half centuries of undisturbed toleration" (Starr, 1939, 283; 1; 8). (It would be useful here to read Appendix 1.)

The fate of Christian slaves owned by Jews was a test-case (Linder, 1987, 79-85). It was considered inappropriate for Jews to rule over Christians and, on the other hand, Jews were obligated by halachic law to convert their slaves: it was a meritorious act.

(i) Jews must not own Christian slaves (Theodosian Code 16.9.1; Justinian Code 1.10.1). The penalty for such ownership was relatively light.

(ii) In 438 CE, a Jew who converted a Christian slave would be subject to both confiscation of property and the death penalty (Theodosian Code 48 and 54, laws which were given validity in the Justinian Code) (Linder, 1987, 80ff).

(iii) Church buildings were recognised as sanctuaries for runaway Christian slaves (Theodosian Code 39 and a similar law in the Justinian Code 61) (Linder, 1987, 83).

Various policies were inconsistent, for example different laws decreed that Christian slaves who were seized from Jewish owners were given over to the church, or the State should own confiscated slaves, or that they should be freed, or that Christians should pay to redeem them. Between 415 and 423 some concessions were made, for example that Christian slaves could be inherited and that some such slavery was permitted to continue in Africa (Linder, 1987, 83f).

In summary: every effort was made to prevent Christians from converting, or from being converted to Judaism but efforts to convert Jews and pagans to Christianity could even, and did include, forced baptisms.

.9. Anti-Jewish Laws Also Effected Judaeo-Christians

In 548 the Talmud was prohibited, along with rabbinic exegesis, which influenced the way the Scriptures could

legally be interpreted. As this deprived Jews of their religious rights (they had also lost civil and military rights) there was a

rebellion in Israel in 556. Its failure caused many to flee to Persia where Judaeo-Christians joined the Nestorians and Samaritans to fight beside Cosroe II of Persia against the Byzantine Empire in 604. This army occupied Jerusalem in 614 and stole the wood of the True Cross from the Church of the Holy Sepulchre (Testa, 1992, 28f).

Various Judaeo-Christians who had remained in Galilee were removed by Emperor Heraclius when he re-established Byzantine control and, in 630, he rescued the relic of the Cross and carried it back to Jerusalem in triumph. His victory was short-lived as the Muslim Arabs penetrated the Holy Land from 638 and many citizens accepted Islam while others broke from both Rome and Constantinople and formed Monophysite national churches: *"Armenian, Syro-Jacobite, Coptic-Egyptian and Abyssianian"* (Testa, 1992, 29).

In 787 the Second Council of Nicaea excommunicated Christians who would not renounce the Sabbath and other Jewish ways, which finally removed remnants of the Ebionites and Judaeo-Christianity in general (Testa, 1992, 30).

.10. The Armenian Church

Christianity came to Armenia early, through the efforts of Gregory the Illuminator (257-331) an Armenian prince who had been captured and raised as a Christian in Caesarea (now Kayserai), in Cappadocia. With the conversion of the ruler, Tiridates III (238-314), the people followed. Temples became churches and pagan priests were baptised and quickly ordained. Gregory the Illuminator went to Cappadocia to receive ordination and to recruit teachers of the faith to return with him. Then he became Catholikos of the nation; a hereditary office. Caesarea continued to have oversight over the fledgling Armenian church up to 374, during the episcopacy of St Basil of Caesarea (c.330-79). Occasionally Armenian rulers (King Pap, in 373, and Jazdgerd II, c.450) reverted to paganism and harshly persecuted their Christian subjects (Wand, 1961, 245).

Over the centuries, Armenians have also been persecuted by Persians, Arabs, Turks and Russians. As Persia, which was Nestorian, annexed half of Armenia in 390, Armenia chose to be Monophysite, but at times they have been in communion with Rome. Rome is still influential, although Armenia's liturgy is largely based upon St Basil's Cappadocian rite (perhaps designed by his sister, St Macrina).

.11. Babylon/Iraq and Persia/Iran

After the day of Pentecost, Christianity was taken in every direction, including along the Persian Royal Roads, which ran from south-western Iran to Babylon and Northern Mesopotamia, where the Asian regions had been conquered by Alexander the Great. In the Middle Ages the Silk Road ran from Syria to Persia, to Uzbekistan, Kurdistan and China, which facilitated the flow of the gospel to the East, although the Nestorians had evangelised the Far East since before the 8th century (Jenkins, 2008, 50, 52).

.12. Ancient Persian Christianity

Theodore of Mopsuestia (c. 350-428 CE) was of the 'Antiochene school of thought', which favoured literal interpretation of Scripture (rather than allegorical interpretation, which was popular in Egypt). He emphasised Christ's human nature in the long-lasting controversy of the two natures of Christ (the divine and the human). *"To him Christ was a man who became God rather than God who became man"* (Wand, 1961, 220).

Nestorius (Patriarch of Constantinople from 428 to 431) popularised these ideas and denied the Virgin Mary the title theotokos (Mother of God) because she was only the mother of Christ. Nestorius was opposed by the Alexandrian school led by Bishop Cyril of Alexandria (c.429 CE) and by Pope

Coelestine (422-32 CE) who excommunicated Nestorius. In response, a party of Eastern bishops excommunicated Cyril of Alexandria but the Emperor Theodosius stepped in and deposed three bishops from office: Cyril, Nestorius and Memnon of Ephesus, who were all temporarily arrested. Nestorius was exiled to his monastery and then to Egypt but Cyril and Memnon were restored (Jenkins, 2008, 219-223).

Nestorius' teachings were readily accepted in Persia, becoming entwined with nationalism and national independence. Rome and Persia had been long-time enemies and when Christianity became the official religion in both empires raids and warfare continued. Persia was as Christian as the Roman Empire, although the ancient Zoroastrians and government officials opposed it and attacked Armenian Christians in the 5th century (Robert, 2009, 145 and 8, 9, 19).

.13. Babylon

In about 550 CE Cosmas the Monk visited the great city of Babylon, writing: 'among the Bactrians and Huns and Persians and the rest of the Indeans, ... and throughout the whole land of Persia there is no limit to the number of churches with bishops and very large communities of Christian people, as well as many martyrs (confessors?) and monks also living as hermits' (McCrindle (trans. 1897), Christian Topography of Cosmas Indicopleustes).

Islam overtook the area in the 7th century and serious violence occurred between the two religions centuries later, especially during the Crusades (Robert, 2009, 24).

.14. In More Modern Times: Iran and Iraq

Persia (Iran) claimed neutrality during WWI, but in 1914/1915 Turkish and Russian troops entered almost unopposed, ravaging the country and requisitioning food and livestock.

British soldiers soon followed and successfully captured Baghdad (in nearby Iraq) in March, 1917. They expelled the Turks and defeated Persian armed resistance. After the Bolshevik takeover in Russia (October, 1917) the Communists negotiated peace with Turkey and Germany but, as the Russian army withdrew from Iran, it burned crops and even bazaars. Due to a severe drought, famine ravaged Northern Persia/Iran. The British purchased what wheat there was because it was cheaper than bringing wheat from America and had the advantage of freeing up cross-Atlantic shipping for other war-related cargo. Almost half of Iran's population died of starvation and disease (between 8 and 11 million people). The same percentage died in nearby Lebanon, due to drought and a great locust plague (Stone, 2017, 71-74). Starving Armenians had been forced out of Anatolia by Turkey's policy of cleansing the Ottoman Empire of its Christian (Assyrian, Armenian and Greek) citizens. They dragged their emaciated bodies into Northern Iran but there was no spare food. Turkish soldiers, in hot pursuit, massacred thousands of them at Basra, but British troops escaped by boat across the Caspian Sea.

Since then it has been difficult for Christians to evangelise a country that had been so badly treated by Christian nations (Russia and Britain). The accusation by various high-profile Muslims (such as Dr Mohammed-Gholi Majd), that Britain bore the main blame and had a deliberate policy of genocide[21] is highly contentions and discounts historical facts for polemical ends.[22] This is not to say that Britain was blameless, or benevolent towards Iranians, but the kind of killings of civilians because of their ethnicity, as the Turks clearly did to Christians in World War I, cannot be substantiated (Jenkins, 2008, 162).

A positive contribution was made by Henry Martyn (1781-1812), an Anglican chaplain to the East India Company. He translated the New Testament into Hindustani, Persian and Arabic, the Psalms into Persian and the Anglican Book of Common Prayer into Hindustani (Robert, 2009, 48; 'Martyn, Henry', in ODCC).

Recently, the ancient Christian churches of the East have become scapegoats for such failed policies of the Western powers as the US invasion of Iraq in 2003. Since that invasion, clergy have been kidnapped and churches in Iran and Iraq have been destroyed. The Chaldean Catholic Archbishop, Paulos Faraj Rahho of Mosul (Iraq), was murdered in 2008. At that date only 3% of Iraq's population was Christian. Chaldeans, who are in communion with Rome and practise an ancient Eastern rite, are the most numerous (Philip Pullella, Rome, and Aseel Kami, Baghdad, online).

Iranian Christians are tenacious and faithfulness: the underground church is growing under persecution. The Christian NGO Open Doors estimates that there are 15,000 Roman Catholics and 500,000 other Christians in Iran today (Pullella and Kami, online). The use in church of the Persian language, Farsi, is forbidden to prevent Muslim conversion and such converts *are subject to extreme persecution*. Even converts who flee overseas fear the secret police (Rode, Open Doors, online).

Some observers say that the Iraqi Church is growing under wartime conditions (Murre-van den Berg, online) but Anglican cleric Canon Andrew White ('the Vicar of Baghdad') recently said that in *the cradle of Christianity,*" churches, manuscripts and artefacts are being wiped out (Lane and Thomas, online). White led the only Anglican congregation in Baghdad: St George's Cathedral. Mainly widows and children, they fled with thousands of others to refugee camps in Jordan. Some have moved overseas, some have returned home and some depend on foreign donations to survive.

6.10. Conclusions

In the East, church dignitaries often had a complex and conflicted relationship with the secular powers (the Byzantine Emperors) and often suffered terribly while trying to maintain the independence of the church. Yet the Eastern Church was protected from Papal punishment or interference by those same Byzantine Emperors. Ecclesia was two large independent bodies, both weakened by the split. The consequences for Eastern Christians were negative when Islamic armies progressively conquered most of the region in the mid-7th century and eventually overran Constantinople in 1543.

Questions:

(1) Why do you think that the Church in Iran is growing today?
(2) Why did Nestorianism have such appeal in the East?

Chapter 7
Iconoclasm and the Great Schism

<u>7.1. Iconoclasm</u>

When the Byzantine armies were not experiencing the success that was expected, Emperor Leo III (717-741 CE) supposed that Heaven was displeased, possibly because icon-veneration was idolatry after all. In 726 Leo began by destroying the image of Christ on the Chalke Gate to the Imperial Palace. A certain Theodosia and other ordinary women were said to have died in its defence.[23] Leo and his successors, his son, Constantine V (741-775 CE) and his grandson, Leo IV (775-780 CE), banned icons and images from churches. Many monks, and even a greater proportion of nuns, resisted, as also did some lay-people.

Plate 7.1.
Apse, Hagia Sophia. Istanbul (867 CE).
Public domain.

Icons were hidden, which was dangerous, but most were destroyed or whitewashed over. Whereas golden mosaics featuring the Madonna and Child had previously graced the apse in most Byzantine churches, they were replaced by huge crosses. Evidence of this remains in St Irene's Church in the grounds of the Topkapi Palace, in Istanbul (Talbot, 1998, ix). Twenty-four years after icons were restored for the second time (in 843 CE) the mosaic of the Madonna and Child was replaced in the apse of Hagia Sophia, Constantinople's Great Church (Plate 7.1) as in many other churches after Iconoclasm.

The most dangerous period for iconophiles had been under Constantine V who forced iconophile nuns and monks to marry; or blinded or exiled them. He tortured an abbess, Anthousa, and her nephew, an abbot. Abbots were paraded through the hippodrome of the capital to be spat upon and cursed. Some monks were executed and imprisoned and monastic property was confiscated. Constantine V's son, Leo IV, was a milder iconoclast, who released monks from prison (Talbot, 1998, x-xi; xi-xiv). Leo IV died under suspicious circumstances leaving his wife Eirene (a secret iconophile) as regent for their nine-year-old son, Constantine VI. There followed a brief period under Eirene in which icons were restored (787-815 CE). Eirene had her son blinded in 797 and he eventually died as a result, so that she became sole ruler from then until she was ousted in 802 by the usurper Niceophorus I (802-813). Leo V (813-820), who was followed by another usurper, Michael II (820-829 CE), reinstated the ban, which stood until 843 (Talbot, 1998, xiii).

Between 842 and 856 the Empress Theodora was regent for her infant son, Michael III (852-867) and in 843 she was able to restore Orthodoxy, this time permanently. Thus two imperial widows, Eirene and Theodora, were essential to the survival of sacred art to the East. The first was the Empress Eirene,

mother of (and regent for) Constantine VI ('ruler' from 790). The second was the Empress Theodora, mother of (and regent for) Michael III [842-867]. Each reversed her deceased imperial husband's decree banning icons. Both women had political reasons for supporting icons, which dovetailed with their personal inclinations (Talbot, 1998, x-xxi; Herrin, in Samuel and Jones (eds) 1982, 56-83).

Plate 7.2.
Icon of the Triumph of Orthodoxy
British Museum: public domain in its country of origin and other countries
and areas where the copyright term is the author's life plus 100 years or less.

A valuable 14th-century icon celebrating 'the Triumph of
Orthodoxy of 843 CE' (which is now in the British Museum)
shows (in Plate 7.2) that the Eastern Church came to venerate an
ordinary iconophile woman. This icon depicts the Empress Theodora and
young Michael III (top left) and beneath them St Theodosia, the woman
who (tradition maintains) was martyred for, as noted, physically defending
an icon of Christ during the first period of Iconoclasm. She is shown on the
far left holding an icon of Christ.

7.2. After the Triumph of Orthodoxy

The Age of Iconoclasm is regarded as a Byzantine 'Dark Age' and the
restoration of icons resulted in an economic and cultural renaissance. There
was a flowering of artistry in every medium, including church decoration,

and under Patriarch Photios the amazing and huge Madonna and Child (Plate 7.1) was replaced in the apse of Hagia Sophia. Because monastics had supported the people's cause, against the emperors, they became popular and monasticism flourished in wealth and numbers. This, in turn, expanded secular and religious education in every discipline, notably manuscript copying and illumination and the production of sacred literature. One staunch supporter of icons and a notable voice, Theodore, abbot of the large Stoudios monastery in Constantinople (which is now a ruin) led the way, reforming their liturgy and practices and encouraging manual labour and the composition of hymns and prayers (Cunningham, 2002, 32f).

<u>7.3. Conclusions</u>

Today icon-piety endures for both women and men and the theological basis of Orthodoxy is firmly established and excludes excesses such as idolatry and the 'vain repetition' of holy images. The Eastern church does not accept three dimensional images (that is, statues). Icons are expected to, and continue to be, vehicles for women's spirituality, although women are under-aware of female contributions to the history and traditions associated with icons.

Christianity flourished in the East but the Eastern church was wracked by various heresies, some of which were not heresies at all but linguistic difficulties or personality conflicts. The most dangerous competition for Orthodoxy came from Arianism because Arian sympathies were held by certain luminaries, such as Constantine the Great, Bishop Eusebius of Caesarea and Bishop Eusebius of Nicomedia, who baptised Constantine on his deathbed. Furthermore the Emperor Constantius II held Arian convictions and persecuted those with orthodox opinions.

Constantine the Great created the Christian Byzantine Empire and, as the eastern frontiers extended, so did Christianity. The Empire's enemies included Sassanians, Turks, Arabs, Bulgarians, Moguls and, eventually, various other Muslims. As the army became weaker, enemies reached the very walls of the city, which provided protection, as during Avar attacks on the city between 619 and 629, when an icon of the Virgin Mary and items of her clothing were paraded on the walls of the city (Cameron, 1978, 79, 89; Whittow, 1996, 239). The Empire was most extensive in the 6th century, after which its boundaries gradually shrank until only the city, itself, survived.

At first the defensive walls of Byzantium had protected only the inner city area - the Sultanamet (near the Palace) but as the city grew Constantine built a wall further out and in 403 Theodosius II built a stronger and longer wall with 95 It was destroyed by an earthquake in 447 but was restored and strengthened with a great dry moat. In the mid-9th century the defensive towers.

A Sea Wall was built close to shore to make a sea-borne invasion difficult. The city walls were often strengthened (as in the 7th and 9th centuries) and were all that saved the city in the 14th century and for another century.

Plate 7.3.
Walls of Constantinople restored in 2006.
Photo by Bigdaddy. Licensed under Creative Commons Share Alike Attribution 3.0 License.

As noted above, the weakening of Byzantium's military power was intimately connected to another feature of life in the 8th and 9th centuries. Byzantium was also wracked by internal controversy: over icons, which were banned during First and Second Iconoclasm by various emperors who blamed military weakness upon the sometimes questioned practice of venerating icons. After both of these periods, as noted, it was an Empress, with imperial power as regent, who restored icons to churches and to private piety.

7.4. Early schisms and moves towards separation

From the efforts of Constantine the Great both state and church powers had struggled to keep unity between the East and the West because, ideologically, Ecclesia should be a monolith. In fact, this had never quite been the case, even in the days of controversy between Paul and Peter and between

Paul and Barnabas. There had often been differences between the East and the West, notably over the date of Easter (known as the Quartodeciman Controversy) in which the Asian

churches (led by Bp. Polycrates of Ephesus) followed the Apostle John and the Jewish date of Passover on whichever day that fell. The rest of the church kept Easter on a Sunday, claiming to follow St Peter. Pope Victor of Rome threatened to cut off unity, until Irenaeus of Lyons (in Gaul) and other bishops appealed for peace (Stevenson, doc. 125, 147-151; Eusebius, H.E. V. 23-5). Another disagreement was over the use of a single Latin word filioque meaning 'and the Son'. This is sometimes called the 'Double Procession Controversy'. From about the 6th century in Spain and the 8th-9th century in France these words were added to the creed *"the Holy Spirit, the Lord, the Giver of Life, who proceeds from the Father and the Son"*, whereas, in the East, the Holy Spirit still proceeds only from the Father. This was a source of great controversy (Cunningham, 2002, 35).

Another difference (which may now seems barely significant) was that, in the West the elements were consecreated by 'the words of institution' said during the gospel-narrative of Jesus' Passover event, whereas, in the East, the consecration

n coincided with the invoking of the Holy Spirit ('Consecration, The Prayer of', in ODCC). There were other schisms over the centuries, such as in Rome over Novatian, the anti-pope. His baptism was challenged by Cornelius of Rome because he was sprinkled when ill and not rebaptised by immersion (Jensen, 2012, f/n. 38). His hard-line against the lapsed in the Decian persecutions of c.250 CE was challenged and/or disliked. Also in Carthage there was disagreement when Bishop Cyprian violently disagreed with Stephen of Rome over the readmission and rebaptism of the lapsed during previous persecutions. Communion between them had been broken (but short of excommunication) although Cyprian remained a dedicated champion of Rome ('Cyprian, St', in ODCC). Also in Rome, Pope Damasus (304-94 CE) struggled with his competitor, Ursinus, and won because the Emperor Valentinian exiled Ursinus (Frend, 1967, 517). In North Africa the Donatists' elected a rival to Bishop Caecilian in 312/ 13 CE (Haight, 2004, 206) and in Corinth when 'Clement of Rome' had intervened to try to sort out differences between groups (as noted in Chapter 23.3 of

Volume 1 this series). In fact, discord and individualism tended to prevail. A thirty-five-year-long EastWest schism occurred from 484 CE over cultural differences and Christology (Haight, 2004, 213). Furthermore when Pope Benedict XIII judged the 'Disputation of Tortosa' in 1413-14 (discussed in Appendix 2, below) he was not actually the Pope but only one of three rival claimants to the Holy See (Maccoby [ed.], 1982/ 2006, 91).

There was a background of theological difference between the East and the West, which was almost inevitable, given that they wrote and preached their theology in different languages. Some of the heavy controversies could only have taken place in Greek because Latin was incapable of some of the nuances of the richer Greek language.

Plate 7.4.
Hagia Sophia, 1852, by lithographer Gaspare Fossati. Public domain.

Latin was St Augustine of Hippo's language (395-430 CE) and he was not at home in Greek and had difficulty with the more obscure controversies (Cameron, LRE, 1993, 190). This led him into numerous theological errors. These were embraced by the Latin Church throughout the Middle Ages, but the Eastern Church was shocked, for example, by Augustine's stress on original sin (Tomkins, 2003, 61f; Cameron, LRE, 1993, 150).

From the death of Theodosius the Great in 395 CE the government of the empire had been split along linguistic lines, with two emperors governing the parts, so a similar division of the church was almost inevitable.

As early as Constantine the Great's reign Rome and Constantinople were antagonistic to each other. In the early-6th-century the patriarchs of Alexandria and Antioch, and the more recently created Patriarchate of Jerusalem, all rejected the decisions made at the Council of Chalcedon in 450 CE, which had followed the teachings of Pope Leo, as explained in his letter or Tome. Leo taught that the two complete natures in Christ were *"unmixed, unchanged, undivided and inseparable"* (Boer, 1976, 171).

7.5. The Great Schism of 1045

Eventually the Eastern bishops all repudiated Chalcedon and embraced Monophysitism, despite the fact that (except for the two representatives of the Pope at Chalcedon) all of the five-to-six-hundred prelates who attended Chalcedon had been Eastern bishops ('Chalcedon', in ODCC). By contrast, the Popes remained firmly Trinitarian but they were powerless in the East because the Byzantine emperors supported the local patriarchs, although Rome remained in communion with the East. Despite a long period of disharmony over the issue of papal supremacy, the church did not finally split between the East and the West until the 'Great Schism' of 1045 when Pope Leo IX and Patriarch Michael I of Constantinople excommunicated one another. The Patriarchs of Jerusalem, Antioch and Alexandria sided with Constantinople, so the church clearly split between the Greek-speaking East and the Latin West.

7.6. The Fourth Crusade

Any possibility of reconciliation with Rome faded on April 9, 1204 when the sorry saga of two Christian powers fighting each other began.

The wealthy and beautiful city of Byzantium was invaded, and looted for three days. As noted in Appendix 1, the Crusaders set up a Latin Kingdom in the city, which lasted until 1261 when the Byzantines regained their capital.

Questions:

(1) What were the reasons for the Great Schism?

(2) In your personal opinion, how should the lapsed be treated after the persecution is over?

Chapter 8
The 'Dark' Ages

8.1. The Spread of Monasticism

The first Egyptian hermit was Paul the Hermit (Paul of Thebes) who, like St Cyprian of Carthage, went into hiding during the Decian persecution (c.250 CE) (History of Monasticism, online). When he died, Paul the Hermit was buried by St Anthony, who from c.285 CE, had formed hermit-type monasteries, in which monks lived independently but close to each other and met weekly, each Sunday. This became popular and spread to Scetis near the Nile Delta and from Egypt's eastern desert into the Sinai and Palestine.

Plate 8.1.
Hermitage, Zilve Valley, Cappadocia.
Photo: D. Campbell, 2007.

The most extreme example of a total hermit was the Syrian saint, Simeon Stylites (c.390-459) who lived on top of a pole, standing on one foot, for over forty years ('Simeon Stylites, St.', in ODCC). From his lofty heights he exerted great power, even writing "a violent letter" to effectively rebuke Theodosius II for being soft on Jews and pagans (Holum, 1982, 125).

This lifestyle choice was copied by various other ascetics including Symeon the Stylite, who, in the 10th century carved a three-storey hermitage for himself in the tufa pillars of Cappadocia, (Plate 8.1) (Rodley, 1985, 193). Symeon also prepared a cave-tomb there, inscribing it: "Christ is the gate of those who are here: Who banishes sadness and heralds joy", plus a long epitaph which confirms his emulation of Simeon by concluding: "While yet alive I dug this burial cave. Receive me, tomb, as you have the Stylite" (Kostof, 1972, 47-50).

A circuitous route took the eremitic monasticism of hermits to France (to John Cassian in Marsailles and St Gregory in Tours) then on to Ireland, north to Iona in Scotland, then to Lindisfarne and Jarrow in England, and back to Europe (Luxeuil, Bobbio and Montecassino, near Rome) (Oden, 2007, 52-55 and Map 5).

<u>8.2. The 'Dark' Ages in Britain</u>

Christianity probably arrived in Britain with the Roman army and traders in the 1st or 2nd century CE, long before St Augustine, who became Catholic bishop of England, was sent from Rome in the late6th century to convert the English.

Celtic tribes lived throughout Gaul, North Italy and Britain and their English Church was sufficiently well organised and in touch with Europe to send delegates to the Synod of Arles (in 314 CE) and to the Council of Ariminium (in 359).

Celtic services appear to have been individualised and were often varied by each bishop and were apparently more charismatic and extemporaneous than in the Latin Church.

The monks did not observe parish boundaries (nor political boundaries) but evangelised at will. They practised extreme asceticism but did not have the exaggerated respect for virginity that the Latin church embraced (Clarke, 1961, 92f). Monks could be married and the historian and monk, Bede, was probably married as his writings suggest. Some Celtic monastic rules and ecclesiastical rites have survived in Latin and some prayers and hymns are known. For example, see Andy Dahlburg, 'The Celtic Monk.' Online.

Plate 8.2.
St Martin's Church, Canterbury.
Public domain.

The first Celtic church buildings were made of wood, which have not survived but monastic churches were often of stone, financed by local nobles. These churches were often so narrow that internal columns were not necessary, so aisles were not created. The typical plan had three parts: a nave, a chancel and an apse. Side chapels or towers to the North and/or South helped to buttress the outer walls. 'West-works' were

developed at the west-end, such as one or two towers and/or a Great West Door. St Martin's, Canterbury (Plate 8.2), which was built in Roman times, has a similar layout. It is the oldest continually used parish church in Britain. Roman brickwork is in situ in the north and south walls and the characteristic thin Roman bricks are in secondary use, elsewhere.

In the later-5th century, the pagan Anglo-Saxons decimated Christian towns and villages in the East of England, which then had to be reevangelised (Hill, 2007, 164). The Celtic Church survived only in Cornwell, Wales, Scotland, Ireland and the Isle of Man. Interestingly, the names of English rivers vary from entirely Celtic names in Wales and the West of England, to a mixture of names in the middle of England, to Germanic names in the East where Viking and Anglo-Saxon influence was strongest (Thomas, 1971, 37; fig. 20). This reflects the demographic changes as earlier inhabitants were pushed westwards by the waves of Norse invasion on the East coast ('Celtic Church', and 'Patrick, St.', in ODCC)

8.3. St Ninian

Ninian (c.360-c.432) was the son of a Christian chieftain of the Britons. He was educated in Rome and consecrated bishop (probably by Pope Siricius) to become a missionary to the pagan Picts of Southern Scotland. He built a white stone church at Whithorn and a monastery from which his monks evangelised Scotland and which later became an important town and a centre for pilgrimage ('Celtic Church', and 'Ninian, St.', in ODCC). Many Irish scholars, including St Finbarr/Finnian of Moville, went across the North Channel for training at Whithorn (Bruce, 1958/1962, 385).

8.4. St Patrick.

Patrick was led by a vision to the Irish as Gods' ambassador. Although little is known about them, there had been

Christians in Ireland from the earliest days, as various oratories indicate. These include the illustrated windowless A-frame, field-stone building called the Gallarus Oratory, which is on Dingle Peninsular just north of the Skellig Islands (Robert, 2009, 152 and 144, citing Patrick's Confessions 11).

Plate 8.3.
Oratory, Dingle Peninsular. Public domain.

Patrick visited the scattered Christian communities of Northern Ireland to bring them closer to the rest of Christendom and encouraged the use of Latin (although he spoke it poorly). He was said to have baptised thousands of people, including the parents of St Brigid/Bride of Kildare ('Bride, St.', in ODCC). Patrick evangelised Ireland's pagan West, despite the opposition of the pagan Druids and he founded numerous monasteries and churches, including the Cathedral of Armargh (in 444 CE) which soon became the educational and administrative centre of the Irish Church. Irish monasteries preserved scholarship in both Latin and Greek (Robert, 2009, 158).

"The story of the conversion of the Irish is inseparable from the spread of Irish monasticism, and the launching of missionary journeys by the great Irish missionaries of the Middle Ages" (Robert, 2009, 157).

Patrick wrote two extant documents in Latin. The first was a letter to the blood-thirsty British chieftain,

Coroticus, (apparently a Christian) (Robert, 2009, 155, citing St Patrick's Letter to Coroticus, Ludwig Bieler (trans.). Patrick's command of Latin was sufficient to

roundly condemn Coroticus for his slaughter and enslavement of newly baptised converts (some still in their baptismal robes) and including many dedicated virgins. Many were sold to the pagan Picts and Scots "where sin abounds, openly, grossly and impudently" (Robert, 2009, 155, citing Letter to Coroticus 3).

In 450 Patrick wrote his "Confessions", an apology against his detractors (Robert, 2009, 145-49). It sets forth his beliefs: in the Trinity; in the oneness ('brother-and-sister-hood') of all baptised believers; in Christian charity; in renunciation and in perpetual prayer. Patrick is the patron saint of Ireland: revered by both Catholics and Protestants ('Patrick, St.', in ODCC). A century after Patrick's time monasteries controlled the Church and abbots, not bishops, were the principal religious leaders. The Pope was even called 'the abbot of Rome' (Bruce, 1958/1962, 385).

<u>8.5. St Patrick and Women</u>

Patrick defended women's decisions, even against their fathers. In particularly he upheld their vows of chastity and he protected women against enslavement. He encouraged women's leadership roles, especially those of high-born and royal women, who readily converted and became prominent in his work and in governing monasteries. Abbesses could control nuns and monks, which gave them greater power than bishops, and they became spiritual and political advisors to men (Robert, 2009, 157). Eventually there were both women and men at the famous abbeys of Whithorn (Scotland), Kildare (Ireland) and Whitby (England) (Bruce, 1958/1962, 394f; f/n 4).

<u>8.6. St Nona and her son, St David</u>

(i) St Nona/Nonnita/Nun/Nonna (born c.483)

St Nona, who was St David of Wales' mother, was named after St Nona, the wife of St Gregory of Nazianzus the Elder and the mother of three saints and the aunt of two more. St David was brought up in Llanon, a village named after Nona, and where she founded and ran a convent (Rees, 2003, 128f; 135; 145f; 209; 225; Ford, 'St. Non', 2001; 'Non of Wales', from the BBC). Upon travelling to Cornwall ('little Wales') Nona built an altar for Christian worship, although some think that the altar was a portable stone, which monks carried around with them. In any case, the village came to be called Altarnun (altar of Nun or Nonna). The shaft of a 6th century Celtic Cross stands in the cemetery of the 15th century church of St Non (often called 'the Cathedral of the Moor')[24] (although some date the cross-head to the 10th-11th century). The decorated Norman font is from the 11th century.

Plate 8.4.
Trewick Home of Digory Isbel. Public domain.

In later times, a hamlet, Trewick near Altarnun, became a base for John Wesley's itinarant ministry. Here a stonemason, Digory Isbel, built a chapel and 'prophet's chamber' for

Wesley and his assistants, and as a base for their ministry to nearby places (Plate 8.4). Therefore the area became a Methodist stronghold and later became central to the Cornish Revival.

(ii) Saint David

St David is the patron saint of Wales. He was born in about 500 and lived to a great age (died c. 601). He built the monastery at Menevia (that is, St David's) and was its abbot. It became a renowned seat of learning, and sent out missionaries into Ireland. David presided over a synod of the Welsh church at Brevi and may have been a bishop.

<u>8.7. St Finnian of Clonard (born c.470/80 - 549 or 552)</u>

Finnian was a native of Leinster, Ireland. His first teacher was St Fortchern of Trim, a disciple of St Patrick. In Wales, Finnian's teachers included St David, St Gildas the Wise[25]

Plate 8.5.
Beehive cells, Skellig Michael, County Kerry.
Photo. by Rob Burke. File is licensed under the Creative
Commons Attribution-Share Alike 2.0 Generic license.

and St Cedoc, and, in Gaul/France he was influenced by Martin of Tours (c.316-397) and John Cassian (c.360-435), who

had both had direct links with Egypt. In Gaul, Finnian could not have met either Martin of Tours (who had been dead for a century) or John Cassian (who had died decades before Finnian's birth) but Finnian visited their monasteries and was probably familiar with their writings. Finnian's Penitentiary, for example, was based upon the works of St Jerome and John Cassian (both of whom are saints of the Eastern Church) ('Finnian', in ODS III, 1992).

Finnian's work was basic to Western monastic rules, including St Benedict's rule (Cassian, John, in ODCC). He had already spent thirty years studying in Welsh monasteries, mainly at Minevia with St David, and had founded monasteries at Rossacura, Drumfea and Kilmaglush in Ireland before becoming a travelling missionary there (Lapa, online).

The King of Leinster, Oengus, granted him land for a monastery, after which he built another monastery at Dunmanogue in County Kildare. Finnian founded oratories and a communal hermitage on Skellig Michael/ Sceilg Mhichil, off the County Kerry coast (Plate 8.5). Similar eremetic-monasteries can be found in the Outer Hebrides and the Northern Isles (Thomas, 1971, 94). The Skellig Michael site was occupied by Augustinian monks from the 6th to 13th century, and remains, but to visit it, one must climb 670 steps up an almost inaccessible crag on Skellig Michael, the

previously mentioned larger Skellig Island, off the coast of County Kerry, Southern Ireland. This monastery, with two rectangular oratories, six beehhive huts, rough crosses, a herb-garden and (later) a 12th-century church (Brown, 2006, 103)

and Verzone suggests that it indicates what Lindisfarne might originally have looked like (Verzone, 1968).

Finnian then studied and taught for years in Kildare under the great founding abbess, St Brigid/Bride, who, as noted, had

been raised in a Christian home by followers of St Patrick.

St Brigid was said to have received episcopal ordination and to have performed miracles ('Bride, St', in ODCC). She was well able to teach men because communal (coenobitic) monasticism had been established in Egypt in the early 3rd century and double monasteries were a tradition inherited in Ireland from the Eastern Church.[26] In the socially and physically rough and rugged conditions of Ireland and Scotland it was most suitable for women to live under one roof and have a contingent of men for additional safety and security.

In 520, Finnian founded the monastery of Clonard on the River Boyne in County Meath, near Leinster. It began as a clay and wattle hut and church (very Irish) and grew so much that up to 3,000 monks had studied there (Gratton-Flood, 'The Twelve Apostles of Erin (1913)', in Catholic Encyclopedia 1914). They followed the strict and ascetic rule of the Celtic Church, based upon Egyptian models: for example, Finnian's pillow was a stone, he slept on the floor, ate bread and herbs and permitted himself a little beer or whey on festival days so that one of his disciples said that he became emaciated ('Biography of Saint Finnian', Irish Ecclesiastical Record Vol. 13, 1892, 810-815; Lapa, online, 2).

Finnian, himself, has been described as a wonder-worker ('Historical information on Clonard', online). The Celts were not Catholics as the Celts were fiercely independent and had not submitted to Rome. Study of the Scriptures was essential and each monk carried the gospel as they went out to found churches and monasteries (as Columba, a pupil of St Finnian, did). Finnian's sister, St Regnach, became an abbess, at Kilreynagh, near Banagher, in King's County. St Finnian's vita was written in the 10th century ('Historical information on Clonard', online).

8.8. St Finnian of Moville (c. 495-579)

This St Finnian was educated at Dromore and St Ninian's monastery at Whithorn, in Scotland. He had made a pilgrimage to Rome and obtained a rare Latin manuscript before returning to Ireland. He established the monastery of Moville in County Down (c.550) of which he was abbot, and then established another at Dromin (in County Louth). He became famous as a scholar and teacher ('Finnian of Moville', in ODS; 'Finnian, St', in ODCC).

8.9. St Columba/Colum Cille

Columba (c.521-c.597) was from royal Irish families on both sides. He was a tall, powerful man, a poet and bard with a loud, melodious voice. Columba was trained in the Irish monastery of St Finnian at Moville and later he studied under Finnian of Clonard in the Abbey of Clonard, in County Meath ('Columba', in Farmer, ODS,; 'Columba', in ODCC; 'Catholic Ireland.net: St. Finnian', online).

Columba became a priest, an abbot and a missionary and founded monasteries at Derry, County Londonderry, at Durroe (c.540/46) and probably at Kells, in County Meath, which became the centre of the Columban Order when Iona was devastated by Norsemen in the ninth century (Bruce, 1958/1962, 387; Brown, 2006, 106).

One tradition asserts that Columba and Finnian of Moville violently opposed each other over the ownership of a copy Columba had secretly made of a manuscript (probably the psalter of Jerome's Vulgate) which, as mentioned,

Finnian had obtained in Rome. The High King of Ireland adjudicated the case and found in favour of Finnian (Jackson, 1989, 9). Columba opposed the king so that, in 561, two battles were fought, which resulted in loss of life ('Columba', in

ODS). Perhaps it was even a bloodbath and Columba came to regret it and his poem in the text-box indicates (Brown, 2006, 105ff).

Columba either emigrated or was exiled in 562. Following Jesus' example, he took twelve companions to undertake missionary work in Scotland. Working out of the monastery he founded on the Scottish Island of Iona, near the territory of his kinsman, the King of Dál Riada, Columba evangelised for thirtyfour years (Jackson, 1989, 8). He converted Brude, King of the Scots, and, in 574, Dál Riada succeeded Brude as high king. Columba returned only once to Ireland, to found a monastery at Durrow, County Offaly ('Columba, St.', in ODCC).

Part of Columba's poem of exile:

I ever long for the land of Ireland
Where I had power.
An exile now in midst of strangers,
Sad and tearful.

Woe, that journey forced upon me,
O King of Secrets,
Would to God I'd never gone there, to Cooldrevne.
    (Cúl Dremne was the battlefield.)

St Columba was noted for diplomacy between the tribes, performing miracles, founding several churches in the Hebrides, reviving monasticism, teaching missionaries, writing hymns, books and poems and positively participating in local politics.

A prayer of St Columba of Iona:
Kindle in our hearts, O God, the flame of that love which never ceases,
    That it may burn in us, giving light to others.

May we shine forever in Thy holy temple.

Set on fire with Thy eternal light.

Even Thy son, Jesus Christ, Our Savior and Redeemer.

St Columba died in Iona on June 9, 597, just months after Augustine had landed in Kent to teach the Celts the Catholic way. Columba's vita, or, more correctly, his hagiography, was written by a later Abbott of Iona, the learned St Adamnan/Eunan (624-704) ('Columba, St', in ODS; 'Adamnan, St', in ODCC).

8.10. St Columbanus

St Columban/Columbanus (550-615) was a Celtic abbot and missionary who left Ireland to travel, via England, to Gaul where he established Celtic-style monasteries. This was strongly opposed because his rule was Irish/Egyptian, not Benedictine/Western, so Columbanus and his monks were driven out of Burgundy in 610. They rowed up the Rhine River to Lake Constance, in Switzerland, but were forced into the Alps. Again they were opposed, although St Gall decided to remain and become a hermit (at present day St Gall) while the other monks moved to North Italy (History of Monasticism. Christian hermits: 3rd-4th century A.D., online).

In Bobbio, Italy, their monastery became a centre for learning. Throughout the 'Dark' Ages of the 5th to 8th centuries, Celtic monasteries in Ireland were noted for scholarship, especially the teaching of Greek, and the translation of Greek texts and for copying the Latin Fathers. Columbanus expressed the lifestyle of his monks: "He who says he believes in Christ aught to walk as Christ walked, poor, humble and always preaching the truth" (Bosch, 1991, 237).

The 'Monastic Rule' ascribed to Columbanus seems genuine and provides clues about his strict form of Celtic monasticism which included corporal punishment and self-mortification

('Columbanus, St', in ODCC; Brown, 2006, 113). St Columbanus also composed a Penitentiary,

strongly influenced by the earlier example composed by St Finnian (Lapa, online). His other surviving works include some letters, poems and a Latin rowing song (Brown, 2006, 112).

Plate 8.6.
The priory of Lindisfarne, painted by Thomas Girtin, 1798.
Public domain.

8.11. St Aidan

From 597, St Aidan continued Columba's evangelism in Northern England. From the Island of Iona St Aidan also undertook many missionary journeys into mainland Scotland. In 635 he was invited by King Oswald of Northumbria to revive the work there. Aidan was consecrated bishop in 635 and crossed to the North-East of England to set up a monastery on Lindisfarne Island.

The monastery was built of oak and thatch (which was later replaced with sheets of lead) (Bede, III, 23). Individual huts would have been built around a common hall, based on the eremetic monastic system designed in Egypt by St

Antony/Anthony (c.251-c.356) (whose vita, as noted, was written by St Athanasius ('Antony, St. of Egypt', in ODCC). At Lindisfarne, they even called their centres "the desert" ('Celtic Monasteries', online). St Aidan died in 651, thirteen years before the Synod of Whitby was held.

8.12. Four Brothers: Ss Chad, Cedd, Cynibil and Caelin

The Celtic Church was strong in the north of England and monks and their monasteries formed the backbone of its expansion and strength. Four brothers (Chad, Cedd, Cynibil and Caelin) who were disciples of St Aidan at Lindisfarne, all became famous priests, two of them bishops (Bede, III, 23). In 664 Chad was a Celtic deligate at the Synod, which was held in the double monastery of St Hild/Hilda of Whitby, near Lindisfarne, to settle the issue of the true date of Easter (Tucker, 2016, 20). Indeed Chad supported the Celtic position but he translated between the parties and accepted the pro-Roman outcome.

Caelin had become chaplain to King Oswald's son, Ethelwald, but Chad and Cedd were great evangelist and founders of monasteries (Chad, St and s.v. Cedd, St, in ODCC). St Cedd, "a wise, holy, and an honourable man" (Bede, III. 23) was given land by King Ethelwald to build a monastery at Lastingham, near Whitby in Yorkshire, but he could not complete the project because he was appointed Bishop of York by King Oswy.

He left Lastingham, which his brother Cedd took over as abbot, but Chad's appointment to the see of York was challenged and overturned by Bishop Wifrid, who had been absent in France to receive his consecration to that see so Chad humbly retired to Lastingham. Soon, however, he became bishop of the Mercians,

establishing his seat at Lichfield, North Yorkshire ('Chad, St' [also 'Caedda'], in ODCC). St Chad died in 672.

In 654 St Cedd became bishop of the East Saxons and built monasteries at Tilbury and at Bradwell-onSea where a little chuch he built, St Peter's, is still standing (Brown, 2006, 178ff).

8.13. St Augustine

In 596 Pope Gregory the Great sent Augustine to evangelise England, perhaps because St Columbanus's foray into Europe had drawn papal attention to the strength of Celtic adherence to the Eastern date for Easter (Brown, 2006, 111ff). As noted, the Celtic churches had been evangelised by monks such as Patrick, Columba and Aidan who had organised churches into diocese long before. This is evidenced by the three bishops from across England who had attended the Synod of Arles of 314 CE/AD; from York, London and one other, probably Lincoln when all three towns were Roman camps (Bruce, 1958/1962, 353; Wand, 1961, 248).

Celtic Christianity was not based on parish churches but on monasteries moreoover in southern England Christianity was stronger amongst the Romans than amongst the indigenous peoples so that, when the legions were withdrawn from England to defend Rome, in 407 CE, many of their churches fell into disuse. These included St Martin's, Canterbury (Plate 8.2) which the Kentish King (Ethelbert) permitted Augustine's papal missionaries to use (Thomas, 1971, 96). Ethelbert's French wife, Queen Bertha, and her chaplain, Bishop Liudhard, had been using St Martin's for their devotions before Augustine took it over. Not long afterwards the King was baptised into his wife's Catholic faith. Augustine travelled to Arles in Gaul to be consecrated (Latin/Catholic) Bishop of England and was given authority to consecrate Catholic bishops throughout England, including a metropolitan bishop for York

(Bruce, 1958/1962, 398). York and London were, in fact, already the chief episcopal seats of the

English/Celtic church.

More Latin clergy arrived from Rome in 601 (Thomas, 1971, 96). Augustine and his companions (some of whom became bishops) tried to negotiate with the Welsh and Irish churches over their 'incorrect' dates for observing Easter. The Celtic Church calculated Easter by following the Eastern Church, which believed it was following St John the Apostle, so the Celts remained antagonistic to the Latins, who claimed to follow St Peter.

As will be show below, most Celts, including St Hilda of Whitby, reluctantly submitted to Rome at the Synod of Whitby in 664 CE on the orders of King Oswy who chose to follow Rome. This virtually ended the 'Easter (or Paschal) controversy'. From then on, but gradually, the Latin Rite also prevailed, as did their method of tonsuring monks ('Whitby, The Synod of', in ODCC).

8.14. St Hild/Hilda of Whitby

St Hilda was of the royal family of Northumberland and had been raised and educated in King Edwin's palace. Her foundation near Lindisfarne was noted for scholarship and, as abbesses of Whitby, which was a double monastery, she controlled and taught both nuns and monks. Hilda obviously taught well because five Whitby monks became bishops (Tucker, 2016, 20).

St Hilda had staunchly supported the Celtic position at the Synod of Whitby (664 CE) which Colman, Bishop of Northumbria, presented to King Oswy. The Celtic Church believed that this position was bequeathed to them by St John the evangelist but King Oswy believed that there should be one rule on earth for all Christian: it was just a case of deciding which one (Bede, III. 25).

The priest, Wilfrid, speaking in English, supported the Roman usage, saying:

"he (St John) literally observed the Law of Moses at a time when the Church was still greatly influenced by the synagogue, and the Apostles were not able immediately to abrogate the observances of the Law once given by God..." [lest they give offence to the Jews, many thousands of whom believed, all being zealous observers of the Law...] *"But when Peter preached in Rome, remembering that it was on the day after the Sabbath that our Lord rose from the dead and gave the world the hope of resurrection,*

he realised that Easter should begin at moonrise on the evening of the fourteenth day of the full moon. This was in accordance with the Law and was John's own practice" (Bede, III. 25).

When King Oswy heard that Peter had been given the keys of the kingdom of heaven he asked the advocates for each side if it was true. When they agreed he said:

"I shall obey his (Peter's) commands in everything.....

otherwise, when I come to the gates of heaven,

he who holds the keys may not be willing to open them" (Bede, III. 25).

Whereas St Cedd accepted the Catholic position, when bishop Colman knew that he had been defeated he left his see, took his loyal disciples from Lindisfarne Abbey, and any others who dissented, and returned home to Ireland. Three years after the Synod of Whitby he went to Scotland where, in 667 CE, he established a monastery on the Island of Iona for Scots and another one for thirty English monks on an island off the coast of Ireland (Bede, IV. 4).

Rome increased its sway in England and Ireland, for example consecrating archbishops and receiving bishops from Britain for ordination (Bede, IV.1). In 668 Pope Vitalian sent an abbott,

Hadrian, with the new Archbishop, Theodore, to Britain to guide him through Gaul and to ensure that he did not introduce into Britain any Greek customs that conflicted with the teachings of "the true faith". The fact that Theodore was tonsured in the Eastern manner (across the front) rather than in the Latin circular manner, indicated his background and training although he was fluent in both Greek and Latin, and very learned (Bede, IV. 5).

Interestingly, in 670 CE, Theodore, as Archbishop of Canterbury, gathered the bishops together for instruction in canons of the Holy Fathers he chose the ten most important and, of them, his first choice was: "that we all unite in observing the holy day of Easter on the Sunday after the fourteenth of the moon of the first month" (Bede IV. 5). At that time, the Latin Church calcuated months according to the Jewish calendar, which is a lunar calendar, in which Passover falls in the first month of the Jewish religious year. Another new rule was that monks should stay at home and not wander around, as was the Celtic model of mission (in the manner of the apostles).

<u>8.15. The English Language</u>

Caedmon was a poor, uneducated shepherd, who was given the gift of composing sweet poems and songs from

Scripture in his native language, English. He was invited by St Hilda to join Whitby Abbey where he would have opportunities to use his gifts for the glory of God (Tucker, 2016, 21, Bruce, 1958/1962, 409).

There Caedmon set much of the Bible into songs. Hilda's action witnesses to the freedom of worship that characterised Celtic monasticism and Caedmon and the others established

English as a medium both for evangelising pagans and for worshiping God (Tucker, 2016, 21). Sacred music (meaning in Latin) was only known in Kent until a singing-master,

Eddi, was invited by Wilfrid (who had successfully advocated the Roman way at Whitby and was *the first bishop of English blood*") to teach the Catholic way of life throughout England. Eddi came to be called Stephen of Northumbria, (Bede, IV. 2). The singing of Gregorian chant was brought to England by a *"skilled exponent"*, Putta, who was consecrated

Bishop of Rochester. He had studied in Rome *"under the disciples of the blessed Pope Gregory"* (Bede, IV. 2).

8.16. Celtic Manuscripts

Celtic artwork and the decoration of Latin texts are famous. Along with manuscript copying these are great gifts from the Celtic monasteries. Some show Byzantine stylistic

influences and the lavish use of gold, with jewels set into their covers. Most have 'carpet-pages' of Celtic interlaced designs and images of the four evangelists and/or their

symbols (man, ox, lion and eagle) as well as decorated letters, geometric patterns and imaginative beasties.

Small gospels were carried on a monk's person but large ones were used in processions and displayed on altars. The oldest example is thought to be the gospelbook named after Archbishop Ussher of Armagh (600-610), but it is relatively unadorned like the Cathach of Columba, which is similarly dated (610-620). A cathach is 'one who fights', that is, it became a talisman in battle such as the Byzantine armies used when they paraded icons and the Virgin's robe on the walls of Constantinople when foreign armies were at the gates. Part of the text of the Cathach of Columba may have been writtern by St Columba, himself and it is said to be "the oldest surviving manuscript of Celtic Insular style of Art" ('Illuminated Manuscripts (c.600-1200)', online, 8).

The Book of Durrow (c.650-80) is lavishy embelished with spirals, tracery and trumpet ornamentation: an artistic development. On Lindisfarne Island the monks who wrote the Lindisfarne Gospels (690700) also created the Durham Gospels ('Illuminated Manuscripts (c.600-1200)', online, 8).

Another masterpiece, but which was taken elsewhere, is the Antiphonary of Bangor (680-91) which was taken to St Denis in Gaul (c.811) and then to Milan, where it is preserved as MS G.S.INF. Biblioteca Ambrosiana. It is the oldest document to be written in Irish miniscule font and is not a gospel but a collection of hymns and poems: a window into Celtic spirituality.

Other examples include the Echternach Gospels (690-715) which may have been started in Northumberland and completed on the Continent under St Willibrord (658-737) who established a Celtic-style monastery at Echternach, in Belgium (Thomas, 1971, 104) and the St Chad or Lichfield

Gospels (c.730) which was created in Ireland, although it is now in Lichfield Cathedral Library, England.

Similarly the Codex Amiatinus was created in Northumberland (c.715). One copy is now in Florence.

Originally, three of them were created at the request of Abbot Ceolfrith: one was taken to Rome on his pilgrimage in 716, as a gift for the pope and two were for monasteries at Wearmouth and Jarrow. Of them, one is lost and parts of the other are in the British Library ('Illuminated Manuscripts, (c.6001200),' online, 9).

The Book of Kells, which was commenced on Iona c.800, was probably removed because of Norse raids and completed decades later in Ireland. It is the most famous and the most lavishly decorated and illustrated of the twenty-six extant examples from the period 600-1000 (Plate 8.7) (Brown, 2008,

112).

The small Book of Armagh (807-08) is exceptional for its fine miniscule script by Ferdomnagh under the direction of Abbot Torbach of Armagh and for its content: a full Latin New Testament (the Vulgate of St Jerome) and documents relating to St Patrick and a 'life' of St Martin of Tours. Some of it is in Irish (Brown, 2008, 10-11).

Twelve more extant illuminated psalters, missals, gospels and hymn books are dated 1000 to 1200. Both English and European (known as Carolingian and Ottonian style) manuscript illumination developed from Celtic roots (1000-1500). Secular works (in Greek and Latin) were also copied and illustrated. Their survival laid a foundation for the Renaissance (Brown, 2008, 13-14).

8.17. Destruction by the Vikings

The first Viking raid on Britain occurred in 787. In 793 Vikings destroyed the monasteries of both Lindisfarne and Jarrow. In 794 the first Viking raids on both Ireland and Scotland occurred. In 800 Vikings raided the monastery of Iona killing 68 monks. In 851 Vikings sacked Canterbury Cathedral in

southern England and, in 861, they sacked the German and French cities of Cologne, Aix-la-Chapelle, Worms, Toulouse and Paris. In 865 hundreds of their ships invaded: bent on conquest and settlement (Cockburn, 'Vikings Feared for a

Reason', online). In 874 they begin to colonise Iceland.

Celtic monasteries were vulnerable because monks didn't fight back, monasteries were built close to the coast and they housed items of gold, silver and precious jewels: costly and easily transported away (History Hit, 'Why did the Vikings Invade Britain?', online).

8.18. Alternative Monastic Rules: St Benedict

St Benedict of Nursia, near Rome, (480-547/550 CE) was an Italian hermit whose following grew into twelve monasteries of twelve monks each. Benedict moved to

Montecassino in 525 where he wrote his Rule. Cardinal Newman said of Benedict that, after Alaric and the fierce

Attila (the Hun), had broken the world, the monks revived it:

"(He) *found the world, physical and social, in ruins and his mission was to restore it in the way, not of science, but of nature*" (Bosch, 1991, 239-40, citing Newman, 1970, 410).

During the 'Dark' Ages, Benedictine monasteries multiplied throughout Europe because the Emperor Charlemagne, who wished to standardise education in his realm, made the Benedictine rule standard for all monasteries in his empire (Hart [ed.], 2000, 64).

Benedict's rule was both profoundly spiritual and very practical. Thus:

"*The Benedictines rule has been one of the most effective linkages of justice, unity and renewal the church has ever known*" (Bosch, 1991, 239, citing Henry, 1987, 274).

Benedict taught: the blessedness of the ordinary (in which God can be found); becoming attentive and mindful; attending to the call of the Holy Spirit (including through other people); stability (staying right where we are); saying 'yes' to the Holy Spirit, and the blessings imparted by life's rhythms (Ringma, 'Contemplation and Action: Towards a Missional Spirituality', online).

Saint Benedict's Monasteries were places of learning, morality and spiritual and intellectual life and force. These monasteries multiplied through family-like communal spirit, devotion to manual labour and only moderate asceticism. Benedict's rule made good sense, was practical and not given to extremes. St Benedict articulated the principles of poverty, chastity and obedience but Benedictine rule did not demand such harsh privations as were practised in the East (Wand, 1961, 212). Undue suffering is not required ('History of Monasticism', Christian hermits: 3rd-4th century, online, 3). As the Holy Roman Emperor, Charlemagne (742-814) had been crowned by Pope Leo III, on Christmas Day, 800, his power was both secular and religious. He charged the church with all education throughout the Holy Roman Empire imposing the Benedictine model so he sanctioned Benedict's order. Charlemagne also imposed one liturgy, one script ('Carolingian miniscule'), one legal code and one Franco-Roman culture (Heer, 1967/68, 120; 12-13).

Benedict and his sister, St Scholastica, are said to have established convents a short distance apart and were buried together at the famous monastery of Montecassino, in Itay.

<u>8.19. Irish Monasteries Become Roman Catholic</u>

Celtic Christianity endured for longer in Ireland than in England but King Henry II of England was give permission by Pope Adrian IV to subdue Ireland and in 1172 "all of the historic Celtic monastic orders which had flourished in Ireland independently for over seven centuries, were declared dissolved", (Heer, 1967/68, 12).

In the Celtic Church, monastic women had a greater role than those of the Roman Catholic Church. There were dual monasteries, virginity was not stressed, and some Celtic monks were married (Monk Preston, 'Were Celtic Monks

Married?', online). Although they used Latin, the Celtic

Church was not Roman Catholic but when the Benedictines

took over Irish monasticism they applied Catholic liturgies and disciplines and their own monastic rule: celibacy was mandatory and males and females were separated.

<u>8.20. Discussion</u>

Celtic monks were noted for poverty and avoiding avarice, for simplicity of life, giving everything to the poor and eating their meagre food infrequently, fasting often. They walked everywhere and avoided riding. They came into a village only "to preach, baptise, visit the sick, and, in short, to care for the souls of its people" (Bede, III. 26).

Celtic Christianity was noted for flexibility, including of its liturgies, its use of local languages, its oneness with nature and care for the environment, its missional orientation, its Celtic music, poetry and art. It adhered to the Early Church, especially to St John, and to Eastern monasticism, which was dominant throughout Britain in the 4th to 6th centuries.

The Celtic Church grew by evangelising the people through itierant missionaries and consolidating through the monasteries which provided education, food and medical care. It gathered (in community and study) so that it could scatter (in evangelising across the land). The Irish saw no obstacle in using their own language to share the Godspell (gospel or good news) "giving them the oldest European written vernacular" (Bosch, 1991, 111). Before the Celtic

Church submitted to Rome it was not, strictly speaking, part of Christendom because the state and the church were not equal in governance.

In the Roman Catholic Church, the blending of monarchy with Christian leadership was justified on Old Testament grounds

and Christianity took root best where the tribal chief or local king was baptised (Robert, 2009, 27). The Celtic bishops and monks had no secular power, only influence. Therefore it may have much to offer to the Church of post-Christendom when its history becomes well known. Benedictine spirituality also has much to offer and is now considered suitable for Protestants (Okholm, 2007). Benedict's monasteries, which were widespread, provided a framework in which the Germanic and Viking barbarians evolved as Christians ('History of Monasticism', Christian hermits: 3rd-4th century A.D., online, 3).

<u>8.21. Long-term Conclusions</u>

Recently there has been a renewal of interest in non-dualistic spirituality which encompasses all of life, in which the body (action) is not separated from spirit (our very being). Celtic-style monasticism, which teaches simplicity, purity and obedience, fits these parameters; but it also seriously promoted mortification of the flesh (self-punishment and extreme fasts).

Marginalised people, ex-church-goers and divorced persons tend to be attracted to the openness and reconciliation aspects of modern Christian communities. Their monastic vows have a modern twist: poverty and celibacy are not required, but married people "must show deep respect for the other person" and "not treat sex as a cheap commodity" (Ashby, 'Call from God leads to global Celtic fellowship'). This principle is sorely needed in all of our nations these days where sex has become recreational.

Various modern groups, which are developing as 'new friars' (friars being more outward-going than monks). Examples include the Community of Aidan and Hilda at

Lindisfarne; Northumbria Community in England; Urban Neighbours of Hope (UNOH) and Peace Tree Community

in Perth, Western Australia. The spiritual practices of UNOH include Scripture, Solitude, Spiritual guides,

Hospitality, Worship, Servant-hood, Living Among the

Poor, Discipleship and Just Stewardship. In fact, justice in

all its ramifications is an important emphasis in modern Christian spirituality, putting into practice love of one's neighbour. A recently produced book relevant to Australia is "Celtic Spirituality in an Australian Landscape" by British cleric Rev. Ray Simpson and Australian Baptist pastor, Rev. Brent Lyons-Lee (2013/2019).

The Iona Community, founded in 1938 by Rev. Macleod (later Lord Macleod), achieved the rebuilding of the Iona church and then the supplementary buildings during the Great Depression and after WW II. Now the Iona Community specialises in community development and church renewal and has members, friends and associates. Thousands of visitors and pilgrims visit the island of Iona annually (Jackson, 1989, 14f; 19f).

Even without joining a community, the principles which enliven Celtic spirituality can and should be adopted: reject materialism, consumerism and coveting; do not be a shop-a-holic; avoid the ostentatious display of wealth; judiciously distribute money and avoid its opposite (being tight fisted); wear simple clothing (designer clothes, handbags and shoes are a wealth trap); be modest and teach modesty to your children from an early age; adopt hospitality, generosity and charity towards the poor; support evangelism and mission at home and overseas and help to do mission; plant a church; develop a life-long love of study; embrace the gospels; avoid the pull of the world; and enjoy nature and the simple things of life (like Celtic music). Praise God in the open air and in the beauty of nature.

<u>Questions:</u>
What aspects of Celtic Christianity make it attractive today?

(1) Which response to the Synod of Whitby was right, St Cedd's or Bishop Colman's?

Chapter 9
The European Middle Ages

.15. <u>Background</u>

When William the Conqueror arrived in England from Normandy in 1066 and was successful against the English under Harold Godwinson he allocated vast estates as rewards to his barons. The farmers who had tilled their lands for hundreds of years were either dispossessed or were reduced to servitude under the feudal system. They were also reduced to poverty, but were expected to tithe to the Latin Church. King William's Domesday Book kept tabs on everyone and everything so that he could accurately impose heavy royal taxes. The European Middle Ages was a period of great struggle for economic survival, except for the religious and secular heirarchies.

.16. <u>Pope Gregory VII's Reforms</u>

From the death of Pope Gregory I in 604 through to the later 11th century Christianity gradually extended from its base in the old Roman world. In the 7th century it faced the encroachments of Islam in previously Christian areas such as Egypt, the Levant and Spain.

In 800, when the Pope crowned the Frankish King, Charlemagne, Emperor of Rome, the supremacy of the Church was being trumpeted. Charlemagne exerted local authority in unity with the Latin Church, but, because he divided his kingdom between his sons, unity gave way to sibling rivalry and hostilities, which fractured social cohesion.

The clergy included the ancient clerical orders (deacons, priests and bishops) but cardinals were added to the hierarchy to help govern the church and to elect popes.

Papal claims to authority [which were increasingly promoted from Tertullian (c.220) to Pope Damasus (c.384)] depended upon large and strong administrative structures, which Medieval popes were determined to enhance (See Chapter 23.3 and 23.7 of Volume 1 of this series Synagoga's

Heritage: Tabernacle, Temple, Synagogue and Church, Justin Campbell and Deslee Campbell; Haight I, 2004, 270ff and 340).

By the High Middle Ages, the Pax Romana was long gone and with it the transport, communications and legal systems which it had once provided. The parish system had become part of the feudal system, in which local landlords (kings, dukes and/or nobles) built and owned churches and chose the clergy, who were often neither ordained nor even literate. Village priests were often neither celibate nor continent. As social disorder increased and communications with Rome became difficult, local bishops, who were often well educated and wealthy, "became local authorities, they governed cities and administered justice" (Haight I, 2004, 270).

In 909 the autonomous monastery at Cluny was established by William the Pious, Duke of Burgundy. It was answerable only to Rome and the movement spread across Europe. Whereas Charlemagne had regarded Benedictine abbeys as his vassals, any such arrangement could not be true of Cluniac monasteries ('Gregory VII, St.', in ODCC).

In 1073, Hildebrand, who had been a monk at Cluny, was elected Pope as Gregory VII (1021-85). He instituted a reform program and appointed papal legates to enforce his requirement, which included the ordination of clergy, celibacy of clergy and abolition of simony (purchasing a

living). Numerous secular rulers objected, as this reduced their powers, but the German king, Henry IV, was forced to submit and do penance for his resistance.

After the Archbishop of Ravenna (as Anti-Pope) had besieged Rome for two years, Gregory VII (who was canonised as St Gregory VII in 1606) was forced to flee to Salerno, where he died.

These centuries saw the great achievement of the construction of the magnificent Medieval Gothic cathedrals. Many people had feared that the world would end at the turn of the millennium but, when that didn't happen and life went on, there was a blossoming of creativity and cathedral building. *"Between 1170 and 1270 more than 500 great French cathedrals were built in the Gothic style"* (Fremantle, 1969, 127).

As the power of the Latin Church increased so did its need to retain power and to ruthlessly quell dissent and alternative religions, for which it increasingly relied upon the Medieval Inquisition (c.1184), the Papal

Inquisition set up in 1232 by Gregory IX (Count Ugolino, who was pope from 1227 to 1241) and the Spanish Inquisition set up under Pope Lucius III (November 11, 1478).

The Middle Ages were characterised by mighty upheavals including the strengthening of Papal power when Innocent III (1198-1216) styled himself 'Vicar of Christ'. "This term implied according to later interpretations that it was wholly necessary for one's salvation to be subject to the Roman Pontiff" (Rosenthal, JQR 47.1, 1956, 58 citing Ault, 1935, 373). Antagonism towards the Jews, that had developed in the late-9th-century, is discernible in the iconography of many beautiful and majestic Gothic cathedrals that were being built throughout Christendom, in iconography from that period, as has been noted in Chapter 1, and in many paintings (Kühnel, JA 1920, 1993-1994, 115).

9.3. The Importance of Assisi

One of the enduring features of Medieval Europe, which is of much interest now that a Pope has chosen to adopt the name Francis XVI, was the establishment in 1208 of the Franciscan Order by St Francis of Assisi (c.1181-1226) (Galli, 2002, 65).

As Benedictine monasticism grew in Europe new religious orders were being formed, such as the Franciscans (from 1208) and Dominicans (from 1217). The Dominicans, or Blackfriars,

were founded by the Spaniard Dominic, formerly Bishop Domingo de Guzman (Galli, 2002, 65; 91). Being mendicant orders (whose friars moved outside their monastery and begged for their food, with bowl in hand) they were in marked contrast to previous Catholic orders. The new orders became large and powerful and their friars became the hard fist of the Papal Inquisition (from 1232) by which Pope Gregory IX planned to combat heresy. [The first Grand Inquisitor in Spain was a Dominican, Tomas de Torquemada (1420-1508)] ('Spanish Inquisition', in ODCC).

St Francis and St Dominic were very different from each other. St Francis was unusual in that his vision involved harmony, justice, extreme poverty and love of nature. Pope Gregory IX fostered both orders and also the Poor Clare nuns, founded by St Clare, who was a protégée of Francis.

Pope Gregory IX was a Machiavellian and complex character who coerced Francis to modify the Franciscan rule. He believed that these monastic orders would reform the church from the bottom up, while he was trying to reform it from the top down. Cluniac monasteries were directly responsible to the papacy, which made them useful tools against 'heresy' and also in foreign missions (Galli, 2002, 136). The Papal Inquisition formed part of Gregory IX's 'reforms' and he canonised St Francis (in 1228) - then the best-known Franciscan friar, St Anthony of Padua (in 1232) and St Dominic (in 1234).

9.4. Clare (also Clara) of Assisi (1193/1194-1253)

Clare, a wealthy sixteen year old orphan who heard St Francis preach at Assisi, decided to run away from her uncle's control, and her suitor, and secretly follow Francis in poverty and austerity. After making her confession she donned a habit and veil, made a vow of obedience to Francis and was tonsured by him. Francis restored an old church and created a convent there, at San Damiano, making Clare a reluctant abbess at only 21 years of age, from 1216.

Her rule for the order (the Poor Ladies, who became the Poor Clares) was the first rule to be written by a woman (Mursell [ed.], 2003, 110f; Galli, 2002, 110-111). Despite their uncle's violent opposition, Clare's sister, Catherine, soon joined her taking the name Agnes so that she is now known as St Agnes of Assisi. Their mother's friend, Pacifica, joined the order and later, Chare's mother and youngest sister, Beatrice, also joined (Galli, 2002, 105-107).

Clare founded daughter houses in Perugia and Florence, in Italy, and others in Germany and France. She was known for sanctity, excessive fasting, subjecting her body to strict discipline, having mystical experiences and for her effective healing prayers - and for her besotted devotion to Francis. "St Clare cared for St Francis towards the end of his life and was with him when he died in 1226" (Galli, 2002, 105; 110; Anonymous, 'St Clare of Assisi Biography').

Clare lived for a further 27 years. Her extant writings include: a letter to a Sister Emendrude and four to Lady Agnes of Prague, daughter of the King of Bohemia; as wsell

as a lengthy blessing and her Testament, which was written for her fellow sisters. Her Testament stressed poverty and the humility which she, herself, exemplified and it also contained some biographical details of St Frances, written after he had departed this life ('Testament of Saint Clare', online). Her writings and the record of her miracles ensured that her example was useful to Rome right through the Reformation and beyond (Galli, 2002, 110f).

Clare refused to let her order own property so the wily and hard-headed Pope Gregory IX withheld approval of their strict rule of abject poverty. Two days before her death, however, Pope Innocent IV consented ('St Clare of Assisi', in Encyclopaedia Britannica). St Clare was canonised by Pope Alexander IV in 1255, like St Francis, just two years after her passing (Galli, 2002, 111).

9.5. Ecclesia in the Thirteenth - Fifteenth Century

In 1215 the Fourth Lateran or Great Council passed seventy canons, which elevated the Church in dominance and militancy (Rosenthal, 1956, 58). The eight Crusades against Islamic control of the Holy Land took place in this era (see Appendix 1). As noted above, the Papal Inquisition, and later the Spanish Inquisition, were used against Muslims, Jews and proto-Protestants.

As noted below in Appendix 2, seven official disputations and attacks upon rabbis who defended the Talmud took place in Medieval Europe. There was intermittent persecution of Jews and those who read the works of Maimonides (Plate 9.1, below) (whose books were burnt by the Dominicans in 1232). Attacks upon 'heretics', such as the Cathgars/Albigensians of Southern France were such that they were virtually wiped out (Rosenthall, 1956, 61). Critically, the split with the Eastern Church in 1045, discussed in Chapter 7 and known as the 'Great Schism', continued.

From 1294 to 1303 Pope Boniface VIII ruled. He quarrelled with Philip of France when each competed for secular power, which split the Latin Church into French and Roman factions. Boniface issued Unam sanctam: the ultimate power-grab. "It is altogether necessary for every human being to be subject to the Roman pontiff" so that Philip sent soldiers against the aged Pope in an effort to dethrone him. This was unsuccessful as the Pope was protected by the people of his home-village (Shelley, 1982/1996, 217ff).

A Frenchman, Clement V, became Pope in 1305 and moved his seat from Rome to a new palace at Avignon, France, where six successive French popes would reside, under the influence of the powerhungry French court. This 72-year-period was known as 'the Babylonian Captivity'. Building the grand Avignon palace and the loss of revenues from the Papal States virtually bankrupted the papacy, which resorted to selling indulgences and livings (livelihoods) (Shelley, 1982/1996, 219ff).

Later Popes attempted to return to Rome (Urban V in 1367 and Gregory XI in 1377) but, subsequently, Urban VI (in Rome) was so unpopular with the cardinals that a rival pope, a Frenchman, Clement VII, was elected and he settled into the papal-palace at Avignon. Each national church backed one or other pope. Riots, tumults and civil unrest broke out but Canon Law prohibited reunion unless one or both Popes agreed to co-operate. "It was left to universities, kings, bishops, dukes and just about everyone else to decide who was the true Vicar of Christ" (Shelley, 1982/1996, 220f).

In 1409, a general council met in Pisa, Italy, to elect a substitute pope, Alexander V, but the other two refused to step down, which resulted in three rival popes. Eventually the Council of Constance in Germany (1414-17) dismissed all three rivals and elected Martin V, a candidate whom all accepted. The theory of 'counciliatism' had become a fact: councils were indeed superior to popes (Shelley, 1982/1996, 220). Ever since the first council in Jerusalem, it was believed that the Holy Spirit guided councils and was present in the unity of the body (Evans, 2002, 63).

Although the Church of England asserted in the thirty-nine articles of The Book of Common Prayer that General Councils may err, and sometimes did err, in both East and West inerrancy was held (at least theoretically) to be true of the seven earliest councils, called the Oecumenical Councils: Nicaea, 325; Constantinople I, 381; Ephesus, 431; Chalcedon, 451; Constantinople II, 553; Constantinople III, 680/1 and Nicaea II, 787 ('Oecumenical Councils', in ODCC), most of which had been called to consider heresies, such as Arianism and Nestorianism. Pope Martin V, however, immediately demolished the power of the Council of Constance, which had selected him. Naturally these upheavals made governance of the Church less than successful and internal criticism increased, notably as the papacy became grossly immoral and greedy (1417-1503) (Shelley, 1982/1996, 223).

<u>9.6. The Jews in Medieval Europe</u>

The situation for Jews in Medieval Europe varied considerably as central Europe was politically fragmented into city-states and small principalities. Relations with the

Jews were more present problems than, for example, what was happening in far-away Constantinople (now Istanbul). In general, a fragile toleration of Jews was the norm. The Great Council of 1215 decreed that Jews must wear distinctive clothing - the distinguishing yellow patch and horned cap (Rosenthal, 1956, 59; Heer, 2000, 155).

In Spain there had been a 'Golden Age' of harmony, but it was permanently shattered by a terrible wave of mass killings of Jewish communities and leaders across the country, which began in 1391 and changed Spanish Jewry permanently:

"The Jews were no longer so necessary to the kings and the aristocracy of Spain because their functions as bourgeoisie and bureaucrats had been taken over by others." (Maccoby,

1982/2006, 83). Because Jews were resident in every city and had been integral to commercial life, relations with them were an important factor in European society. St Augustine had taught that Jews should not be killed but scattered everywhere with their Scriptures so that the Church would keep their testimony concerning the Messianic prophesies and so that Jewish converts could teach the Hebrew language and help interpret the Old Testament (Rosenthal, 1956, 59, citing

Augustine, City of God, XVIII, 46). Jews were relatively more numerous in the Middle Ages than they are now because the Nazi Holocaust would later kill one third of Europe's Jews. Because they were probably the only non-Christians whom most people ever met Jews were viewed with suspicion and, if they prospered, with jealousy. Jews were blamed for every

problem and every evil. In England in c.1144 Jews were accused of desecrating the Eucharist and killing children (such as St William of Norwich) to use their blood at Passover ('William of Norwich, St.', in ODCC). The 12th century, a

relatively positive period for the Jews of Europe, was marred in England by the burning of the Jews of York within the castle in 1189. In 1255 Jews were blamed for the death of Hugh of Lincoln (Little Saint Hugh). A century later, Jewish communities were blamed for the Black Death of 1348-50 and hundreds were massacred.

As mobs of Crusaders progressed towards the Holy Land they attacked Jews before even leaving Europe. Moving East, they killed Muslims, Jews and even Byzantine Christians. (Because the Byzantine capital, Constantinople, was conquered and pillaged by the Crusaders in 1204 it was weakened and fell prey to the Turks in 1453).

In the 13th and 14th century Jewish converts to Christianity challenged Jewish scholars to publicly debate them in front of kings or popes. As noted in Appendix 2, there were at least seven disputations including at Burgos, Avila and Pamplona in 1375, and Granada (c.1430), but the three which are most important and are detailed in Appendix 2, are: Paris (1240), Barcelona (1263) and, later, Tortosa (141314).

The 12th century saw the beginning of the ghetto system in which Jews clung together and even, at times, walled themselves in. On the advice of the Dominican convert, Friar Petrus/Pablo Christiani, who had who disputed with Nahmanides in Barcelona in 1260 "Louis IX (of France) enforced the wearing of a 'Jew-badge' in 1269" (Maccoby, 1982/2006, 80). This practice would be followed whenever Europeans wished to distinguish Jews from others.

Forced baptisms and death sentences were common, especially immediately after an official disputation between Jews and Christians, but by and large European Jewish communities withdrew from others and adopted rigid, orthodox views and lifestyles.

Plate 9.1.
Statue of Maimonides, Cordoba.
Photograph by D. Campbell, 1996.

Some great Jewish philosophers and scientists emerged in the Middle Ages, such as Maimonides of Cordoba (1135-1204) (called Rambam) who was a physician, philosopher and Talmudist, and Nahmanides of Genoa (1194-1270) (who was called Ramban). He was the Talmudist, Kabbalist and philosopher who debated at the Barcelona Disputation, barely escaping with his life (Maccoby, 1982/1996, 39).

At the age of thirteen, Maimonides (Rambam) fled with his family from the fanatical Muslims from North Africa and Nahmanides (Ramban) fled from Spain three years after the Barcelona Disputation of 1263. Both eventually moved to

Muslim controlled lands where they were welcomed

(Blech, 2004, 151). Nahmanides (Ramban) lived in Acre and founded the famous Ramban Synagogue in Jerusalem ('Nahmanides,' in Jacobs, 1995). Maimonides lived first in Fez (Morocco) and then in Alexandria and Cairo (Egypt), although the family travelled extensively in the Holy Land from 1164/5 to 1166.

Maimonides was a descendant of King David and also of Judah the Prince, who first edited the Mishnah, so it was fitting that his greatest work was his Commentary on the Mishnah. His best know popular work is his thirteen principles – Ani Maamin – I Believe (Mangel, 1985, 57f; 13;24f).

Plate 9.2.
Restored Crusader Church, Abu Gosh, Israel.
Photograph: J. Campbell, 2019.

A great Christian struggle against Judaism continued, including persecutions and seizure of property. Leaving behind their property, European Jews (and Muslims) were

expelled: from England in 1290; France in 1182, 1306 and 1394; Hungary in 1349 and 1360; Germany in 1348 and 1498;

Lithuania in 1395 and 1445; Austria in 1421; Spain in 1492, Portugal in 1497 and the Papal States in 1569 (Heer, 2000, 255; Blech, 2004, 142;

'Anti-Semitism in Medieval Europe', Encyclopaedia Britannica). As a result, Turkey, Egypt, Poland and Russia became centres of Jewish life, although Russia required that Jews live in 'the pale of settlement', in the extreme West.

Because Maimonides later lived in Egypt many of his letters and writings were preserved in the Cairo Genizah of the Ben Ezra Synagogue. This repository also contained hundreds of Jewish Medieval documents of many types, including wills and marriage contracts (Ketubot) dating from the 9th century, onwards. Many of the commercial documents of Jewish and Arab merchants, who plied their trade throughout the Mediterranean and who were essential to commerce, were deposited in the Cairo Genizah. In Europe, because Christians were forbidden to charge interest on loans, Jews had an essential role in money lending and, then banking, some details of which have also survived in the Genizah, which has proven to be a treasury of information about Medieval trade and commerce.

In the 15th century the really hard times began for the Jews of Europe. The Spanish Inquisition (14791820) was set up (with papal approval) by Ferdinand V of Aragon (1452-

1516) and his wife, Isabella I of Castille, the parents of Catherine of Aragon, first wife of Henry VIII of England. It specifically dealt with suspect conversions: of Marranos, who had been forced to convert from Judaism, and Moriscos, who had converted from Islam. As noted, in 1492, all of the Jews of Spain were expelled by Ferdinand and Isabella: although some Marranos of Spain and Conversos of Portugal remain today (still secretly Jewish, or semi-Jewish). The Spanish Inquisition was also used against Protestants.

With the start of the Crusades the last vestiges of Concordia with the Jews (and certainly with Muslims) were destroyed.

The first Crusade in 1096 unleashed a wave of anti-Semitic

violence in France and the Holy Roman Empire, including massacres in Worms, Trier and Metz ('Anti-Semitism in Medieval Europe', in Encyclopaedia Britannica).

Plate 9. 3. Atlit Crusader Castle. Public domain.

The eight Crusades, which are described in Appendix 1, were mounted until 1270. They resulted in the early deaths of thousands of Europe's fighting elite, children and people of other faiths. The aim of the Crusades was to take back the Holy Land from the Muslims. This was briefly achieved, making pilgrimage to holy places easier. Pilgrimage to Jerusalem, Rome and other shrines was undertaken to earn time out of Purgatory and was an essential part of Medieval spirituality. The matter was urgent because of the belief that, by preventing pilgrimage to Jerusalem, Muslims were forcing Christians to spend more time in Purgatory, before reaching Heaven.

Numerous remnants of Crusader's building activities can be found in the Levant, including the fortified underground City of Acco/Acre, churches and a string of fortified castles with chapels: Beaufort in Lebanon; Montfort/Starkenberg in Israel's far North; Nimrod on Mt Hermon; Castel Pilgrim/Atlit on the North Coast (Plate 9.3); Belvoir overlooking the Jordan Valley and, in the Old City of Jerusalem, the Tower of David and the ruined German Hospitaliers' Church. Abu Gosh, near Jerusalem, boasts two Crusader-period treasures: the restored church (in Plate 9.2) and the semi-ruined castle called both Aqua Bella and Ein Hemed. Jordan's fortified Crusader castles include Al Aljoun and Al Kerak, but the largest Crusader monument is Krak des Chaveliers, in Syria.

9.7. Discussion

The Inquisition operated out of Rome throughout Christendom. It was established to suppress the Jews, Muslims and alternative Christian movements and operated against the Albigensians/Cathars in France and Italy, the Bogomiles in Bulgaria as well as the Jansenists

and Huguenots in France. The secular arm worked in tandem with the church, from 1232/33 in that, when Inquisitors condemned a person for heresy, he/she was handed over to the secular powers to be tortured into a confession and perhaps burnt at the stake anyway.

On the fringes of the church there had been a steady growth of criticism (for example, against hypocrisy, monkish laziness and graft) and voices promoting alternative religious ideas such as mysticism and proto-Protestantism (Hill, 2007, 216f). Examples of mystics include Meister Eckhart and Bernard of

Clairvaux, whose hyms are still sung, including 'O sacred head sore wounded', 'Jesus the very thought of Thee', 'Jesu, Thou joy of loving hearts' (Vos, 1994, 70f). Examples of proto-Protestants include the Waldensians, who followed Peter Waldo of Lyons (d.1217); the Lollards (who followed John Wycliffe of Oxford University); the Hussites of Bohemia (who followed the martyr John or Jan

Huss/Hus of the University of Prague who was excommunicated in 1411 and burnt at the stake in 1415) and followers of William Tyndale (who translated the Bible into English from Hebrew and Greek, and was strangled and burnt on October 6, 1536) ('Huss, Jan' and 'Tyndale, William', in ODCC). Wycliffe was not executed but his books were burned and his bones were dug up and burnt in 1428 ('Wycliffe, John', in ODCC). All of this indicates Roman Catholic abhorrence of their views.

Throughout the Middle Ages, many thousands, even millions, were killed for believing divergent doctrines. All of the followers of these proto-Protestants were

persistently persecuted. No one can possibly know how many people, both Christians and Jews, died at the hands of Roman Catholic persecutions but a figure of sixty-eight million was given by W. C. Brownlee, in Letters in the

Roman Controversy, 1834, cited by Plaisted, Estimates of the Number Killed by the Papacy in the Middle Ages and Later (2006) online.

Roman Catholic monks even killed members of their own order, for example, the Spiritual Franciscans, who practised extreme poverty, quarrelled with the more lax monks (the Conventuals) over property ownership. Four Spirituals were burned in 1318 for asserting that Franciscans must not own a granary or a wine cellar. Other deaths followed. The quarrel continued until 1517, when Pope Leo X permitted them to divide into two separate bodies: the Observant Franciscans and the Regular Franciscans (Clarke, 1961, 218f).

Fault was not exclusively Catholic: when non-Catholics gained political power they also persecuted their opponents;

but fewer, less frequently and much less successfully. Ecclesia was wracked with internal strife in the Middle Ages. Amongst the hierarchy there was political infighting, manipulation, intrigues, brutality, poor leadership, nepotism, financial extortion of the poor, fornication and murder. Martin Luther said that the church "is spoiled and robbed by the princes and prelates, they give nothing but take and steal ..... the church is more torn and tattered than a beggar's cloak" (Martin Luther, Thesis 59 of 95, 2017, 122).

Jews were intermittently ostracised, persecuted, expelled and executed. Lone voices demanding reform (and the right of everyone to read the Bible in their own language) were violently quelled. The outward appearance of the unity of the Latin Church was only maintained by brutal repression: but that was about to change.

9.8. Prelude to the Reformation: The State of the Catholic Church

So much depended upon the personal qualities of the Pope and the length of his reign if he was competent and wise, but the tendency has always been to appoint old men and, in the Middle Ages, many manipulated themselves into office and ruled for personal gain and to promote relatives and friends. A succession of such popes meant decades of disaster. Ecclesia's greatest achievement was the building of many magnificent gothic-style cathedrals in Europe.

9.9. The Black Death

The bubonic plague swept through Europe in the mid-14th century, killing one third of everyone and half of all priests (Hill, 2007, 214). The Grim Reaper became a morbid

preoccupation in art and black humour. A drastic manpower shortage resulted and with it the collapse of the feudal system of land cultivation, higher wages and civil unrest. Urbanisation increased and an urban middle class of

merchants, traders and craftspeople grew. This gathering of populations into urban centres would facilitate the spread of new, reformist ideas, as well as of diseases when the plague reappeared. In German cities the Catholic population set upon Jews, "in the belief that the plague was a malignant device of the Semitic race for the confusion of the Catholic creed". Hundreds of thousands of Jews were burnt so that many others fled to Poland (Fisher, I, 1964, 335).

Question:

(1) Why were the Middle Ages tumultuous centuries for both Judaism and Christianity, with millions dying?

(2) Which one of the three disputations noted in Appendix 2 was the worst for Jews?

Chapter 10
The Renaissance and the Protestant Reformation

<u>.17. The Renaissance and Humanism</u>

The Renaissance (rebirth) was a gradual development in the 15th to 16th century. It was a revival of learning, notably classical learning, an interest in man, nature and art, prompted by growing scientific enquiry and in turn, increased knowledge in many fields (C. P. S. Clarke, 1961, 262). This accompanied a flowering of classically inspired art and architecture and a new optimism about learning, including using experimentation and logic to make discoveries and mathematics to create new architecture. Christian Humanism and the study of Greek and ancient classical texts, early Christian (patristic) literature and the Bible in its original languages helped prepare the way for the Reformation, for example, Luther used the translations of the French humanist, Lefrèvre, in his university lectures (Grimm, 1954/1959, 67). It revealed that the early church of the gospels was very different from the Latin Church they knew.

The Renaissance has entered the European consciousness mainly through its art and its famous artists and architects: Michelangelo (1475-1564), Raphael (1483-1520), Bramante of Urbino (1444-1514), Brunellesco (1379-1446) and the great master, Leonardo Da Vinci (1452-1519). These worked to build or decorate churches and monasteries: even their aristocratic patrons of Florence and Venice chose religious subjects. Christianity gave birth to the Renaissance in equal measure with Classical Antiquity, indeed the Church (Ecclesia triumphant) was virtually the creator of western civilization (Kenneth Clark, 1969/1971, 262).

<u>.18. Erasmus of Rotterdam (c.1466-1536)</u>

Erasmus was a scholar and a theologian who searched for the simple gospel of Jesus. He translated the New Testament and also the Greek speaking Church Fathers into classical Latin (in thirty volumes). Erasmus lived in Holland, Italy, Belgium, France, England and Switzerland while escaping the threat of war, his accusers and the victims of his wit. His Praise of Folly (1509) attacked belief in the miraculous powers of images, indulgences and the sanctity of ignorance and dirt (C. P. S. Clarke, 1961, 263). For a time, in England Erasmus became Lady Margaret Professor of Greek and Theology in Cambridge University and he was a close friend of Sir Thomas More and Bishop John Fisher, both of whom became Catholic martyrs under King Henry VIII. In Basle, Switzerland, Erasmus lodged with the scholar and printer John Froben and his son Jerome, who published all of Erasmus's translations and writings, some posthumously.

Erasmus was a contemporary of Martin Luther and, although he debated with Luther in writing and in person, he repeatedly claimed, when accused of being 'a Reformer', that he had never read Luther's works. Erasmus urged moderation on both the reformers and the conservatives and he, himself, could see both points of view. He hated violence and quarrels, and desired church unity (C. P. S. Clarke, 1961, 264). Erasmus maintained loyalty to the Catholic Church and believed that faith and reason are not opposites. Despite his loyalty, the Council of Trent branded him a heretic and some of his books were placed on the Index of Prohibited Books. After his death, in Basel in 1536, his books were banned by Pope Paul IV (in 1559) and Pope Sixtus V (in 1590).

.19. Galileo Galilei (560-1642)

Galileo was a highly influential Renaissance figure, called "the father of modern physics" (Whitehouse, 2009, 219). Einstein called him "the father of science" (Einstein [Bargmann, trans.], 1954). He studied philosophy, medicine and mathematics.

Galileo's work was based upon careful, repeated experiments, observations using a telescope and a microscope of his own design, mathematical calculations and rational philosophy. His story is continued in Chaprer 12, below, where it demonstrates the Inquisition in action.

<u>The Protestant Reformation in Europe</u>

<u>.20. Martin Luther in Germany (1483-1546)</u>

The European Reformation is notionally dated from October 31, 1517, when the German Augustinian monk and academic, Martin Luther, apparently attached his ninety-five theses or beliefs upon the door of the Castle Church of Wittenberg (Bettenson, DCC, 260-68; The Reformation – Facts & Summary – History.com, online). Such an event did not, however, arise in a religious vacuum. As early as the 12th century preaching friars and other popular preachers, such as Henry of Lausanne, Tancred of Antwerp and Peter of Bruys, had actively and eloquently preached against infant baptism, images and crucifixes, corrupt clergy and the excessive wealth of the church, much to the annoyance of local parish priests and bishops (McManners (ed.), OIHC, 209ff). Erasmus of Rotterdam, other humanists and Renaissance philosophers had also questioned Catholic dogma and clerical power.

Luther's teachings included: justification by faith alone (not at all by good works), the priesthood of all believers,

the denial of papal primacy and opposition to the selling of indulgence by which people could purchase a reduction of time in Purgatory, for themselves, after death, or for deceased relatives immediately. Luther was angered when the Dominican friar, Tetzel, began to sell indulgences locally. Luther also opposed clerical celibacy, Masses for the dead, pilgrimages, monastic vows and communion of only the bread, rather than the two elements.

His theses were circulated in German and Latin and a

pamphlet war broke out. This could have seemed like a typical Dominican versus Augustinian brawl as Tetzel produced his own theses about papal authority but it was the start of something much greater (MacCulloch, 2003, 120f).

When Luther read the opinions of the Bohemian, Jan Huss, and agreed with them danger seemed very real as Huss had been burnt as a heretic a century previously (Tomlin, 2012, 88f; 92ff). Luther was threatened with excommunicated by the Papal Bull Exsurge Domine in 1520 but he publicly burned the bull at the gate of Wittenberg, like an ancient prophet (McCulloch, 2003, 124). He published three major articles: Address to the Christian Nobility of the German Nation, The Babylonian Captivity of the Church and The Freedom of a Christian (McCulloch, 2003, 124-7). These attacked the corrupt papacy (which he called the Anti-Christ) and the Latin Church (which he called Babylon). The pope could not ignore these. Luther was excommunicated on January 3, 1521 and summoned to the Diet of Worms (April, 1521) (which published the Edict of Worms). Luther was commanded to recant. Luther's works were put under an imperial ban by Charles V. He survived by being kidnapped and secreted in the fortress of Wartburg Castle where he lived in disguise, protected by the Frederick the Wise (14631525) the Elector of Saxony (Bettenson [ed.], 1968, DCC, 279-283).

Luther translated the Bible into popular German prose, a welcome and enduring achievement, which enhanced a sense of German identity and culture ('Luther, Martin', in ODCC). He also composed many memorable hymns and translated others from Latin. Many are still sung. He also played the lute,

sang well, married an ex-nun, Katharine von Bora, and fathered five or six children. In 1523 Luther showed sympathy for the Jews by writing "That Jesus Christ was born a Jew" (Blech, 2004, 156-159, citing Marcus, 2000). In 1542-43, however, probably because he had failed to make converts

amongst the Jews, he also wrote the vicious tract "*Against the Jews and Their Lies*", which called for the burning of synagogues, Jewish homes, schools, Talmuds and prayer-books. This influenced the Lutheran public. In the late 19th

century, in both Austria and Germany, anti-Semitism became organised, with its own political parties ('Anti-Semitism in Medieval Europe', in Encyclopaedia Britannica) and in the 20th century the blood-libel accusation and Luther's virulent threats were later widely quoted and practised in Nazi Germany (Bergen, in Rittner, Smith and Steinfeldt (eds), 2000, 49).

10.5. Huldrych/Ulrich Zwingli in Switzerland

Huldrych Zwingli (1484-1531) was a Catholic priest who adopted Protestant doctrines in about 1519 in Switzerland. In 1524 Zwingli married. In 1525 the Catholic Mass was suppressed in Zurich and paintings and images were

removed and churches were whitewashed. From 1524-5 Zwingli accepted the purely symbolic meaning of Holy Communion, which led to a complete break with Lutheranism as Luther believed in the 'real presence'. At

first Zwingli saw no point in baptising infants who knew neither good nor evil, except if they were close to death ('Zwingli, Ulrich [or Huldrych]', in ODCC). Zwingli had more trouble with the Anabaptists (one of whom was beheaded and two were drowned) than with the Papacy (C. P. S. Carke, 1961, 276). In October, 1531, five of the Swiss canons that dissented from Zwingli's views mounted an armed attack. Zwingli carried his customary sword and, being the chaplain, he carried the banner. He died in battle on October 11, at the age of forty-seven.

10.6. John Calvin in Switzerland

John Calvin (1509-1564), who was born Jean Cauvin, was tonsured at the age of twelve. He became a jurist and humanist turned reformer, who broke with Rome in 1533.

He wrote his multi-volume *"Institutes of the Christian Religion"* in Geneva, while in exile from his native France. The first edition

(in Latin) was completed in 1536 and edited for the final time in 1559 (McManners, OIHC, 1990/1995, 258).

Both Calvin and Luther preached justification by faith only (sola fide), in Christ alone (solus Christus), which happened in an instantaneous transaction with God (McManners, OIHC, 1990/1995, 259). This became the basis for Protestantism. Calvinism was more radical than Lutheranism in theology and in praxis and paved the way for the restrictions of Puritanism, for example games and dancing were forbidden in Geneva ('Calvin, John', in ODCC). Thus Geneva became a "theocratic regime of enforced, austere morality" (McEwen, John Knox: Scottish Religious Leader, 1, online). Calvin is remembered for the doctrine of predestination: that the elect were chosen by God to be saved. The term

'Reformed' was came to be attached to Calvinism only, and not Lutheranism.

10.7. John Knox in Geneva and Scotland

John Knox (1513-1572) was born and died in Scotland but he spent years elsewhere. As a youth he was captured and taken as a galley slave to France but was ransomed by England. Being a priest he became a chaplain to the boy-king Edward VI in 1531 and helped revise Cranmer's Book of Common Prayer. He embraced the Reformation in about 1547 but, when Mary Tudor became Queen of England, he fled to Frankfurt and then to Geneva (McEwen, 'John Knox: Scottish Religious Leader', 1, online).

In Geneva, Knox met John Calvin and became Calvin's friend and disciple.

Plate 10.1.
Woodcut of John Knox. Public domain.

Here (in 1558) Knox wrote the pamphlet "first blast of the trumpet against the monstruous regiment of women"

against women in authority, which, he taught, was against natural law and the law of God (McEwen, 2-4, online). In his preaching he particularly attacked the arch-catholic

Queens, Mary Tudor and Marie/Mary of Guise. The latter, Marie (1515-1569), was a member of the formidable French Guise family, who staunchly opposed Protestantism in

France. Marie had married King James V of Scotland, but soon becoming regent for her daughter Mary Queen of Scots because King James died after only four years of marriage. (From 1558 to 1560 Marie had been married to her first husband, Francis, the son of the French King).

Knox also later clashed with Mary Queen of Scots. When Elizabeth I became queen, however, Knox tried to eat humble pie by dedicating a commentry to her: but Elizabeth refused to let him even enter her kingdom ('Knox, John', in ODCC).

Plate 10.2.
*Mary of Guise. Scottish National Portrait Gallery, attributed
to Correille de Lyon. Public domain.*

With the consent of the town council of Geneva, Calvin invited Knox to put reformation moral principles into place in Geneva. Knox transformed the city into the hub of European Protestantism and a refuge for many, such as hundreds of English refugees from Queen Mary Tudor of England: although some opponents in Geneva were

tortured and executed ('Calvin, John', in ODCC). Knox was an eloquent, logical preacher. He valued education, care of the poor and strict morality. The trail of wreckage against Christian art works left by the

Covenanters, French Huguenots and, a century later, by the English Puritans, was only indirectly connected to Calvin's teachings (McManners, OIHC, 1990/1995, 9).

In Scotland, John Knox and five others wrote the Scottish Confession, which the Scottish Parliament ratified in 1560. This ended Papal control of Scotland but itself was replaced by the Second Scottish Confession or Scottish Covenant in 1581, which was more anti-Catholic. Calvinism was firmly established in Scotland by an act of parliament in 1592 ('Scottish Covenant', in ODCC).

In Scotland, Knox was at the centre of contemporary religious and political turmoil. His friend, George Wishart (a Scottish reformer) was burned for heresy in 1546 by the powerful Catholic Cardinal, the Archbishop of St Andrews (McEwen, 4, online). Another Protestant friend, James Stewart, Earl of Moray (pronounced Murray), was murdered in 1570, also by a Catholic opponent: a nephew of Archbishop Hamilton. Moray was the ambitious, illegitimate half-brother of Mary Queen of Scots, who was her advisor but opposed her marriage to her Catholic cousin, Lord Darnley.

When Mary fled to England Moray became interim regent of Scotland (McEwen, 4, online) and may have organised Darnley's murder before forcing Mary to abdicate so that he, himself, became regent for her infant, James VI (Amie Gordon, Daily Mail, 14/15 Jan., 2019, online).

Plate 10.3.
Mary Queen of Scots by François Covet (c.1558).
Public domain.

10.8. Conclusions

It is impossible to do justice to this watershed period, these huge topics and the issues they generated. The Reformation period has governed the direction and fate of Ecclesia for five centuries. The 16th century had been an era of chaos: social, political and religious. Europe was wracked by religious wars in which many thousands died. These became more political wars than anything else: wars for power and influence and to impose one doctrine or

another upon Christian people but, as the heavy fist of Catholic domination began to lift in the 16th century because of both internal reform and external pressure, the

Reformation prospered. Individualism, scepticism and anti-clerical tendencies also increased, trends that had existed, underground, in the

Middle Ages but which gradually emerged as the social climate thawed. Eventually choice in religion could lead to the complete rejection of religion, which has been increasing in the West ever since and is bearing bitter fruit, as discussed in Chapter 24.1, below. In 150 years, ideas of religious reform had swept across Europe engulfing some of the Germanic states, Switzerland, the Netherlands, Scandinavia, Scotland and as will be seen, England.

Questions:

(1) How can the life of Galileo Galilei be interpreted?

(2) Which of Martin Luther's many ideas was most revolutionary?

Chapter 11
Protestant Christianity in England

<u>Henry VIII and his three children</u>
<u>11.1 Henry and the 'king's great matter'</u>

King Henry VIII (1491-1547) appealed to the Pope for an annulment of his marriage to his first wife, Catherine of Aragon, the mother of his daughter, Mary Tudor. He had fallen in love with Ann Boleyn, who refused to be his mistress and Catherine had been unable to produce a male heir, which the kingdom needed. Because the Papacy had originally granted Henry permission to marry Catherine (his teenage-brother's widow) it would have lost prestige by reversing that decision, so the Pope played for time.

Eventually, in 1529, Henry took his Vicar General, Thomas Cromwell's, advice. He convened parliament and placed his predicament before it. Parliament agreed to separate from Rome and established the King as the head of the English church *"as far as the law of Christ allows"* (The Act of Supremacy, 1534, Bettenson, DCC, 318).

Henry VIII was a charming and able statesman who largely took the church, the country and the parliament along with him. The following statutes were passed to finalise the break with Rome (Bettenson, DCC, 305-321).

The Submission of the Clergy (1532) - to Henry's will.

The Restraint of Appeals (to Rome) (1533) - which were now forbidden.

The Dispensations Act (1534) - Moneys sent to the king, not to Rome.

The Supremacy Act (1534) - Henry is the head of the Church of England.

Abjuration of Papal Supremacy over clergy (1534).

Henry dissolved the monasteries and seized their property and, in 1536, he decreed that the Bible should be available in every church, for parishioners to read (The Reformation – Facts & Summary – History.com, online). Henry was, however, no Protestant. After the above Acts he then enacted the Six Articles of 1539 known as "the bloody whip with six strings" (Bettenson, DCC, 328f). These upheld Roman Catholic doctrines: transubstantiation (that the bread and wine do become the body and blood of Christ), communion in only one kind, vows of chastity and widowhood, private masses, confession to a priest and clerical celibacy: so that even Archbishop Thomas Cranmer was forced to 'put away' his wife in 1539. (The Church of England had abolished clerical celibacy in 1549 under Edward VI.)

11.2. King Edward VI and his regents

Eventually Henry VIII had a son, a frail boy, Edward VI (1537-1553) who became king at the age of nine so that the Protestant Lords Protector ruled in his name. They were Edward Seymour, Duke of Somerset, and then John Dudley, Duke of Northumberland. Both were Protestants but were enemies. Under Edward VI, Archbishop Cranmer's Book of Common Prayer was introduced and the Church of England was established as the official church, but with Calvinist leanings, although the work of Reformation in England was incomplete. Edward ruled for only six years and all of his potential heirs to the throne were women: the Catholic Mary Tudor, her younger sister, Elizabeth (a Protestant), Mary Stuart of Scotland (who was Catholic and half French) and Lady Jane Grey; but Henry VIII had previously nominated his oldest daughter, Mary.

11.3. Lady Jane Grey: Queen for nine days

John Dudley, the Duke of Northumberland, persuaded the

boy-king, Edward VI, to contravene Henry VIII's will and bequeath the throne to his Protestant cousin, Lady Jane Grey,

the daughter of Lord Henry and Lady Frances Grey of Suffolk, rather than to his Catholic sister, Mary Tudor, who (like

Princess Elizabeth) had been declared illegitimate by Parliament. At about fourteen years of age Jane Grey lived with the Princess Elizabeth and Katharine Parr, the devout Protestant dowager queen of Henry VIII, who soon secretly married her old love-interest, Sir Thomas Seymour. Before Katharine died in childbirth Jane Grey, too, had become a deeply convinced Protestant (Hanson, online).

For £2,000 Thomas Seymour purchased from her parents the right to choose Jane Grey's husband as he was planning to marry her to the boy king. Thomas Seymour was opposed by his brother Edward, who was Lord Protector. Both Seymours were, however, hated by John Dudley/Northumberland who connived to have the King execute Thomas Seymour and then moved to take over the government and to arrest Edward Seymour (Hanson, online).

As Edward VI was clearly dying Dudley/Northumberland wanted to marry his son, Guildford Dudley, to Elizabeth but she was too wise to comply. Then Jane's parents consented to Guildford's proposal and persuaded Jane to marry him, with verbal and physical abuse. Dudley persuaded the Privy Council, the Archbishop of Canterbury, the King and relevant officers that they did not want a Catholic queen and Jane Grey became Edward's heir.

When Edward died in July 1533 it was kept secret for two days, except from Jane who apparently said, *"the crown is*

    not my right and pleaseth me not. The Lady Mary is the rightful heir" (The Attempted Coronation, online). Jane was taken by barge to the Tower of London where the crown jewels and royal apartments were made ready and her parents insisted that

    she obey them and comply. She was crowned queen but

    never again left the Tower.

Nine days later there was such spontaneous, nationwide, popular support for Mary that the Privy Council had a change of heart (The Attempted Coronation, online).

Plate 11.1.
Queen Jane Grey. Public domain.

In 1553, when John Dudley, Duke of Northumberland, had declared himself a Catholic and received the Mass, Jane Grey had written him a critical letter denouncing him as *"the deformed imp of the devil"*, *"an unashamed paramour of the AntiChrist"*, *"an apostate"*, *"a cowardly runaway"* and *"seed of satan"*. For her part Jane was faithful and courageous. Jane wrote to John Feckenham, Dean of St

Paul's Cathedral, who was sent to persuade her to recant: *"I ground my faith upon God's word, and not upon the church.... The faith of the church must be tried by God's word, and not God's word by the church, neither yet my faith."*

Mary Tudor, who ousted a crowned queen and assumed the throne in 1554,[27] delayed the execution of the newly-weds (Hanson, online) but Dudley's return to Catholicism and his recantation did not save him (nor his son). Mary executed him. Some suggest that Dudley's motives when he passed himself off as a Protestant were either convenience, or greed for church lands (Elton, 1959, 210) but he may just have been afraid. His motive in securing Queen Jane's coronation was to become the real power behind his son and therefore the throne.

Jane's father, the Duke of Suffolk, had been pardoned when he distanced himself from Jane's cause and indeed he proclaimed Mary on Tower Hill (Elton, 1959, 213) but when he joined Sir John Wyatt's Protestant rebellion against Mary, in 1544, his fate, too, was sealed, along with those of young Jane, and her young husband Guildford Dudley ('Henry Grey, Duke of Suffolk', in Britannica).

Jane and Guildford, had been pawns in a great anti-papist scheme devised by ambitious men: John Dudley, who had forced his son to marry Jane; her father, the Duke of Suffolk, and of Sir John Watt/Wyatt, who raised a Kentish army against Mary - attempting to re-establish Jane. Jane was a danger to Mary Tudor and she and Guildford paid with their lives, in 1554 (Hanson, online).

<u>11.4. Queen Mary Tudor and Phillip of Spain</u>

Mary Tudor (1516-1558) was Henry VIII's oldest child, who was raised as a devout Catholic by her mother, Catherine

of Aragon. A year after becoming England's queen, Mary

chose to marry the heir to the Spanish throne, who was also a Catholic. For this reason and because it made England an adjunct to a foreign power, Parliament did not accept the marriage. As Northumberland had feared, Mary surrounded herself with Catholic advisers, repealed all of her brother's and her father's antiCatholic legislation and turned England back to Rome (Fisher, II, 1964, 525f).

Amongst the hundred of Protestants who were burnt as heretics during her five-year-long reign were

Bishops Latimer and Ridley and Archbishop Cranmer.

<u>11.5. Queen Elizabeth I (1533-1603)</u>

Unlike her half-siblings, Queen Mary and Edward VI, Elizabeth I had a long life, from 1533, and a long reign, from 1558. Having inherited a kingdom that was greatly divided along religious lines after thirty years of turmoil, Elizabeth ruled for forty-four years, which enabled her to calm the controversy, cement her position, successfully defy the Pope, break any connection with Spain, defeat the Spanish naval armada (in 1588) and reconcile the populace to Anglicanism as 'the middle way'. By 1559 she had implemented the "Elizabethan Settlement" by both the Act of Supremacy of 1534, which reestablished the status-quo devised by her father, Henry

VIII, and the Act of Uniformity (1559) which managed to pass though both Houses of Parliament, by a slim margin. Elizabeth became Supreme Governor of the Church of England, not its 'head'.

As all but one Catholic bishop refused to take the Oath to Elizabeth they were replace by those who would. This emptied the House of Lords of bishops who had been hostile to Elizabeth, which made government much easier for her, although many laypeople in the House of Commons had Catholic sympathies (Trueman, 'The Religious Settlement of 1559', online).

Weekly attendance at Church of England services was compulsory, as was the Church of England Prayer Book of 1552 (S-cool Youth Marketing Limited, 'The Religious Settlement', online). Bible reading was widely promoted and Bibles were required to be placed in churches.

They were the Geneva Bible in English, translated by Protestants in Geneva, including Miles Coverdale (1488-1568) who had already completed an important translation of his own (Renwick, 1958/1962,

130ff). Bibles were readily available in the vernacular because of William Caxton's development of the printing press in 1477. Public readings helped ordinary folk to absorb religious belief, not just rote learn it.

When Pope Pius V excommunicated Elizabeth in 1570 she suppressed the Mass and took stronger anti-catholic measures ('Elizabeth I', in ODCC). When she discovered a plot involving her prisoner, Mary Queen of Scots (the mother of James, who later became the first Stuart king of England), she reluctantly ordered that Mary be beheaded in the Tower of London on February 8, 1587.

Many of the returnees from Geneva, and other exiles from Europe, were Calvinists and/or strict Puritans who constantly criticised Elizabeth's 'middle way' including anything of 'popery' such as clerical robes, making the sign of the cross and using written prayers (Trueman, online).

<u>11.6. Conclusions</u>

Elizabeth's policies reversed Mary Tudor's, but utilised a mixture of both Henry's and Edward's innovations, which satisfied neither Catholics nor extreme non-conformists who had returned from exile (Trueman, online). The Church of England Prayer Book of 1552 and weekly attendance at Church of England services was required;

and policed. Bible reading was promoted, and Bibles were required to be placed in churches and chained down. Bibles were widely available in the vernacular language because of Caxton's development of the printing press (1477) which facilitated the vernacularisation of religious belief (C. P. S. Clark, 1961, 321-325).

With the Reformation the sacramental economy of the Catholic Church, the hierarchical structure, priestly celibacy and monasticism were unnecessary and the difference between clergy and laity almost disappeared.

Questions:

(1) What were Elizabeth I's main achievements? Was the Elizabethan Settlement successful?

(2) From the information about John Calvin in Chapters 10 and 11 in what ways has he influenced Ecclesia today?

Chapter 12
The Catholic Counter-Reformation

<u>12.1. Catholic Responses</u>

In the early-16th century there were stirrings for reform within the Latin Church so that, in 1537, a commission of reforming cardinals presented the Pope with the report De Emendanda Ecclesia (McManners, OIHC, 239). Therefore Catholic historians prefer to call the period 'the Catholic Reformation', rather than the 'Counter Reformation'..

In effect the measures recommended in 1537 were too late: sixteen years previously Luther had already been excommunicated, Calvin's 'Institutes' had been written, and Erasmus was already dead.

The move towards Protestantism was in full swing.

The Catholic Church countered the growing threat from Protestantism with a multi-pronged counteroffensive:

1) The Inquisitions continued to be used.

2) The Council of Trent was assembled (1562-63).

3) The Jesuit Order was approved by Pope Paul III (in 1540).

4) The Index of Prohibited Books was drawn up.

5) The examples of Saints, such as Theresa of Avila and Clare of Assisi, were promoted.

<u>(i) The Numerous Inquisitions.</u>

The first of the inquisitions is known as the Medieval Inquisition (c.1184) under Pope Lucius III. The Papal Inquisition was set up by Gregory IX (Count Ugolino, who was pope from 1227 to 1241). In 1232 the burning of heretics became the law in the Holy Roman Empire (Heer, 1967/68,

173). There was also a Roman Inquisition, a Portuguese Inquisionion, a Genoan one and a Spanish one.

The Spanish Inquisition was set up in November 1478 by

Ferdinand V of Aragon (1452-1516) and his wife, Isabella I of Castille (the parents of parents of Catherine of Aragon, Henry VIII's first queen) with the approval of Pope Sixtus IV. The first Grand Inquisitor of Spain from 1493 was Thomás de Torquemado who was close to King Ferdinand and Queen Isabella as he was their confessor. About 2,000 people were burned alive for heresy due to his diligent scrutiny ('Torquemado, Thomás de', in ODCC). The Spanish Inquisition was active in Spain from 1479 to 1820, including against converted Jews and Moslems who might be continuing with their traditions and against all and any Protestants. As can be seen, Inquisitions were was not confined to Spain but its heresy-hunting activities and trials extended to Italy, France and those German states which remained Catholic. Protestant German states and the Netherlands (Holland) were beyond Rome's reach.

(ii) The Council of Trent.

The Council of Trent met in 1562 to reassert Papal power over all secular rulers, including the Holy Roman Emperor. The Council denied that the Bible is the only source of Christian truth and denied the right of interpretation to anyone but the church. It condemned 'justification by faith alone' and reaffirmed the seven sacraments and the idea of original sin (Tomkins, 2003, 154). The dictates of the

Council of Trent would prevail in Catholic countries.

iii) The Jesuits.

Inigo (later Ignatius) Loyola of Spain (1491-1556) wrote The Spiritual Exercises. In 1540, with St Francis Xavier, Blessed Peter Faber and four others, he vowed poverty, chastity and pilgrimage to Jerusalem, founding the Society of Jesus as the

Pope's special and zealous servants on the mission field and in Europe: an obedient army to do Pope Paul III's bidding.

They specialised in running schools and gaining powerful

positions in the Courts of Europe and in universities (Tomkins, 2003, 151; 'Ignatius Loyola, St', in ODCC).

Loyola was twice denounced to the Inquisition and imprisoned. The Jesuits were expelled from Portugal in 1759 and Spain and from France in 1764 after a failed assassination attempt on Henry IV. They were suppressed in England by Henry VIII (c.1545) and in the whole Catholic Church by Pope Clement XIV (1773) until restored in 1814. Secular European powers were always wary of them (Mursell [ed], 2003, 203).

Plate 12.1.
Meeting of the Council of Trent
Creative Commons Attribution Share Aike 3.0. Unported license.

<u>4) The Index of Prohibited Books.</u>

All of the writings of the reformers were banned in an attempt
to stop the spread of their ideas.

5) <u>Clare of Assisi (1193-1253) and Theresa of Avila (1515-1582)</u>

These two remarkable women so embodied strict Catholicism and influenced others to do so, by teaching, writing and by example that they helped defend Catholicism, even long after their deaths. Both ladies established women's orders of greater strictness than was customary and themselves embodied devotion. Interestingly both women spoke of being 'converted' or of having conversion experiences.

The church used hagiographies of female saints to encourage devotion, vocations and Catholic women in general towards piety and obedience to the Church. As previously discussed at 9.4. above, St Clare founded her own order, the Poor Clares. Her extant writings indicate her spirituality which was upheld as exemplary for Catholics. Neither she nor Teresa of Avila is normally seen as part of the Vatican's counter-offensive against Protestantism (Lutherans and Calvinists were all the same to Teresa) but their offensive was one of love. If Theresa of Avila could have given her soul to save even one of them she would have because, for her, salvation and Roman Catholicism were the same.

Yet Theresa of Avila was constantly at odds with its hierarchy. She disobeyed her Rule by leaving her convent in secret, roaming the countryside, engaging in financial wheeling and dealing and she even led an armed band of bodyguards against her motherhouse. She also practised extreme asceticism. She lashed herself "until the walls of her cell dripped with gore" (Tucker, 2016, 73). Theresa made a most remarkable impression upon the Catholic world in a church and a society in which women were rarely influential. Only celibate women had any standing, so Theresa had to have been a nun. She, like Clare of Assisi, was also a mystic and both were strong, independent women.

As a Carmelite nun Theresa was shocked by the laxity of convent life so she worked to establish a new house with a primitive (strict) rule, called St Joseph's. Here Theresa wrote The Way of Perfection. Theresa experienced visions and ecstasy and her spiritual life deepened until, in 1572, it reached the state of 'spiritual marriage'. Theresa combined mystic experience with ceaseless and energetic activity, working to found reformed Carmelite houses for nuns and friars (know as the Discalced/Barefooted Carmelites) in many places. Her ideas were much influenced by Egyptian eremetic monasticism, which was very demanding. She forfeited all but the barest necessities with self-imposed solitary confinement, flagillations and strenuous asceticism.

As a Carmelite nun Theresa experienced the visions, ecstasy and indescribable raptures for which she is well known. Less well known is her conversion experience which came in a

momentary flash at age 41 and with it a visionary tour of hell (inhabited by the souls of poor Protestants) and many

torments and temptations (Tucker, 2016, 73f).

Plate 12.2.
The 'Ecstasy of St Teresa' in the Cornatro Chapel, by Bernini (1645-52). Public domain.

The Baroque marble statue of her by Gianlorenzo Bernini was inspired by her testimony in which she saw an angel with a large golden spear:

"I felt as if he plunged this into my heart several timers, so that it penetrated all the way to my entrails. When he drew it out, he ... left me totally inflamed with a great love for God. The pain was so severe it made me

moan several times. The sweetness of this intense pain is so extreme there is no wanting" (Teresa's Life, cited by Tucker, 2016, 74).

Teresa's writings, including Foundations, Life and The Interior Castle, may have been her greatest legacy.

"She was the first to point to the existence of states of prayer intermediate between discursive meditation and ecstasy... And to give a scientific description of the entire life of prayer from meditation to the so called 'mystic marriage" ('Teresa of Avila', in ODCC).

There was no lack of miracles to prove her sanctity so Teresa was canonised only 40 years after her death at age 66. She became Spain's first female saint who was not also a martyr: a remarkable example for nuns and others to follow ('Teresa of Avila', online). Her writings, disseminated within the church, were highly spiritual and thoroughly Catholic so therefore were useful propaganda for a church under siege. Similarly St Clare of Assisi was quickly canonised: just two years after her death (Galli, 2002, 111).

<u>12.2. One Example of the Counter-Reformation in Action.</u>

Consider the life of philosopher and scientist, Galileo Galilei (1564-1642). It well illustrates aspects of the Counter-Reformation in action. In 1614 he was accused of heresy for his support of the Copernican theory, 'heliocentrism': that the Sun was the centre of the solar system, not the Earth (Nicholas Copernicus [1473-1543] had developed this theory, which was fully published in 1543 just before his death.

Plate 12.3.
Galileo, by Justus Sustermans c.1640,

National Maritime Museum, London, Caird Collection. Public domain. Galileo was found guilty in 1616 and forbidden to advocate these theories but, in 1632, Galileo published "Dialogue Concerning the Two Chief World Systems", which is a discussion for and against Copernicus. It appeared to attack the Jesuits and his supporter, Pope Urban VIII, who was not amused, and Galileo was summoned to Rome by the Inquisition. He was again found "vehemently suspect of heresy", compelled to recant under threat of torture and publicly withdrew support for heliocentrism. He was sentenced to permanent house arrest. His writings were placed on the Index of Prohibited Books and some remained on it until 1835, long after his ideas, adopted by Sir Isaac Newton (16421727), had become accepted (Clarke, 1961, 372).

Galileo's experiences were the Counter-Reformation in action.

12.3. Long-term Conclusions

The fracturing of Ecclesia became more extreme after the Reformation. Today, Ecclesia is made up of an estimated 34,000 denominations, worldwide, and within each there is a multiplicity of beliefs on every topic.

There are about sixty million Christians (Tomkins, 2003, 245). Each has become his/her own priest, as Luther proposed. Ecclesia's government is no longer centralised nor politically powerful (although the Papacy endures) but even Rome no longer persecutes people for heterodox beliefs. The ideals for which the reformers preached, worked and died have become the inheritance of Ecclesia, worldwide.

12.4. Long-term Conclusions

Some, such as Payton Jr, (2010, 246-259) suggest that the Reformation was a tragedy: that the church should have

remained "one", as Jesus prayed (John 17:22) but oneness of spirit and heart were lacking while ever individuals felt trapped in an institution that was anything but Christian, in theology and behaviour.

1) In any case, centuries before the Reformation the church had already split into two: with 'the Great Schism' between East and West in 1045.

2) There had been divisions in the Early Church from the start: whitewashed over - rarely mentioned and never preached about. It was not right, but Christians are imperfect humans too. In New Testament times, the Hellenists had criticised the Hebrews (Acts 6:1), Paul had a falling out with Barnabas (Acts 15:39), Paul accused Peter of hypocrisy and opposed Peter to his face (Gal. 2.11-13), Paul and the 'circumcision party' disagreed and the Judaeo-Christians were soon marginalised as Greek philosophy, combined with Roman authoritarianism, began to penetrate Christian thinking.

The Patristic period was by no means all unity and family-hood. Even in the first centuries it was riddled with heresies,

schismatics and divisions. In the 4th century Eusebius named 47 leaders of contemporary heresies (H.E., 420-21).

Not all heretics were excommunicated. Although he was an influential Church Father, Tertullian formed his own Montanist sect later in life, which was schismatic in its rigorous praxis rather than its beliefs ('Tertullian', citing Tertullian, On Fasting, 1, in ODCC). Origen, an influential Church Father, believed that eventually God would restore the created order to perfection, including Satan (NDT, 1988, 702) and Origenism was declared heretical three hundred years after Origen's death, being condemned by the Second Council of Constantinople in 553. ('Origen and s.v. Origenism', in ODCC).

3) There had always been 'dissenters' in the Latin Church - dissenters in spirit, if not in body: women like the poor rejected soul, the nun Héloise, who despite her inner torments, conformed so well that she became a prioress (Tucker, 2016, 25ff); the scholar and visionary who was sealed in with an anchoress for thirty years, Hildegard of Bingen, who became an abbess; the mystic and miracle worker, St Theresa of Avila, who was examined by the Inquisition; and the teenager, Clare of Assisi, who was besotted with Francis and became the founder of the Poor Clares; as well as men like St Francis who was

married, not to his beautiful Clare, nor to the Church, but to 'Lady Poverty' (Tucker, 2016, 37-41; 69-75; 27-32; 28-32, respectively).

In modern times St Mary of the Cross MacKillop, who founded an order, was excommunicated by her bishop (until the Pope intervened) and another bishop expelled her from his diocese: but she pressed on with her work.

4) The Reformers had no option but to flee the Latin Church: they were excommunicated, with prices upon their heads. Persecutions and death penalties were a disgrace to Christianity: practised by many groups at times (except, perhaps, the Quakers).

(5) The thousands of different denominations that exist today may be criticised by 'the world' (who need an excuse to reject Christianity anyway) and the sceptical, secular press in the West but they proclaim and demonstrate the liberty enjoyed in democracies: 'Freedom of Religion'.

<u>Questions:</u>

(1) Which aspect of the Catholic Counter-Reformation was the most helpful and which was the most destructive?

(2) Why have the Jesuits been so successful? and so controversial?

Chapter 13
Oliver Cromwell and the Wars of Religion

<u>13.1. Scotland and England Unite</u>

After a period of relative calm achieved by Elizabeth I's long reign the fact that she was childless was the cause of ongoing problems so that the 17th century was a period of convulsions for Ecclesia in the British Isles and, it transpired, in Europe as well.

The end for Mary Queen of Scots has been noted but the son she and Lord Darnley had together, James VI of Scotland, was Elizabeth I's second cousin and heir. When Elizabeth died, in 1603, he travelled South to assume the title James I of England, hence the 'United Kingdom', which is still holding together - by a thread. His mother, Mary Queen of Scots, was, of course, baptised and raised as a Catholic by her widowed French mother, Marie/Mary of Guise, and she grew up in France, but when the Scottish queen was imprisoned in England the boy, James, was raised by Presbyterian nobles. The Stuart dynasty always walked on a knife's edge between the requirement to be supreme governors of the Anglican Church and their natural inclinations and historical ties to Rome.

James I's lasting contribution to Christianity has been 'the King James Version' or 'Authorised Version' of the Bible which was published in 1611 ('James I', in ODCC). His lasting contribution to English social life has been fireworks on November 5, in memory of Guy Fawkes and the Gunpowder Plot in which some disappointed Catholic leaders tried to assassinate the king by blowing up the opening of parliament. Guy Fawkes was executed.

The Stuart position was so tenuous that James I's son, Charles I, went to war against parliament and the 'Roundheads', led by Oliver Cromwell. A combined force of Scots and

Roundheads defeated the Royalists in 1643 and 1645. King Charles I was beheaded on January 30, 1649 for financial mismanagement, overriding parliament in raising taxes, waging war against his own people and the injustices of the 'Star Chamber' (a cruel justice system).

13.2. Oliver Cromwell

Oliver Cromwell became a cruel, puritanical dictator, suppressing Catholicism, forbidding long hair, bright clothing and amusements, crushing the Irish (who were Catholics) and imposing military law. From 1658, his son and heir, Richard Cromwell, was so incompetent that he resigned, leaving a political vacuum. Parliament was recalled and chose to restore the monarchy.

13.3. The Restoration

Amid great acclaim, King Charles II entered London on May 29, 1660 to resume the Stuart monarchy and to be head of the Church of England. The Restoration was a time of gaiety, frivolity and laxity at court, but neither for Catholics nor for Puritans because "parliament .. contained a majority of hot Cavaliers (royalists) burning for revenge on the Puritans, and especially the Puritan ministers" (Clarke, 1961, 372).

13.4. John Bunyan (1628-1688)

John Bunyan was a poverty stricken tinker who had served in Cromwell's parliamentary army from 1644-1647. He lived a degenerate life until he read about 'justification by faith alone' in Luther's Commentary on Galatians. He became a Baptist by immersion in 1653, a deacon in 1655 and then a preacher, but

he was a Puritan in theology (Timeline, online). In 1658, at thirty years of age, he was imprisoned for preaching without a license, along with many other Baptists, Independents and

Quakers; including the founder of the Quakers, George Foxe, whose Book of Martyrs inspired Bunyan ('John Bunyan. Church History Timeline', online). John Bunyan was released after twelve years and became pastor of a Bedford Baptist church but was again imprisoned for six months (in 1675) on the same charge. While imprisoned he lived on starvation rations which may have damaged his health as he died aged sixty. He wrote sixty books, including Grace Abounding to the Chief of Sinners and The Pilgrim's Progress (a popular book in Britain and in rural America).

Plate 13.I.

William III and Queen Mary II. Public domain.

13.5. The Bloodless or Glorious Revolution

King James II (the second son of Charles I) became king in 1685 despite having converted to Catholicism about fifteen years previously. His appointments and regulations favoured Rome, which angered parliament. He imprisoned the

Archbishop of Canterbury and seven bishops in the Tower for seditious libel when they refused to obey his instructions on

matters of religion. Parliament decided to act. The King's son-in-law, the Dutch Protestant, William, Prince of Orange and his troops landed in 1688 and James II fled to France. William was invited to rule with his wife Mary, a Stuart princess. This became known as 'the bloodless revolution'. When James II raised a Catholic army he was defeated in Ireland at the Battle of the Boyne in 1690. With the reigns of Queen Mary II and her husband William III (1688-1702) and then of Mary's sister, Queen Anne (1702-1714), the British knew that they had avoided a bloody civil war, giving peace and prosperity a chance ('James II', in ODCC).

13.6. Wars of Religion in Europe

Religion was the cause of much armed conflict throughout Europe. The causes of these conflicts were rarely simple and were often mixed in with conflicts over dynastic successions, land ownership, politics, revenge, mutual obligations, egos and power.

3.7. Anabaptists

As noted, the Anabaptist movement arose in the 16th century, a time of great turmoil. In 1525 the first known adult baptism of modern times was performed by Conrad

Grebel near Zurich, virtually as a protest against his mentor, Zwingli's, reluctance to institute reforms (Estep, 1963/1975,25f; 'Anabaptists', in Encyclopaedia Britannica, online). Zwingli had withdrawn his support for the Anabaptists and for

rebaptism (Oyer, 1964, 203f; Estep, 1963/1975, 14). He "refused to accept their strict Biblicalism and doctrine of a free, confessional church" (Grimm, 1954/1959, 266). The Anabaptists disagreed with Zwingli's belief that baptism was similar to circumcision: membership of a religion. They interpreted baptism as a symbol of a person's regeneration,

faith and future obedience to Jesus Christ (E. Scott, 1995, 3, online). Zwinglians turned against Anabaptists, persecuting the Swiss Brethren.

13.8. Baptist-type leaders

Six founding Anabaptist-style leaders of the 16th century and their groups are:

1) Thomas Müntzer (in Wittenberg from 1521) claimed special revelation and influenced the Quakers with his teaching of 'Inner Light', i.e., that each person's inner light was sufficient to guide the conscience and give revelation (C. P. S. Clarke, 1961, 362).

2) Balthasar Hübmaier and then Denck were the leaders of the Swiss Brethren in Zurich, Switzerland, from 1525. Even before becoming an Anabaptist Hübmaier wrote, "the burning of heretics is an invention of the devil" (Estep, 1963/1975, 197).

He and Grebel were the first to determine the congregational form of government: when Hübmaier resigned as priest his congregation reelected him as their minister (Estep, 1963/1975, 191). He had been a friend and student of Zwingli, but the latter imprisoned him, forcing him to recant. Hübmaier fled to Moravia but was extradited to Austria and burnt in Vienna on March 10, 1529 ('Hübmaier, Balthasar', in ODCC).

3) Jacob Hutter (d.1536) was the leader of the Moravians/Hutterites, who held their property and children in common (E. Scott., online, 8, citing Clasen, 1972, 295). In Tyrol, Hutter had reported that 700 persons were executed, exiled or fled to Moravia, leaving property and children behind, but they were expelled to Liechtenstein. He was tortured and burned (Estep, 1963/1975, 92-95).

4) Melochior Hoffmann (1500-1543) a German and former Lutheran preacher founded the Melchiorites or Hoffmannites in Germany and the Low Countries (that is, the Netherlands, Belgium and Luxenburg). In 1533, he was sentenced to life imprisonment and died there, aged 43 ('Hoffmann, Melochoir', in ODCC).

5) John of Leiden/Jan Matthijs (d.1534) led the Munster group with an iron fist, forcing baptism upon everyone. He introduced the death penalty for adultery but finished up with polygamy. In 1535, the starving city was captured and the leaders were mutilated and killed, including the new leader, Jan Beuckels (Tomkins, 2003, 148f).

6) Menno Simons (d.1561), a Catholic priest, who planted Mennonite churches in Holland and Germany. He survived twenty-five years as a wanted man (Tomkins, 2003, 149).

<u>.21. Anabaptist Martyrs in Europe</u>

Michael Sattler was a Benedictine monk, who became an Anabaptist after reading the New Testament. He preached in Strasbourg/Strasburg and Horb. "Early Swiss and German churches owe their doctrinal and organizational stability to his work" (Estep, 1963/1975, 41). The Catholic King of Austria had decreed a 'third baptism' for Anabaptists (i.e., drowning). In 1527, one of the charges against Sattler was that he had

taken a wife. In his defence he said that marriage was an ordinance of God and that there was gross immorality among priests and monks. His witness was steadfast. In 1528, Sattler was tortured and burned. His death noble was forgiving and

pure. His faithful wife was drowned. Mass executions were common and in Altzey police hunted Anabaptists and

executed them on the spot; yet they increased in number (Estep, 1963/ 1975, 46f; 49).

.22. <u>Anabaptist Beliefs</u>

Anabaptists did not have defining beliefs and practices but some ideas are common: the separation of church and state, adult (or believers') baptism and a repudiation of infant baptism as erroneous and worthless, refusal to swear oaths or pay taxes, a return to the New Testament church in baptism and Holy Communion, and withdrawal from the corrupt and evil society. Love for the Word of God and holiness of life were key characteristics (Estep, 1963/1975, 1-8; E. Scott, online, 6). All overt acts of sin were censured, including by shunning, but not by force (Estep, 1963/ 1975, 187).

Anabaptists took the 'Great Commission' seriously and the Hutterites developed the most extensive missionary work. Many Anabaptists believed that the second coming was immanent. Some were pacifists but others, such as Hübmaier believed in 'the Sword' if the government demanded it, and they fought valiantly against oppression (Estep, 1963/1975, 192f).

.23. <u>The 30 Years War</u>

This thirty years of religious warfare in Central Europe lasted from 1618 to 1648 and killed twentypercent of the German population (Robert, 2009, 35). By 1648 only Catholics, Calvinists and Lutherans were permitted in the Holy Roman Empire under the terms of the Treaty Peace of Westphalia, which ended The 30 Years War (1618-48) (E. Scott, online, 303f). The Anabaptists missed out completely and were persecuted by all state churches, Catholic and Protestant.

They had been opposed by Martin Luther and his colleague, Philipp Melanchthon (1497-1560) and persecuted by Zwingli. Tens of thousands of them were put to death, but Anabaptist

preachers were convicted and energetic and the movement spread rapidly, despite the obvious cost.

.24. <u>Political Outcomes</u>

Both Roman Catholics and Protestants agreed to suppress the Anabaptists at both the Diets of Speyer

(1529) and of Augsburg (1530). The Peace of Augsburg (1555) gave rights only to Lutherans, not Calvinists. The Huguenots of France were ruthlessly crushed, for example in the St Bartolomew's Day massacre of 1572 which killed 5,000 to 10,000 in French cities in a few days ('Bartholomew's Day, Maassacre of St.', in ODCC).

Henry IV of France (a Protestant who converted to Rome to secure the throne) had issued the Edict of Nantes which granted French Huguenots the right to practise the Reformed Religion in certain designated areas (Vos, 1994, 212, note 24; Bettenson (ed.), DCC, 302) This saved many lives but decades later these rights were withdrawn by Louis XIV (1685) so that the industrious Huguenot remnant left France for Protestant lands (Fisher, I, 1964, 445).

Trouble between rivals for imperial power led to war in Bohemia/ Hungary, Moravia and Austria by 1618. Imperial and Catholic forces defeated and then ruthlessly crushed Protestantism in Central Europe by 1623, before turning their attention to Denmark's Protestants (1624-29) then Sweden's (1630-34) and the German states (1635-48) (Vos, 1994, 106).

The Peace of Westphalia ended The 30 Years War but the devastation and deaths of the period 1618 to 1648 had so weakened the disjointed German-speaking states, both economically and militarily, that it would leave them open to Napoleon's eventual attacks (Fisher, I, 1964, 442ff). France, however, emerged from its religious conflicts even stronger than previously. Catholicism had triumphed in Spain, Austria, Bohemia and Poland and in some parts of Germany: a situation that remains much the same today.

13.13. Conclusions

Anabaptists opposed 'popery' and the Magesterial Reformers (who established national churches). They aimed to model their practices upon the New Testament Church, as they understood it (E. Scott, online, 3). They remained faithful to their unique, individualistic doctrines and interpretations despite terrible persecution from Catholics, Lutherans and Calvinists (Payton, Jr., 2010, 213).

The movement was foundational or important to many denominations, including Mennonites, Amish, Hutterites,

Quakers, Dunkards, Baptists and Brethren groups. Many of these groups remain separated from regular society and preseve their personal, individualistic zeal but others have joined mainstream life.

13.14. Important Roman Catholics of the 17th Century

(i) Brother Lawrence of the Resurrection (c.1605/1611-1691)

Lawrence was born in France, perhaps in about 1611, the time of the Authorised Version of the Bible in England, but his life was lived in France in the bosom of the Latin Church. He a Carmelite monk, a cook and a sandal-maker. (Even though the order went barefooted, sandals were worn in the snow). As with many of the individuals discussed in these pages, Lawrence made a great contribution to posterity through his writing: in this case his books. One is re-published in English as "The Practice of the Presence of God". Maximes spirituelles (Spiritual Maxims) (1692) and Moeurs et entretiens du F. Laurent (1694) were published postumously. Lawrence found that his personality was more comfortable with short personal prayers than with constructed, formulaic prayers. He designed five simple skills that anyone who is dedicated to a life of communion with God could learn and follow (Frost, 2006, 64-70). Archbishop Fénelon (who is noted below) quoted from Lawrence's maxims so they undoubtedly influenced Madam Guyon during her long solitary imprisonment, as also detailed below.

Maxims from Brother Lawrence include: Guard your heart with extreme care to retain piety: Keep the soul's gaze fixed on God in Faith; Do all for the love of God; Offer short prayers to God; Value the presence of God.

(ii) Madam Guyon (1648-1717)

After Madam Jeanne-Marie Bouvier de la Motte Guyon's husband died in 1676 she travelled throughout France and

Switzerland, privately teaching her mystic beliefs. Numerous Catholic bishops expelled her from their territory. She mixed in French court circles where her patron was Madam de Maintenon, the mistress and then secret second wife of Louis XIV (Knight, 2012, online). Her disciples at court were exemplary people of piety.

Another ardent defender of Madam Guyon and her frequent correspondent was Archbishop Fénelon, who had tutored the King's grandson. Despite her connections, Madam Guyon was imprisoned in the Bastille twice: for seven months from January 9, 1688 and for seven years from Christmas Eve, 1695, the final two years being in solitary confinement. Madam Guyon's autobiography is available in the Christian Classics Ethereal Library.

Plate 13.2.

Madam Jeanne Guyon. Public domain.

Two books by Madam Guyon that are avialable in English from Dialogue & Documents from the Past are "The way to God" & "A Short & Very Easy Method of Prayer". All of her books were placed on the Index of Banned Books and she was forced to recant (Missler, online).

John Wesley read her autobiography in English, "The Life of Madam Guyon," and was sufficiently influenced to condense it and republish it for wider consumption. Wesley said of her: "How few such instances of exalted love of God, and our neighbour; of genuine humility; of invincible meekness and unbounded resignation" (Knight, 2012, online).

13.15. Conclusions

In a century and a half, ideas of religious reform had swept across Europe engulfing some of the Germanic states, Switzerland, the Netherlands, Scandinavia, Scotland and England. The 16th century had been an era of chaos: social, political and religious. Europe was wracked by religious wars in which tens of thousands died and which became more political wars than anything else: wars for power and influence and to impose one doctrine or another upon Christian people.

The 17th century was heralded by the accession to the English throne of Elizabeth I. It became a period of trade, manufacturing and economic growth, political stability, scientific discoveries and social change.

Gas street lighting, chimneys, brick houses, window-glass, sash windows, forks, tea, chocolate, coffee, coffee-houses,

grandfather clocks, padded chairs, armchairs, bookcases, chests of drawers, walnut and mahogany furniture, veneering and inlays, men's wigs, newspapers, women's magazines, and female actors became commonplace. Cities were dark, dangerous, dirty and unsanitary and the bubonic plague struck in 1603, 1636 and 1665 (Lambert, online).

Questions:

(1) Why were the Stuart kings of England frequently attracted towards Catholicism?

(2) How did James VI of Scotland become James I, of England?

Chapter 14

American Christianity:

<u>Founding Fathers, Great Awakenings, Modern Baptists</u>
<u>14.1. The Mayflower and the Founding Fathers</u>

Ferdinand and Isabella of Spain had sent Christopher Columbus to discover new worlds in 1492, decades before Europeans, including the Spanish, attempted to settle the lands that he discovered. Even then, the first colonies failed (from Spain's first attempt in 1526), even losing every person to starvation, conflict with native Americans and disease: but the Dutch, Spanish, French and English governments could see that settlement held promise and all eventually established, or approved of, colonies in North America.

Even though Martin Luther had survived his bold challenge to the Latin Church, and Lutheranism had flourished with the help of local princes and rulers (electors) it did not mean that religious freedom flourished in Europe.

In England, Elizabeth I's Act of Uniformity of 1559 resulted in a heavy fine for those absent from Church of England services on Sundays and holy days (DCC, 330-336, notably 33f).

Prison and even execution for sedition were imposed upon for those who conducted illegal 'separatist' services; for example Robert Browne, a leader of non-conformist or separatist services was a wanted man who survived, but his colleagues,

John Greenwood and Henry Barrows, were executed in 1593 under Elizabeth I. In Europe, two factors (a new

continent and religious persecution) combined to result in the emigration of religious dissenters and nonconformists.

Some nonconformist followers of Robert Browne, called 'Brownists', moved from England to Holland and then to America, where Jamestown, Virginia, (settled in 1607) was the only colony to have succeeded, so far. Virginia was strongly Church of England, anti-Catholic and a Crown

Colony, until religious freedom was decreed by the American Constitution in 1730 ('Religion in the 13 Original Colonies', online).

Plate 14.1.

Mayflower in Plymouth Harbour, by William Halsall, 1882.

In the Pilgrim Hall Museum, Plymouth, MAS, USA. Public domain.

The Mayflower anchored in Provincetown Harbour on 11/11/1620 with twenty-eight members of the 'Brownist' congregation from Leiden, led by William Brewster; with 174 others. They cooperatively wrote the Mayflower Charter, "the seed of American democracy", elected John Carver as their first governor and found a site for a settlement. Many died, including Governor Carver, but the colony of Massachusetts struggled on ('Religion in the 13 Original Colonies', online).

The Colony of Rhode Island was founded by Roger Williams, a dissenter from the Puritans of Massachusetts, who had been

banished by them. The new colonies of Connecticut, New Hampshire and Maine were founded for similar reasons.

Delaware had originally been founded by Sweden (in 1637) and the Dutch founded New York (in 1604) and New Jersey (in 1702). These fell into the hands of the English and religious toleration was granted to all Christians there, except that Protestantism was favoured in New Jersey ('Religion in the 13 Original Colonies', online).

14.2. Conclusions

Many small and dissenting congregations fled together from one city or state to another in Europe and eventually found sanctuary in America.

By 1702 each of the thirteen colonies granted rights and/or financial assistance to a particular denomination (i.e., 'established' churches). For example, Virginia, Maryland, New York and North and South Carolina were Church of England/Anglican; Massachusetts, New Hampshire and Connecticut were Congregational and, although Pennsylvania was founded by Quakers under William Penn, and a religious oath was required by officials, there was no official religion there ('Religion in the 13 Original Colonies', online). People of different faiths and 'dissenters' (such as Baptists) were sometimes persecuted.

All financial advantages for religions were abolished, however, after the War of Independence, when the United States was created as a secular state, and the 14th Amendment to the Constitution was passed, on July 28, 1868. Freedom of religion and the separation of church and state became fundamental principles in America ('Religion in Colonial America: Trends, Regulations, and Beliefs', online).

<u>14.3. Six reasons for the disestablishment of churches</u>
(as suggested by Vos, 1994, 129ff)

1) The variety and numbers of immigrants from many denominations, and/or of no religion.

2) Many were proprietary colonies which were tolerant, having been founded to make money.

3) The Awakenings and Revivals were a levelling influence.

4) The frontier and pioneering work were also levellers, breeding individualism.

5) Thinly spread populations lacked churches and resisted paying for their services.

6) Anglicanism (which had been important) was in ruins, its churches were sacked during the War of Independence and its clergy fled to England.

<u>.25. The First Great Awakening in America (1730s and 40s to c.1770).</u>

An earthquake in New England in 1727 was significant for religion, and the Great Awakening may have been ignited by such trials as wars, economic crises and famines. These may have been background forces but they cannot account for the particular pathway that was followed without reference to the people whose genius enlivened the age, especially Jonathan Edwards, George Whitefield and the Wesley brothers.

Jonathan Edwards (1703-1758) and Revival in Massachusetts

Jonathan Edwards' own record of events in his congregation in Northampton, Massachusetts, indicates that an admonition about the behaviour of the youth in late 1733, and the sudden

deaths soon after of two young people in early 1734 were significant. Also, the death of an old man: "was attended with many unusual circumstances, by which many were much moved and affected..." (Jonathan Edwards, 'A Fathful Narrative (1737)', in Kidd, 2008, 32ff). What this strage sentence means remains an intriguing mystery.

Plate 14.2.
Jonathan Edwards. Public domain.

Then a girl of questionable repute was gloriously redeemed. News of it spread like lightening as she witnessed to many, both children and even the elderly and some African-Americans. Everyone was talking about religion and pressing into the kingdom of heaven, thronging to house-meetings and churches. There was joy and many tears. Whereas religion had been dying, "ready to expire" there were now expectations of the end of the world. People were suddenly convicted of sin and joyously changed (Kidd, 2008, 34-36).

In November, 1734, Edwards preached on "Justification by Faith Alone", which resulted in revival in Northampton and along the Connecticut River Valley ("Jonathan Edwards' by

Schafer, Encyclopedia Britannica). Many reported dreams, visions, spiritual journeys, trances and visits to Heaven (Kidd, 2008, 13; 73f). Some cried out, wept or fell 'under the power' as though dead. Edwards 'fire-and brimstone' preaching is best illustrated by his sermon, "Sinners in the Hands of an Angry God." (The Independence Hall Association, '7b.The Great Awakening', online).

The radical preachers criticised incumbent clergy ('dogs that can't bark') as unregenerate. One preacher, James Davenport, was a very colourful character'. He had previously been arrested for sedition. He was charged with libel/slander against other clergy, although he was declared insane and released (Kidd, 2008, 3).

He was given to street parades and often led crowds of African-Americans and Native Americans and poor white folk singing through the streets of colonial New England. In 1743, Davenport arrived in New-London, Long Island, with an ulcerated leg and seemed quite deranged, gathering religious books, clothing, ornaments and jewellery to be burnt. He took off his plush breechers to burn them until a woman snatched them up, threw them into his face and demanded that he dress decently. It was written up in the Boston Evening Post as 'James Davenport's Book and Clothes Burning,' (Kidd, 2008, 107). Davenport's followers melted away. When his fever improved he apologised in person and in writing and moderated his behaviour (James Davenport, 'Confession and Retraction', in Kidd, 2008, 109ff).

From 1741 to 1746, Edwards combined his love of philosophy and his scholarship (he tutored at Yale College and earned an M.A.) to write apologies (that is, defenses) for the Awakening.

"Edwards' ability to combine religious intensity with intellectual rigour and moral earnestness, the cosmic sweep of his theologica

l vision, his emphasis on faith as an 'essential' response to reality, his insistence that love is the heart of religion, and his uncompromising stand against all forms of idolatry are some of the reasons his life and writings are again being seriously studied" (Schafer, Encyclopedia Britannica, online, 4).

<u>14.6. George Whitefield (1714-1770) and Revival in America</u>

George Whitfield, an ordained Anglican itinerant preaching deacon, had previously been an actor and brought his dramatic delivery and powerful voice to his work, preaching to England's common people in the open fields. He also advertised his meetings as he would have his stage roles. He preached

'rebirth', salvation and damnation and he welcomed all-comers. Thousands were converted and their preachers were called *'New Lights'*, while the staid and unemotional were called *'Old Lights'*. These differences led to schisms in congregations and differences of opinion on many political issues (Chen, online).

Plate 14.3.

Rev. George Whitefield. Public domain.

From 1739 until his death in America in 1770 Whitefield visited America many times with even more effect than in Britain, coming on the back of Jonathan Edwards' earlier successes in Massachusetts.

<u>14.7. Conclusions</u>

The First Great Awakening was a national event: everyone was effected. It has gone down in history as the greatest of all revivals but in America it mainly influenced established church members in the old colonies along the Atlantic Coast. As a result there was much splintering of the older churches and great changes in relative strengths and weaknesses.

Many new denominations were born, including in the original thirteen colonies. They were mainly 'Separate' and Baptist churches. In only forty years (1740-1780) Baptist churches grew from from 96 to 457, at the expense of the Anglicans and Congregationalists. Baptists' numbers overtook

Congregationalists and Methodists by 1850 (although a revival of Methodist numbers occurred by 1890) ('Cause and Effect The First Great American Awakening', online).

The American Revolution, which began in 1775 (until 1783), was greatly influenced by democracy and cultural currents inspired by the First Great Awakening: that the king was a tyant and a foreigner, and that government was a contract from God direct to the people. The notion of contract had been present in the Mayflower Compact and "grew to link religion and politics in the colonies" ('04 Significance of the Great Awakening: Roots of Revolution', online). Collective action and volunteerism was also stimulated (Chen, online).

The Great Awakening stimulated education: Yale had been founded in 1710 but Harvard (1740), William and Mary (1740), Princeton (1746), Brown/Rhode Island (1764), Rutgers/Queens College

(1766) and Dartmouth (1769) were established by different denominations after the Awakening ('Cause and effect', online).

Whitefield, Edwards and Davenport were all slave owners but believed that slaves should be treated humanely and instructed in Christianity (Kidd, 2008, 19).

14.8. The Second Great Awakening in America (c.1797/99-c.1869)

Throughout Church history, after every revival or outbreak of religious devotion there is a period of quiet: so also in America. That quiet lasted from 1770 to 1800, perhaps because people were preoccupied with the war against the British, which lasted for eight years.

American preachers who had been influenced by the revival began to move south where there were fewer churches and

many more people of colour. Although the Atlantic Coast was not entirely ignored, the Second Great Awakening favoured frontier-people and those beyond the Appalatian Mountains and the Mississippi River. Camp meetings were an early feature, when thousands of people gathered in the wilderness, from near and far, to hear a visiting revivalist. The first, organised by Rev. James McGready was held in Logan County, Kentucky (1797-99), another was held in Kentucky in 1800 (New World Encyclopedia , online).

The largest ever, attended by 20,000 people, was held in Cane Ridge, Kentucky, in 1801. One was held in Hancock County, Georgia in 1803 and one in Upper Canada in 1805 (Mursell (ed.), 2003, 286f). These were revivals, but also social outlets and marriage markets for the socially isolated.

Towards the end of the Second Great Awakening the American Civil War occurred, 1861-1865, by which time camp meetings had ceased. Christianity penetrated the frontier lands because the war resulted in the opening up of lands beyond the Mississippi and the disestablishment of all churches in all states. Disestablishment freed people to become more evangelical and many abandoned predestination in favour of every soul's freedom to choose to

be saved. The message of spiritual equality between the races accompanied the religious revivals (Kidd, 2008, 25; 19). African-Americans could preach (D. J. Bingham, 2002, 144). Native American preachers included Samson Occom, a Mohegan Indian who became a pastor and a missionary

(Kidd, 2008, 4f; 'I Believe It Is Because I Am a Poor Indian': Samson Occom's Life as an Indian Minister', online). Even women could be preachers and leaders (Brekus, 1998). Numerous preachers were illiterate, which resulted in much extemporaneous preaching by lay-people (Mursell (ed), 2003,

287. The egalitarian thrust of the Awakenings meshed with optimism, Protestant individualism and Revolutionary ideals to form the American character. By 1760 evangelists who made inroads inland were more interested in Baptist informality than Episcopalian formalities and elitism was scorned ('Cause and Effect: The First Great American Awakening', online)

<u>14.9. Charles Finney (c.1792-1875)</u>

Finney, an American, became a schoolteacher in New Jersey. When he began to study law he attended a Presbyterian church but was skeptical about God, unanswered prayer and eternal destiny (Lawson, online). As Finney studied the Bible he went into the woods one day and experienced a dramatic conversion (Mursell (ed.), 'Christian Spirituality', 2003, 287).

Within days, he met the Lord Jesus Christ face to face... as one sees any other man.. he wept aloud at Jesus' feet and bathed his feet with tears. He recorded:

"I received a mighty baptism of the Holy Ghost. Without any expectation of it, without ever having thought that there was any such thing for me, without any recollection that I had heard the thing mentioned by any person in the world, the Holy Ghost descended on me in a manner that seemed to go through me, body and soul. I could feel the impression, like a wave of electricity, going through and through me. Indeed it seemed to come in waves of liquid love... it seemed like the very breath of God" (Lawson, online).

News spread throughout his village and that evening (and every night afterwards) everyone gathered in church, mysteriously drawn, waiting to hear Finney speak.

From then on he abandoned law for prayer, fasting and preaching. It is estimated that, from 1858 to 1859, 600,000 persons were brought to Christ in revival.

Plate 14.4.

Charles Finney. Public domain.

In 1833 Finney became a Congregationalist and later President of Oberlin College, which trained people for the ministry and which had become America's first co-educational college, in 1833 ('The Struggle for Public Schools', online). His legacy includes his Autobiography, Lectures to Professing Christians, Lectures on Revivals and Systematic Theology.

Finney held that Christians must ardently seek perfection while also working to bring Christ's millennial kingdom into earthly reality. He demanded constant frenzied work for God (Lawson, online). Finney's atonement theology was not Calvinism (i.e., strict predestination) but is called New Calvinism because he held to people's free agency and moral responsibility (Lawson, online). Finney, was a world-famous evangelist, visiting Britain to preach.

It is said that in the Second Great Awakening he used to provoke conversions with protracted meetings and the 'anxious bench' on which enquirers sat until they 'broke throught' (D. J. Bingham, 2002, 145) - but Finney needed no prompts to convict people of sin, many, even hardened atheists, fell down with tears of repentance by being in his presence. "In London, England, between 1,500 and 2,000 persons were seeking salvation in one day in Finney's meetings" (Lawson, online).

14.10. African-American Spirituality

African slaves in America came from 50 different language groups. After the Second Great Awakening many slaves adopted Christianity because it gave them hope and it

gradually helped mould them into a community, and provided literacy classes. Some illiterate Afro-Americans became famed preachers, developing a unique spirituality based upon redemption through suffering, the brevity of life, eternal rewards in Heaven and identification with the poor and oppressed (Raboteau, 1989, 38). They expressed this spirituality in their unique musical genre: the Negro Spiritual. "Go down Moses", with the words "*let my people go*", the song "*Steal away to Jesus*", which hinted at escaping to the North and "Wade in the Water" (to put dogs off the scent) reflect their illegal underground meetings (Kidd, 2008, 113). Their songs expressed their faith, longing and fears.

"*In post-Civil War America, a burgeoning black church played a key role strengthening African American communities and in providing key support to the civil rights movement*" (Masci, online).

When all American slaves were freed in 1863 that was just step one in their struggle. Religion dovetailed with politics to

achieve first freedom and then civil rights. Rev. Dr Martin Luther King Jnr. exemplified this blend. Even in 2014 53% of African-American Christians attended black Protestant churches, but more so among older people (63%) (Masci, online).

Plate 14.5, by J. Maze Burbank.

Second Great Awakening Methodist revival meeting 1839. Public Domain.

14.11. Discussion

The Second Great Awakening saw an increase in conversions, in church menbership, and in the number and type of Protestant churches in the South and West of America. (Catholicism or 'popery' was considered un-American.)

There was also a growth in societies that promoted education, missions, pacificism, women's rights and the abolition of slavery: all issues which mainstream America wrestled with for decades afterwards (D. J. Bingham, 2002, 144). After more than a century the old denominations had become staid and a new nation seemed to require a renewed wind of faith.

14.12. Outcomes

Camp meetings were characterised by prayer, dancing, singing, 'speaking in tongues' and by preachers who competed with each other in skill, enthusiasm and numbers of converts. Christianity spread into new areas and unevangelised fields by people who were willing to leave the comforts of home, to bring Christianity and social contacts to people in remote locations. The Awakenings encouraged attendance at church and the founding of churches and of denominations.

Many Separatist churches resulted, including the American Baptists, Primitive Methodists, Church of Christ, the Christian Church, Disciples of Christ and the Seventh Day Adventist Church ('Great Awakening', in ODCC: New World Encyclopedia, 1;3).

14.13. European Baptists

The origins of the modern Baptists are shrouded in mystery because of the persecution they endured and because of the paucity of surviving documentary evidence, which was destroyed if it endangered people. The established churches

held the high ground and cooperated with rulers to impose their own churchmanship practices as widely as possible

. English Baptists probaby developed from the Puritans, but, after the monarch (Charles II) and the nobility were restored in 1660, some of the distaste for Oliver Cromwell fell upon Puritans and Baptists alike. Persecutions followed the restoration of the monarchy.

The first Baptist service in England was held in Spitalfields in 1612 under Thomas Helwys and they became known as General Baptists ('Baptists', in ODCC). The key spiritual practices and beliefs, which gave rise to the English Baptist movement, remain central including: the authority of Scripture, believers' baptism by immersion, the Lordship of Christ, the priesthood of all believers, liberty of conscience, separation of church and state and Regenerate Church membership (i.e., only the 'born again' could be members).

In Britain, Baptist members and churches increased in numbers in the 18th and 19th centuries, largely through a climate of greater toleration and deliberate evangelism by itinerant evangelists or 'messengers' amongst the villages. The harvest fields of the Celtic church (Wales, Cornwall, Northern England and Ireland) were reploughed and evangelistic missions were held in the cities. Baptists also became involved in social issues: the abolition of slavery, Sunday Schools for the poor, prison reform, such as John Howard (1726-1790) and foreign missions, starting with William Carey (see Ch. 18). Theological differences often tore Baptist groups apart, for example the great preacher Charles Spurgeon, who led a large London church in

1887, withdrew from a union of the Particular Baptists and the New Connection Baptists. Issues that created problems could include immersion, the Trinity, the person of Christ, open versus closed membership, open versus closed Communion, Calvinism (in that predestination discouraged evangelism) versus Wesleyanism (free will or Armenianism) and (amazingly) the singing of hymns.

Luther's reformist interpretation of a doctrine now called the "priesthood of all believers" has recently been challenged by Canadian authors Roger Helland (a Baptist) and Leonard Hjalmarson (a Mennonite) (Helland and Hjalmarson, 2011, 60f). By a close study of the key Biblical texts on the issue (I Peter 2:4-5 and 9-12) they conclude that it is the church (and not the individual) who has priesthood. "*It is the priesthood of all believers not of each believer*" (Helland and Hjalmarson, 2011, 65, f/n. 20, citing Bennett, 1993, 104).

This is a significant challenge to standard Baptist interpretation, that each individual is his own priest, with access to the Father through Jesus, the Great High Priest, and having the right to private judgement in interpreting Scripture and to profess and declare his own religious opinions (Moore, 'Baptist Distinctive - Fundamental Baptist Institute').

Could Helland and Hjalmarson's proposition lead to a reversal - back to the days of Bishop Ignatius of Antioch, who wrote in his Epistle to the Trallians that nothing should be done except through the bishop (pastor/leader)? (Andrew Louth [ed.], Early Christian Writing [Staniforth, trans.] 1987, 79). This is an astonishing proposition which counters centuries of Protestant conviction, so the implications are enormous. Now consider the Baptist's main proof-text for "the priesthood of all believers" (I Peter 2:4-10). This epistle was written to God's elect, "*strangers in the world*" (v.1) who were addressed as "dear friends" [plural] (v.11). Together, these people were told that they constituted a group of "*living stones*" who were in the process of "*being built together into a spiritual house*" (v.5) and "the people of God" (v.10). This certainly looks like a church in process, not an individual, but time will tell if the extreme individualism of American Protestantism will ever be modified.

Questions:

Do you think the 2nd Great Awakening influenced the Civil War and if so how?

(1) Why are Baptist churches so dominant in the American church landscape?

(2) How was Finney's New Calvinism compatible with the American spirit?

Chapter 15
Revivalism in Britain

<u>.26. Earliest Revival Movements</u>

Revivalism actually started amongst Presbyterians in Scotland in the 1620s, in Bristol and London in 1637, and then among Kingswood coal miners. Religious enthusiasm amongst churchgoers in Protestant countries in Europe was also revived in the 17th century and, by the 18th century, this was to reach greater heights, mainly through George Whitefield and John Wesley.

<u>.27. The Evangelical Revival</u>

The start of the Evangelical Revival predates the pairs of friends John Wesley and George Whitefield, as well as William Wilberforce and Pitt the Younger, although they all became part of it with their religious enthusiasm and dedication to social justice (such as prison reform, abolition of slavery and concern for the poor).

The politicians (such as Pitt and Wilberforce) were central to what was called the Clapham sect, many of whom were devout Anglicans but using their money, position and power as pioneers of social reform, education and the civilization of the Irish. The Reformation and Protestantism had given the English a social conscience (Clarke, 1961, 441). This was an age of missions and missionary activity: the Society for the Propagation of Christian Knowledge (1699), the Society for the Propagation of the Gospel (1701), the Baptist Missionary

Society (1792), the London Missionary Society (1795), the Church Missionary Society (1799), and, into the 19th century, the British and Foreign Bible Society (1807) and the London Society for Promoting Christianity among the Jews (1809) which was founded by the Clapham Sect. The China Inland Mission was not founded until 1865 (Rack, 1989/ 2002, 472; Clarke, 1961, 501).

.28. John Wesley (1703-1791) and Jabez Bunting (1779-1859)

As noted above, revival was already afoot when the Wesley brothers, John and Charles, were ordained as Anglican clergy in about 1735. They were much influeced by the Moravians, who taught a 'conversion experience', which John Wesley embraced (or which embraced John) in 1738. John taught 'the second blessing' or a work of the Holy Spirit. He also embraced the teaching of 'full sanctification' as a gift from God, after he encountered numerous examples of it from 1758, although he did not claim to have received it himself (Rack, 1989/2002, 334-342). As will be noted below, a number of the international revivalist preachers and even more missionaries followed this doctrine (Pollock with Randall, 1964/ 2006/2013, 1ff).

This teaching became one of Methodism's unique contributions to the Church but it was very similar to an old idea, which had featured in the writings of Jovinian (died c.405) and Pelagius (born c.380). These two monks demanded that both the church and each individual (not just the chosen few) should aspire to perfection (Markus, 1990, 39-42). They had opposed the prevailing double standard (a higher expectation for celibates) and had fought with St Jerome and

St Augustine over the issue. The 4th century had been a heady era of intense theological debate amongst the famous (Patristic) names. The difference in Wesley's teaching was that perfection was a gift, bestowed from Above.

Following the example set by the great preacher George Whitefield, John Wesley began preaching in the open air in 1739, with great success. He travelled widely in Britain on horseback, preaching 40,000 sermons altogether. Because Wesley soon realised that his converts needed ongoing nurturing, as well as attending Holy Communion in their local Anglican church, he set up a system, which became a denominaton after his death (Turner, 2005, 1).

Plate 15.1.
John Wesley by John Russell.
Public domain.

This system began with young lay-preachers (his assistants) who were attached to a 'circuit' of small cell groups/class meetings, which they moved between. Cell groups formed 'societies'.

The lay-preachers were formed into an annual Conference, a decision making body, which later elected a new President each year. 'Preaching Houses' were eventually built and legally registered as dissenting places of worship, for their own protection from local violence (Turner, 2005, 2).

Each 'society' developed various combined gatherings: Moravian style Love-Feasts (which were testimony meetings with bread and water); Puritan style Covenant Services (for an annual rededication of one's life) and the Watchnight (an all-night vigil). The normal 'Connexion' or Preaching Service consisted of a sermon, singing Charles Wesley's hymns and extemporaneous prayer. Members were required to attend their local Anglican Church for Holy Communion (Turner, 2005, 2). Wesley taught three main doctrines: repentance, faith and holiness and he opposed Calvin's doctrine of predestination, which caused him to break with his friend and colleague, George Whitefield, in 1741, and also with his mentors, the Moravians (Turner, 2005, 1; Rack, 1989/2002, 333). When Wesley died in 1791 a young Jabez Bunting soon became the main preacher and the main voice at the Methodist Conference, which, with the Legal Hundred (a body of 100 senior clergy who could veto decisions of Conference) became the ruling establishment. Jabez Bunting, as Conference President, also dominated every committee.

On Wesley's death (1791) there were 72,467 official Methodist members in Britain: 60% of whom were women. The men were from the artisan class, or shopkeepers, farmers and household servants. There were 43,265 members in America ('Wesley, John', in ODCC).

Athough laypeople were supposed to have equal say Jabez Bunting, who was politically conservative and autocratic in style, was often called "*the pope of Methodism*" (Richard

Brown, online). Bunting's policies led to constant fracturing of unity: often over trivial issues.

The Methodist New Connection had formed as early as 1797, to give power to the laity. The Camp Meeting Methodists formed in 1807 to continue the 'frontier revivalist style meetings' which Rev. Lorenzo Dow had brought over from America because such 'enthusiasm' was condemned by the Methodist Conference. Rev. Hugh Bourne and Rev. William Clowes were expelled when each began camp meetings in about 1810. In 1811 these two formed the Pimitive Methodists, a denomination that was successful in evangelism and, in 1843, sent missionaries to Australia and New Zealand ('Primitive Methodist Church', in ODCC).

Early in his ministry Jabez Bunting had approved of revivalism: if it was quiet and respectable. In fact it was he who had developed techniques which stimulated revival and concluded that "Holy Spirit inspired movements (are) triggered by apostolic praying, potent preaching and ardent proclamation." (Orr, 1976, 205). Prior to this it had been thought that revivals occurred haphazardly (Piggin, 1984, 8990).

15.4. The Awakening in England

In 1803, the aforementioned English Methodist preacher, Rev. Lorenzo Dow, had participated in the camp meeting in Georgia and took reports back to England. Methodist ministers in England, including Rev. Hugh Bourne, organised a series of 17 similar meetings from 1807 to 1811, but the preaching was from the Bible, not extemporaneous.

As noted, because Methodists disapproved, Hugh Bourne and William Clowes were expelled and the Primitive Methodist Church was founded, but camp meetings

continued in England through the 19th century (New World Encyclopedia, online, 4-5).

<u>15.5. More Trouble in the Wesleyan Ranks</u>

The Bible Christians were not a 'breakaway' but were formed to conduct extended revivals - but they were refused entry to the Wesleyan Connection because of the independent character of their charismatic leader. The Protestant Methodists withdrew because they wanted organ music; the Wesley Methodist Association withdrew because they wanted lay control of finances; six-hundred Cornish people formed the Teetotal Wesleyan Methodists to ensure a non-alcoholic Holy Communion and 40,000 others became United Methodist Free Church members. In 1849, the Wesleyan Methodist Reformers were created when James Everett was expelled, and, in 1857, they jointed with the Wesley Methodist Association to become the United Free Methodist Church. There were also Calvinistic Methodists (who followed Whitefield's teaching, rather than Wesley's). All of this upheaval consumed time, energy and resources and Methodism slowly ceased to attract enquirers. Also, its social base in agricultural areas was changing and, from 1832, the Church of England repaired the broken parish system, organised churches for the new industrial towns and grew (Brown, online).

Some of the smaller groups became Congregationalists and, in 1932, the Primitive Methodists joined with United Methodist and the Wesleyans to form the Methodist Church. Many were gathered in when the United Church in Britain and the Uniting Church in Australia were formed, the latter by a union of Congregationalists, Methodists and most Presbyterians in 1977.

<u>15.6. Conclusions</u>

In Britain, the 18th century began with a new dynasty, the Protestant Hanoverians, German descendants of James I. The end of the century coincided with John Wesley's death. It was a remarkable era for Britain marked by colonial expansion, industrialisation and urban expansion and the growth of wealth and British naval power. With colonial expansion came the so-called 'white mans burden': being responsible for other peoples, part of which entailed their spiritual welfare, which led to the formation of many missionary societies. For Ecclesia, it was a period of a social conscience associated with Protestantism and a constitutional monarchy, with the rule of Parliament becoming secure; all trends which continued into the 19th century.

Questions:

(1) Can you suggest reasons why early Methodism fragmented easily?

(2) Do you think that Jabez Bunting's leadership style helped or hindered Methodism?

Chapter 16
Post-Reformation Spiritualities

<u>16.1. Background</u>

By considering some of the leaders and their spiritual views and some of the lesser lights of the 17th to 20th century a feel for the spirituality of the age may be grasped. Although after the Reformation there was a great diversity of opinions about any and every subject, a common thread in Christian thought has been the Grace of God in redemption of the soul which leads to changes in lifestyle and an inner peace, or even joy.

A great proportion of the more memorable Christians are Roman Catholics, possibly because the celibate life has afforded them time for spiritual pursuits: contemplation, prayer and writing and perhaps because that denomination has well developed mechanisms for publicising their saints and a long tradition of honoring them.

<u>16.2. Pietism</u>

Perhaps Pietism dates from Thomas à Kempis (c.1380-1471) who wrote The Imitation of Christ, or perhaps from the Lutheran, Johann Arndt (1555-1621) and his influential book True Christianity which influenced both Philip Jacob Spener (1635-1705) and Professor August Francke (1663-1727), but the term 'Pietism' was not coined that early (Helland and Hjalmarson, 2011, 80).

Pietism is often dated to the late 17th century when Philip Jacob Spener published Pia Desideria in 1675, in Germany (translated into English by Theodore G. Tappert, 1964).

It proposed a heart religion to replace the head religion of cold, formal Lutheranism. Spener proposed: more use of the Bible, exercise of the priesthood of all believers, putting Christianity into practice and clerical education that would teach piety, right conduct and preaching, rather than academic theology. Spener influenced the aforementioned Professor Francke, whose sister, Anna, advised him to read Johann Arndt's True Christianity, a book that made Catholic-type mysticism available to

Lutherans (Helland and Hjalmarson, 2011, 75-81). Afterwards, Professor Francke effectively applied Pietism to many good works and charities.

The flame of Pietism (primarily love of God and love of others) and teaching of 'the indwelling Christ' was passed to the Moravians, Wesley and the Methodists, the Salvation Army (which began as an arm of Methodism), Quakers, Mennonites, the Christian and Missionary Alliance, the Keswick holiness movement and Holiness and Pentecostal movements in the U.S.A. and Europe. Pietism influenced individuals, such as Jonathan Edwards, Dwight L. Moody, Hannah Whitall Smith, Ruben Torrey and John Wesley, and the thousands who heard them preach or who read their books (Helland and Hjalmarson, 2011, 81).

<u>16.3. The Enlightenment</u>

In the 18th and 19th Centuries, while Methodism had gained ground in Britain and Pietism in Germany, a new force was developing among intellectuals, especially in Germany: the Enlightenment. In many respects this resembled the Renaissance, being an academic movement based on rationalism and scientific inquiry. It finally swept away the remnants of medievalism and superstition.

England was at the forefront because personal freedoms in

England had been enhanced by the Restoration of the

Monarchy in 1660 and the so-called 'Bloodless Revolution' of 1688, in which parliament had selected the Stuart princess, Mary, and her husband, William of Orange, from the Netherlands, to rule Britain jointly.

Secondly, in England, writers such as John Locke (1632-1704) upheld rationality, taught that people have natural rights, which are inalienable, and championed freedom of religion. In Paris, the writings of the 'philosophes', such as Jean Jacques Rousseau (1712-1778), were acclaimed by the populace and society women who developed a café culture for the discussion of radical new ideas and ideals. The philosopher Voltaire (1694-1778) was their hero.

As scepticism increased the miracles of the Bible were read with scepticism and Jesus was reduced to being a good moral teacher. The Creator, 'God', was most likely to be regarded as Unitarian (not as a Trinity) - one who set the laws of the physical world in motion and then left it to its own devices (Walker, 1959, 479-483).

In Germany, a university lecturer in mathematics, Christian Wolff (1679-1754) popularised the ideology and theology of the German Enlightenment in teaching that the universe was a giant machine, which operates by mechanical laws. They taught that these can be deduced by 'pure reason', which is a higher principle than revelation and with which humanity can increase in perfection. German Pietism was deeply offended and in 1723 Wolff was dismissed by King Frederick William I, but restored in 1740 by Frederick the Great (Walker, 1959, 481).

<u>16.4. France: Revolution, Terror and Dictatorship</u>

With the French Revolution (1789-1799) the radical

thinking and revolution led to a reign of terror, with

anarchy, bloodshed and the abolition of the monarchy, the aristocracy,

clerics and religion. The motto of the new French Republic was Liberty, Equality and Fraternity (Brotherhood) but its result were repression and dictatorship by the Committee of Public Safety which under Robespierre, instituted a reign of terror (9/1793-7/1794) that even took him to the guillotine, in 1794. Soon after the Revolution Napoleon emerged to make himself dictator - conquering much of Europe and even beseiging Acco/Acre in Israel on his way to Egypt. Among the vast changes that Napoleon initiated, such as decimal weights, measures and currency, his Civi Code of 1804 emancipated the Jews of Western Europe and brought them out of the ghettos. Jewish communities were transformed, which led to their increased prosperity, assimilation, intermarriage, secularisation and conversion rates (Aish.com, online).

America absorbed much French republican ideology so that open-mindedness and tolerance gradually increased in both America and post-revolutionary France. In America, each person was born free and equal: if they were white, male and owned property, but that was accepted as the way things were.

A direct connection led from rationalism and analysis to academic dissecting of the Bible: first into its division into genres (such as history, law, letters, apocalyptic writing

etc.). This led on to a detailed analysis of the texts themselves: where, and from what, were they composed - asking questions the medieval churchmen had never thought to ask. Especially in Germany 'biblical criticism'

(or analysis) became a huge intellectual industry that consumed the energy and time of generations of the ablest minds, and continues to do so. The various 'quests for the historical Jesus', the first of which began (as Chapter 18 will show) with Albert Shweitzer, follow naturally on from the Enlightenment.

16.5. Progressive Conclusion

The Enlightenment was an age in which reason, critical thinking, science and rationalism were pushing faith and religious traditions to the side: in a word, humanism. Reason triumphed over revelation. Open-mindedness, religious tolerance and anti-clericalism were hallmarks, first in Germany and increasingly in America and post-revolutionary France. In America, at least in theory, people (white people) were free and equal.

Plate 16.1.
St John Henry Newman, National Portrait Gallery.
published (or registered with the U.S. Copyright Office) before 1/1/1924.

16.6. John Henry Newman (1801-1890)

Newman was an Oxford scholar, an Anglican cleric and the leading spirit of the high-church Tractarian or Oxford Movement which aimed to defend Anglicanism against liberal theology, the lure of Roman Catholicism and reform movements. In this he was closely associated with two other founding member, E. B. Pusey and John Keeble (after whom Keeble College Oxford is named). As rector of St Mary's Oxford, Newman influenced the religious life of Oxford and the whole country, before resigning in 1843 to retire into semi-monastic life ('Newman, John' , in ODCC).

Oxford Movement members were influenced by the Romantic Movement, Medieval Christianity and especially the Early Church Fathers, whose writings they began to translate from 1838 under a collection called 'Library of the Fathers'. Newman was influenced by Calvinism but, like a number of his friends, he was gradually drawn towards Roman Catholicism, converting in 1845 and returning to academic life in Dublin University and then Oxford ('Oxford Movement', in ODCC).

Although Newman was not a bishop he was created a cardinal in 1879 and became known as John Henry Cardinal Newman. Almost a century later his teachings (which reflected his Anglican past) would influence the Second Vatican Council (1962-65). His poems include "Lead Kindly Light" and "Praise to the Holiest in the Height." In total, "his life was a continuing, prayerful search for truth, for integrity of thought, faith and action" (Mursell (ed.), 2001, 219. He became a saint in the Roman Catholic Church in 2019.

16.7. George Müller (1805-1898)

As a student this remarkable German man was influenced by fellow-students to become a Christian so that he experienced a remarkable conversion at the age of twenty. His wayward behaviour instantly changed and he devoted himself to the

work of the Lord. In 1829 he moved to London to work for the Society for Promoting Christianity among the Jews.

Ill health forced Müller to move to Tiegmouth where, for two years, he became a Plymouth Brethren preacher who lived by faith. When he moved to Bristol his life's work really began. He founded an orphanage for up to 2,000 children which became world famous as a faith ministry, while Müller, himself, became well known as a man of prayer.

In his old age he and his second wife spent seventeen years on a speaking tour of Europe, America, India, Australia and China while family members cared for the orphans ('Müller, George', in ODCC).

16.8. Fanny Crosby (1820-1915)

American, Fanny Crosby was blind from infancy or birth. She was born-again at the age of thirty. She played the piano, wrote poetry and composed the lyrics of over 8,000 hymns, forty of which are still popular, including *"Blessed Assurance"*, *"Pass me not"*, *"Safe in the Arms of Jesus'*, *"Rescue the Perishing"*, *"To God be the Glory"* and *"Jesus Keep Me Near the Cross"* (Tucker, 2016, 185-188). Her beliefs centred on the Cross of Christ and closeness with Jesus. She also believed in Christ's future millennial reign on earth.

In 1858 Fanny married Van Alstein or Alstine, a musician and organ virtuoso who also was blind and, early in their marriage, he composed tunes for Fanny's poems (athough later they lived separate lives). Her only child died in infancy (Ruffin, 1995, 69). Her musical friends included Phoebe Knapp, who wrote the music for "Blessed Assurance" and William Bradbury who also composed melodies for her and

published them. His music was sneered at by highbrow critics but loved by the masses (Ruffin, 1995, 77f).

During the Second Great Awakening Fanny and Van lived in New York and became involved, working with Ira D. Sankey's crusades from 1876 until Sankey's death in 1908 - which popularised her light, happy hymns and did much to make Sankey's evangelistic campaigns a success (Mursell (ed.), 2001, 288f). She wrote popular songs in support of the Unionist cause during the American Civil War and was an organist, harpist, preacher and lecturer. Hundreds visited her for prayer and conselling (Ruffin, 1995, 7f; 74.).

Plate 16.2.
Fanny Crosby. Public doman.

16.9. Hannah Whitall Smith (1832-1911)

Hannah, was raised a pious Quaker and, with her husband, Robert Pearsall Smith, was converted in 1858. They were influenced by the Wesleyan-based Holiness movement, "a

revivalst creed based on sanctification by faith and the direct experience of salvation" ('Hannah Whitall Smith', in Britannica). They both became popular speakers at holiness meetings in the U.S.A. and Britain. Hannah believed that Christianity should make people joyful, not given to the morbid self-examination of the Puritans (Mursell (ed.), 2001, 300f).

Hannah is remembered for her best-seller, "The Christian's Secret of a Happy Life" (1875). This little book is full of wise advice, including that Christian workers should engage in neither selfcongratulations nor recriminations.

"in the life of trust neither will troube us; for, having committed ourselves in our work to the Lord, we shall be satisfied to leave it to Him, and shall not think about ourseves in the matter at all" (Whitall Smith, 1942/1977, 137).

16.10. Charles Haddon Spurgeon (1834-1892)

Spurgeon was from a long line of independent preachers and he became a Baptist in 1850, the year in which he preached his first sermon. At the age of seventeen he was appointed a pastor. He became so renouned as a preacher that eventually a huge church had to be built for him in London: 'The Metropolitan Tabernacle'. His published sermons continued to be widely read.

16.11. Arthur Tappan Pierson (1837-1911)

Arthur Tappan Pierson, an American, became a close personal friend of Charles Spurgeon and, in 1891, was invited to London to lead the Metropolitan Tabernacle for three months when Spurgeon went to the Meditaerranean for his health.

As Spurgeon was 'called home' in France, Dr Pierson remained the pastor at The Tabernacle for two years before the vacancy could be filled, although he was a Presbyterian, and not yet a Baptist until 1896 (Christianity.com, 'Arthur T. Pierson, Illustrious Heritage', online).

Arthur Pierson was descended from Abraham Pierson, a non-conformist preacher in early Massachusetts. Arthur's parents, Stephen and Sallie Pierson, were devout

Christians and abolitionists and named the ninth of their ten children after Arthur Tappan, a famous abolitionist. Arthur Tappan Pierson and his wife, Sarah Frances Benedict, had two sons Delavan and Farrand, and five daughters (Helen, Laura, Louise, Ann and Edith) all of whom served the Lord in the USA/Britain and foreign fields such as Japan, India and Central America (Kwang He Lee (ed.), 2007).

Arthur Pierson was a great preacher, an expert at story telling and the use of apt illustrations, an exponent of the Word and an adversary of 'New Theology' and Higher Criticism (Maclean, 2012, online). Among his many books, In Christ Jesus was the most widely read.

Dr Pierson had attended Hamilyton College (1857) and Union Theological Seminary (1860-63). After decades of ministry, in 1903-04 he was awarded an honarary Doctorate in Divinity by Knox College. He and Sarah had been married in 1860 and he was ordained to the Presbyterian ministry the same year. They were close friends of D. L. and Mrs Moody.

Dr Pierson was a missiologist who understood better than any the state of world missions. He founded the magazine The Missionary Review of the World, a work which his older son, Delavan, took over. He passed into glory at the age of 74 while on an extensive tour of the mission fields of the Orient.

As well as missionary work, Dr Pierson was a keen supporter of the new Student Volunteer Movement in America and Britain, and of homes for orphans, especially those of his close friend George Müller, in Bristol, England.

He wrote two relevant biographies: those of George Müller

and of George's son-inlaw, James Wright. After watching the new Keswick Conventions from afar for two years Arthur became an ardent supporter and often preached at Keswick Conventions on two continents (Maclean, 2012, online).

Arthur Peierson was not only close to many spiritual movements of his day but he helped to initiate or to nurture them. His legacy has, however, paled in the light of great people who were his closest friends.

<u>16.12. St Mary of the Cross (MacKillop) (1842-1909)</u>

Mary Helen McKillop became Australian's first and only Catholic Saint. She was beatified on January 19, 1995 by Pope John Paul II in Sydney and canonise by Pope Benedict XVI on October 17, 2010 in the Vatican, as St Mary of the Cross.

At Penola, in South Australia, with Bishop Sheil's approval, she had founded the teaching order of St Joseph of the Sacred Heart, recruiting ordinary young women who could endure poverty, the privations in outback Australia and teach the poorest children without complaint. On September 22, 1871 Bishop Sheil excommunicated her (for alleged insubordination) until 21/7/1872, nine days before he died: but that is now interpreted as a sign of her sanctity.

In 1873 Mary (by now Mother Mary MacKillop (sic.) visited Rome and obtained papal approval for her Sisterhood. She visited schools throughout Europe before returning

to Australia in 1875. She was asked to leave the diocese by Bishop Reynolds and moved the headquarters to North

Sydney. *"In journeys throughout Australia she established schools, convents and charitable institutions"*.[28]

Mary devoted herself to the poor, immigrants, 'battered women' and to exposing pedophile priests (ABC television 'Regional News', April 10, 2021). Mother Mary of the Cross (MacKillop) was noted for affection, charity, determination and holiness and a Pilgrimage Route called the 'Aussie Camino', from Portland in Victoria to Penola in South Australia, has been established.

Plate 16.3.
Mary MacKillop, 1869. Public domain.

16.13. St Thèrése of Lisieux (1873-1897)

Louis Martin, and his wife Azelie-Marie Guerin, had nine children. Thèrése, who was born FrancoiseMarie Therese, was their youngest. Their five children who survived were:

Marie, Pauline, Cêline and Thèrése who all became Carmelite nuns and Léonie, who joined the Order of the Visitation. When Thèrése was only four years old her mother died of breast cancer and she became a serious child who was emotionally fragile, having to be withdrawn from school and taught at home by Cêline. Through a severe illness and ongoing frailty of body Thèrése endured severe physical sufferings. Later, before her father's death, Thèrése grieved the loss of his physical and mental health as he was committed to an asylum.

Thèrése was a particularly devout child. On Christmas Eve, just before her fourteenth birthday she had a vision, which she always called 'my conversion'. This vision, of the new-born Christ Child, filled the darkness of her soul with light and healed her of undue sensitivity.

After many requests (even to Pope Leo XIII while on pilgrimage to Rome) Thèrése was granted a special exemption to enter the Carmelite convent of Lisieux, at the age of fifteen. Three of her sisters and a cousin had entered, or would later enter, while (as noted) a fourth sister joined the Order of the Visitation. Thèrése loved the daily round of the religious life, especially the liturgies and the readings from Scripture. She took her vows at the age of seventeen. One priest noted that it was easy to direct Thèrése because the Holy Spirit was leading her.

Thèrése developed her own spirituality which she called "the little way of spiritual childhood" believing that to be admitted to the heavenly banquet one must be trusting, like a child, with absolute self-surrender, into the arms of the good God. Her 'way' taught perfection in small things, every-day.

Plate 16.4.
St Theresa of Lisieux.
Public domain.

She said "*to do good without God's help is as impossible as to make the sun shine at night.*" Thèrése was noted for her prayer life:
"*with me prayer is a lifting up of the heart, a look towards Heaven, a cry of gratitude and love uttered equally in sorrow and in joy: a word, something*

noble, supernatural, which enlarges my soul and unites it to God ... I just tell the Lord all that I want and he understands me."

Her way of coping with attacks of 'the enemy' was:

"I turn my back on the foe, hasten to my Saviour, and vow that I am ready to shed my blood in witness of my belief in Heaven."

Thèrése is often called *'the little flower'* in English. She had indeed been delivered from extreme sensitivity because she radiated joy to her fellow nuns with her outgoing nature and love for others. As she was dying Thèrése was able to say, "I have reached the point of not being able to suffer because all suffering is sweet to me."

Thèrése's autobiography, L'Histoire d'une ane (Story of a Soul), and her The Little Way For Every Day: Thoughts From Thèrése of Lisieux are available in English. Her writings and

her many letters were widely circulated among Carmelite monasteries.

Miracles of healing and prophecy followed. Because of her particular interest in China and friendship with Carmelite nuns and priests ministering in China Thèrése is the patron saint of foreign missions and of Russia. Thèrése is a Doctor of the Church (one of only three women doctors) not because of any great intellect or learning but because she introduced a new element into doctrine.

Thèrése was canonised as Saint Theresa of the Child Jesus and the Holy Face by Pope Pius XI, in 1925, only 28 years after she had died of TB at the age of 26. She is a co-patron of France with Joan of Arc ('Teresa of Lisieux', in Lives of the Saints [John Crawley & Co]). Thèrése's parents, Louis Matin, a watchmaker, and Azelie-Marie Martin, a lace-maker, were remarkable. In 2015 they became the only Catholic couple who were not martyrs to be canonised together. The family motto was, "God must be served first". A case for the canonisation of their third daughter, Léonie, is being considered.

Plate 16.5.
Louis and Azelie-Marie Martin.
Public domain

16.14. The 'Keswick' Movement (1875)

In 1875, the interdenominational Keswick movement, and its week-long Convention, commenced in the village of Keswick, England, to promote practical holiness ('Keswick Convention', in ODCC). It reached a height after WWI (c.1919), spread to the U.S.A., Australia and elsewhere, and continues. The movement was greatly influenced by Wesley's teaching on personal holiness and it is often called

'the Keswick holiness movement'. Its hallmarks were deeply Protestant: the Word of God as inspired and infallible; the personality and power of the Holy Spirit; Jesus Christ's atoning death; the priesthood of all believers; simple and spiritual worship; separation and self-denial for Kingdom purposes and the Lord's return (Maclean, 2012, online).

A great many of the great missionaries and preachers of the last two centuries have been influenced by Keswick, for example Dr Church of Africa: Rev. Norman Grubb, evengelist; Dr Arthur T. Pierson, pastor, and his seven missionary children; Amy Carmichael of India, Hannah Hurnard in Israel and Rev. Geoffrey Bingham of Australia and Pakistan: all noted below.

16.15. Hannah Hurnard (1905-1990)

Hannah Hurnard, a Quaker, had French Huguenot forebears. As a child she was habitually depressed with nightmares and anxieties, which increased with the arrival of World War I. Hannah stammered badly but, later, in her writing, she followed her literary parents and her grandfather, who was a poet. As pacifist Quakers the Hurnards were spurned but they turned their large garden into a soldiers' meeting place with high tea and a tent for evangelistic rallies (Wood, 1996, 30).

As a teenager Hannah had been an angry, surly rebel but a spiritual experience at a Keswick Convention in 1924 was

followed by two years at Bible College and evangelising experience in downtrodden English villages. Being a quiet Quaker Hannah avoided charismatic excitement but she had a love relationship with the Lord Jesus Christ (Wood, 1996, 30).

Hannah volunteered to work in the Anglican Hospital (now the Anglican School) on the Street of the Prophets, Jerusalem (Plate 16.4) and worked there as a house-keeper through Israel's 1948 War of Independence. Hannah was deeply invested, emotionally, in the land where Jesus had lived and was the first Christian worker after the birth of the State of Israel to visit New Zealand where her brother lived; and she became a popular speaker while there (Wood, 1996, 138). Later she and her numerous co-workers travelled throughout the land ministering to Arab and Jewish villagers; but she was never a paid missionary. She travelled widely and ministered in New Zealand, the U.K. and the U.S.A.

Plate 16.4.
Anglican Hospital, Jerusalem, now a school.

Photograph by D. Campbell. 1989.

Hannah wrote devotional books, accounts of her travels throughout Israel, two autobiographies and a book on prayer. She, herself, was the Miss Much-Afraid of "Hinds' Feet on High Places". The book was her own early spiritual journey.

Hannah also wrote: Mountain of Spices, Watchmen on the Walls, Wayfarer in the Land, The Hearing Heart, The Kingdom of Love and God's Transmitters.

Hannah became a complete vegan and then a fruititarian, which reduced her weight and her heath alarmingly (Wood, 1996, 170f). She was a self-confessed mystic who allegorised the Bible in her own fashion. Her spirituality underwent change over her long life and therefore the thrust of her worldwide teaching changed. Later in life, she interpreted her lack of success amongst Jews and Arabs as failure and she was influenced by the theological disquiet that many gentiles experience when evangelising the 'people of the Covenant'. Her final book had to be privately published because it explained her views, which were unorthodox, much as Origen's universalism had been (and he had believed in the eventual salvation of even the devil) (Wood, 1996, 206).

<u>16.16. Saint Teresa of Calcutta (1910-1997)</u>

Mother Teresa, who was born in Albania, became a Loretto nun. She worked as a teacher in a girls' school in India until she received a call from

God; which was as natural as it was supernatural. After two years, and helped by three of her former students, she was authorised by the Pope to commence the Missionaries of Charity, a new work in the teeming streets and slums of Calcutta, now Korlkarta (Tucker, 2016, 243-245). There she cared for the poorest of the poor, enabling them to die with dignity, between sheets rather than in the gutters.

Mother Teresa's work expanded to every settled continent and she was awarded the Nobel Peace Prize in 1979 and was justly regarded as a saint long before she died in Calcutta in 1997. She was canonised in 2016 as St Teresa of Calcutta by Pope Francis.

16.17. Saint John Paul the Great (1920-2005)

The Polish Pope, John Paul II, had the longest papacy in the 20th century. He arriving at a crucial time in world history, as,

having been trained in an underground seminary, he worked behind the scenes to rescue Catholic Poland from the grip of Communism. He adhered to traditional Catholicism in very conservative ways slowing down the great changes of the Second Vatican Council (discussed in Chapter 20), for example he reemphasised devotion to Christ's Incarnation and to Mary as the Mother of God (Mursell [ed.], 2003, 335f; 365). He refused to rethink divorce, celibacy and women priests. He opposed liberal theology, for example, Hans Küng, who had been arguing against papal infallibility, lost his licence to teach and Rome insisted that his university dismiss him, which they did (before they re-employed him).

Wisely, John Paul II cautioned against the fashion of adopting spiritual practices, ideas and techniques (ascetical practices and meditation) from other religions and he stressed personhood: that one, irreplacable individual in relationship with God (Tomkins, 2003, 238).

Pope John Paul II visited Jerusalem in March 2000 to confess and ask forgiveness verbally and in "We Remember", a formal document. He was canonised on 26/4/2014 by Pope Francis as Saint John Paul the Great.

16.18. Conclusions

In every generation each unique individual has had to travel a pathway to Christian maturity and their own intimate relationship with Christ Jesus. In many cases this has been a tortuous road. There is a golden thread running between the above cases in that all of them benefited from their reading of the Bible and the books of previous Christians, even those from other denominations. Many of them wrote hymns that

people still sing, or preached sermons that people still read, or wrote books that are in print generations later. Some of their remarkable lives have been featured in films and documentaries. Many of them knew each other or were somehow connected as is demonstrated by a careful study of

the links between the 18th-19th century abolitionists and reformers as well as in the spread of the gospel from Britain to Australia to New Zealand to Solomon Islands and Vanuatu, as Chapter 18 will show. Despite their flaws and mistakes, all who feature here contributed to the overall welfare of God's world.

Questions:

(1) Why was St Thèrése of Lisieux canonised so promptly?
(2) What long-term effects has Pope John Paul II had on Christianity?

Chapter 17
Social Progress

<u>.29. The Needs</u>

In the 18th century, much of the need for social reform in Britain stemmed from its success. It was foremost in colonisation, industrialisation and modernisation. Thus the worst excesses of this success were manifestly obvious by the 19th Century: a harvest of poverty, slum-dwellings, exploitation of child-labourers, the working classes and poor women, while the rich landowners and industrialists became rich with 'new money'.

Christian denominations in the post-Reformation world were constantly multiplying and many of them devoted time and energy to reforming the social conditions of their particular era. Often the smaller denominations were engaged in welfare work out of all proportion to their size. The fabulous wealth of the 4th-century elite Roman Christians was no longer available so middle-class Christians combined to form societies to achieve financial strength-in-numbers. Societies that were dedicated to missions are noted in Chapter 18 but there were many others devoted to worthy causes and charitable work from Christian motives. Reformers were usually interested in more than one issue of social justice, for example William Wilberforce was committed to many causes, not just the abolition of slavery and the women who worked for equality in education also worked for equality of voting rights (as suffragettes). Universal literacy would go hand-in-hand with suffrage as literacy was considered a prerequisite for careful assessment of political issues. In any case, in England political power could not be extended to the poor, who needed to keep to their place in the social structure.

The whole world benefited from the work of thousands of dedicated Christians for whom love of neighbour was a Divine calling.

<u>.30. The Capham Sect (c.1792-1834)</u>

The Clapham Sect was a group of Christians who had wealth, status and/or a social conscience that grew out of their faith. They were Evangelicals of varied types: William Wilberforce was a Wesleyan and his closest friend and fellow parliamentarian, Henry Thornton (1760-1815) was a Calvinist. These two were the first to live in the London suburb of Clapham. Wilberforce, his wife Barbara, the Thorntons, and Charles Grant (1746-1823) lived on the Thornton's estate at 'Battersea Rise House' from 1790.

Of the names below some were just frequent visitors, others were fellow-abolitionists. The Clapham group formed around the Clapham Anglican church and various Evangelical Anglican clerics including Rev. Henry Venn (1725-1878), his son, John Venn (1759-1813) who was rector of Clapham from 17921813, and William Dealty (1775-1847). John Newton was an Anglican cleric, as were Thomas Gisborne (1758-1846), Charles Grant (1746-1832) and Charles Simeon of Cambridge (1759-1836).

Other members of the Clapham Sect were Granville Sharp (1735-1813), John Smith (1764-1846) and two important women, Hanna(h) More (1743-1833) a teacher, writer, poet, abolitionist, suffragette and social reformer and Katherine Horky (1834) an evangelist.

Wilberforce and four others were members of parliament: Edward Eliot (1758-1797); James Stephen (1758-1832) and William Smith (1756-1836) who was a Unitarian and Thomas Buxton (1786-1845). Buxton was P. M. William Pitt The Younger's brother-in-law and was also connected to the Pankhursts by marriage. Pitt the Younger was a frequent visitor but not a member (Gathro, for Knowing and Doing, 2001, online).

The group produced a magazine, The Christian Observer, which was edited by a former save-owner Zachary Macaulay (1725-1797), who had been the governor of Sierra Leone, a colony which the group had founded. In 1802 John Shore (Lord Teignmouth [1751-1834]) the retired governor-general of India joined the Clapham Sect.

As the list of illustrious people shows, the group had money, political 'clout' and widespread denominational connections in Protestantism. They were inter-connected by friendship and marriage, which enabled them to be more effective than their numbers would suggest. All were dedicated to public service and philanthropy. They founded and/or supported many societies devoted to specific issues, and charities to help prisoners, factory workers, refugees and foreigners in distress. Their concern and commitment was to the social welfare of Britain and the abolition of first the slave trade and secondly, slavery itself.

Trading in slaves throughout the British Empire was outlawed by the Slave Trade Act of 1807, but the victims remained in slavery. Many of the original Clapham Sect (Wilberforce, Hanna(h) More, Thomas Buxton, Lord Teignmouth, William Smith, Thomas Gisborne and William Dealtry) lived to see the total emancipation of slaves by the Abolition Act of 1833.

17.3. William Wilberforce (1759-1833)

Wilberforce resided with Henry Thornton until he married Barbara Spooner, after which he lived close by. Wilberforce overcame ill health to become a tireless organiser and researcher who put consistent pressure on the British political system for the benefit of slaves and others in need. He donated to at least seventy charities and missionary societies. William Wilberforce had two passions: the abolition of slavery

and moral and social reform in Britain. His biography cum manifesto was constantly republished in America and Britain

and translated into five foreign languages (Gathro, 2001, online). William Wilberforce was supported by a close community and many influential people (including the Prime Minister Pitt the Younger, Charles James Fox, a great orator, and not a few women) who each worked for the cause but it is Wilberforce who is remembered as the dedicated Christian individual who made a worldwide impact for good. Anglicans, Quakers and Methodists were in the forefront and the 19th-century evangelical revival movement in the Church of England had far reaching consequence up until today.

17.4. John Newton (1725-1807)

This English ex-captain of slave-ships wrote the immortal words of "Amazing Grace", which are his lasting legacy, expressing his personal spirituality. Christ's grace (his unmerited favour) had elevated Newman from a low ebb of wretchedness, spiritual blindness, lust and near starvation so that he became a defout Christian and then an Anglican clergyman.

After he was press-ganged into the Royal Navy, Newton happened upon a copy of Thomas à Kempis's Imitation of Christ, and, during a terrible storm, he turned to the Lord as at his late mother's knee. At the end, which he was expecting immediately, he would be led safely Home.

Newton abandoned the seafaring life and for seven years, with the help of his mentor, George Whitefield, Newton taught himself biblical languages and divinity. He was eventually ordained, ministering in the poor village of Olney and then in a smart London parish. His popular sermons and hymns were published and Newton, who had learned much in the school of hard seamanship, was noted for wise counsel. For example he counselled William Wilberforce, who was

facing a crisis of direction, that he could serve God in politics and make a difference (Wilberforce, 1797/2006, 11). Under Wilberforce's influence, Newton slowly came to realise that

the enslavement of God's children, of any colour, was wrong: they were not just a commercial commodity like any other, as he had previously thought. To further the cause of social justice he helped Wilberforce, P. M. William Pitt and the Privy Council by detailing the abuses of slave trading (Armstrong, Christianity Today, online).

John Newton is remembered, with William Wilberforce, as a champion amongst many leading abolitionists but there were many hundreds hammering away against this inhumanity.

17.5. Granville Sharp (1735-1813)

Granville Sharp, another leading Clapham Sect member, was a civil servant, a layman of no particular station or wealth. He demonstrated a warm heart and a persistent character in that, after he had seen a Negro slave being cruelly treated in the streets of London, he was fired up and did not rest in his campaigning until he had obtained the parliamentary verdict that rid Britain of the evils of slavery (Fisher, II, 1964, 1123).

17.6. Henry Venn (Jnr.) (1796-1873)

As noted above, the Clapham group formed around the Clapham Anglican church and especially its clergy including Rev. Henry Venn (1725-1878) and his son, Rev. John Venn (1759-1813) who was rector of Clapham from 1792-1813. John Venn was one of the founders of CMS and presided at its foundational meeting, so naturally the missionary society had an Evangelical Anglican orientation. John Venn's son, Henry, spent his youth in the Clapham rectory amongst the greats of the abolitionist movement, including Wilberforce, whose work in parliament led to the opening of India to missionary work in 1813, when Henry Venn Jnr. was an interested young freshman at Cambridge. He also became a clergyman and, from 1841 to 1872, he was Honorary Clerical Secretary for CMS, which meant that he ran its day-to-day activities (Shenk, online).

By the mid 19th century no philosophy of mission or 'missiology' had been formulated a task to which Henry Venn applied himself. For example he was "implacably opposed" to the methods employed among the Melanesians by Bishop

Selwyn (whom you will meet in 19.3B below) (Davidson, online, 15). Selwyn wrote that CMS was "a mere society organized to supply the deficit of life and action in the church itself" (Davidson, online, 32). Bishop Selwyn believed that the missionary bishop and his priests and brothers were the mission, whereas Venn feared 'episcopal autocracy'.

Henry Venn Jnr. believed that the emphasis should be upon the deepening and strengthening of the life of a community as the starting point for witness to the world and he held a strong conviction that the Holy Spirit would guide the fledgling churches (Shenk, online, 37).

Venn developed the principles [that were later adopted as the 3-Self-Movement in Communist China - see 20.2(d) below]. These principles or aims were self-government, self-support and selfpropagation. Under Venn's leadership CMS became a powerhouse for world evangelism, notably throughout the British Empire.

17.7. Slavery in Britain and America

British slavers were the most successful taking about two million kidnapped Africans into the British colonies between 1680 and 1786. Great ports grew rich from slavery, the Royal Navy depended upon it for manpower and British business flourished because of it. The vested interests seemed unassailable, yet Britain was first to abolish all enslavement throughout its vast Empire, which was so extensive that the sun never set on it (Fisher II, 1964, 1122).

Change was achieved because of democracy, parliamentary rule, Christian humanitarianism and the loss of the American colonies, which were strongly pro-slavery. Abolition came in three stages. First, enslavement within the British Isles was abolished in 1772 (Fisher II, 1964, 1122). Then the slave trade itself was abolished in 1806 but there were still slaves in the British Dominions, such the West Indies, until 1833 (Fisher II, 1964, 1122). Slavery never penetrated Australia, nor its offshoot, New Zealand, thanks to the first Governor of New South Wales, Arthur Phillip. In Australia, convicts did provide years of free labour but their sentences were often reduced and they could even eventually be granted land.

The Arab slave trade, centred on Zanzibar, was particularly terrible but Britain managed to have its great slave-market closed in 1873 and the high seas were patrolled by the Royal Navy, which seized human cargo (Fisher II, 1964, 1125f). The Seychelles Islands, previously a French and then a British colony, were populated with such freed slaves.

As noted Britain, the biggest offender, was first to abolish all enslavement throughout its Empire, but, despite the example set by Britain, conditions for slaves were bad in Portugal and America, although Spain treated its slaves relatively better (National Museums Liverpool, online). As noted, British warships confiscated the cargo of slave-ships, which made the trade uneconomic, but to abolish slavery in America took a civil war over five summers of fighting.

Slave-trading was banned in America from January 1, 1808 but slaving-vessels continued to ply their trade illegally for fifty years (National Museum Liverpool, online). Slavery was a boom industry in France, Spain and Cuba but in 1831 France, and in 1835 Spain, imposed effective penalties against slave traders. The trade flourished in Cuba until 1862 with the last human cargo docking in Cuba in 1867 (Fisher II, 1964, 1125; National Museum Liverpool, online).

Because the American War of Independence had intervened British reforms did not apply in America. In 1857 the Supreme

Court of the United States ruled that "slaves were subhuman property with no rights to citizenship" (American Battlefield Trust, online) and it was not until after the American Civil War had been won by the Unionists of the North that slavery could be abolished throughout the United States, by the 13th Amendment to the Constitution (December 5, 1863). America's founding fathers and early presidents were not abolitionists, for example Thomas Jefferson owned 600 slaves and George Washington owned at least 300. At least twelve presidents had at times owned slaves and eight did so while in office. Many slave-holders fathered children by their slaves, including Thomas Jefferson (HISTORY, 'How Many U.S. Presidents Owned Slaves,' online). Abraham Lincoln (president from 1850) always maintained that the Civil War was not to free slaves but to preserve the Union because South Carolina and then six other states had withdrawn from the Union (in March, 1861) (American Battlefield Trust, online) and, after hostilities began on April 12, four more states seceded. Lincoln refused to enlist black volunteer soldiers, "proving to northern whites that their race privileges would not be threatened" (People & Events, 'Civil War and Emancipation', online).

17.8. Women Abolitionists

Some women were in the forefront of the anti-slavery cause, including Sojourner Truth, Harriet Beecher Stowe, Harriet Ross Tubman and Mary Ann Shadd Cary. Harriet Tubman and Mary Cary both recruited black soldiers for the Unionist cause, after the first Emancipation Proclamation of 1863, which freed slaves in Confederate states but left a million slaves in Unionist territory in bondage. It did, however, open the military to black recruits (American Battlefield Trust, online).

17.9. Sojourner Truth (c.1797-1883)

Isabella Baumfree (Sojourner Truth) was the youngest of ten or more children. Her Parents, James and Elizabeth, were both slaves of the Baumfree family in upstate New York so their children were born into slavery. Isabella was raised to value family and God. The older children were sold on; only Isabella and Peter remaining with their parents (Allred,

'Sojourner Truth', online). Isabella, herself, was sold five times before marring Thomas, a fellow-slave of the Dumont family. She had five children with Thomas but ran away with her youngest child, Sophie. Upon finding that the Dumonts had sold her son, Peter, to Alabama, even though he had already been freed when New York emancipated all slaves in 1827, she bravely sued in court and won his return (Lewis, 'Sojourner Truth', online). Isabella changed her name to show her belief in the truth.

Sojourner's most famous speech, "*Aint I a Woman*", was delivered at the Women's Rights Convention in Akron, Ohio, in 1851 (Tucker, 2016, 136). She was six feet tall and a powerful public speaker. Even though Dutch was her native language, she could speak with a southern accent for effect. In mature years she worked for women's rights and suffrage and met President Lincoln and General Ulysses Grant (Allred, 'Sojourner Truth', online).

<u>17.10. Harriet Beecher Stowe (1811-1896)</u>

The American novelist and writer of religious poetry, Harriet Beecher Stowe, a friend to Sojourner Truth, wrote about her in the Atlantic Monthly and wrote an introduction for Sojourner's autobiography (Lewis, 'Sojourner Truth, online). When Sojourner disapproved of what Harriet had written about her in the newspaper she sent Harriet a copy of her Narrative (biography) and a photograph of herself so that only the truth would appear in print (Berry, Black History Month', online).

Harriet Beecher was the daughter of a Congregationalist minister who became president of Lane Theological Seminary. Her husband, Rev. Calvin Ellis Stowe, was a seminary

professor and eminent biblical scholar. Harriet is famous for the novel, Uncle Tom's Cabin, which was published as a serial from 1851-52 and then as a book (1852) to dispel the myth (which was promoted in the South) that slaves were happy with their lives. In 1853 she published A Key to Uncle Tom's Cabin, a collection of testimonies and documents supporting the case against slavery and in support of her novel, which was embraced in the North and in Britain but reviled in the South.

<u>17.11. Political Rights for Dissenters, Catholics and Jews in Britain</u>

Democracy was impossible whilever the female proportion of the population had no hope of being enfrancised, along with 'dissenters' who were opposed to laws that required attendance at Church of England services. It has previously been noted in connection with John Bunyan that Dissenting Christians (Nonconformists) were jailed after the English Reformation because of Elizabeth I's Act of Uniformity of 1559. These disabilities became the concern of social reformers.

Catholics could not vote, inherit property, own land, hold civil or military office or freely practise their religion. After the Restoration of the Monarchy conditions were even worse for Puritans and Catholics, that is, until Protestant monarchs ruled Britain again.

In Ireland a Catholic could not vote and could have his land taken by his nearest Protestant relative. When the Protestant monarchs William of Orange and Mary Stuart arrived in Britain, however, the Act of Toleration of 1689

was passed, which granted freedom of worship to Nonconformists. By the First Relief Act of 1778 British Catholics could own land and, in 1791, could freely practise their religion. In Ireland the Relief Act of 1793 gave Catholics the franchise and admitted them to civil office although an anti-Catholic oath was still required of Irish parliamentarians ('Catholic Emancipation', in Britannica, online).

The Act of Union of 1801, which united Britain with Ireland, was significant because British law prevailed. Irishman Daniel O'Connell was able to force the House of Commons, Prime Minister Wellesley (the Duke of Wellington) and the Home Secretary (Robert Peel) to pass the Emancipation Act of 1829 which admitted Catholics to Parliament in London and to most public offices. By the Religious Disabilities Act of 1846 Roman Catholic schools and churches could be built and the last restrictions upon Dissenters and Catholics were removed, except for university admission. This only came with the Universities Tests Act of 1871 ('Catholic Emancipation', in Britannica, online).

The Religious Disabilities Act of 1846 also gave Jews rights to education, property and the administration of charities. In 1858 David Solomons, the first Jewish Lord Mayor of London, campaigned for the Jewish Relief Act which gave full civil and political rights to Jews. Thus Baron Lionel de Rothschild was able to take his seat in the House of Lords in 1858. Benjamin Disraeli, a Jew, became Prime Minister in 1868.

Universal suffrage for women was an entirely different challenge, as will be shown.

17.12. John Howard (1726-1790)

Although a convinced Calvinist and a dissenter by persuasion John Howard accompanied his second wife to

the local Church of England every Sunday. In 1783, he became High Sheriff of Bedford, which was possible because he outwardly conformed to Anglicanism. Through his work Howard became aware of the afflictions of prisoners. First he obtained salaries for jailers so that they no longer had to extort fees from prisoners. After visiting many jails and hospitals, in 1777 John Howard wrote The State of the Prisons which led to the Reform Act of 1777. He visited prisons throughout Europe and wrote Account of the Principal Lazarettos of Europe, in 1789 (Howard, John, in ODCC).

17.13. Elizabeth Fry (1780-1845)

Elizabeth (Betsy) Gurney, the daughter of John Gurney (1749-1809) and Catherine Barclay Bell of the Barclay banking family, grew up in Eartham Hall with her six sisters and six brothers: her siblibngs were: Joseph, John, Priscilla, Samuel, Catherine, Richenda (wife of Rev. Francis Cunningham), Louisa, Hannah (Mrs Buxton), Rachel and Daniel. Betsy was a devout Quaker and one of the most remarkable of British women. Altruism developed in her from the age of twelve as she helped her older sisters care for her younger siblings after their mother's death.

In 1798, Betsy was inspired by the work and preaching of an American Quaker (William Savery) and then by Priscilla Hannah Gurney and the preaching of Deborah Darby, in 1799.[29] Betsy began by visiting the sick and setting up a Sunday school in the laundry of their home.

In 1800 Betsy became Mrs Fry when she married Joseph Fry, a 'plain' Quaker and wealthy merchant of the chocolate-making Frys, who later become a banker. Elizabeth had eleven children (and eventually twenty-five grandchildren). One daughter, also called Betsy, died in 1815 at age five, but the others all reached aduthood. Her health suffered after every childbirth, notably her ninth (in 1814) and her eleventh (at the age of forty-two).

Mrs Fry was acknowledged as a Quaker minister in 1811 and, in 1813, she and Anna Buxton, her sister Hannah's sister-in-law, visited Newgate

Prison where conditions for women and their children were appalling.[30] In 1817 she set up the Association for the Reformation of the Female Prisoners in Newgate. Their combined achievements included clothing for prisoners, schooling for their children, separation of the genders, separation of prisoners according to their crime, female supervisors for women prisoners, provision of religious instruction and secular education and useful employment ('Elizabeth Fry', for Britannica, 2019 online).

Elizabeth and Joseph Fry had three periods of financial difficulty: in 1813, 1816 and 1828 when Joseph Fry was declared bankrupt. He lost his business, his reputation, his membership of the Society of Friends and all of his Quaker friends and customers. The family was left destitute and under suspicion of spending bank deposits on their charity work (and they may well have had poor accounting practices). Elizabeth resolutely continued her work with compassion for the poor and needy (Intriguing History, 'Elizabeth Fry', online).

Mrs Fry, in 1818, was the first female to present evidence to a Parliamentary Committee. The Home Secretary, Robert Peel, persuaded the House of Commons to pass the Gaols Act of 1823 which banned male guards, irons and manacles for women and included chaplaincy visits. The number of hanging offences was reduced from 200 to 100 (Spartacus Education, 'Elizabeth Fry', online). As a consequence, this increased the pressure to transport convicts to penal colonies. Eventually, in 1835, inspectors were employed to ensure that jailers obeyed the regulations and by 1840 the number of hanging offences had been reduced to only five.

Mrs Fry worked tirelessly for improvements in female convict-transportation including approval for all of a mother's children under seven to stay with her and that nursing mothers were not be transported until their child was weaned. For twenty-five years she visited convict ships bound for Port Jackson (mistakenly called Botany Bay) to encourage the women and bring them parting gifts made by her supporters.

This work began in 1818 when she visited Newgate Women's Prison on the eve of the departure of some women to sail on the Maria. Normally the women would have rioted, trashed and burnt everything but Elizabeth and her companion spent time calming them and promising to go with them to the ship. While women from other prisons might arrive in hand-cuffs, irons and/or chained together no

Newgate women would travel in irons and Mrs Fry also arranged for the privacy and protection of closed coaches rather than the usual open waggons (as though they were going to the gallows).

While the Maria lay in the Thames River for six weeks the Ladies Committee visited often and set up a school for the fourteen children and organised the women into classes of twelve, with monitors. Industrious habits were encouraged by the gift of a large bag for each woman's clothes, as well as a Bible, two aprons, a cap and a bag of sewing materials. Pins, needles, cottons, scissors, spectales, two pounds of patchwork pieces and more items were included (for making patchwork quilts which could be sold for the high price of a guinea) ('Elizabeth Fry History's Heroes? 1780-1845', online).

In 1842 Mrs Fry managed to have matrons sent on the convict transport Garland Grove. Mrs Fry's charitable work included soup kitchens, homeless shelters, better housing for the poor and reform of mental asylums. With her husband, her brother (Joseph John Gurney) or her daughters

Rachel and/or Katherine, she travelled in Europe, Ireland and throughout Britain advising on prison reform and writing reports. She wore herself out with travel and work and was greatly distressed whenever her pleas to save women from the gallows were unsuccessful.

Mrs Fry attended the inaugural meeting of the British and Foreign Bible Society and held Bible readings in Newgate Prison (Spartacus Education, 'Elizabeth Fry', online). Between 1824 and 1836 she set up libraries in every isolated station for the coast guards. In 1834 Elizabeth began to oppose the silent system of sensory deprivation imported, like solitary

confinement, from America - because of the toll these practices took on prisoners' mental health. She was also committed to the abolition of slavery. In 1840 she attended the World Anti-slavery Convention in Exeter Hall and she hosted

antislavery meetings in her own home. Mrs Fry met royalty: Queen Charlotte, Queen Victoria and King Frederick William IV of Prussia, who visited Newgate prison and her home. She also founded a nursing school at Guy's Hospital, which inspired her distant relative, Florence Nightingale, who took a team of Mrs Fry's nurses to the Crimeam War ('Elizabeth Fry', in Britannica, online).

In 1843 Betsy's neice, Harriet, died and in 1844 there were more deaths: a grandaughter; her sisterin-law, Elizabeth Fry; her grandson, Gurney; her son William and his daughters, Emma and Juliana; a neice and her infant son. Betsy Fry's relatives were her loved ones and her strongest supporters. In her grief her own health was declining. In February, 1845, her brother-in-law, supporter and Member of Parliament, the anti-slavery campaigner, Thomas Fowell Buxton, died.[31] Betsy, herself, died sixmonths later, in September.[32]

Elizabeth Fry was a dedicated Christian altruist who devoted her life to what would now be called 'social work'. She saw only one gospel, not two. Loving God and one's neighbour was the true gospel. In 1846 her daughters Rachel and Elizabeth edited her Memoir in two volumes: Rachel Elizabeth Cresswell and Katherine Fry (eds), Memoir of the Life of Elizabeth Gurney Fry (1848).

<u>17.14. Charles Dickens (1812-1870)</u>

Charles John Huffam Dickens, the mature writer, was the product of England's 'dark satanic mills'. His father, John Dickens, a naval clerk, had been in debtors' prison, a low point on the social ladder, so that, at age twelve, Charles, the oldest son of ten children, had to work in a boot-polish factory. Although an inheritance enabled all debts to be paid Charles had to leave school at fifteen to work as an office boy. He became a freelance journalist and then a court stenographer, gaining valuable background material for his novels Bleak House and Dealings with the Firm of Dombey and Son. From his life's experiences Dickens gained his

perceptions of human character, exploitation of workers, degrading living conditions and distinct social classes. These insights colour his work and make his characters

memorable. Mr Micawber of David Copperfield was based upon his father (Charles Dickens Info, 'Charles Dickens Biography', online).

Plate 17.1.

Slum conditions, Whitechaple, London, 1872. Public domain.

Dickens was notably perceptive, insightful and observant. He saw hypocrisy all around him as people tried to adopt the veneer of piety without commitment. He was a devout Christian who believed in doing good and living by

the Golden Rule: "do to others what you want them to do to you." He wrote a special book for his own children, to teach them his religious and moral principles, which was only published after they had all died (in 1934).

Dickens is remembered as a social reformer but he was motivated by the Biblical view of social justice.

He was so convinced of the need for reform that, even when he was ill, he travelled, even across to America, to present his works on stage and speak against exploitation, poverty, cruelty, ignorance and especially slavery. The characters that he popularised, especially the children, drove his message home: Oliver Twist, David Copperfield, Nicholas Nickelby and Little Dorrit.

Dickens was popular in America where the lack of international copyright law enabled others to profit from his work. When he visited America he was not impressed with his treatment by the press. He was horrified by slavery, the spitting of tobacco, the vulgarity and the sharp practices. Dickens set two of his novels in the United States: American Notes (1842) and Martin Chuzzlewit (1843-44). In the former he criticised American life as being culturally backward and materialistic ('Charles Dickens: British Novelist', in Britannica, online).

<u>17.15. The Church During Queen Victoria's Reign</u>

Queen Victoria's fifty-four year reign has been exceeded only by that of Queen Elizabeth II and both reigns have been periods of great change, including in the churches of Britain and the world. A young Victoria became queen shortly after the Great Reform crisis had been successfully negotiated by William IV, her uncle, and when 40% of the world's land mass was under her control. In 1840 Victoria married Prince Albert

of Saxe-Coburg-Gotha. They had nine children many of whom would marry into one of the non-Catholic royal or aristocratic families of Europe; but Albert died in 1861, leaving her a widow for forty years.

.Naturally the Queen's emphasis upon family-life influenced British society and morality. These days it is fashionable to concentrate upon Victoria's relationships with other men but while Albert lived she was devoted to him.

The Victorian Era was a time of rapid urbanisation in England and the expansion of great industrial towns such as Liverpool, Birmingham and Manchester. New-money was being made by self-made men in their own way, at the expense of the little people. Small government and Free-Trade principles prevailed. 'User pays' attitudes predominated: for example, even the great women's activist, Millicent Fawcett, approved of education but opposed free schooling, free school meals and the 1925 introduction of family allowance payments (Howarth, online). As Britain benefited from the glories of the Empire, living standards were slowly improving and with it crime and immorality declined but little wealth trickled down to the very poor.

Church attendance was the standard and the needs of the vast Empire bothered Christians and motivated them to support the burgeoning number of missionary societies: to carry the 'white man's burden'. The 18th century Evangelical Revival had been an age for the founding of charities, missions and missionary activity, a continuing trend into the 19th century, so there were many worthy causes for the growing middle class to support.

17.16. Model Villages and Estates

Some philanthropic employers and industrialists attempted to alleviate the living conditions of their workers

by providing housing in well-planned estates or villages. The first example was New Lanark in 1799,

established by a Christian, Robert Owen (1771-1858), on a picturesque site on the Clyde River in Scotland where cotton was milled. Owen's aims were progress and

prosperity for all: education, childcare,

recreation, personal betterment and social harmony. New Lanark is now a UNESCO world heritage site and now

weaves wool not cotton (New Lanark Trust, 'Robert Owen', online).

In England, the Quaker families who made chocolate were enlightened employers. The Frys, who invented the chocolate bar, paid their employees above expected levels. The Rowntrees founded the model village of New Earswick and made adult education a priority. The Cadbury family built 140 workers-cottages near their factory at Bournville (where infant mortality was half that of nearby Birmingham) and they introduced a 5-day working week ('Quakers in the world, Chocolate Makers', online).

Non-Quaker manufacturers, such as soap-manufacturer William Lever (1851-1925) also built model villages. At age sixteen William had avidly read a moral treatise on the promotion of selfimprovement and against materialism: Samuel Smiles, Self-Help (1859). Ever afterwards he effectively applied the wisdom of self-help and time-management to his life and business. William had been educated at Bolton Church Institute and was a Congregationalist ('Quakers in the world', online). Between 1899 and 1914, with 30 architects, he built Port Sunlight, a social experiment for 3,000-4,000 people. It included 900 semi-detached houses with gardens, a technical institute, hospital, church, museum, library, gymnasium, heated pool, cafeterias and, because he was a freemason, a lodge room (Faulks, 'William Lever', online).

From 1917, Lever was a peer and, from 1922, a viscount (Viscount Leverhulme). As a Liberal MP, he introduced the Old Age Pension Bill and was a generous philanthropist supporting education, research and the arts.

17.17. William Booth (1829-1912) and the Salvation Army

Two years after William Booth's conversion experience in 1844 he became a revivalist preacher (at age 15). He married Catherine Mumford in London in 1855 and soon left the Methodist church to found the Christian Mission which majored on evangelistic, rescue and social work.

William was dedicated to help alcoholics. His sympathy for the poor developed while he was apprenticed to a pawnbroker at the age of thirteen ('Booth, William', in ODCC).

The Mission was heavily dependent on volunteers, many of whom were reformed prostitutes, and it became the Salvation Army in 1878 with William as its first General ('Salvation Army', in ODCC). In 1890 Booth wrote In Darkest England and the Way Out which suggested such remedies as farm colonies and rescue homes for social evils. When he begged on the streets and preached on street corners he was jeered at, but after he was invited to the coronation of King Edward VII, who supported his work, his status rose and his good work was welcomed. In 1912 he was succeed as General by his son, William Branwell Booth (1856-1929) ('Booth, William', in ODCC).

17.18. Catherine Booth (1829-1890)

Catherine Mumford married William Booth in 1855 but not before she had established that they were equal as Christians and people. From the beginning she was involved in the work of the Salvation Army. Catherine Booth was involved in the temperance movement and had a particular concern for prostitutes and their children so that homes for unwed mothers were one of the first social services the 'Salvos' set up. "Without her enormous influence, it is difficult to imagine where the organization would be today." (Tucker, 2016, 152).

Plates 17.3 and 17.4.
Catherine Booth, c.1890 and Evangeline Booth.
Public domain.

Mrs Booth preached in her husband's church to a mixed congragation, which was considered shocking, and she became a regular preacher in c.1860's. Her dynamic preaching was very effective and appealed to large crowds in London's wealthier West End. Her work supported the family, while William's concern was with the poor and slum dwellers. Even while bearing eleven children Catherine worked tirelessly to inprove people's lives and bring them the gospel. Catherine wrote a book in support of women preachers: Female Ministry: Or, Women's Right to Preach the Gospel.[33] This couple set the standard for married couples in the Salvation Army who, even now, are required to be equally trained and equal participants in ministry. All of their children were inolved in Christian ministry, notably William Branwell Booth, Ballington Booth and Eva/Evangeline Booth.

17.19. Evangeline Cory Booth (1865-1950)

In London, Eva Cory Booth was known as 'the White Angel of the Slums' as she grew up doing the work of the
Salvation Army. In 1888, at the age of 23, she was given charge

of the Army's International Training College and command of all Army forces in the Home Counties around London ('Evangeline Cory Booth', in Britannica).

Eva became Evangeline when she went from England to North America first in Canada and then (in 1904) in the United States. Evangeline was the most notable of the Booth children as, although a woman, she became General of the Salvation Army. By this time the Salvation Army had spread worldwide so that, because the movement required complete self-denial and 'unquestioning obedience' of all members, technically they were all subject to her.

Evangeline was the Salvo's fourth general and worked from her HQ in New York where her brilliant organizing skills shone. She put Army finances on a secure footing, so that the first national drive raised $16,000,000. She greatly expanded the services provided: residences for working women, homes for the aged, canteens for servicemen, hospitals, and schools. After the San Francisco earthquake and fire of 1906 the Salvation Army began disaster relief work. In 1923 Evangeline took American citizenship. Evangeline Booth was a gifted musician and a composer of hymns that were published as Songs of the Evangel in 1927. Like her parents she was a writer, publishing The War Romance of the Salvation Army (with Grace Livingstone Hill) in 1919, Towards a Better World (in 1928) and Woman (in 1930). In 1919 she was awarded the Distinguished Service Medal for her relief services for soldiers and others ('Evangeline Cory Booth', in Britannica).

17.20. (Dr) Thomas John Barnardo (1845-1905)

Thomas Barnardo was born in Dublin, Ireland, the fourth child of a Quaker mother and a German-born Sephardi-Jewish father who converted to Christianity as an adult.

At the age of twentyone Thomas went to London to study medicine and prepare for missionary service in China. He did not complete his degree but, appalled by conditions for waifs and strays in London, he stayed to apply himself to the problem (Banerjee, online).

Before his early death, at age 60, and using only donations, amid great political and economic difficulties he had established 90 homes for children based upon Christian principles, was caring for over 8,000 children, and had rescued, educated and trained 59,384 children (Banerjee, online).

<u>17.21. Universal Elementary Education In England</u>

During the Reformation in England, because the monasteries had been destroyed by Henry VIII, education was disrupted. Afterwards, all education was provided by either the Church of England or by small cottage 'dame schools' run by poor but genteel single women such as Hanna(h) More in her early adulthood.

In 1780, the Sunday School movement was commenced by Robert Raikes (1735-1811) so that on Sundays a paid teacher could educate the children of those too poor to pay school fees, at least sufficiently to read the Bible. The ideology was that all Christian people should be literate, if not numerate. Societies for Promoting Sunday Schools in the British Dominions began in London in 1785 and a similar one in Philadelphia, U.S.A., in 1791 (Walker, 1959, 470f).

It gradually became obvious that children left to roam the streets every day became petty criminals and, as adults, they were virtually unemployable, except in agricultural settings. Cities needed a dutiful, industrious, literate workforce. In towns and cities, fear of crime was a strong motivator for establishing schools, as was Christian charity and a desire that people could read the Bible for themselves, which lay at the heart of Protestantism and American individualism.

France lagged behind Britain until 1881-2 when it introduced universal, compulsory, secular, free education to age 13, that

is, 30 years before compulsory, free education was available in England. Even New South Wales introduced compulsory schooling before England. [34] In 1850 the male literacy rates in England (of 64%) was lower than in Prussia (93%).

Plate 17.5.
First King's School, Parramatta. Public domain.

In England, it was not until the Education Act of 1870 that the Crown acknowledge the responsibility of the state for universal elementary education (mainly literacy, simple aritmetic and domestic and useful skills) but it took twenty years for the Act to be fully implemented. In 1870 male literacy was at 60% but it rose to over 90% by the end of the century, thanks to the Act (Boos, 'The Education Act of 1870, online). The state continued support for indepeded schools.

Plate 17.6.
The first King's School, today.
Public domain

17.22. Education In Early Australia

Many children accompanied their convict-mothers when they were transported to 'Botany Bay' and keeping them usefully occupied was a priority of church and state for fear that they would become offenders, like their parent(s). Some of the street urchins of Sydney had been convicts themselves, as convicts could be as young as eight years old.

Some education was begun three years after the first settlement. The first school was established in 1798 by the colony's first chaplain, Rev. Richard Johnson, in his church beside Sydney Harbour. Classes were held in each corner of the narrow, cross-shaped wooden church, the nave of which measured 11m by 5m. Rev. Johnson had brought out a font, communion vessels and a communion table from England, but pews were rough benches, badly suited to children. Johnson assumed that education would be one of his many tasks as he also brought 150 copies of Dixon's Speller after which the Creed, the Ten Commandments and the Lord's Prayer would be mastered (Kotlowski, 2006, 29f). The 3Rs, morality and religion were taught. From here on the churches virtually monopolised Sydney's education system.

Until 1848 Sydney was served by independent schools for the affluent which were established by the churches: the (Anglican) King's School at Parramatta (1832), St Mary's at the Roman Catholic cathedral site (in 1824) and Sydney Grammar School in College Street (1857). A substantial buiding in College Street was constructed c.1850 and occupied by the University of Sydney while its campus was being built and the Sydney Grammar School moved in when it was vaccated.

The first church-run school for girls, in 1858, was St Vincent's Catholic College at Potts Point. All four church schools (King's, SMCC, Grammar and 'Vinnies') are still functioning.

The secular University of Sydney was founded in 1850 for "Sydney's male middle-class meritocracy"; but it did not

enrol women until 1881. From 1833, the Sydney Mechanics' School of Arts provided a library and lectures and classes for both genders (Sherington and Campbell, 'Education', Sydney Journal 2 (1) 6/2009, 4f, online).

The state system of day-schooling expanded in country towns where the churches had little money, the first being built at Newcastle East, in 1816. After the National Board of Education was begun in 1848 public schools were built in Sydney: Botany, c.1849; Fort Street in 1850; Cleveland Street in 1856 and Bourke Street in 1866. Some were called 'superior' public schools and provided secondary education free of charge (Sherington and Campbell, 'Education', Sydney Journal 2 (1) June, 2009, 3).

Governor Lachlan Macquarie (1762-1824) had decided, soon after arriving in the colony, to establish townships along the fertile Hawkesbury River (in 1810). He selected sites for five towns: Wilberforce, Pitt Town, Windsor, Richmond and Castlereagh and each was to be provided with the basis for a civilized society: an Anglican church, a school-house, a school, a courthouse, a guard house and a gaol. The Windsor courthouse and church are still in constant use as is the Wilberforce church with its schoolhouse and school next door (Plate 17.7). Thus these villages, only some of which flourished, were given state schools decades before any were built in Sydney.

After a way across the Blue Mountains had been found by Gregory Blaxland, William Charles Wentworth and William Lawson in 1813 and a road had been cut, Governor and Mrs Macquarie made the arduous journey by coach in 1815. They chose a site on a fertile plain for a city (Bathurst) marking out the future school, church and a burial ground. Governor Macquarie similarly founded Liverpool and Campbelltown.

Of the three explorers, Lawson was noted as a prominent Presbyterian and founding member of the local British and Foreign Bible Society, Wentworth (although of

convict heritage) became a politician in the first legislature and Blaxland's descendants are still fulfilling important roles.

As well as teaching Christian principles, Governor Macquarie was committed to morality and family life, sobriety, church attendance and the construction of buildings (about 200 of them), tollroads and toll-houses (one of which survives in Windsor). Along with Rev. Marsden, William Lawson and Judge Advocate Wylde the governor launched the British and Foreign Bible Society (1817) then the Benevolent Society of New South Wales (1818) and, thirdly, the Sunday school movement.

Plate 17.7.
Schoolhouse and church, in Wilberforce. Photograph: D. Campbell, 2015.

While churches ran most of the schools in Sydney Town, the State was building schools in country towns. Public schools in Sydney were slow to be built. According to Sheringham, and Campbell ('Education' Sydney Journal 2(1) 2009, 3) there were only three by 1849 compared with fifteen in country locations. In 1814, Governor Macquarie also

established Native Institutes at Parramatta and Black Town for aboriginal children ('Lachlan Macquarie: visionary and builder', online). The aim was "to effect the civilisation of the aboriginals of N.S.W." and "to render their habits more domesticated and industrious" (Marsden's Letter to the Editor of the Sydney Gazette, online).

Although Macquarie was from a poor family he had attended the Royal Edinburgh High School but in the colony he was grappling with mere elementary education (Kotlowski, 2006, 41). Macquarie had diligently dedicated himself to the colony and during his twelve year term of authoritarian governorship (1810-1822) the colony had grown from 11,000 people on the brink of starvation to a prosperous colony of 40,000. While still a penal settlement it was also a thriving agricultural, pastoral and commercial centre with clergy in every country district, schools based upon Christian principles and institutions to care for the needy. The need for vocational and commercial studies influenced education.

Commissioner John Bigge was sent out from England to investigate and report on complaints against Macquarie (initiated and advised by John Macarthur and his old regimental mates) (Macarthur, John 1755-1834, in Dictionary of Famous Australians [DFA]). Bigge recommended that a legislative council be established to advance democracy but Macquarie took Bigge's negative report very personally. He returned to London a spent man and died two years later, at age 62, while preparing his final report. He had, however, put the colony upon the sound footings upon which it grew and prospered.

After the passing of the Public School Act of 1866 more schools were built in Sydney and State aid was provided to all schools until 1880. In that year the Public Instruction Act was passed, which attempted to make school attendance compulsory. In 1880 the Church of England agreed to give up

its elementary schools but Catholic schools remained

independed and expanded with the growth of parish schools, taught by Mother Mary MacKillop's sisters of St Joseph of the Cross in remote areas (Sherringham and Campbell, Sydney Journal 2 (1) June, 2009, 3 and 5-6; DFA, 1992/95, 166-157). The Public Instruction Act created the crime of 'truancy' but many children needed to earn money (especially during harvests) and school fees, which were not abolished until 1906, were prohibitive for many families.

<u>17.23. The Female Factory and Orphanages</u>

All that remains of the Female Factory at Parramatta is a brick wall but in colonial Sydney it had been a very important institution and most of the convict women spent some time there, even if it was only for the birth of a baby, just as poor Enlish women entered a work house: both were safer than delivering without assistance. At times the Female Factory for Convict and Destitute Women at Parramatta was well run, despite overcrowding and having criminal residents and their numerous, often poorly disciplined children. Small children stayed with their mothers in the Female Factory until they were seven years old, when they were removed to a boys' orphanage, which began in Sydney in 1803 but was relocated to Cabramatta, near Liverpool, away from the city's temptations. It taught employment skills and apprenticed lads to carpenters and boat builders and the like.

Between 1788 and 1796, while Philip Gidley King was Lieutenant Governor on Norfolk Island, he had established an orphanage that fed half of the girl children on the island; which was supposed to be Sydney's food-bowl. As Governor of New South Wales from 1796, King was acutely aware of the critical problem of the colony's street urchins and abandoned, homeless children (Ramsland, 1986, citing Ramsland

online).[35] In Sydney Town about one third of female children were abandoned by their parent(s) so orphan

asylums had to house them. In 1803, Governor King picked up 103 girls from the streets and provided them with 'protective enclosure' to safeguard their morals. The first girls' residential home, established in George Street Sydney, was known as Mrs King's Orphanage because his wife took such a keen interest.

Plate 17.8. Parramatta 'reform school', Parramatta.
Research Services, Parramatta City Council.

From 1813 to 1818, Governor Macquarie built a larger facility on the banks of the Parramatta River, which

continued to take in girls who were exposed to moral danger. Initially, the aim was to teach domesticity and to

find them husbands. Land grants were given as an incentive to marriage, as cohabitation was undesirable and a detriment to their future children (Ramsland, 'Childrens

Institutions', online).

A second orphanage was built further along the Parramatta River, near the Female Factory. Later it became at Roman Catholic orphanage, then a 'reform school' or prison for wayward teenagers and eventually the Norma Parker women's prison (Plate 17.8). In 1826 a third asylum, the Female School of Industry, was set up by Governor Darling's wife, Eliza, and her Ladies' Committee as a private charity (Ramsland, 1986, 11-21).

By 1832 there were 1,025 illegitimate children in the colony, not all destitute but in danger of abandonment because there was no provision for divorce and remarriage; servicemen returning to the U.K. took only legitimate offspring; and if convict parents were repeat offenders they would be sentenced to hard labour in Port Macquarie, Morton Bay or Newcastle, but without their children. The Benevolent Society of N.S.W., Australia's oldest Charity (from 1813) then established the Society for Destitute Children in 1852 and used Juniper Hall, Paddington[36] (renamed Ormond House) to house and educate 103 children of 'dissolute characters' until 1857 when a sandstone asylum was completed on 40 acres in High Street, Randwick to accommodate 400 children, and 800 by 1863.[37]

<u>17.24. Public Education in America</u>

In America, education began in the original thirteen colonies especially amongst the Puritans who ran their own schools. Education was not a matter of public concern in America until after the American Revolution/ War of Independence (1775-1783) when Thomas Jefferson unsuccessfully argued for schools that would be paid for by taxation.

Massachusetts had a public education system from 1647 but it fell into decline by 1830 when Horace Mann (1796-1859) a lawyer, became involved. He was a member of the

Massachusetts House of Representatives from 1827 to 1833 and a state Senator from 1835. He became President of the Senate in 1836 and Secretary of the revived and reformed

Board of Education from 1837. He travelled to Europe to study education in Prussia and elsewhere and developed an enlightened theory of pedagogy, including free, comprehensive, compulsory and secular schooling, free of corporal punishment. His plan included teacher training (which he started in 1839). His ideas were bitterly opposed by clergy, parents and teachers, but for different reasons, although numerous other states adopted various aspects of his praxis (Britannica, 'Horace Mann', by L. A. Cremin).

At the same time Henry Barnard of Connecticut (1811-1900) a Yale graduate who went on to study

Law, became an educator and jurist. He was a member of the State Legislature of Connecticut (183770) and created a state board of Education and a teachers' institute (in 1839). He founded and edited a relevant journal before becoming Commissioner of Education for Rhode Island from 1845 ('Henry Barnard', Britannica).

Barnard returned to Connecticut in 1849 and took charge of a normal school (i.e., teachers' college) at New Britain and edited 36 volumes of the American Journal of Education (1855-1881). Like Horrace Mann, Barnard toured Europe to study education abroad and from 1867 to 1870 he became America's first Commissioner of Education ('Henry Barnard', Britannica).

Robert Smalls (1839-1915), a daring but illiterate slave of the McKee family in Beaufort, South Carolina,

escaped to freedom during the Civil War (1861-1865) before becoming a naval hero. After the Unionist victory, Smalls concerned himself with civil rights and the welfare of freed slaves, purchasing a building in Beaufort for a school for them. He taught himself to read and write and entered state and then

national politics. He wrote the state legislation that

provided for South Carolina to have a free, compulsory, public education system (Pat Wigington for ThoughtCo. 4/12/2018, online).

Although Horac Mann's theories of pedagogy influenced praxis in numerous states, free compulsory schooling did not become nation-wide until 1918, decades after this was achieved by France, England and Australia (Watson, for HowStuffWorks, 2019, online).

<u>17.25. Voting Rights: British Campaign for Women's Suffrage</u>

Christianity played a greater role in British campaigns against slavery and poverty than in women's rights. Universal suffrage was not achieved in Britain until 1928 although it had been achieved in New Zealand in 1841 and in Australia (for non-aboriginal people) in 1902. Today, adult women in some nations are still without voting rights.

In Britain, campaigns for women's rights to a university education, to own property, to enter parliament, to control their own bodies and lives, to be guardians of their own children and to vote were long, bitter and often violent. Enfranchisement is attributed in particular to two remarkable, dedicated women leaders, speakers and prolific writers. The more moderate was Mrs Mellicent Fawcett (1847-1929) (Oxford University Press 'Fawcett, Dame Millicent Garrett, online) and the more militant was Mrs Emmeline Pankhurst (1858-1928) (Purvis, 2001 and online).

Mrs Millicent Fawcett's had one daughter. Her husband, Henry, an economics professor at Cambridge, was a liberal member of parliament (who died in 1884). Mrs Emmeline Pankhurst's husband, Richard Pankhurst, a Doctor of Law, practised in Manchester and died in 1898.

They had two sons and three daughters. At first the three Pankhurst girls aided their mother's work but eventually only Chrystabel, later Dame Chrystabel Pankhurst, remained with Emmeline. Her son Frank died at age 4; Harry died at 21;

Adela went to Australia, married and had four children and Sylvia and her son, Richard, lived in Ethiopia.

Both Millicent's and Emmeline's husbands were highly educated, supportive and liberal-minded and left behind a distraught widow and family.

Mrs Millicent Fawcett became president of the National Union of Women's Suffrage Societies (NUWSS). Its 50,000 active members stayed within legal boundaries. Later she became a Dame of the Grand Cross of the Order of the British Empire (Lewis, 'Millicent Garrett Fawcett,' online).

After 1912, Mrs Pankhurst's 'suffragettes' of the Women's Social and Political Union (WSPU) became increasingly violent. They burned empty buildings, blew up postal-pillar-boxes and planted bombs so that they were brutally treated by the police and jailed. When they resorted to hunger, thirst or sleep strikes the government, fearful that they would become martyrs, introduced 'cat and mouse' legislation, whereby ill prisoners were released, but rearrested when they recovered.

Women's activism ceased during World War I. Their entry to 'male' jobs was an economic necessity and enhanced their claims for equality of pay and a more public

role and profile. Both Mrs Pankhurst and Mrs Fawcett supported the war effort but declined to campaign for enlistments. Both women cared deeply about poor women's lives. Mrs Pankhurst became a Poor Law Guardian and was appalled at conditions in poorhouses for children, pregnant women and the aged (Pettinger, online). Men with socialist, communist and radical leanings were more sympathetic to women's rights. Male parliamentarians often had complex agendas but, in 1918, six million British women achieved the vote, based upon education, property ownership and/or age and in 1925 women won control of their own children (Blessedimp, online).

From childhood, Christianity influenced both Mrs Fawcett and Mrs Pankhurst but during the years of campaigning, religious motivations were less significant than

liberal ideals, democracy and in Emmeline's case, socialism. Richard Pankhurst had begun life as a Baptist but he married

Emmeline Goulden in a free church. They occasionally attended a Church of England but he became an agnostic and was buried as a Unitarian. Emmeline Pankhurst converted to Catholicism in her last year of life. Mrs Fawcett had become an agnostic and "cast aside her mother's evangelical religion", although she later returned to regular worship in the Church of England (Blessedimp, online).

<u>17.26. Discussion</u>

Both Mrs Fawcett and Mrs Pankhurst believed that having women in parliament would bring about change for poor

women but this is not necessarily true. For example, in

America today the gap between rich and poor is growing and Americans near the top of the income ladder earn 8.7 times more than those near the bottom, the largest discrepancy (and the highest incomes) being among Asians (10.7 times) (Geiger, in News in the Numbers, online). "Many of the poorest people, even within the most wealthy nations, have become poorer" (Hughes, 'The 3rd Millennium etc.', online). In the USA, 5.6 million children with one or two working parents live in poverty: an increase of 30% between 1989 and 1994 (Hughes, online; Sine, 1999, 164) and in pre-Covid Britain more than 20% of the population "lives below the poverty line after housing costs are taken into account, even though most of these households are in work. Nearly one in three children live in poverty...." (Parkington, in The Guardian, Sept. 5, 2018). It is expected that food insecurity and homelessness will increase for the poorer classes after the economic consequences of the Covid19 pandemic are complete: and social unrest may accompany that poverty.

17.27. Conclusions

The 18th to 19th centuries in Britain was the high point of

Ecclesia's influence towards social betterment, characterised by an unprecedented social conscience associated with Protestantism and a constitutional monarchy. As, however, the rule of parliament became secure and Britain's economy benefited from industrial development and raw materials from her vast and growing colonies the social welfare of the lower-classes did not automatically benefit: quite the contrary. Wealth did not 'trickle-down'.

Christian denominations in the post-Reformation world were constantly multiplying. Often the smaller (non-conformist) groups devoted time and energy to social reform out of all proportion to their size. Often the leading altruists were women who pushed the boundaries of societies' expectations to meet dire needs. The fabulous wealth of the 4th-century elite Roman Christians was not available so middleclass Christians achieved financial strength-in-numbers by combining together to form societies, many of which were devoted to charitable causes from a Christian perspective.

Questions:

(1) Why was the 19th century such a period of social action?
(2) Which is more important: universal education or universal suffrage?

Chapter 18
19th Century Revivals in Australia

.31. Introduction

Despite the common belief that Australia has never had a revival, there were many scattered small revivals, mainly in the capital cities where revivalist preachers from Britain or the U.S.A. were able to gather a large audience and rent suitable facilities. The missioners were already skilled and experienced.

Due to the discovery of gold in various states in the mid-19th century Australia's population expanded rapidly. Disappointed miners drifted back to the cities towards the end of the 19th century as the easily accessible gold was depleted. There was also an increase in the conservative middle-classes and 'free settlers', compared with the dwindling numbers of ex-convicts and the children of convicts (given that transportation of British convicts to the Eastern States of Australia had ceased before 1850).

.32. Matthew Burnett

The British evangelist, Matthew Burnett, campaigned for twenty-five years, from 1864 to 1889, in the Eastern States and in the new colony of South Australia, which was founded by free settlers in 1836. Burnett's methods were flamboyant, using entertainments, brass bands, banners, flaming torches and dramatic torchlight processions. He preached 'temperance', that is, he campaigned for voluntary abstainance from alcohol, and his work influenced legislation controlling hotel hours in South Australia, assisted the formation of the Salvation Army there (in 1880/81) and led to the use of grape juice in Wesleyan services (Hilliard, 1982, 17).

Numerous others evangelised South Australia in the late 19th century so that Wesleyan membership increased by

16.6% in that state in the three years, between 1881 and 1884, and Baptist membership increased by 11% (Evans, 2005, 16, 43, 75, 116-9,186, 187, 297, 313, 348, 403).

.33. William G. Taylor

William Taylor evangelised from 1876 in New South Wales (Evans, 2005, 16, 43, 75, 116-9,186, 187, 297, 313, 348, 403). He founded Sydney's Central Methodist Mission and was its first Superintendent (1884-1913). Its headquarters, the Lyceum Theatre, had been purchased by the philanthropic politician, Ebenezer Vickery, who gave it to the Methodists (Piggin, 2004, 63). Taylor also founded the Sydney Methodist Holiness Association in 1885 and was its first president (Evans, 2005, 75). He was one of a small number of tireless, long-term workers and, from 1900 to 1902, he was head of the organising committee for the (then forthcoming) Torrey-Alexander Crusade.

.34. Mrs Emilia Louise Baeyertz (1842-1926)

Emilia Aronson was born into a Jewish family in North Wales but became a resident of Australia in 1864. She married an Anglican, Charles Baeyertz, in 1865, had a son Charles in 1867, and soon a daughter, Marion, but she was widowed in 1871 (Evans, 2007). Through this tragedy she converted to Christianity in 1872 and became the teacher of factory-girls' groups and young boys' groups (Evans, 2007, 157).

Then, reluctantly and almost by accident, she became an evangelist. Eventually she held meetings in country towns throughout mainland Australia as well as Tasmania, New Zealand and, then, the U.S.A., Canada and Britain. Mrs Baeyetz was a very successful evangelist for the Praye

r Unions, the Evangelistic Society of Victoria (Evans, 2005, 16; 22; 143) and the Y.M.C.A. overseas (Watson, c.1894, 11; 96; 99; 110; 114; 118; 120 and 123).

Having been raised in an orthodox Jewish home Mrs Baeyertz often said, "I will never allow anyone to speak in my presence disrespectfully of Judaism" (Evans, 2005, 100). She believed in the near advent of the

Lord, the return of the twelve tribes to the promised land, the conversion of all Israel and their mission to the gentiles, and the reign of universal righteousness in the millennial age (Evans, Emilia Baeyertz, entry under Los Angeles, undated). She preached evangelising sermons based on Jewish themes such as 'The Jewish Day of Atonement', 'The Two Offerings of Cain and Abel', 'the Judgement of the Great White Throne' (from Isaiah 6 and Rev. 22) and 'the Jewish Passover' as well as on 'Baptism of the Holy Ghost' (Baeyertz, Six New Addresses, 34-40 and Twelve Addresses delivered by Mrs. Baeyertz, undated, online, 81-87).

Jewish people flocked to Mrs Baeyertz' meetings in Melbourne and she particularly appealed to young women (Hilliard, 1982, 14). She denounced 'worldly amusements' and preached John Wesley's doctrine of 'entire sanctification' (also called 'scriptural holiness') This type of holiness was not self-denial or self-control but a gift from God, given during a crisis experience through complete surrender to God (Evans, 2005, 68-71). For her Passover sermons Emilia Baeyertz used a table, set out as a modern Jewish family would celebrate the Feast: very novel and memorable. (Address in Auckland by Mrs Baeyertz, in Robert Evans, Emilia Baeyertz, unpaged).

> Mrs Baeyertz preached only once in Sydney, for the Y.M.C.A.: a service for men (Watson,

c.1894, 80). When she was in Toronto, Canada, (c.1890/91) Mrs Baeyertz recommended the policy of co-operation between denominations saying:

> *"You have so many fine Christian men and women in your city. If*

> *they were only just a little more united. In Melbourne we work together, and accomplish much more than if we were to work in*

> *separate or rival organizations"* (Watson, c.1894, 123).

The U.S.A. had begun to adopt this policy, following the 'Great Awakening' of the 1850s.

Mrs Baeyertz was a deeply private person with a cultured speaking voice. She had great spiritual depth and her spirituality included the following: faith in God; 'full surrender' ('entire sanctification'); personal prayer; praise and intercession; endowment of the Holy Spirit; 'wrestling in prayer'; the 'prayer of faith'; 'rejoicing in weakness'; 'respect for and obedience to the Scriptures'; 'retaining communion with God' (called 'keeping the heart') and 'separation from the world' (Evans, 2007, Ch. 5). Mrs Baeyertz travelled widely and evangelised for forty-one years. Among her responders were two young men, John J. Virgo, in Adelaide, and Thomas C. Hammond in Ireland. Virgo became an international evangelist for the Y.M.C.A. and T. C. Hammond became Principal of Moore Theological College in Sydney (Evans, 2007, Ch. 7). Typically her responders stayed true. Mrs Baeyertz retired in England in 1918, at the age of seventy-six, and passed into Glory in 1926.

<u>18.5. Mrs Margaret Hampson</u>

In 1883, Mrs Margaret Hampson evangelised in Melbourne, Adelaide and Sydney and, in 1884, in Tasmania and Victoria (Evans, 2005, 3-7; 50). Her knowledge of

poverty and drunkenness in the slums of Liverpool, England, motivated her preaching of 'temperance', which led her to stress total abstinence from alcohol and the taking of 'the

pledge' not to drink (Evans, 2005, 39; 44; 50). Margaret Hampson's Melbourne meetings were a great sensation. Her Adelaide campaign was greeted by a spirit of religious excitement and anticipation of revival (Hilliard, 1982, 15f).

Mrs Hampson introduced some new ideas into her ministry, such as counsellors, an enquiry room and the importance of ongoing fellowship for new Christians. These procedures were so sensible and effective that they have become standard practice (Evans, 2005, 20).

<u>18.6. Rev. George Grubb (ministry Down-Under: 1890-92)</u>

The 'Wild Irishman', George Grubb, was a Church of Ireland cleric. An Irish-American, he was sent to Australia by the Keswick movement with the message of 'higher spiritual life' (Reed, 2007, 120). He faced opposition in Wellington, New Zealand, but cathedrals in Melbourne, Sydney and Goulburn were opened for some remarkable outreach-meetings from 1890-1892. Grubb promoted 'full salvation' and 'baptism in the Holy Ghost'. In the late-19th-century, evanglelical Protestantism came under the sway of a "preoccupation with the Spirit" and "an energetic holiness movement, compounded of personal piety and millennial doctrine" (Piggin, 1996, viii). Grubb was more successful in Victoria than in Sydney but some Victorian converts moved North including R. B. S. Hammond and H. S. Begbie who became leading clerics in Sydney.

Evangelism and foreign missions became more popular and Grubb's report to CMS in London resulted in Church Missionary Associations being started in Victoria and New South Wales. CMS "quickly became a major vehicle for the revivalist and Spirit-driven enthusiasm for missions which Grubb had kindled" (Judd and Cable, 1987, 151).

<u>18.7. Rev. Ruben Archer Torrey with Charles Alexander</u>

In 1901-02, Ruben A. Torrey was president of the Moody Bible Institute. He was Dwight L. Moody's successor when he toured in Victoria and other states with Moody's soloist and songwriter, Charles Alexander (Piggin, 2004, 59).

These two established the formula which evangelist Billy Graham and his song leader George Beverley Shea utilised in the mid 20th century: massed choirs, soloists, skilled accompanists, congregational singing from a song book and simple, catchey and/or emotionally laden songs (Mansfield, in Hutchison et al. (eds), 1994, 126). Prior to the Torrey Crusade a dozen committed men in Sydney had devoted themselves to prayer for fifteen years. In Melbourne, before the crusade, every home had been visited and fifty local evangelists preached in thirty tents and twenty church halls, as well as the Melbourne Town Hall and the Exhibition Hall. By Torrey's own account 8,642 conversions were recorded (Piggin, 2004, 61; Evans, 2005, 340ff). Charles Alexander returned alone in 1907 and conducted 'choir practices', and again with Wilbur Chapman as speaker, in 1909 and 1912 (Piggin, 2004, 60).

The Torrey-Alexander Crusade was the high point of revival preaching in pre-war Australia. William Taylor, who was well acquainted with the task, identified four outcomes: a deeper desire for the Word of God, more one-on-one personal work, organised evangelism by local congregations and closer coperation between denominations (Evans, 2005, 350f).

18.8. Miss Isabella Leonard

Miss Isabella Leonard was an American holiness preacher c.1886. Like Mrs Baeyertz, Miss Leonard preached John Wesley's approach to holiness (Evans, 2005, 3; 75; 116). Following her missions, Methodist Holiness Associations were formed in Sydney (1885/6) by William Taylor (see above) and also in Victoria in 1889 (Evans, 2005, 75).

18.9. Mrs Janet (Sarah Jane) Lancaster

In 1909, Mother Lancaster withdrew from Methodism. She purchased an old temperance hall in North Melbourne, renamed it The Good News Hall, and ran the first permanent

Pentecostal congregation in Australia (Chant 1973/84,

36, 65; Piggin, 1996, 65; Piggin, 2004, 65f). In 1926, faced with diminishing numbers, Mrs Lancaster launched the Apostolic Faith Mission and stepped down to make her husband the 'lead pastor', as convention opposed women leaders even though women founded thirty-seven of the first Pentecostal churches in Australia (Elizabeth Miller, Ph.D. thesis, 2015, 144). After a decade the Mission combined with the Pentecostal Church of Australia to form the Assemblies of God (now Australian Christian Churches), which began with c.1,500 members in 1937 (Elizabeth Miller, 2015, 57-58). By 1945 membership had fallen to 1,200, but Melbourne and other cities were so disrupted by WWII that this decrease is not surprising.

Visiting evangelists Aimee Semple McPherson (who founded the Church of the Four-Square Gospel), Smith Wigglesworth and Adolfo C. Valdez were hosted by Good

News Hall but they distanced themselves from it after deducing that it was "Christadelphian in character" and had "embraced false teaching and doctrine" (Duncan,

1947, 4-5). In Pentecostalism, women-evangelists were quite acceptable and Mrs Lancaster continued to campaign widely and her daughter, Leila, and her husband W. A. Buchanan, had an important ministry in Queensland (Chant, 1973/1984, 37f; Hutchinson et al. (eds), 1994, 104; Elizabeth Miller, 2015, 142, citing Chant, 2011, 263-300).

<u>18.10. Simultaneous Tent Missions</u>

Australia was influenced by reports from the 1859 Welsh and Irish revivals. Much prayer for revival occurred in the later 19th century in Sydney and amongst goldminers in Victoria. The year 1901 was important as the year of Federation - when Australia became a nation. Thanks to a philanthropic

politician, Mr Ebenezer Vickery, who purchased twelve tents and financed a tent-meeting crusade, 1901 was also the year of an innovation in missions. In Sydney, up to 200 open-air

meetings were held every night for a fortnight and several thousand people professed conversion (Piggin, in Hutchinson and Campion (eds), 1994, 188). In the following two years evangelism was simultaneously carried out in fifty country towns (Piggin, 1984, 135). In the coal mining villages of the Illawarra area, 2,735 decisions were made and the pit ponies stopped work because swearing ceased and the ponies could no longer understand their instructions (Piggin, 2004, 63).

David O'Donnell and Robert Robertson held tent meetings throughout New South Wales and over seventeen thousand people made personal responses (Evans, 2005, 294f). O'Donnell continued campaigning until 1914 and his

favourite themes were said to be 'receiving the fullness of the Spirit' and 'the blessings of sanctification' (Evans, 2005, citing The Spectator of July 12, 1895, 464). In

1903, the politician Ebenezer Vickery imported the English evangelist, John Leafe, to campaign for twentytwo months and, as noted, he purchased the Lyceum Theatre in Pitt Street, Sydney, spent £27,000 on alterations, and gave it to the Methodist Church (Evans, 2005,296; Walsh, 'Vickery, Ebenezer (18271906)', in ADB, 6, online). Altogether, the Simultaneous Tent Missions resulted in 25,000 conversions or enquirers (Piggin, 1984, 135ff). In Victoria, results were even greater when Ruben Torrey and Walter Geil campaigned (Piggin, in Hutchinson and Campion (eds), 1994, 188).

<u>18.11. Conclusions</u>

The 19th Century was a period of numerous revivals in Australia, mainly in the Eastern States and South Australia. Important outcomes were: a decrease in alcohol consumption and crime, increases in church membership, the growth of

missionary societies and of inter-denominational organizations. As though the Holy Spirit was determined to break through, Pentecostal type experiences, including

glossolalia (speaking in tongues) often occurred, sometimes to everyone's surprise. The many revival preachers who taught 'a second blessing' included: Emilia Baeyertz; John MacNeill (who wrote The Spirit Filled Life); George Grubb; Mother Lancaster; David O'Donnell and Robert Robertson. Although Methodists were the major driving force in the campaigns, they did not oppose this type of preaching at the time. 'Baptism in the Spirit' passed under the radar and was generally confused with 'entire sanctification' as it was often reported or recorded under such euphemisms as "manifest tokens of God's grace", "deep things of God" or seekers after Holiness who "stepped into blessed enjoyment of this grace" (Evans, 2005, 119 and 20, f/note 20, citing the Weekly Advocate of 30/1/1886, 355; Piggin, 1984, 89).

A second feature of all of these revivals was concerted and long-term prayer, by the missioners, local prayer groups and American intercessors.

While Australia's population doubled between 1881 and about 1912 in that period Baptist church membership grew by 210%, Methodism by 228%, the Churches of Christ by 718% and the Christian Brethren by a huge 1,093%.

In Australia, Catholicism remained apart but other denominations tended to co-operate in social reform and evangelism: social cohesion and volunteerism have always been national qualities. This co-operation helped to prepare for the Billy Graham Crusade, of 1959.

<u>18.12. Long-Term Results of 19th Century Revivals</u>

There were many long-term benefits to morals and social welfare but many revival campaigns failed to prosper in the long term. In the 19th Century, the need for follow-up and spiritual formation was poorly understood, moreover small suburban and rural churches had insufficient manpower to schedule Bible-studies and home fellowships for closer discipleship and training: too few leaders for too many 'babes in Christ'. Possibly the greatest problems were the disappointment of mundane life after the revivalists had gone home, opposition from husbands and/or secular family members and the resurgence of old temptations, such as alcohol.

Many souls wilted for want of spiritual refreshment, or perished in World War I (1914-1918) or were ground down by the depressions of the 1890s and of 1929-35, and/or capitulated to secular and sceptical forces, which were always strong in Australia. Australia's spiritual soil has always been hard; but perhaps only its outer layer.

18.13. Discussion

Each unique individual has had to travel a pathway to maturity. Every generation of Christians has to forge it

s own intimate relationship with Christ Jesus. In many cases this has been a tortuous road.

There is a golden thread running between the above cases in that all of them benefited from their reading of the Bible and the books of previous Christians, even some from other denominations. Many of them wrote hymns that people still sing, or preached sermons or wrote books that people still read. Some have been featured in films and documentaries. Many of them knew each other or were somehow connected,

as is demonstrated by a careful study of the links between the spread of the gospel from Jerusalem to Britain to Australia to New Zealand to Solomon Islands and Vanuatu, as

Chapter 19 will show. Another feature of Ecclesia has always been the importance of family, noticed in the case of Jesus' earthly family which carried on his leadership after the Resurrection. The importance of inheriting leadership has been noted in connection with the Booth family and the Pankhurst family, and even in colonial Australia and Solomon Islands. Despite their flaws and mistakes, all who feature here contributed to the overall welfare of God's world.

Questions:

(1) What historical and social differences were there between colonial Australia and New Zealand that might have influenced the course of Christianity and the churches in each?

(2) Why does it seem the 'Australia has never had a revival'?

(3) Why were revival preachers always imported into Australia from overseas?

Chapter 19
Missions to the World: Oceania and Africa

.35. Introduction

"*Mission is an activity of God Himself*" (Bosch, 1991, 389). As this book demonstrates, the Christian narrative is a story of mission. God is on mission and He asks His people to partner with Him in His redeeming work in the world. This shapes the church and determines its character. The church is on mission rather than mission being one of a number of ministries of the church (Guder and Barrett (eds), 1998. 4). The very first missionaries were the apostles who obeyed the Great Commission: to "*go into all the world and preach the gospel*" (Mat. 28:19-20). Local oral tradition holds that St Mark founded the Egyptian Church, c.50-60 AD/CE (Gabra, 2002, 6) and that St Thomas founded the Mar Thoma Churches in South India, where three groups now use Syriac and their vernacular languges ('Malabar Christians', in ODCC). In the pre-Reformation days the Latin Church sent monks and other missionaries to any far away lands that were known (such as to the Far East, Ireland and England) and the Moravians and Anabaptists were ardent, early Protestant missionaries.

.36. Missionaries to the Pacific: Australia

(A) Rev. Richard Johnson (1753-1827)

Rev. Richard Johnson, an Anglican, was recommended by Clapham Sect members Wilberforce, Thornton and John Newton to become the chaplain to the First Fleet and to the British colony of Port Jackson/Sydney Town.

He was the first Christian cleric to set foot in Australia. Richard and his young wife sailed to the colony in the First Fleet under Captain (later Governor) Arthur Phillip.

On February, 3, 1788, four days after landing at Sydney Cove (27/1/1788) Johnson held the first divine service in

Australia under a large tree and then celebrated Holy Communion in a markee on February, 17 (Manning Clark, I of III, 1988, 87).

Johnson's duties were complex and competing and included: moral rehabilitation of the depraved; attending the execution of the condemned; social work; conducting Anglican services for convicts, settlers and the military alike; conducting funerals, marriages and baptisms; religious education and promoting conversions. As well, he established formal education, c.1798. He was made a magistrate and was appointed to a committee to begin an orphanage. He supported Sunday Schools and befriended aborigines, including a girl, Abaroo, whom he took into his family of two children. Because he had been a farmer in England and to produce food for the colony he grew vegetables and was the first person to grow grain in Australia. He owned eight cows and two oxen (Cable, 'Johnson, Richard (1753-1827)', ADB, online).

When Governor Phillip departed for England he left Major Grose in charge, a man who constantly criticised Rev. Johnson and removed him from the bench, although he was reinstated by the next Governor to arrive, John Hunter. Because the bureaucracy was slow to approve funds, Rev. Johnson was forced to build a wooden church on Church Hill with his own funds, which angered Grose. Rev. Johnson had opened the school in that church, the cost of which was refunded by the new governor. Unfortuately it was burnt down, because convicts disliked compulsory 'Sabbath observance' (Cable, 'Johnson, Richard (1753-1827)', ADB, online).

The Johnson family and Governor Hunter sailed home in October, 1800, arriving in May, 1801. Evangelical Anglicanism had been firmly established in Sydney by Rev.

Johnson and his assistant, Rev. Samuel Marsden, who had arrived in Sydney Town in 1794. The colony was

becoming settled and with the arrival of many young convict women (who had survived the disease ridden women's ship of the second fleet known as 'the floating brothel') normal domesticity was possible. Women and children brought a civilizing influence although about one third of female children were abandoned by their parent(s).[38] Many convicts who had served their time were given grants of land for farming: something they could never have aspired to in Britain.

Later, Johnson was concerned that he had not evangelised successfully. In Sydney he had been an important official, welcome at every table, but back in England he was forced to accept employment as a curate. He was unhappy that he was not rewarded for his thirteen-year-long service in the colony with money, preferment or promotion, by either the church or the government. Although he had retired from Sydney for health reasons he lived on in the south of England for about twenty-six years, pre-deceasing his wife by four years (Cable, ADB, online).

<u>(B) Elizabeth Macarthur (1766-1850)</u>

Mrs Macarthur was one of the first gentlewomen to arrive in Sydney. She was probably the most outstanding woman in the colony: certainly one of impeccable reputation and Christian faith and one with excellent business and farming talents. Just 30 months after the First Fleet had landed Elizabeth and her husband, Lieutenant John Macarthur, and their ailing young son, arrived on a convict transport ship of the Second Fleet.

Plate 19.1.

Elizabeth Farm House, Parramatta. Photograph:
D. Campbell, 1964.

On the long voyage Mrs Macarthur had given birth to a daughter who had not survived. Mrs Macarthur went on to deliver seven more children in the colony, six of whom survived to adulthood. They were raised at 'Elizabeth Farm' at Parramatta, which Mrs Macarthur described in glowing terms as: *"a very excellent brick building"* while their small landholding of 100 acres

(40 hectares) was "fruitful" and had an excellent climate. John did so well that another 100 acres was gifted to him and he was always supplied with convict workers.

Elizabeth wrote: *"Our gardens with fruit and vegetables are extensive; and produce abundantly. It is now spring and the eye is delighted with a most beautiful variegated landscape: almonds, apricots, pear and apple trees are in full*
bloom; the native shrubs are also in flower and the whole country gives a grateful perfume... The greater part of
the country is like an English park, and the trees give to it the appearance of a wilderness, or shrubbery commonly
attached to the habitations of people of fortune."

Whereas other English women longed for home, Elizabeth was able to see the beauty in her surroundings: its native flowers and its olive-green evergreen trees. She taught her three surviving sons to love the country of their birth although they went to England for their education because (as noted in 17.22) there was very little in the way of schooling available in the colony this early. Elizabeth, who had been well-educated herself, placed great value upon education: both spiritual and secular.

Mrs Macarthur ran a well organised home and wrote interest-filled and charming letters about the voyage, life in the colony and about her children and grandchildren. From 1801 John spent four years in England attempting to clear his name because of his financial scheming and political scandals.

After John Macarthur returned from England in 1805 he was constantly suspicious that his wife had been unfaithful during his absence. He developed an abiding hatred of governors and constantly connived (sometimes successfully) to have them recalled and/or disgraced, including Hunter; King; Bligh; Macquarie and Darling; as well as the Chief Justice, Sir Francis Forbes, and his own commanding officer, Lieutenant-Colonel Paterson. It was Macarthur who ingratiated himself with Commissioner Bigge and gave negative advice about Governor Macquarie.

In 1809 Macarthur, who had resigned from the military, was again in London because of his involvement in the arrest of Governor Bligh by soldiers of the Rum Corps but he and the other civilian rebels were returned to Sydney to be dealt with there (Steven, 'Macarthur, John (1767-1834)' in ADB

II, online).

Macarthur had tried, unsuccessfully, to sell his holdings but during both absences Elizabeth took over control of their many pastoral ventures and the convicts who worked them. She steered everything towards financial success, while he courted favours and made deals in England.

Elizabeth constantly wrote to her husband about wool and merino sheep breeding and urged him to consider staying

permanently in Australia: and to the boys, who had sailed with their father in 1801 for their schooling.

John Macarthur acquired more properties, building "Bella Vista" in a commanding position west of Sydney from which Elizabeth could count the seven hills of Seven Hills and then constructing a grand Georgian residence, "Denham Court", on their property at Camden. Elizabeth continued her life-long devotion to her husband and her Christian faith enabled her to weather his bouts of anger and melancholia by "giving thanks to God in everything." It is often more challenging for married women to be saintly than for cloistered virgins. Eventually Governor Bourke stated that John had been "pronounced a lunatic" but for the last few decades of her life Elizabeth preferred to live separately, in their cottage at Parramatta (Plate 19.1) and was a widow for her last sixteen years there (Conway, 'Macarthur, Elizabeth (1766-1850)', in ADB II, online).

<u>19.3. Missionaries to the Pacific: New Zealand</u>

(A) Rev. Samuel Marsden (1765-1838)

Samuel Marsden was the second cleric to arrive in Sydney Town. His patron in England was William Wilberforce who greatly influenced his life, and therefore the Anglican

Church in Australia. Although Marsden visited England he made Australia his home and lived to see many substantial churches built, the most important being St Phillip's Church Hill, St John's Parramatta and St Matthew's Windsor, but his greatest work was in New Zealand.

The story of white contact with the Polynesians of New Zealand, the Maori, began with the explorer Tasman's visit in 1642. Over a century later, in 1789, Captain James Cook landed, along with a Tahitian, Tupia, who could

communicate with the Maori. Near the Bay of Plenty Cook took possession of the land for Great Britain before sailing south to find a separate island. Despite the large number of warlike inhabitants, who were also cannibals, Cook landed and also claimed the South Island for Britain. He then sailed westward and found the coast of Eastern Australia, which he followed northward and mapped.

While the future Governor King had been on Norfolk Island he had been gifted two young Maori chiefs whom he treated well and soon took home. In 1806, an even greater chief, Te Pehi, was brought to Sydney and entertained by the governor. Thus Governor King decided to send his friend, the Anglican chaplain Rev. Samuel Marsden (assistant to Rev. Richard Johnson from 1794) to take the gospel to the Maori. Marsden had met Te Pehi when they were both dinner guests of Governor King (Marsden's Letter to the Editor of the Sydney Gazette, online). Meanwhile French adventurers and various traders, whalers and sealers were making trouble with

the Maori by offending their complex taboos and were often killed and eaten for it. As pay-back the crew and

passengers of the ship, 'Boyd', were killed and eaten. Furthermore, after Te Pehi had returned home he was caught up in such trouble: after rescuing a white woman and three youngsters from slaughter he was killed for it (Jose, 1914, 260-66).

Rev. Samuel Marsden built St John's Church in Parramatta (Plate 19.2), which is now a cathedral. The only original features are the twin towers the design for which Governor Macquarie's wife, Elizabeth, chose, copying her former church in Reculver, Kent. When Marsden, as the first rector, officially opened the church in April, 1803, he preached on the text: "But will God in very deed dwell with man on the earth? Behold Heaven and the heaven of heaven cannot contain thee, how much more less the house which I have built."

The Marsdens returned to England in 1807, to argue for a CMS mission to the Maori, which Samuel guided to establishment: clearly a dangerous endeavour (Marsden's letter to the Editor of the Sydney Gazette, online). CMS

accepted William Hall and John King as missionaries and, shortly afterwards, Thomas Kendall was accepted.[39] In 1813, Marsden purchased the brig Active to facilitate the venture but the new Governor, Macquarie, tried to prevent him from going. Eventually Macquarie was persuaded to take more control over New Zealand. In 1814, he appointed Thomas Kendall as resident magistrate (basically governor). Kendall, Hall, King and their families, with livestock, tools and workmen, sailed aboard the Active to make a settlement at the Bay of Plenty in the North Island of New Zealand, under Chief Hongi's protection. They stayed for many years and Kendall reduced the Maori language to writing and wrote the first book in Maori (Marsden's letter to the Sydney Gazette, online).

Thus, Christianity came to New Zealand on Christmas Day, 1814, when Rev. Samuel Marsden, preached at Oihi Bay,

Rangihoua on "behold I bring you good tidings of great joy" (Luke 2:10) (Ballantyne and Blackman, online). Marsden, who represented such para-church organizations and missions in the Pacific region as the London Missionary Society, the Church Missionary Society and the British and Foreign Bible Society believed that the Maori were intelligent, with more potential than the Australian aborigines.

Although Marsden was sometimes prevented from leaving Sydney by Governor Macquarie, he sailed to New Zealand seven times between 1814 and 1837 (Ballantyne and Blackman, online). He was a busy man: at times he was the only clergyman in New South Wales, performing a

ll weddings, funerals and baptisms, and he was also a magistrate from 1795. Marsden was required by the Governor to be involved with the Female Factory for

Convict and Destitute Women and also the boys' orphanage and school. He also opened a Sunday school and established a seminary in Parramatta for Maori. Marsden was an excellent crop farmer as well as a successful sheep breeder, to whom King George III gave a flock of merino sheep. He wrote reports on agriculture in the colony for Governor King and for the botanist Sir Joseph Banks (who had sailed with Captain James Cook when he circumnavigated New Zealand and discovered Eastern Australia, in 1770).

In 1820, the Maori chief, Hongi, went with Magistrate Kendall to England where King George IV gave him valuable gifts, which he later sold in Sydney to purchase 300 muskets, powder and shot because tribal warfare had become less a sport and more a deadly power-struggle. With these firearms Hongi conquered many tribes, exacerbating the conflicts because other Maori also obtained guns (Jose, 1914, 268f).

In 1830, the most appalling incident, which spurred Britain into concern and (delayed) action involved a trading ship, with its British captain who hired the ship out to another

ambitious chief, Rauparha, who sought revenge for the death of his uncle. With the connivance of the British captain, the chief of the Kaipot tribe, and his family, were deceived and kept prisoners aboard the ship while the Kaipot tribe was slaughtered. The victims were cooked in the ship's galley for a cannibal-feast (Jose, 1914, 270).

As a consequence, James Busby was sent from Sydney to New Zealand in 1833 as Resident and, in 1835 he gathered all tribal chiefs in the North into the United Tribes

of New Zealand. Violence continued, however, but between Maori and Pakeha (white people). This mainly concerned the purchase of land: signed over in exchange for *"scissors, combs, beads, sealing-wax and Jew's harps"* while the chiefs fought over the trinkets (Jose, 1914, 271).

French warships in the area and French attempts at settlements stirred London into action. On February 6, 1840, the so-called land sales were nullified by Busby and Governor Gipps in Sydney, the treaty of Waitangi was signed with twenty-six chiefs. This gave sovereignty to the Queen of England, citizenship to all New Zealanders, full possession to their lands to the Maori, but with the government having the first right to purchase land (Jose, 1914, 273).

By the time of Marden's last visit to New Zealand in 1837, CMS had established over sixty schools there. Back in New South Wales, some complained that Marsden neglected his clerical duties (MacDonald, online, 3). In both New South Wales and New Zealand, as more settlers arrived, "the secular Empire came to prevail over religion" (MacDonald, online) as the many civic roles that were imposed on Marsden in Sydney and Parramatta indicate.

Marsden did good work in New Zealand and is revered there (Yarwood, 'Marsden, Samuel (1765-1838)', in ADB, 3, online). In Sydney, his achievements are almost forgotten. He argued with the Catholics, the Presbyterian cleric, Rev. John

Dunmore Lang, and most of the Governors (especially Macquarie, who favoured 'emancipists', that is, ex-convicts who had 'done their time'). He was an entrenched rival of sheep breeder, John Macarthur, and was called 'the flogging parson' by ordinary folk because he was a very hard magistrate (Yarwood, 'Marsden, Samuel (1765-1838)', in ADB, 3, online).

Marsden's Family

Mrs Marsden delivered a child during the voyage in 1794. She gave birth to five daughters and a son and became disabled by a stroke during childbirth in 1811. (Yarwood, 'Marsden, Samuel (17651838)', in ADB, 3, online).

In May, 1813, Thomas Hassall, who became the Marsden's son-in-law and who was the eldest son of Rev. Rowland and Elizabeth Hassall, had the distinction of opening the first Sunday school in Australia, in his father's rectory. In 1815 Thomas became the first Australian candidate for Anglican ordination, having trained in England under the guidance of Rev. Charles Simeon of the Clapham Sect, who was assisted by William Wilberforce (Rev. Samuel Marsden's patron). A letter from the governor's wife, Elizabeth Macquarie, in support of Hassall's future ministry, facilitated his ordination, which took place in 1821 before he returned to the colony.

Thomas became Rev. Samuel Marsden's curate at St John's Parramatta (Plate 19.2) and married Ann Marsden in 1822. Thomas then ministered in various towns including Port Macquarie, where he built the Anglican church.

He built Heber Chapel on 'Denbigh', his own estate in Cobbity, naming it after his much-loved bishop, the hymn-writer, Reginald Heber, who died as a missionary bishop in India.[40] Thomas Hassall then built St Paul's Church, Cobbitty. His parish was so vast that he was called '*the galloping parson*'. Like his father-in-law, Rev. Samuel Marsden, Thomas was a keen sheep-breeder: perhaps because he was not English-born but a local. He was a popular parson, with a remarkable record of conversions. He received an MA from the Archbishop of Canterbury and was popular with Bishop Grant Broughton, in Sydney ('Hassall, Thomas', in ADB, online).

Rev. Thomas and Mrs Ann (Marsden) Hassall had eight children, including Rev. James Samuel Hassall (1823-1904) who became a pioneer clergyman in New South Wales and Queensland and Miss Eliza Marsden Hassall (1834-1917). Eliza was keenly involved in the British and Foreign Bible Society and co-founder of the Young People's Scripture Union. As noted in 17.6, above, the Clapham Sect of Evangelical Anglicans were intimately associated with CMS, with which Samuel Marsden was connected through his patrons, Wilberforce and Simeon. At the request of CMS London Eliza Marsden founded and ran Marsden Training School for Women Missionaries, in Sydney, which sent out many women missionaries, the first being Eliza's niece, Amy Isabel Oxley, who went to China in 1896. Eliza, who was made a life-member of CMS, London, greatly contributed to the Christian education of young people and carried her grandfather's legacy into a new century, retiring in 1903 (Teale, 'Hassall, Eliza Marsden (1834-1917)', in ADB, online).

(B) Sarah Selwyn (1809-1907) and George Selwyn (1809-1878)

Sarah Harriet Selwyn (1809-1907) was born to Sir John and Lady Harriet Richardson. In 1841, Sarah's husband, George Augustus Selwyn (1809-1878), became the first bishop of New Zealand, a diocese that also included the Melanesian Islands (MacDonald, online). The population was sparse and scattered as, at that time, there were only about 2,000 white settlers in all of New Zealand: but having a bishop was the next step, following the success of CMS and Rev. Samuel Marsden's missionary efforts.

Sarah was reluctant to go, although she would not stand in the way of what her husband thought was right. She called her new home at the established CMS base at

Waimate, near Auckland, a 'wooden box' as it was all made
of Kauri Pine: but she transported all her furniture, including her
beloved piano, in crates from Eton College, England. From the first, the
Maori called her 'Mother Bishop' ("Mata Pihopa") but others called her
"the deputy bishop" as she was so important to the bishop's work while
he was away or at sea. Mother Bishop was remarkable: she supervised all
of the stores every week, entertained house guests, nursed her terminally
ill chaplain to the end, made matches and organised weddings, travelled
widely (despite being a poor sailor) oversaw all of the students of St John's
College (which her husband had founded) and planted 2,000 trees in St
John's Bush.

Bishop Selwyn did not begin to visit the islands until 1847 but
altogether he spent 22% of his time "yachting around the islands" which
annoyed the white settlers in New Zealand (Davidson, online, 16).

When Bishop Selwyn established St John's College, Auckland, the
Selwyn family moved there and it became "the key and pivot of all his
operations" (Davidson, online, 11, end/n. 10). Charles Abraham and his
wife Caroline, who was Sarah Selwyn's cousin, arrived in 1850 and Charles
became principal of St John's College, of which he had been a major
benefactor from the start. Caroline Abraham (1809-1877) was a gifted
watercolourist, who has left numerous landscape paintings of the Auckland
area (MacDonald, online). In 1859, Charles Abraham became the first
bishop of Wellington, N.Z.

Sarah and Caroline took into their homes Islander girls who were
betrothed to students at St John's College. The first two Melanesian girls,
who arrived by boat with Bishop Selwyn, were wearing only "very skimpy
petticoats made... by the bishop himself out of a coloured
counterpane".[41] The ladies taught them Christianity and domestic
skills and showed the shy young girls a loving
Christian home: so different from the violence, polygamy and
infanticide they had known (Crawford, online, 27; MacDonald, online, f/
notes 93-98).

Together the Selwyns visited England three times. In 1855 the Bishop
appealed for extra missionaries and John Coleridge Patteson (the future

Bishop of Melanesia) responded. He became a teacher in New Zealand and began his study of local languages.

The Selwyns were caught up in the Maori versus British government conflict over land purchases, seen by Maori as breaking the Treaty of Waitangi, and which was called the Taranaki War (1856-65). In 1863-4 Bishop Selwyn accompanied imperial troops as their chaplain, which damaged his reputation with the Maori who felt betrayed when a village sheltering women and children was attacked. He also lost favour with the, now dominant, settler class. By 1866 co-operation between Maori and Europeans had ceased (MacDonald, online, f/note 90). "Missions and the Maori church had fallen away and what remained had been relegated to the periphery." (Selwyn, in Crawford, online, 92).

The Selwyns returned to England in 1867 when George became Bishop of Lichfield, until his death in 1878. In New Zealand, Sarah Selwyn was considered frail and vulnerable and was described as quiet and lonely, perhaps because, at first, she had no social equals there. By contrast, the Bishop was strong and an excellent sailor, but Sarah outlived him by twenty-nine years (MacDonald, online, f/notes 19, 21- 26).

Also living in retirement in Lichfield from about 1870 were Sarah's relatives, Caroline and Charles Abraham (the

former Bishop of Wellington, N.Z.) and the Selwyn's friends

from New Zealand, Bishop Edmund and Mary Hobbhouse (from Nelson, N.Z.) and Sir William and Lady

Mary Ann Martin. These three couples were the major benefactors for the building of Selwyn College in Cambridge University. In 1893, a similarly named college was built at the University of Otago, Dunedin, N.Z., in 1893 (MacDonald, f/n 107).

Sarah Selwyn had always kept a journal and had written many letters home, although they had taken from three to six months to arrive. She transformed these into her memoirs during her widowhood.

Two of the Selwyn's four children survived and were sent back to Eton College be educated. The second son, John Richardson Selwyn, became Bishop of Melanesia for fifteen years from 1877. John's first wife, Clara, died in 1877, shortly after the birth of a girl who survived only briefly (Crawford, online, 37). Bishop John remarried. He became Master of

Selwyn College, Cambridge, but retired c.1893 with poor health. He died aged only 54.

19.4. Missionaries to the Pacific: Solomon Islands

(i) Beginnings in Solomon Islands

The nation 'Solomon Islands' is Christian today, with many denominations, but Christianity began with a British-initiated Anglican presence and a French work by Marist Fathers. The Anglican work was begun by two capable bishops, Selwyn, the previously mentioned first Bishop of New Zealand and Melanesia, and then John Coleridge Patteson, the afforementioned unmarried teacher, who became the first Bishop of Melanesia.

From 1925, two aspects to the Anglican work developed: white missionaries from England and New Zealand, as clergy, and local native men who volunteered as evangelists with the Melanesian Brotherhood.

(A) Ini Kopuria

In 1925, Solomon Islander Ini Kopuria felt God's call to found a monastic order. With Bishop Steward's help,

Kopuria, aged 25, renounced possessions, marriage and freedom of action and donated his ancestral land for a Mother House at Tabalia on Guadalcanal Island. He chose to utilise local men to evangelise village people. In 1926 six brothers joined the Melanesian Brotherhood, dedicating themselves for a set term of four to nine or more years, to work as evangelists. The bishop was the Father of the Brotherhood so all of the racial groups were coordinated under episcopal leadership.

At first the Brothers evangelised more quickly than the bishop could staff villages with clergy so that the villagers slipped back into paganism. Eventually this became obvious and the Brothers stayed longer in a village than the original three months. The Brothers selected lads who could be sent away by boat, for training in St John's College, New Zealand (founded, as noted above, by Bishop Selwyn) and later on to the school on Norfolk Island. After 1867 primary and then high schools were built at various locations within the Solomon Islands and eventually, only the most senior boys and their future wives went to Norfolk Island. Their marriages took place in the beautiful Chapel of the Brotherhood on Norfolk at the end of the academic year (Crawford, online).

Melanesian Brotherhood brothers who withdrew and married were usually catechists in their own villages, wherever it was safe to do so, although some were martyred upon their return home. By 1947 there were 81 native priests and deacons (Oxford Dictionary of Anglicanism, IV, Global

Western Anglicanism, 337). The churches were called 'schools' and 'schools' became centres of village life.

The small number of local women whom the Anglicans educated (those who then married leaders and native clergy) could also teach.

They were also village midwives and mothercraft teachers, gradually eliminating infanticide and decreasing

infant and maternal mortality. Previously 40% of babies had died: largely because women had given birth alone, out in the bush ('Mothercraft: Melanesia: The Solomon Islands and New Hebrides', London, 1949, 4, online).

(B) English Speaking Anglican clergy

Single men were preferred, as the death rate among white women in the Islands was high, although women made good teachers and nurses, which were basic to the Anglican mission. Single women did not work in the Islands until 1905, but worked for the Melanesian Mission, little noticed, on Norfolk Island and in New Zealand. The Melanesian Mission was male orientated and favoured men so it tended to marginalise women or ignored them, notably in the case of Elizabeth Colenso, a missionary whose husband left her for a local woman. She persevered on Norfolk Island, ran the Mission's laundry and sewing room, trained the girl students for domestic work and personally cut and sewed all of the boys' clothing. Mrs Colenso also constantly corresponded with donors and exstudents. She was crippled with arthritis before she retired to England, but her lowly work hardly rated notice (Crawford, online).

A Christian village could be easily identified: everyone wore clothes (a skirt or shorts), there were lots of children and the village was clean and tidy. Polygamy had originally been universal and on some islands cannibalism and head hunting were practised. Warfare between tribes and the different language groups had previously been incessant.

(C) Bishop John Coleridge Patteson (1827-1871)

Bishop Patteson had been principal of St John's College, in Auckland. When a new see was created he inherited all of Melanesia from Bishop Selwyn, in 1861. The Diocese of Melanesia included Solomon Islands, New Hebrides and the Popondetta area of Papua-New Guinea. By then Patteson had

learned to speak twenty-three languages of the Pacific Islands and despite the dangers by sea and from the fierce tribespeople, for ten years he visited his island diocese on his vessel, Southern Cross. ('History of the Melanesian Brotherhood', online). Unfortunately he and a companion were killed on Nakupu, a Santa Cruz Island, on September 20, 1871, apparently as 'pay back' for the hijacking of five islander lads by white slave-traders. The missionaries were not eaten because cannibalism was not practised by that community. Their bodies were set adrift by the islanders and retrieved for a Christian burial service.

In Britain, the martyrdom of a bishop aroused great interest in missions and in the Pacific Islands and led to the speedy passage of the Pacific Islander Protection Act to regulate the native-labour trade ('Patteson, John Coleridge', in ODCC; MacDonald, online, f/n 105).

(D) S.S.E.M. and Florence Young (1856-1940)

Florence Young was born in New Zealand but lived in Australia. In 1882 she established schools for Pacific Islander workers on her family's property in Queensland.

Called Kanakas, these workers were indentured labourers on the Young's sugar plantation: although many of such workers were virtually slaves who were 'blackbirded' (hijacked) into working on plantations in Fiji and Queensland. Florence then became an evangelist among them and also a missionary in China. She founded the Queensland Kanaka Mission, which made thousands of converts. In 1904 the Solomon Islands Mission was formed. Now called the South Sea Evangelical Mission (S.S.E.M.) it was formed in a central base at One Pusu on Malaita (Mala). Florence, herself, bravely went to Malatia: perhaps the first white woman to do so. Many of the Kanakas were from the Island of Malatia: a warlike and vigorous people, many of whom became strong Christians and potential leaders while they were away.

Florence Young evangelised on Malatia, in China and in Queensland, moving between the three places as the Lord led her. She survived the Boxer Rebellion in China, which, in total, claimed the lives of 188 missionaries and children (Piggin, 2004, 69).

In 1906 Australia implemented the notorious 'White Australia Policy' and many Islanders were sent home: to face hostility and even martyrdom (Piggin, 2004, 69). Her 'boys' begged Florence for help but the Lord gave them a Holy Spirit revival so they went home as fearless Christians.

.37. Conclusions

The above servants of the Lord went into all the world to preach the gospel, a calling which dates back to Jesus' 'great commission' of Mat. 28:19-20. Their obedience and faithfulness is memorable as they nobly bore privations, ill health and death. The calling was difficult for women and children, among whom the death rate was high but, despite the many obstacles, the church spread across the globe

. Even in recent years, adult missionaries and/or their children have been martyred, for example, in April of 2003

some Melanesian Brothers were tortured and seven were murdered after the Townsville Peace Accord was signed between the government of Solomon Islands and armed insurgents, beause the Brothers had tried to negotiate peace.

In every Christian era there have been courageous people who carried the flame of the faith to other, scattered people groups. They spread the knowledge of Jesus, along with education and health-care, into the most remote and barely known places and then passed that torch on to others in the next generations, often their own surviving children. In some denominations such transmission is formalised and is called 'apostolic succcession' but, even without a formal name,

the Good News has been passed from person to person for two thousand years and others have been challenged by its call. Every Christian is called to actively participate because

missionaries cannot do it alone.

They need encouragement, volunteers, emails and letters, money, prayer and Christmas gifts. Keeping the home fires burning is part of the task, too. In these difficult times, every Christian should seek God for their own small (or even large) apostolic calling.

.38. Missions to Africa

Ecclesia in sub-Saharan Africa is large and still growing quickly. The Gospel arrived on the continuent in Apostolic times and until the Muslim conquest of the 7th century, North Africa had a thriving but heresy-troubled church. Alexandria, Carthage, Hippo and Fustat (Old Cairo) were great urban centres of Christianity and the expansive desert a great centre for monasticism. Now there are over 400 million Christians on the African continent.

(A) David Livingstone (1813-1876)

Dr David Livingstone was a pioneer of medical and educational work in South Africa where white people, who opposed British efforts to help Africans, burnt his mission and his precious library (Robert, 2009, 84). Once he witnessed slave-traders killing 400 natives. He moved up to Central Africa and later explored the inland, discovering Lakes Shirwa, Nyassa and Bangweulu. He explored the Zambesi River and its tribularies and the Upper Nile.

Livingstone published his findings, his letters and the popular book "Missionary Travels and Research in South Africa" but, unfortunately, the Muslim and Portuguese slave-traders, whom he opposed, used these writings to find the Africans whom he wished to help (Robert, 2009, 83ff). One must always be aware that there may be unseen consquences of one's decisions and best intentions. Livingstone was famously found, much emaciated, in the wilds of Africa by H. M. Stanley of the New York Herald. He died two years later in Africa where his heart was buried, as requested. His body was taken to London for burial in Westminster Abbey ('Livingstone, David', in ODCC).

(B) Albert Schweitzer (1875-1965)

Albert Schweitzer was born in Alsace. He became a theologian, preacher, church organist, philosophy lecturer, musicologist and a unique interpreter of Bach's music. He

studied medicine and with his wife, Helene, who was a nurse, he went to central Africa where he built and ran a

hospital and, later, a leper colony. He was interned as an enemy alien in France in World War I after which he wrote his "Philosophy of Civilization" (1923) in which he expounded belief in reverence for all life. In 1930, he wrote

"The Mysticism of Paul the Apostle" but he is more famous for writing "The Quest for the Historical Jesus" in 1906 and for receiving the Nobel Peace Prize in 1952 ('Albert Schweitzer', in Britannica, online).

19.6. The Church in Uganda

The Ugandan church has been built on the blood of its martyrs. Christianity was welcomed in the 1870's by King Mutesa however his son, Mwanga, (king from 1884) opposed the presence of all foreigners.

In 1885, when the first Anglican Bishop to be appointed to Bugunda, James Hannington, was coming, he was killed by Chief Luuba on the King Mwanga's orders.

Then Mwanga's first native victim was the king's senior advisor, J oseph Rugarma, (d.1885) who was beheaded for criticising the king's debauchery and the killing of Bishop Hannington. Three pages, Joseph

Mukasa Blaikuddembe, (d.1885) Mark Kakumba and Noah Serwanga were killed for refusing the homosexual demands of Mwanga (a serial rapist) (Matsiko, 'The Uganda Martyrs of Namugongo – the full truth behind this historic event' Anglican Communion News Service (ACNS) January 12, 2015).

In 1885, 23 Anglican and 22 Catholic young men were murdered for their faith and because they also refused the king's homosexual demands. "These included his headman, Charles Lwanga and a thirteen year old page,

Kitzito" (Uganda National Media, 'The Valley that witnessed Bishop Hannington's death', online). (Those with European names had obviously been baptised). About two or three hundred minor chiefs and others were also killed from 1885 to 1887 (Reed, 2007, 42). Alexander

Mackay, a Presbyterian minister, wrote that Mwanga "had copied homosexual behaviour from Arabs of his court" (Matsiko, online). The king's Christian pages were speared, hacked to pieces and burnt alive at Namugongo and two more were later speared at Paimol in Northern Uganda. The Catholic victims were canonised by Pope Paul VI in 1964 (Uganda National Media, online) and he visited Uganda in July, 1969 (Ihunnia, online).

In 1976-77, under President Idi Amin, Archbishop Janani Luwum and the Roman Catholic Monsignor were martyred in Kampala and many students and staff were tortured and crippled for life, and soldiers were killed for attending Mass. Law and order broke down, with even police and soldiers rampaging, looting and killing. There were many other Christian martyrs in Uganda's history (Kiefer, 'James Hannington and the Martyrs of Uganda 29 October, 1885', online; Kevengerie, I Love Idi Amin, 1977, 37-43).

<u>19.7. The East Africa Revival</u>

In the 19th century, East Africa was divided up by the colonial powers (such as Belgium, Germany and Britain) and entry was either physically difficult or politically impossible. Christianity had penetrated Uganda but, by 1890, the Ugandan church was stagnant, with concubinage, drunkenness, immorality and withcraft continuing and with nominal members lacking assurance of salvation (Gehman, online 29; 36). Because the preaching stressed Mark 16:16, church members thought that baptism provided a 'tickets to heaven'.

Revival began in Uganda through the ministry of George Pilkington in the 1890s. When Pilkington held a mission, which began with the hymn "Have you been to

Jesus for the cleansing power?" revival broke out

and hundreds prayed for forgiveness. Again in the

1920s and 30s, when Cambridge University friends Dr Stanley Smith and Dr Leonard Sharp went to Kigezi in S-W Uganda, 300 churches were planted. A background influence was that, prior to 1922, Jack Warren had called for a week of concerted prayer for Uganda and Britain. Stanley Smith then entered Rwanda and the now-vibrant Kigezi (Ugandan) church sent evangelists and teachers to assist him (Gehman, online 29;

36).

In 1927 Dr Church, a supporter of the Keswick Movement, arrived in Uganda in the midst of a famine. In Kampala he met Simeoni Nsibambi, with whom he spent two days in prayer. They received "a share of the power of Pentecost" (Gehman, Eajet, 40 f/n. 15, citing Katarikawe and Wilson, unpblished thesis for Fuller Theological Seminary).

Through Dr Church, the Keswick practices of 'testimonies' (public confessions) and 'second conversion' (or commitment) were to become trademarks of the East Africa Revival (Gehman, Eajet, 40). Nsibambi went on to become a successful full-time evangelist.

Dr Church went to Gahini, Rwanda, to do medical work and revival spread to the Tutsi people there. Teams of preachers began to be formed c.1933 and to fan out from Rwanda. In 1994 in the Rwandan genocide (noted below) many Tutsi Christians died.

The Revival is often dated to June, 1936, in Uganda, but the above details show that its origins were much earlier. Bishop Stuart, from England, became a significant figure who held the Ugandan church together, c.1940-41, when the 'Revived Bretheren' were being criticised by the European old guard and there were schisms in Tanganyika (1953) and Kenya (1958) (Reed, 2007, 24ff; Gehman,

Eajet, 46).

After WWII, the Revival spread to Tanganyika/Tanzania (a former German colony) which borders Rwanda and has a similar language. The new diocese of Central Tanganyika became the special responsibility of CMS Australia, which provided its missionaries from the late 1920s. Rev. George Chambers, founder of Trinity Grammar School, Sydney, was its first bishop, from 1928 (Gehman, Eajet, 123f). A former rector of ours, Rev. T. Geoffrey Croft, who, with Ray and five children, ministered in Central Tanganyika and Victoria Nyassaland for nine years (1958-67). He reported that Africans would meet him along the road and fall down in repentance, seeking salvation.

Another Australian missionary, Rev. Canon David Hewetson, who was very involved in the Revival, ministered in Tanzania from 1961 to 1965, with his wife Ann. In Sydney he had been friendly with Rev. Geoffrey Bingham, who was interested in Keswick-holiness and revival. Bingham, a former Changi prisoner-of-war and story teller, was so impressed by eyewitness reports of the East Africa Revival (brought back in 1950 by Rev. Dr Marcus Loane, a future Archbishop) that from 1953, he commenced revival-style meetings at Holy Trinity Miller's Point, in Sydney,

even though Dr Loane thought that the revival was too African and culturally unsuited to Australians (Reed, 2007, 154).

"The emphasis was on placing everything under the blood, on being fully completely yielded to the Holy Spirit, on constant brokenness" and recalled the Grubb mission of the 1890's (see 18.6 above) (Judd and Cable, 1987, 257f).

The Anglican heirarchy eventually invited African bishops to Australia, including the revivalist Bishop, Festo Kivengere of Uganda, who came with Yohana Omari in 1959 (and again in 1970, 1978). In 1959 they preached in Perth, Sydney, Adelaide, Melbourne and Tasmania and also spent a month with aboriginal mission stations in the North. Similarly, Bishop Festo Olang and Alpha Mohammed came in 1963 (and in 1978) and Gershom Nyaronga also ministered among the aborigines as well as in the cities, in 1963. Three aboriginal leaders visited East Africa in 1978 to see Africans leading congregations. They noted the joy, music and dance of the congregations: African's spiritual riches amid their dire poverty (Reed, 2007, 135; 205).

Having led revival at Miller's Point, Geoff and Laurel Bingham went as missionaries to Pakistan from 1957 to 1966 where revival was also witnessed (Reed, 2007, 156). In 1967 Geoff Bingham founded Adelaide Bible Institute (now the Bible College of South Australia) (Sandleman, 'Tribute to revival preacher,' June 4, 2009).

The Australian churches changed greatly in fifty years and the decades indicate that Dr Loane was too pessimistic. Today we also see: "a mission in reverse taking place as the vitality and vision of African Christianity not only finds foothold in Europe and North America but also challenges the very expression of Christianity in those continents" (Ihunnia, 'How Africa is changing the face of mission', Sedos Mission ; Effa, 'Releasing the Tiger: The Nigerian Factor in Global Christianity,' JBMR 7.4 (2013), 214-18).

(E) Martyrs of Kenya under Mau Mau

In Kenya, in the 1950s the Mau Mau movement
developed within the Kikuyu tribe based upon
legtitimate grievences over land, segregated education and unequal pay between white and black employees (Reed, 2007, 166). It was nationalistic, anti-colonial, revolutionary and anti-Christian. Mau Mau 'terrorosts' opposed the British and killed sixty-three white famers on their own land. The British military fought back, killing 11,000 people. Local Mau Mau killed about 2,000 opponents and coerced others into swearing the anti-Christian, anti-British Mau Mau oath (Reed, 2007, 160):

"I swear that I will renounce Christianity and take up once more my name of Kikuyu. I swear I will never again approach missionaries, go to church or participate in the sacraments. I swear that I will combat the government in every possible way."

Many Anglicans (mainly new converts) were martyred and seventy-five Roman Catholics who also refused to swear were also martyred. An Italian nun who was martyred, Sister Irene Stefani Nyaatha, who evangelised and/ or baptised them, was beatified by the Pope on May 23, 2015 ('Martyrdom calls for Mau Mau Victims', online; Campbell, Modern Christian Martyrs, 2000).

(F) Martyrs of Ethiopia in 1974 when Emperor Haile Selassie was deposed

Ethiopia's 3,000 year old monarchy was believed to have originated with King Menelek, the son of Solomon and the Queen of Sheba (Queen Makeda of Axum). It was ended when the Emperor Haile

Selassie, whose name means "Might of the Trinity," was overthrown by a military coup, led by the Marxist-Leninist junta or Derg, on September 12, 1974 (Hunter, 2014, online). Although 40% are Muslim, Ethiopia had been a Monophysite

Christian country since the 1st century but the Ethiopian

Tewahedo Church (a much respected Oriental Orthodox

institution) was savagely persecuted by the Derg and many Christians fled to nearby countries or overseas.

The Soviet Union openly supported the communist regime with money and arms, from 1975 to 1987 (Hunter, 2014, online).

During WWII Ethiopia had been conquered by the Italians and Emperor Selassie was exiled. The victorious Allies, who had earlier declined to protect the country, restored the Emperor in 1941. He worked hard, travelled widely, promoted the formation of the League of Nations, drew up a new constitution (1955), founded a university in his own palace (1960), built schools, ended slavery and brought in some democratic structures and artfully obtained foreign aid. Because he 'hushed up' the severe drought of 1973 (which killed 100,000 people) the peasantry and the army turned against him, with riots in the capital. The constant border-disputes with Somalia also caused economic and social problems (Whitman, New York Times August 28, 1975, online).

Haile Selassie was probably murdered (on August 24, 1975) despite being guarded by lions and cheetahs and a body guard but he was not properly buried until November, 2000. The communist reign-of-terror that commenced in 1975 lasted until the Derg was driven from power in 1987 (Whitman, New York Times, August 28, 1975, online).

(C) Reginald and Catherine Hamlin

Drs Reginald and Catherine Hamlin were both Christian gynaecologist-obstricians who married in Sydney, Australia, in 1950, before being employed on a three-year contract (1958-61) by the Ethiopia government to work in the Princess Tsehay Hospital in Addis Ababa. With their own money they built a

hostel for girls who were awaiting treatment. They then built a hospital for women patients (mostly teenagers) who had

suffered extreme and damaging labours which resulted in fistulas (tears) in the bladder, vagina or bowel. These difficult labours result in stillbirths and continuous incontinence so such girls are rejected by husbands, families and all of society. While raising funds the

Hamlins delivered babies, performed operations and tried to have a clean, efficient hospital despite the poverty of the country. Meanwhile they learnt all they could about obstetric fistulas, which they had never seen before (Barrowclough, The Good Weekend 8/11/2008 and S.M.H. 10/10/2014, online). After fifteen years of struggle and red-tape, the Addis Ababa Fistula Hospital was opened in 1975, treating patients without charge. The Imperial Patron was Her Highness Princess Tenagne Work.

Together, and with staff doctors, the Hamlins have treated many thousands of patients. The hospital has both received patients and trained fistula-surgeons from around the world and all local trainee-doctors do a period of residence there. Fistual hospitals have been built in various areas of Ethiopia and a school of midwifery has been opened in an attempt to provide trained midwives for every village. Catherine Hamlin once said:

"Jesus never promised us a smooth or trouble-free passage through life, but He did promise to be with us to share the sorrow and the pain" (Hamlin with John Little, 2001/2016, 290).

In 2003 the United Nations launched a campaign to eradicate obstetric fistula, targetting 40 countries. About seven girls per day have surgery at the 'mother hospital',

others receive physiotherapy, counselling, literacy lessons, business-skills, handicraft instruction and certainly learn how to care for their unique conditions. Those who cannot be cured are cared for and given useful work, including in the wards (Little, 2008, 216).

Dr Reg Hamlin died in 1993 but the work continued, unabated. Dr Catherine Hamlin (who was born on the 24th January, 1924) died recently. She was a Companion of the

Order of Australia (1995), a National Living Treasure of Australia and an Honary Doctor of Medicine of the Universities of Sydney, Dundee and Addis Ababa. Dr Hamlin received the Rotary Award for outstanding Research in 1998. She is an honorary Ethiopian citizen and was twice nominated for a Nobel Peace Prize (1999 and 2014) and received the "Alternative Nobel Prize" (nazret.com/blog, 14/10/2009). Catherine Hamlin was renowned for her dedication, humility, gentleness and love for her girls. If she found an ex-patient begging in the street Catherine would takes her back and work out something better. Until the end she continued to live and work at the hospital in Addis Ababa and to oversee the newer, satellite hospitals run by Hamlin Fistula Ethiopia (Australia). Apart from saving and renewing lives the Hamlin's great joy has been to deliver a live baby for their former patients. Reg used to say: "for these girls the wheel of fortune has turned full circle. They have what every woman wants, a live baby in their arms" (Hamlin with Little, 2001/2016, 212). Motherhood was very important to her patients and to Catherine Hamlin whose son, Richard, is involved with the Ethopian work, and is married to, Diana. They have given Catherine four British grandchildren.

19.8. 100 Days of Genocide in Rwanda

On April 6, 1994, the Hutu tribe (the majority) began the killing of 800,000 Tutsis and sympathisers and those who

refused to kill, who included Christians. From 1894 the German colonial masters had favoured the light-skinned Tutsi (the 10% who owned the most cattle) and after WWI the Belgians took over, issuing identity cards allocating one or other of these identities to 90% of the population. Like the Germans, the Belgians appointed Tutsis to all leadership positions (for which they had some experience) but when the Belgian authorities feared a revolution they switched to favouring the Hutu majority.

The plane carrying the President, a Hutu, was shot down on April 6, 1994. On April 7, the Hutu extremists took over the government, purged it of moderates and opponents and began to massacre Tutsis with knives, clubs and machetes. The radio station sprouted hatred and broadcast details of where Tutsi's were hiding and details of their deaths. Identity cards and informers betrayed people. Tutsi women were raped and mutilated. Burials were forbidden: bodies were left to the dogs and rats or thrown into rivers and lakes. The United Nations did nothing (Rosenberg, online).

In July, 1994, a Ugandan-trained militia of exiled Tutsi ex-pats (the Rwanda Patriotic Front) gradually took control of Rwanda, ending the genocide (Rosenberg, online).

19.9. Conclusions

In Africa, missionary development and colonialism occurred at the same time, as the dark interior of the country was opened up. Thousands of language groups made communication difficult and each colonial power taught its own tongue: mainly German, English or French. The Christian denomination of the 'mother' colonial power usually held sway.

With the many exotic tropical diseases and very poor sanitation the need for medical help was extreme so

many of the early missionaries were doctors. Hospitals were built. In Africa, more so than in Asia and the Pacific, there were two reactions to Christianity (both extremes): eiother violent and savage opposition or enthusiastic embrace. Mission education and the embrace of Christianity changed African culture very quickly but many problems continue: tribal violence; the suffering of females through cultural subjugation; diseases and primitive superstitions;[42] enslavement; corruption in politics; endemic corruption of the bureaucracy and now HIV/Aids and other epidemics. It is dangerous to be a Christian today in a number of African countries, notably

Nigeria, Libya, Somalia, Ertitrea, Democratic Republic

of Congo, Mozambique, Cameroon, Central African Republic,

Mali, South Sudan, Ethiopia, Burkina Faso, Angola and Rwanda where mass killings, abductions and/or the burning of churches are commonplace (Christianity Today News and Reporting, Jan. 12, 2021, online).

Questions:

(1) What aspects of Africa made missionary work there notably difficult?

(2) Why is the Church in Sub-Saharan Africa growing rapidly?

Chapter 20

Missions to the World: India, China, East Asia

20.1. Missions to the East: Part i: India (a) William Carey (1761-1834).

William Carey was baptised an Anglican but accepted Baptist teaching upon conversion as a teenager. He was a shoemaker's apprentice who taught school students, pastored a Baptist church and taught himself Latin, Greek, Hebrew, French and Dutch. At the age of nineteen he married his first wife, Dorothy (Dolly) who was illiterate and a 'real home-body'. When his mother visited because their third child (a daughter) had died, she was shocked by their abject poverty (Tucker, in Christianity Today, July/August, 2017, online).

At a ministers' meeting in 1792 Carey preached on "Expect Great Things from God: Attempt Great Things For God", which, as a booklet, became the Magba Carta of the Protestant mission movement (Winter, online). With his help, within months the Baptist Missionary Socierty was formed. The Careys were its first candidates (D. J. Bingham, online, 154).

The Carey family went to India in 1793 when a very reluctant Dorothy was pregnant again. She was ill with dysentry from their arrival until her death after twenty-six years of marriage. When their son, Peter, aged five, had died of dysentry in 1796 Dorothy became emotionally unstable: even more so after her sister, who had accompanied her as her companion, had left to marry an East India Company officer. Her condition deteriorated so much that she had to be kept in a locked room. Carey was very detached from the family and pressed on with one or other of his translations, of which he completed forty-four (Robert, online, 48).

Marital relations continued and Dorothy bore at least seven children. Some say that three died in India, some say

four. Five months and one day after Dorothy's death Carey remarried. His second wife, Charlotte Rumohr, was a Danish resident of India. Because of an accident she was physically disabled and could not speak but she was from a wealthy family and, being well educated, she helped him with his translation work. They were happily married for thirteen years. Carey's third wife, Grace Hughes, was a widow who, for eleven years, cared for him in his old age in India and died the year after he did (D. J. Bingham, online, 154).

Carey's two oldest boys, Felix and Jabez, were ordained for ministry but in 1814 Felix became the Burmese king's ambassador. His father was very disappointed but, by living in Burma, Felix was able to take the gospel to the (now Christian) Keren tribespeople there (Communication from a descendant, John O'Hara, of Queensland. See note on Felix's story in Chapter 20.3.(a) below). Another son, William, and his wife, Mary, were missionaries, as were numerous nephews (D. J. Bingham, online, 154).

Perhaps Carey's greatest contribution was the pamphlet he published in Britain, in 1792, called "An Enquirey into the Obligations of Christians to Use Means for the Conversion of the Heathen", which provided a Christian incentive for missions and helped to arouse interest in the missionary call (Curtis (ed.), 'William Carey', online).

Carey was by no means the only, nor the first missionary to India. The Portuguese were there from c.1500 and the Jesuits, including St Francis Xavier (from 1542) had been active for many decades.[43] Anglican clergy arrived as chaplains for the East India Company from 1614 but

missionary work was against Company policy. Missionaries were not even permitted to sail there on the Company's ships until the British Parliament intervened in 1813 by passing the Charter Act (Robert, online, 48).

This altered the conditions under which the E.I.C.

operated (McGrath, 2013, 274). Carey had to virtually hide in the hills of Bengal for five years, working and learning

the language, because he had no permit to enter the country. He made no converts for the first seven years.

Protestant missionaries, notably Danes and Germans, had been active in India since 1706, and the Moravians already had 120 missionaries there. When the British permitted it, the SPCK took over the

English work, and later the Church Missionary Society (CMS, founded in 1799) sent missionaries (from c.1814). The British started a training college in Calcutta, Fort William College, where Carey taught Indian languages for thirty years as well as translating the Bible into numerous local languages ('India', in ODCC). Between 1813 and 1877 other missionaries arrived: American Baptists, Swiss Calvinists, Scottish Presbyterians, German Lutherans, Americans, Danes and Canadians (McGrath, 2013, 274). Under the British raj English became a commonly spoken language. By an Act of the British Parliament in 1813, all denominations had freedom to operate in India, but were given no material assistance. Missionaries influenced the British to abolish child sacrifices and Suttee/Suti, a practice by which a man's widows were all expected to self-immolate upon his funeral pyre, but which the British outlawed 1826.

In 1947, when India became an independent country, numerous Protestant denominations in the South were united into the Church of South India ('Church of South India', in Bettenson (ed.), DCC, 467-470). Gradually, however, foreign doctors, nurses and teachers were no longer needed and, by 1980, the Indian government refused all of their visa applications.

(b) Anglican Missionary Work in India: Amy Beatrice Carmichael

Amy Carmichael (1867-1951) was a devout Presbyterian who was born in Belfast, Ireland, of Scottish ancestry. After her Keswick holiness conversion she worked among the poor of Belfast and wanted to become a missionary, believing that

was her calling. With Keswick's help she spent the

years 1893-94 with CMS in Japan but ill health forced her to return home. In 1895 Amy went to Ceylon/Sri Lanka and then to India for 55 years; never to return. In Dohnavur, Tamil Nadu, from 1901 she began to rescue girls from temple prostitution. In 1927 the Dohnavur Fellowship (a faith mission) was registered to rescue abandoned and needy children (Murray, in Anderson (ed.), BDCM, 1998,

116).

Queen Mary (Queen Elizabeth II's grandmother) supported her work in 1912 and helped fund a hospital in Dohnavur. Her children called her Amma (mother). A boy's home was added, although since 1982 baby boys must be adopted out. Now there are: 16 nurseries; a hospital; a school; a clock tower; about 500 girls and a bird-bath to mark Ammai's grave.

Amy Carmichael was a poet and prolific writer of devotional popular books. In the final decades of her long years of her suffering (when she was confined to her room

after a fall) she followed the English mystic known as St Julian of Norwich, who was probably an enclosed anchoress at St Julian's church at Norwich ('Julian of Nowich, c.1342-after 1413', in ODCC).

In 1924 Stephen Neill came to work with Amy and persevered for a year. She described their parting as "one of the sadest nights of my life" and wrote, "I long over him, miss him still and want him..." Stephen Neill wrote, "I gave my whole soul to Dohnavur" and "by January 1926 the darkness was complete" and "it took me many years to recover from the injuries and the scars are still there" (Tucker, 2016, 170ff, f/notes 23; 24). Her authoritarian model was extreme and she claimed that her power came directly from God Because Neill had a "hair-trigger temper" love could not survive so that, when he became Anglican bishop of the area, Amy severed her ties with that church (Tucker, 2016, 170-177).

Amy both pitied half-hearted Christians and feared the influence of worldly missionaries. Hers were required to be

dedicated and were not permitted to associate with outsiders (Tucker, 2016, 177). After India became independent, temple prostitution was outlawed in 1948 but Amy's Foundation continued in the Republic of India under the local Church of South India Diocese of

Tirunveli/Tinnevelly.

Amy founded the Sisters of the Common Life, a Protestant religious order devoted to celibacy. Her lengthy ministry in India was undergirded with Scripture and prayer "Her early dedication to holiness practices and her roots in the Keswick tradition helped to guide her strong will and determination in her mission to the children of southern India" (White, "'Ammai" of orphans and holiness author', online).

(c) The Church South India (CSI)

The Church of South India was formed by a union of Anglican, Congregational, Presbyterian and Methodist denominations on September 27, 1947, immediately after Indian Independence although negotians had begun two decades previously. Christians wished to be self-reliant, independent and more united in their witness to non-Christians (CSI Homepage, online).

(d) The Church of North India (CNI)

This Church was formed by the union of six Protestant churches in North India: Anglicans, Methodists, Presbyterians, Baptists, Bretheren and the Disciples of Christ. It has 1.3 million members, 3,500 congregations, and 26 dioceses. Negotiations and plans for the union took over twenty years. Founded in 1970, CNI reflects the growing nationalism of India in the post-colonial era and follows the example set 23 years earlier by Protestants in South India ('Church of North India', in Britannica, online).

(e) Conclusions to this section on India

In India, as elsewhere, Catholic missionaries reached foreign shores early and in relatively large numnbers and for extended periods. As was demonstrated in the Solomon Islands, single males had a greater chance of survival than the married couples usually sent by Protestant missions. In Africa and India, European governments directly or indirectly facilitated the missionary work of particular denominations, leaving permanent reminders of colonial history in their respective dominions.

Questions on Part i: India

(1) Why must baby boys be adopted out from the Dohnavur orphanage?

(2) How has India benefitted from missionary work and how has that work been a disadvantage?

<u>20.2: Part ii: China</u>

(a) James Hudson Taylor (1832-1905)

Hudson Taylor had some medical training before sailing for China in 1853. In 1865, he founded the China Inland Mission. It was an inter-denominational ministry, although mission stations were staffed according to denomination ('China Inland Mission' and 'Taylor, James Hudson', in ODCC). In China, Hudson married Maria Dyer (aged 21) whose late parents had been early missionaries to China. Being fluent in the Ningpo dialect she was a great help to Hudson. In their twelve years of marriage Maria gave birth to

seven or eight children, four of whom survived and became CIM missionaries (Piper, 2014, online).

Maria died of cholera in 1870 and in 1871, Hudson married Jennie Faulding who was a 28 year old CIM missionary. She gave birth to two children (Ernest and Amy) and they adopted another daughter. Jennie ministered to women, edited the Mission's magazine, China's Millions, organised the work of the mission and cared for Hudson in old age. She died in 1904 at age 61 years ('James Hudson Taylor', by Wholesomewords, online).

Hudson Taylor visited Australia in 1892 and two young sisters responded to his appeal for recruits. When they were murdered in China their widowed mother, Mrs Saunders, went in their place (Reed, 2007, 54).

The Boxer Rebellion, which raged against foreigners and Chinese Christians in 1900, was particularly tragic for CIM (now called Overseas Missionary Fellowship) as 58 of their adults, and 28 of their children, were killed (Piper, online, 5).

When Hudson Taylor died in 1905 (at age 73) the Mission had 300 mission stations, 825 missionaries and 25,000 Chinese Christians (Piper, online, 5). Although Catholic missionaries had practised 'indigenisation' - expecting missionaries to dress like the locals, eat like the locals and eat with the locals – Hudson Taylor applied this to Protestant missions. All CIM missionaries lived entirely 'by faith' (McGrath, 2013, 273ff). Hudson passed on the torch of faith and his policies enabled Chinese Christians to assume leadership, despite extreme persecution, especially during the Cultural Revolution of the 1960s. After c.1953, by which year all western missionaries had been expelled by the Communists, the church expanded rapidly, outstripping population growth (Hattaway, 2003, 16f). Chinese Christianity then became a power-house for evangelism (Word From Jerusalem, March 2015, Global Edition).

An estimate in 2011 places the number of China's Christians at 67,070,000 ('Global Christianity', Pew Research Centre's Forum on Religion and Public Life, Dec. 19, 2011, online).

<u>(b) Charles Thomas Studd (1860-1931)</u>

C. T. Studd captained the First XI cricket team at Eton College in 1876 and then captained the Cambridge University team. He and his two brothers were deeply influenced by their father, who had been converted during a 'Moody and Sankey Crusade' two years before his death, in 1879. After a conversion experience, in 1885, C.T. and his friend, Stanley Smith, led the famous 'Cambridge Seven' to China as missionaries with Hudson Taylor. They included: Montague Beauchamp, William Cassels, Dixon Hoste and Arthur and Cecil Polhill-Turner. Before leaving, however, the Cambridge Seven toured university campuses throughout Britain encouraging students to give their lives to missionary service

(The Travelling Team, 'C. T. Studd', online).

When Studd was twenty-five he inherited his father's fortune and prompty gave it to evangelists and missions. He married a Salvation Army missionary, Priscilla Livingstone Stewart, and together they gave away the last of his money (Tucker, 2004, 315) in obedience to Christ's command to the rich young ruler, "sell all that you have and give to the poor". Shortages became an opportunity for God to meet their needs. "God trusts us and is willing to leave his reputation in our hands," Studd said (Graves, MSL, online).

In 1894, after ten years in China, the Studds returned to Britain for health reasons. Then, in 1896-1897, C.T. toured American and British Universities for the newly formed Student Volunteer Movement where students flocked to his meetings and hundreds volunteered for overseas service (Tucker 2004, 315). In 1900, the family went to South India where Studd pastored an English-speaking congregation until 1906 (Bonk, in Anderson (ed.), BDCM, online).

Studd's final missionary call was to the Belgian Congo (now Zaire). Against his ailing wife's wishes and despite his own poor health (and contrary to all medical advice) he was determined to go. He left his wife with their four daughters, made an exploratory trip to Africas in 1910 and returned to found the Heart of Africa Mission (later called Worldwide Evangelization Crucade/WEC). In 1913 C. T. left with his assistant, Alfred Buxton. He returned home briefly in 1916, to obtain new recruits and found that his wife, much improved, was running the home-office. After all, Africa was in Priscilla's blood: her middle name was 'Livingstone'. Their daughter, Edith, joined Studd in Africa and married Alfred Buxton. Then another daughter, Pauline, and her husband, Norman Grubb, (C.T's successor and author of his biography, C.T. Studd, Cricketer and Pioneer [1933]), also joined them (Tucker, 2004, 316). Priscilla visited him in 1928 and died the next year (Ross, online).

To C.T., laziness was a sin in either natives or missionaries. He expected everyone to work eighteen hours a day, as he did. Prayer meetings were held at 4a.m. Studd had human failings too: in his old age he became cantankerous and unreasonable (Bonk, in Anderson (ed.), BDCM, 649).

Studd was noted for various sayings. One was :

"Some wish to live within the sound of Church or Chapel bell.

I want to run a rescue shop within a yard of hell" (Graves, online).

C. T. Studd was buried in Africa, having spent nineteen years soldiering on there - obedient to the task God had given him. Studd's life is an eternal rebuke to easygoing Christianity.

(c) Gladys Aylward (1902-1970)

Gladys Aylward, 'the small woman', was another fearless misssionary. Although the China Inland Mission accepted single women missionaries they would not accept Gladys because she found Chinese hard to learn, but she followed God's call, unaided. Gladys travelled by herself to China on

the Trans-Siberian Railway and by ship and by mule, to assist an older missionary, Mrs Jeannie Lawson, with her work. Together, Gladys and

Mrs Lawson renovated an old inn on a major caravan route to provide hospitality and to tell gospel stories at night.

Gladys began to rescue abandoned children, ending up with two hundred of them, as well as some fellow-workers. After Mrs Lawson died, Gladys was helped financially because the Mandarin of Yangchen employed her as his 'foot inspector', to implement the government's new policy banning the custom of binding women's feet. The Chinese called her Ai-weh-deh, 'the righteous one' (mylordkatie, 'Gladys Aylward - Missionary to China', online).

One faithful convert, her cook Yang, remained with Gladys throughout her ordeals. She had taken Chinese citizenship so, when the Japanese invaded China in 1938, she was reluctant to leave, but, because she had spied for the Chinese, the Japanese put a high price on her head. Therefore, with one hundred children, Gladys walked for twelve days through the mountains to the Yellow River, which a Christian soldier helped them to cross. Eventually they found a train to take them over the border into Siam and the safety of an orphanage. All two hundred children were saved but Gladys collapsed with fever and exhaustion (mylordkatie, 'Gladys Aylward - Missionary to China', online).

After returning to England for surgery in 1947 Gladys was prevented from reentering (communist) China but her mother had organised for her to travel widely in Britain, and the world, to speak about China (Tucker, 2016, 177). In 1957, she sailed to Taiwan where she preached the gospel, founded an orphanage and cared for orphans until the very day she entered Heaven on 1/1/1970 (Mylordkatie, 'Gladys Aylward - Missionary to China', online).

(d) The Cultural Revolution

The Communists had successfully expelled foreign missionaries by 1948 and rejected Vatican involvement within China so the local churches began to organise for themselves. In the 1950s Y. T. Wu developed the Three-Self Patriotic Movement, based upon self-governance, self-support and selfpropagation. The Communist government first sought to control the church but, by August 1966, repression and persecution of anything old (customs, culture, habits and ideas) led to a rampage of destruction and brutality known as the Cultural Revoution. This was led by the Red Guard and lasted a decade but as soon as Mao Zedung died (9/9/1976) members of the 'gang of four', who had masterminded the reign of terror, were arrested. This "opened the way to social, political and economic reconstruction" (McGrath, 2013, 339). Western style Christianity, Buddhism and Confucianism had all been cast aside but communism had proved to be dangerous and untrustworthy. The persecuted church had grown resilient and proved itself faithful. The many unofficial (underground) churches prospered in the ideological vacuum so that up to one third of China's people are now Christians and the Communist Party is ruthlessly tightening its grip on power.

(e) The Back to Jerusalem Movement

The Chinese 'Back to Jerusalem Movement' began in the 1940s through CIM and in the Northwest Bible Institute in remote Shaanxi Province, which had been founded by Alice and James Hudson Taylor II. Mark Ma was the leader of the movement and also the vice-principal of the Institute. The vision was to take the gospel back through the hardest to reach peoples: to evangelise in Tibet, the 'Stans' and all Hindu

and Muslim lands S-W of China and along the Silk Road(s) back towards Jerusalem. This early phase of the movement was stymied in August 1947 when China sealed its western

borders. Of the two male and five women missionaries arrested at the border a few, including Grace Ho, who had been dedicated to God as a baby, survived to old age

(Hattaway et al., 2003, 34ff).

Upon becoming a communist republic, China expelled all missionaries, destroyed churches and temples and persecuted Christians. "A curtain of silence descended across the nation" (Hattaway, 2003, 44). The State aimed to exterminate Christians, as it tried later, during the

Cultural Revolution (1966-1976) but leaders went underground or learnt valuable lessons during torture in prisons,

'refined as by fire'.

One brother, Simon Zo, release from prison in 1988 after 40 years, attended a meeting addressed by Brother Yun who was calling for a renewal of the vision. Simon Zo came forward to tell his story and he laid hands upon Brother Yun for its continuation so that the Movement gained strength in the 1990s under the leadership of Brother Yun, who is known as the Heavenly Man. Other leaders were Peter Xu Yongze and Enoch Wang. The latter was taught by the renowned Christian, Watchman Nee.

Brother Yun said:

"The best way for the Chinese Church to remain strong is to keep it motivated to reach out to the nations of the world. When believers focus on serving the Lord and reaching the lost, God blesses them and the church remains sharp."

Paul Hattaway has been instrumental in publicising the movement in the West through the book *"Back to Jerusalem"*. Also, in 2002, he and Brother Yun wrote "The Heavenly Man: The Remarkable True Story of Chinese Christian Brother Yun". Because of State repression many of the modern-wave leaders have left the country and the movement is working

away, secretly, quietly, like termites, wherever they can (Hattaway, 2003, 107). By accident, much of what communism has done has been positive for Christian missionary work: a highway has been constructed into Tibet, a unified language

has been created, literacy has expanded, living standards have been raised and superstitions and ancestor worship have been suppressed and the church learnt resilience, courage and reliance upon only God.

<u>Questions on Part ii: China</u>

(1) What aspects of Gladys Aylward's personality, history or activities are most memorable?

(2) Should C.T. Studd have given away all of his father's fortune and have gone to China penniless?

20.3. Part iii: East Asia

(a) Christianity in South Korea

In the 20th century, Ecclesia has made more remarkable growth in South Korea than in any other country so that now about 50% of the population may be Christian and Korea is sending out missionaries rather than receiving them. 'Why?' is an intriguing question. Prayer, unity, community, faith and teaching may be the answers.

Two American Protestant missionaries to Korea, Henry Appenzeller (1858-1902) and Horace Underwood (1859-1916) promoted education and so that Western religion was not shunned. Later the West was viewed with favour because it defeated Japan in WWII. (Japan, having annexed Korea in 1910, persecuted Christians and imprisoned and tortured pastors [Goforth, online]). From 1906 to 1917 there was a pentecostal style revival which began in Methodist and

Presbyterian churches with intense corporate prayer followed by the public confession of secret sins. In the year 1907, for example, 50,000 converts were added to the churches (Hattaway, 2003, 337; Goforth, online). "One of the reasons why the Korean Church is so strong and efficient is due to

Bible study. One year 1,400 Bible study classes were held, and 90,000 students were enrolled" (Goforth, online). When one man with a New Testament evangelised in his village the converts learnt that baptism was important but no one knew how it was done. They decided that each would go home and take a bath after which they would meet and form a congregation (Goforth, online).

From c. 1970, David Paul Yonggi Cho and his megachurch (of the Full Gospel denomination) and its prayer mountain had much to do with the expansion of Christianity (Hattaway, 2003, 95ff).

It is well known that pastors' three greatest temptations are 'gold, girls and glory' (that is, finances, females and fame' or, more bluntly, 'greed, lust and pride'). Even the great ascetic, Francis of Assisi, understood these traps. He regarded money as dung. He ordered his followers never to associate with women because (human nature being what it is) one thing leads to another, "no one may counsel them, travel alone with them or eat out of the same dish with them" (Galli, 2002, 95ff).

Unfortunately Yonggi Cho tried to help his son out of financial trouble in 2011, by buying stock from his son at three times their real value. He was found guilty of embezzling $US12 million of his church's money. In February, 2014 he was given a suspended sentence and his son, Hee-jun, was imprisoned (Moon, for Christianity Today, online). Yonggi Cho, then 78 years old and pastor of the world's largest church (and his son) had been ensnared. Christianity continues to flourish in South Korea and, in 2000, it sent out 8,103 missionaries throughout Asia (McGrath, 2013, 337). It may even reach into North Korea.

<u>(b) Burma/Myanmar and The Karen and Chin Tribespeople</u>

Rev. Adoniram Judson (1788-1850) and his new wife, Ann, set out from America as pioneer Congregationalist missionaries but were baptised by immersion upon arrival in India and

switched denominational allegiances before moving on, to Burma (Tucker, in Woodbridge (ed.), 1994, 12f). Felix Carey (the son of William Carey) and his wife were already in Burma when the Judsons arrived in Rangoon in 1813. Christian work in general was directed towards the Buddhist majority, largely in

'safe' territory controlled by the British, areas which expanded in size after the three Anglo-Burmese Wars (1824 to 1885) (Khup Za Go, online, Section B.3.online; Case, 2012, 49).

Rev. Judson was capable and dedicated. He immersed himself in the oral culture and had translated the whole Bible by 1834. By 1849, he had also compiled a Pali-Burmese Dictionary and a Burmese-English Dictionary before his death. He followed the Buddhist way of teaching: in little wayside shelters or 'zayats'. 'Zayat preaching' became central to Baptist evangelism throughout the nineteenth century" (Case, 2012,35). Ann Judson opened a school in 1821 although her health was poor following a still-birth (Tucker, in Woodbridge (ed.), 1994, 33). Through Ann's letters and journals the Judson's became local heroes as Americans experienced their griefs and triumphs and her memoirs were published in 1829 by James D. Knowles as Memoirs of Mrs. Ann H. Judson (Boston: Lincoln & Edmands, 1829).

The first Burmese to be baptised was U Naw, in 1823. Later the Judsons moved to Moulmein, the capital of the Karen/Keren semi-nomadic hill-people, where a revival was afoot. The conversion of the Karen, who today are largely Christian, is attributed to Ann and Adoniram Judson and another American Baptist missionary couple, George and Sarah Boardman. Keren conversions would best, however, be attributed to two Karen men: a tribal elder, A-Pyah Thee, whom George Boardman first called "the old sorcerer", and the first Karen whom Boardman baptised, Ko Tha Byu.

It seems probable that the Karen had previously had contact with Judaism because their monotheistic deity was Y'wa who was omnipotent, and omnipresent. A-Pyah Thee was the proud owner of a sacred book which he was given in about 1818. He believed that would some day it would be read to him. Even though his son managed to learn Burmese he could not read this book, so its secrets remained hidden. In April 1828 A-Pyah Thee heard that an American missionary couple was ministering in Tavoy, one hundred miles away, so he sent a delegation of thirty to ask the missionary to come. Boardman declined to go but gave them a tract in Burmese, which the elder's son was able to read. With his son and the tract the old man went around the village exhorting peole to adopt Christianity. Later they visited other villages (Case, 2012, 19f).

Twelve days later, three men made the long treck back to Tavoy, which coincided with the baptism of the Karen man, Ko Tha Byu, who had been requesting baptism for a long time. It was delayed because of his criminal past, but at the right time he was baptised by Boardman who then permitted him to go to the Karen village while one of the visiting trio stayed with the Boardmans to learn English. When old A-Pyag Thee and his book, with a large entourage, made the treck to Tavoy he was able to discover that his treasure was the English Book of Common Prayer, complete with the Biblical Book of Psalms (Case, 2012, 19f).

Boardman was mainly interested in evangelising the Buddhists of Burma, whose language he had learnt, although he had little success. Therefore he had declined many requests by numerous Karen villagers to visit them before he, his wife and their son, George Jnr. set out. They were welcomed by thousands, many of whom desired baptism. George was already ill when they arrived but he insisted in conducting the baptisms. He was buried in Burma.

In 1824 Adoniram was jailed for eighteen months for 'spying' for the British and in 1826 Ann and their daughter, Maria, died. Adoniram became deeply depressed and lay in the

jungle beside an open grave mourning for them for forty days. After recovering he found a great change throughout the land as the church grew (Tucker, in Woodbridge (ed.), 1994, 30-35).

Meanwhile, Sarah Boardman continued their work in education and, in 1834, she married Adoniram Judson ('Judson, Adoniram', in ODCC). After having eight children in ten years Sarah died (1845). While on furlough in America Adoniram met and married a younger woman, Emily Chubbock, who wrote stories about their missionary work. Adoniram died in 1850, leaving the translated Bible, a church, his wife, three chidren in Burma and others in the USA (Tucker, in Woodbridge (ed), 1994, 35). In 1899, Ann and Arthur Carsons were sent by the American Baptist Mission to minister among the Chin tribes-people. Although Arthur died in 1908, Ann Carsons continued her work until 1920. After Arthur's death, Herbert and Elizabeth Cope arrived in the Chin Hills. Herbert translated the New Testament into Tedim Chin (1931) and today the Chin (called the Zomi Chin) are the largest Christian group in Myanmar (Khup Za Go, online, Section B.3).

Persecution of Christians began in about 1838. Any local Christians who possessed books were beaten, jailed and threated with execution, fined, and/or forced to work for the Buddhist Temple in Rangoon (Case, 2012, 49, citing the American Baptist Magazine, 12/1838, 301-03; 5/ 1839, 101-7; 9/1839, 216; 4/1840, 80-81). Burma gained its independence from Britain in 1948 and has since endured much political turmoil, with tribal groups fighting for independence and communist insurgents who managed to install the Socialist Republic of the Union of Burma in 1962. Buddhism was declared the state religion c.1960. There is a strong history of persecuting religious minorities. When 'the Burmese Way to Socialism', a secular materialist philosophy took control in 1965, Christian schools and hospitals were nationalised, foreign missionaries were expelled by 1965 and Christian printing was curtailed (Khup za Go, online, Section IV).

Myanmar/Burma is strongly anti-colonialist, anti-British and anti-tourism. There are over 100 languages spoken but English, which could have been a unifying force, was dropped from the education system. This turned the country away from modernity when other Asians were trying to learn English to enhance progress. Of the three million Burmese Christians most are Baptists, followed by Roman Catholics. In the 1930s, Assemblies of God Chinese missionaries crossed the border and this is now the fastest growing denomination. Now, hundreds of native missionaries evangelise in the remote mountains.

In 1990 the National League for Democracy (NDL) won the first elections to be held between 1962 and 1990 but the NDL was annulled by the generals. The NDP leader, Aung San Suu Kyi, was imprisoned but there was a short perod of uneasy cooperation between the two with Suu Kyi as a figurehead. When her party won a landslide electoral victory in November, 2020, the military staged a coup and, early in 2021, Suu Kyi was re-arrested on fake charges.

Christians make up 8% of Burma's population but they are mainly etnic-minority peoples of 135 language groups. The many tribes include Mon, Shana, Moken, Nagas and Wa but the Chin, Karen/Keren, Kachin, Rawang, Lisu, Lahu and Lushai are largely Christian (Kauffman, 1990, 187) and are treated much as the Muslim Rohinga of Rakhine State are treated by the Buddhist majority. The headline in one newspaper in 2007 claimed that Burma "orders Christians to be wiped out" (Pattisson and State, in Telegraph Media Group Ltd., 21/1/2007). Both Muslims and Christians in Burma are struggling for fundamental rights of freedom of religion and the Burmese government flouts international law, democracy and even its own constitution.

<u>(c) Cambodia and Laos</u>

In the 21st century, Christianity in Laos and Cambodia is growing quickly. Christians in Laos are under 2% of the

populations, but 3.7% in Cambodia and growing at 8.8% per year ('Cambodians Turning to Christianity', Phnom Penh Post, online). These nations, with Vietnam, were once colonies of France and together were known as French Indo-China so that Catholicism is their strongest Christian denomination. All three countries have been through much suffering and political turmoil: during wars of independence, through the Vietnam Civil War and then through communist insurgency and/or repressive and

persecuting communist governments. All missionaries were expelled from Cambodia in 1965 but returned in the 1970s. During the years of genocide by the Pol Pot regime, middle-class and educated people, those 'tainted' by the

West (including Christians) were killed and others were forced into the countryside to work as slave labourers (Phnom Penh Post, 'Cambodians Turning to Christianity',

online). In the years around 1980 the population actually fell. Before the genocide there were 10,000 Christians but barely 200 survived the genocide (OMF, 'The Growth of Christianity in Cambodia', online, 2016, online).

At present the population of Cambodia of over sixteen million people is 97% Buddhist but Christianity is outpacing Islam (Coggan, 21/1/2016, online). One and a half million people live in the capital, Phnom Penh. With nearly 1,000 births per day and only 267 deaths the population increases by around 267,500 people per year. Christians are currently a small percentage but "Cambodians are flocking to the faith" especially the former Khmer Rouge (Coggan, 21/1/2016, online). They followed Pol Pot and killed 2 million people and destroyed churches and Buddhist temples, but do not wish to die with such sins on their conscience (Burke, 'Khmer Rouge embraces Jesus', The Guardian 24/10/2004, online).

About 1.5% of Cambodians are Catholics but, under indigenous leadership, Christianity is rapidly becoming Cambodianised, with ten large evangelical churches in the country aiming to have Christians in every village by 2021

('Cambodians Turning to Christianity', Phnom Penh Post, online). The countries of the former Indo-China are amongst the poorest in the world, although the communist government in Vietnam is relatively successful.

20.4: Conclusions

Over many centuries missionaries have been sent to East Asia and indeed many were martyred there: but, overall, the rewards for their efforts have been less than those in Africa.

In East Asian each nation is different and nothing is static. Nations with the least government restrictions and social hostilities are Japan and the Philippines, although

zenophobia has limited Japanese interest in Christianity. In countries with low government resistance to Christianity, such as South Korea and Cambodia, the Church is steadily expanding. In countries where nationalism is rising, such as India and Burma/Myanmar, it is becoming increasingly dangerous for nationals to be Christians. In yet other nations, such as China and Pakistan, nationals and even foreign Christians are targetted, persecuted and/or killed.

<u>Questions on Part iii: East Asia:</u>

(1) What aspects of Christianity made it so successful in South Korea?

(2) What factors are contributing to the growth of Christianity in Asia?

Chapter 21

The 20th Century

Azusa Street, War, Depression and More War

<u>21.1. Anointed for Burial?</u>

Before the Great War began in 1914, two remarkable events took place. (1) In 1901, the Pentecostal outpouring (with glossolalia) had been evidenced by a young woman named Agnes Ozman, a Bible student of the former Methodist minister, Charles Parham, in Topeka, Kansas. Rev. Parham's itinerant preaching in the western states resulted in a following of 25,000 people before 1908 (Bartleman, 1925/1980, 15).

An African-American, William Seymour, became Parham's disciple and, eventually, the leader of the first established Pentecostal church (1906-1922) which met in an old warehouse on Azusa Street, in that great ethnic melting-pot, the city of Los Angeles (Plate 19.1). This church notionally marks the start of Pentecostalism in America, and indeed, from here on it became a fixture in the Christian landscape (Tomkins, 2003, 220).

Prior to this, 'Holiness' had been the main renewal movement in America, with Wesley's doctrine of 'entire sanctification/second blessing' being embraced. This was often referred to as a 'Pentecost' experience but 'Holiness' churches were frequently opposed to glossolalia and held aloof from the new Los Angeles movement. Pentecostalism was a major point of division, for example, a prominent Los

Angeles pastor, Phineas Bresee, who had founded the Pentecostal Church of the Nazarene in 1895 as a Holiness church, opposed the Azusa Street revival, which he regarded as a repudiation of the second blessing (Bartleman, 1925/1980,

xiv and 205-08). Breece wrote of this revival: "it is of small account, being insufficient both in numbers and influence... what little influence it has seems to have been mostly harmful" (Bartleman, 1925/1980, 206f, citing Bresee, The Nazarene Messenger XI.24 (December 13, 1906). Today, there are over 250 million Pentecostals in over one million churches and 300 million Charismatics in every denomination, worldwide (Bartleman, 1925/1980, xi).

(2) In 1904-05 the last of the great Welsh revivals occurred, covering Wales with Holy-Spiritled mountain-side prayer meetings and evangelistic gatherings. Many Welsh Revivals, both farreaching and limited, had occurred: in 1739, 1762, 1791, 1817, 1840, 1848-9 and 1860 (Phillips, 1860/1989/2002, 4; Tomkins, 2003, 220). Evan Roberts was the main leader of the Welsh Revival of 1904-05.

Evan Roberts, was visited by, and continued contact with, the Pastor of the First Baptist Church of Los Angeles, Joseph Smale, from 1906 so that the great event at Azusa Street and the Welsh Revival influenced each other (Bartleman, 1925/1980).

<u>21.2. A Climate for Pentecostalism</u>

Pentecostal churches and denominations date from 1906 although Pentecostal manifestations have a much longer history and appeared in various revival periods from the 1st century onwards. The informality and freedom created by the Great Awakenings provided a climate for the growth of American Pentecostal churches. The, now worldwide, movement is still strong in the U.S.A.

Pentecostalism resulted in new churches, such as the Assemblies of God and the Church of the Foursquare Gospel (which stood squarely on conversion, healing, sanctification and glory). Pentecostalism spread, and soon became the

fastest-growing denomination(s) of the 20th century, as will be shown. In England, meetings began in about 1907 and,

in 1915, in Ireland, a group of small meetings were

formed into the Elim Foursquare Gospel Alliance under George Jeffreys. Elim Foursquare is still a formidable denomination. Between 1925 and 1935 a great impetus was provide in Britain by the preaching of Stephen and George Jeffreys and their nephew, Edward Jeffreys ('Pentecostal churches', in ODCC).

Plate 21.1.
Church in Azusa St., L.A. 1907. Public domain.

21.3. Principles of Revival

Certain 'principles of revival' emerged in Wales and Los Angeles. Some people gave themselves to deep intercessions, day and night. Many had a burden for the lost, believing that: "souls are born into the kingdom only through prayer" (Bartleman, 1925/1980, 35) and that such prayer must include repentance, indeed *the depth of revival will be determined exactly by the depth of the spirit of repentance*" (Bartleman, 1925/1980, 22).

People were prepared to cross denominational boundaries in unity (party spirit, sectarianism and prejudice must be eliminated). Services were not regimented and might last many hours. There was an expectation of good things from God. Spontaneous giving of money was a feature. Home prayermeetings and front-porch meetings featured: "Revival *almost always begins among the laity*" (Bartleman, 1925/1980, 21; 30). The sick were prayed for and the walls were decorated with discarded crutchers and canes. There had to be unity in

the city between renewalist groups. Azusa Street began its decline as cold, hard-hearted zeal and fleshly enthusiasm replaced divine love and tenderness of the Spirit (Bartleman, 1925/1980, 159).

21.4. War

As previously noted, the 19th century saw both Christians and humanists concerned with social issues. These included women's voting rights, relocating orphans into the community, banning child labour, providing universal education and equality for women in universities and for Dissenters and/or Catholics in society and politics. Many of these concerns were still present in the 20th century. Politicians were grappling with poverty at home, carrying 'the white man's burden' overseas and demands for independence for dominions and colonies. Compared with previous centuries, the 20th century saw fewer European people attended church but more were on the mission field, preaching to people of colour and making converts (Tomkins, 2003, 219).

Australia was born as a nation in 1901 amid considerable optimism, but within thirteen years the new nation was embroiled in a terrible war on the other side of the world, ostensibly to save 'Mother England'. One in five Australians enlisted, including many fathers with large families to support (or leave behind).

Total war-casualties were horrendous. *"Within months, one and a half million people were dead"* .... *"The war left the west reeling and shattered."* (Tomkins, 2003, 222). The idea of liberal optimism was dead: the idea of moral progress was buried alive with the fallen. Christian religion and spirituality in Europe has never recovered, as Chapters 22 and 23 will note.

<u>21.5. Christian Tragedy in Turkey</u>

On 25/4/1915 Allied troops landed in Gallipoli, Turkey, in a doomed attempt to march on

Constantinople/Istanbul. That same day the persecution of Armenian and Greek populations and other non-Muslim ethnic groups in Turkey began with the deportation of Armenian intellectuals, journalists and leaders from Istanbul to Ankara; by foot. The persecution of Christian minorities quickly expanded, resulting in much suffering, and, was exacerbated by deliberate slaughter so that over amillion-and-a-half Armenians. Many thousands of other Christians did not survive (McGrath, 2013, 287f; Campbell, Modern Christian Martyrs, 2000, Ch. 2).

Armenians had often looked to Christian Russia for assistance, which caused Turkey to try to move them as far from the Russian border as possible; in forced marches without food or water. Their villages were burnt behind them.

After the Communist Revolution (6/11/1917) and the murder of the Russian Czar and his family, Leninist ideology, which opposed all religions, took hold and, in any case,

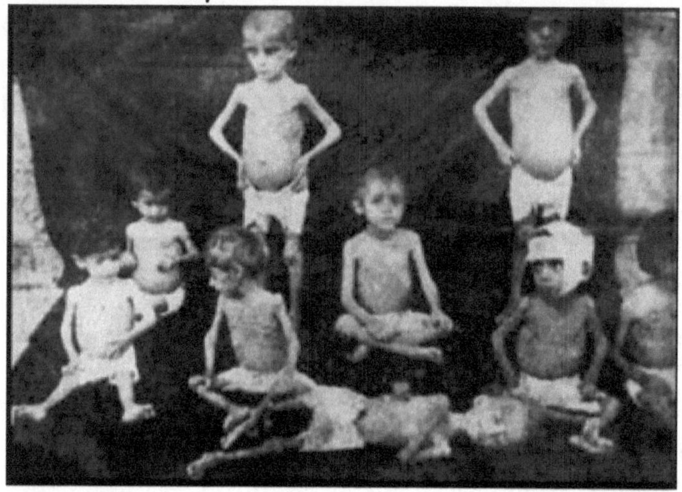

Plate 21.2.
Starving children collected by the Committee of the Middle East, Kharput, Turkey. Photograph by Maria Jacobsen. Public domain.

Russia withdrew from World War I, signing for peace on 3/3/1918. Homeless, starving and dying Armenians were friendless, lost in the fog of war (McGrath, 2013, 288f).

Hitler would later use similar techniques, having learnt that actions committed far away and in wartime did not attract much attention. He seems to have assumed that "his own program of genocide woud not attract international condemnation" (McGrath, 2013, 302).

21.6. Three Jewish Intellectuals Who Shook Christendom

Some of the greatest minds of their age were relatively assimilated European Jews whose ideas and ideologies shook the Christian world on both sides of the Atlantic. They were Karl Marx (1818-1883) the ideaologue behind socialism which produced Russia's atheistic totalitarian communism; Albert Einstein (179-1955) who rewrote the textbook of all previous scientific knowledge and Sigmund Freud (1856-1939) the psychiatrist who first developed psychanalyis. Freud's theories about unconscious motivations, human self and sexuality challenged Christian beliefs about God, humanity and morality. The theories of these three radical thinkers further troubled a world torn apart by wars and economic disasters and helped to spell the end of Christendom through the rampant growth of skepticism and atheism.

21.7. Jews in Europe

In the 19th century, Russian Jews had experienced hundred of pogroms (vicious attacks). These even continued into the 20th century: for example in 1903 and 1905 in Kishinev (now in Moldova) there were two pogroms in which sixty-six Jews in total died and many hundreds of houses were looted (Gilbert, 2007, 10). Because of such pogroms, which were widespread, thousands fled westward into Europe, emigrated to the U.S.A., or walked, overland, to their ancestral homeland, now Israel.

The Jews of the British Empire fought beside their gentile fellow-soldiers in both World Wars. Eight Jews won Britain's Victoria Cross in WWI (Gilbert, 2007, 30). Jewish graves can be recognised in any British Commonwealth War Cemetery by the Star of David on their headstones, for example in the military cemetery on Mt Scopus, Jerusalem, where they lie side-by-side with their comrades. Buried here are 2,180 British, 143 Australians, 50 South Africans, 34 New Zealanders, 40 British West Indians, 3 Turks, 5 Italians, 16 Germans and 60 whose nationalities could not be identified (Gilbert, 2007, 55). This did not, however, endear the Jews to the wider world, except to the ANZACs (Australian and New Zealand Army Corp) who tended to respect 'brothers in arms'.

German Jews fought in WW I for Germany but even having won the Iron Cross earned them no favours from Hitler but Europe had a long history of killing Jews and Hitler's anti-Semitism was in keeping with the tenor of the age:

"Jews all over the world were made the scapegoats for the inflation of the 1920s, the Wall Street crash of 1929 and the ensuing word-wide depression" (Bacon, Illustrated Atlas of Jewish Civilization, 2003, 155).

Plate 21.3.   The Road from Bethlehem to Jerusalem. Photograph: Ian Finnin, 2018.

21.8. Tribute to the ANZAC Light Horsemen

In WWI, General Allenby led troops of the British Empire in Palestine. Throughout 1917 they fought Turks and Germans

up from Egypt through the Levant (Transjordan, Palestine [now Israel] and Syria). On October 31, just over one hundred years ago, the famed 4th Battalion of the Australian Light Horse (recently withdrawn from the disasterous invasion of Turkey, at Gallipoli) had successfully charged the Turkish garrison at Beersheba and taken the town and its ancient wells.

This daring raid opened the way north, straight up to the Holy City, Jerusalem. Providentially, the Balfour Declaration was signed on that very day (Hamilton, 2004, 143). The British Foreign Secretary, Mr (later an Earl) Arthur Balfour, signed a letter to the Jewish Leader in Britain, Chaim Weizmann, to indicate that a Jewish homeland in Palestine was favoured. The letter was delivered to Weizmann on November 4, 1917 (BBC 29/ 11/2001, In Depth). In part it read: "His Majesty's government views with favour the establishment in Palestine of a home for the Jewish people, and will use their best endeavours to facilitate the achievement of this object" (from the Balfour Declaration, Gilbert, 2007, 27).

"Weitzman pulled the Zionists through a brief window of opportunity fated never to reoped again" (Tomkins, 2003, 139).

The ANZAC Light Horsemen fought on past Beersheba and made it possible for the British to fulfil Balfour's promise in that General Allenby walked through the Jaffa Gate to receive the keys of Jerusalem on December 11, 1917.

One British soldier wrote of later capturing "Meggido by 7:30a.m., Nazareth by 2:30 in the afternoon" (Wood, 1996, 30f). The ANZACs, Indians, British and others fought on, North to Damascus, after which the Ottoman war-effort collapsed and Turkey called for an Armistice. Britain was given a mandate over the Holy Land, but it was a 'hot-potato', so for how long would the mandate last?

Plate 21.4. Wilderness terrain near Jericho. Photograph: Ian Finnin, 2018.

As the weeks before the creation of the State of Israel in May, 1948 were to show, Britain did not use her "*best endeavours*" and Israel's independence came with hard fought battles, with Britain appearing to assist the Arabs (probably because Arabs controlled the world's oil supplies).

21.9. Churchill in the Holy Land

After WWI, in 1922, Winston Churchill was sent to Palestine by the British P.M., David Lloyd George, where he received petitions from all of the stake-holders and interviewed them. Churchill was impressed with the Jews' enthusiasm and achievements in a short time but saw that

their security was precariousd and that the Arabs were all violently hostile to new immigrants, especially any Jews from Russia who were possibly Bosheviks (Communists). The Arabs demanded the renunciation of the Balfour

promise. Churchill could not imagine a one-state solution working if Arabs and Jews had an equally representative parliament (Gilbert, 2007, 66, 72 and 74). In 1921, there were

no Jews East of the Jordan River (soon to become Transjordan) but 600,000 Arabs and only 83,000 Jews in the future Israel: although immigration would eventually change those figures (Gilbert, 2007, 51).

Churchill had faith in a future Jewish state. While there, he told them:

"I am myself perfectly convinced that the cause of Zionism is one which carries with it much that is good for the whole world, and not only for the Jewish people, but that it will also bring with it prosperity and contentment and advancement to the Arab population of this country." (Gilbert, 2007, 62). The issues with which Churchill was confronted in Jerusalem in 1922 are still live issues after nearly a century.

> *The Biblical four horsemen of the apocalypse - pestilence, famine, war and death, reappeared in the modern world."*

21.10. The Great Depression

An economic collapse, the worst depression in world history, began in 1929. With the American 'Wall Street Crash' people lost faith in the future of the economy. Despondency and hunger gripped the world for six years, except for subsistence and barter economies. German suffering provided the propaganda platform which enabled Hitler to rise to power and the Jews were scapegoated by the populace and government as they were involved with the Russian Communists (the enemy) and the financial sector of Europe.

21.11. World War II

In a matter of decades, the 20th century was once again involved in war. World War II pre-occupied the developed world in preparing, fighting and recovering from conflict for half a century. Allied troops were once again fighting in the Holy Land.

Hitler's meglomania and Jew-hatred was unleashed upon a stunned world with mass executions as soon as Poland was invaded (Bacon, 2003, 169). Jews were rounded up in every Nazi-occupied country and from every Mediterranean islandthat Germany seized, supposedly to be sent to 'work camps'. Instead, six million Jews were killed by shooting-squads and trucked into concentration camps, or were worked to death in work-camps (such as Auschwitz III, in Poland, and Dachau, in Germany), or were killed in gas chambers with Zyclon B (poison gas) in six extermination camps. In recent decades a Catholic priest, Patrick Desbois, co-founder of Yahad-In

Unum, has found about 800 forgotten and unrecorded mass graves of Roma and Jews in Eastern Europe, so that the figure of six million may be an underestimate. Despite attacks on his methology, the United Nations and Yad VaShem acknowledge Yahad-In Unum as *"the leading research organization investigating the mass execution of Jewish and Roma people in Eastern Europe between 1941 and 1944"* (United Nations press release, November 2, 2012).

The Nazis used six extermination camps, all in Poland, built between 1941 and 1942 for one primary purpose: extermination. They were Chelmno, Treblinka, Sobibor, Belzec, Majdanek and Birkenau (Auschwitz). Hitler's chief intention (the 'Final Solution') was the elimination of all Jews: from Germany; Europe; the Holy Land and the world.

Mechanical means were trialled and refined for this purpose and Jewish slave labourers were forced to carry it out, sometimes even on their own relatives and neighbours.

Gypsies and homosexuals were also exterminated. The disabled were killed until the churches objected (McGrath, 2013, 299-302). Nazi treatment of Jews was the Shoah, the Holocaust (meaning a whole burnt offering).

(The cattle truck, in Plate 21.5, is marked 'Munchen' [Munich]. It had been used to transport Jews to and from concentration camps in Poland and was left on a siding but donated to Israel after the fall of Communism in Poland. It is now a Holocaust memorial at Yad Vashem).

Other nations need not be judgemental as Europe and Britain had a long history of killing Jews. When U. S. President Roosevelt convened the Evian Conference on Jewish Refugees, in July, 1938, Hitler offered German Jewish refugees to the rest of the world but the world was indifferent and many sealed their borders. Canada, the U.S. and Australia refused to take any (Gutman et al., 1988, 128f). Britain eventually accepted many children who arrived on 'Kindertransport' ships. Many Jews escaped Germany illegally or were helped by relatives abroad but most were trapped, or, like Anne Frank's family, did not flee far enough from Germany.

During WW II 25,000,000 Soviet citizens died, out of the total of 60,000,000 dead (MacMillan, 2009, online). Across the world, great cities (like Kiev, Warsaw, Berlin, Dresden, Tokyo and Hiroshema) had been reduced to rubble.

<u>21.12. What was "The Final Solution"</u>

The expression in full is "the Final Solution to the Problem of the Jews". The very existence of the Jewish people was a problem that had to be solved, in Hitler's opinion. Eradication was his solution. There is no doubt that, had his kingdom, the Third Reich, continued, all Jews would have been exterminated.

<u>21.13. Righteous From Among the Nations</u>

Hundreds of families and individuals tried to save Jews and some died for doing so. Many of these "righteous gentiles" were non-religious or were Japanese, Hindus, or whatever. Relatively few Christians loved their neighbour as themselves; despite almost 2,000 years of gospel teaching. Princess Alice, the Duke of Edinburgh's mother, who became an Orthodox nun and who was profoundly deaf, was one of them and the Dutch Ten Boom family are well-remembered. Perhaps that is because Corrie Ten Boom survived the concentration camp and travelled the world to speak about forgiveness and reconciliation and a film made at Mrs Ruth Graham's suggestion, The Hiding Place, dramatised their story.

The whole area around the French village of Chambon-sur-Lignon, its citizens and Pastor Trocmé and Pastor Theis of the Reformed Church of France, cooperated to provide refuge for 5,000 Jews and anti-Nazis when the pro-Nazi (Vichy) government under Marshall Petain controlled Southern France. The local people often escorted Jews along the old Hueguenot escape routes into Switzerland (Sauvage, online) and a Quaker organisation AFSC (American Friends Service Committee) was very active, in providing food for those interned in camps and in rescuing Jewish children.

After the German occupation in November, 1942, the two pastors and a school principal were arrested so Madam Magda Trocmé took over the leadership. The men were released after 28 days but on June 29, 1943, Pastor Trocmé's cousin, Daniel Trocmé, a teacher, and eighteen students were arrested. Daniel Trocmé, the local doctor and five of the students were killed by the Nazis. The area was liberated by soldiers of the Free French on September 2/3, 1944 ('Le Chambon-sur-Lignon', in Holocaust Encyclopedia, online).

If Christians permit themselves to think about the Holocaust for very long they will be confronted with the agonising question: "how would I have acted if I had been in their shoes?" "After the Shoah it is no longer acceptable just to call yourself a Christian. Now you must prove it" (Smith, in Rittner, Smith and Steinfeldt (eds), 2000, 238).

21.14. Jan Karski (1914-2000)

Jan Karski was one gentile who tried very hard to make a difference. In 1942 this Catholic former Polish soldier became a clandestine diplomat for the Polish government-in-exile and the Polish Underground.

He entered the Warsaw Ghetto, which was full of starving and dying Jews, and was begged by its Jewish leaders to take messages to Allied leaders. He also entered

a concentration camp, disguised as a Ukrainian Militiaman, where he saw Jews being beaten, stabbed and crammed into cattle trucks for deportation. In England he met Polish leaders and British Foreign Secretary Anthony Eden. They were not interested. Karski secretly met the

American President, who at least established a War Refugee Board. No military action resulted from Karski's

tireless efforts to save Jews. Dr Karski became an academic in America and married a Jewish dancer and choreographer, Nina, who had lost all her family in the

Shoah. At age 81 she jumped to her death from their balcony, unable to sustain her despair. Yad VaShem awarded Jan Karski "Righteous Among the Nations" status and he received honorary Israeli citizenship. [Information is from Michael T. Kaufman, 'Jan Karski Dies at 86; Warned West About Holocaust', N.Y. Times July 15, 2000; and 'Jan Karski', United States Holocaust Memorial Museum, Washington, D.C., online].

21.17. Short and Longer Term Conclusions

World War II was a disaster for world Jewry and for Christendom (that is, the state-churches). In the Third Reich this meant the Catholic Church, which remained officially neutral although under Pope Piux XII's policy (1939-58) of 'justice and charity' the Vatican did not prevent nuns, priests and other individuals from secretly helping Jews: and many did so (Marrus, 'Understanding the Vatrican During the Nazi Period', in Rittner, Smith and Steinfeldt (eds), 2000, 127ff). Basically the Catholic Concordat with Hitler (the Reichskonkodat of July 20, 1933) meant 'leave us alone and we will leave you alone', which neutralised any Catholic opposition to Hitler, although he repeatedly vioated the treaty (Downey (ed.), 2013, 502).

Many Lutherans were patriotic Germans who became Nazis, although some Christians became part of the Confessing Church which withdrew from the state system. The history of Nazism, and its legacy, belongs to Christians of all denominations (Bergen, in Rittner, Smith and Steinfeldt (eds), 2000, 48).

World War II had accelerated the decline of the old European empires and the rise of the 'super powers' (U.S.A., U.S.S.R. and now China). The mid 20th-century was one of the most difficult periods for the world, ever, and for the Jewish people in particular (MacMillan, 2009, 2). Older Jewish people try to rejoice in their children and grandchildren but they cannot forget the siblings, children, parents and grandparents who were deliberately killed. The Holocaust (the Shoah) is the greatest blight on modern European society: and it happened in the heart of Christendom.

It is a dreadful secret that 25% of Jews in the camps committed suicide and that Jews who survived the Shoah still continue to die by suicide. Jan Karski's wife, Nina, (noted above) was one example. Another was Ági (Agnes), the

mother of teenage diarist Eva Hayman. Agi died with a photograph of her daughter beside her; probably suffering from survivor's guilt (Judah Marton [ed.] 1988).

A recent study (in 2017), that has shocked the Israeli medical profession, found that Holocaust survivors are almost

three times more likely to attempt suicide than their age-peers in Israel. In oldage, survivors become impoverished, are no

longer heroic or 'hungry for life'. They relive their trauma and tend towards depression (Tamara Traubmann in HaAretz 19/8/2005, online).

After Hitler's suicide, the Pacific War was brought to a quick end by the United States with the dropping of an atomic bomb on each of two Japanese cities, Hiroshema and Nagasaki. The end of WW II resulted in an arms race in such weapons by the super-powers, and in the enduring threat of mass destruction.

<u>Questions:</u>

(1) Why is October 31, 1917 remembered for the Balfour Declaration more than the capture of Beethsheba by the ANZACs?

(2) Why might Poland have given Israel the cattle car (in Plate 21.5)?

Chapter 22
Post-war Events

22.1. After WW II

Many millions of ethnic Germans were expelled from Poland and elsewhere, and their women were raped by Red soldiers and others. Two million German women had abortions each year from 1945 to 1948. Millions of children were just abandoned (MacMillan, 2009, online).

After World War II, behind the Iron Curtain, Joseph Stalin (d.1953) "purged hundreds of thousands of Russian Orthodox nuns and priests in an attempt to destroy religious belief" (Robert, 2009, 68; McGrath, 2013, 304f). Hundreds of churches were blown up or burnt down. Atheism reigned. Twenty-two million ordinary Russians and Poles were killed, mainly by starving, imprisoning or working them to death in concentration camps.

WW II was followed by the Cold War. The democratic West and its allies formed one bloc: Russia, its satellite states (with Communist China in the background) formed another. Each feared and distrusted the other and occasionally fought or came close to hostilities (as in the Berlin blockade 1948/49; the Korean War 1950/53; the Bay of Pigs crisis 17//4/1961; the Hungarian uprising in 1956; the Cubal missile crisis of 16-28/10/1962 and the Vietnam War of 1/11/1955-30/4/1975). With the fall of the Soviet Union by October, 1990, symbolised by the destruction of the Berlin Wall on November 9, 1989,[44] the West was able to relax a little.

Plate 22.1.
St Basil's Church, Moscow. Photo: D. Campbell, 1990.

The Russian Orthodox Church, which had been decimated by communism and Stalinism, was given its status and any remaining property back and there was a brief window of democracy in the days of 'glasnost' and 'perestroika' although the economy of the USSR was in ruins (c.1989). Since then fledgling democracy has given way to nationalism under Russia's long-term leader, President Vladimir Putin, who was secretly and illegally baptised as an infant and who has joined forces with the Orthodox Church to the mutual benefit of both in restoring Russia's national pride. In 1989 only three of Moscow's Orthodox churches were functioning. St Basil's Cathedral was closed, even to tourists, but now the bells of St Basil's are ringing out the call to prayer once again. From c.1990, a trickle of Jews were released from their bondage behind the 'iron curtain' as the hard-fought 'Let My People Go' campaign by the West for Soviet Jews to emigrate to Israel bore fruit. Over one million Jews have now made that journey.

"The days are coming says the Lord when men will no longer say 'the Lord who brought the children of Israel up out of the Land of Egypt' but they will

say 'the Lord who brought them up out of every land where he had scattered them' (Jer, 16:14; 23:7).

<u>22.2. A Jewish State Was Established After World War II</u>

The occupation and disarmament of Germany and Japan were the first post-war tasks for the Allies, closely followed by family reunification, relocation and permanent resettlement. These needs were the most critical for the emaciated Jewish survivors still in the camps but with nowhere to go. At least the sympathy of the free world was on their side. On November 29, 1947 a majority in the United Nations voted in favour of a homeland in Palestine for the Jewish people and in May the following year the State of Israel was born.

After their conquests in the Middle East in WW I the League of Nations gave Britain a mandate to govern the area but the task was beyond Britain's capacity or desire. From 1939, under Arab pressure, Britain restricted Jewish immigration into mandated Palestine, turning boats back and relocating Jews to the island of Cyprus. The immigrant ship 'Struma' sank, drowning 769 Jewish refugees. A crisis came when the British navy rammed a refugee-ship re-named 'Exodus' near Haifa and deported its concentration-camp survivors back to Germany (Lourie, in Avi-Yonah (ed.), 2001, 329).

Soon after the war, on 27th November, 1947, the United Nations voted to partition Palestine into a Jewish state and an Arab state. They have quarrelled over the boundaries ever since. Israel's recreation as a state on 14th May, 1948, was a great miracle.

"A people without land, kings, princes or temple for two thousand years, dispersed among all nations, a people mercilessly persecuted down through the ages and repeatedly threatened with
extermination policies, culminating in the final solution (of the Nazis) of the most recent past - this people scattered like 'dry bones' throughout the world, has overnight been reassembled as a nation and has become visible as a state"
(Schlink, 1987, 71).

<u>22.3. Arab-Israel Hostilities</u>

(i) <u>British Withdrawal</u>: In 1928 Trans-Jordan was carved off as a homeland for Palestinians (who are 80% of Jordan's population) and a member of the Saudi Arabian royal family was invited to become its king.

Despite local opposition, the British Mandate continued to govern the remainder until November 27, 1947 when the vote for partitioning the remainder into two states was passed by the United Nations. From then on the Mandate was a 'lame duck' administration as the British prepared to leave while abstaining from maintaining law and order. The previously simmering Jewish-Arab hostilities increased and each side secretly prepared for war. The British flag was finally lowered at midnight on May 14/15, 1948.

(ii) A <u>Nation is Born in a Day</u>: On May 14 David Ben Gurion had declared the birth of the State of Israel as five Arab nations (Egypt, Jordan, Syria, Lebanon and Iraq) were attacking it. Britain withdrew on May 15 and war raged for two months, with 39 different operations. The Jews lost the Old City and Mount Scopus with its university and hospital. The United Nations General Assembly (in a resolution on December 11, 1948 and a vote on Dec. 9, 1949) and the Roman Catholic Church (which opposed Jewish statehood) demanded that Jerusalem should come under International control and the Vatican launched a propaganda campaign against Israel (Crombie, 1991, 228, citing Sacher, Vol.1, 1979, 433). Few expected Israel to survive but it did so, at the cost of 6,373 lives: 2,000 of them civilians.[45]

<u>22.4. Post-war Immigration/Aliyah</u>

(i) <u>Holocaust survivors</u>: These were the first olim (immigrants/returnees) because Israel was established as a homeland and as a refugee for persecuted Jews. It was they who fought the invading armies in the 1948 war.

(ii) <u>Yemenite Olim</u>: A remarkable aliyah occurred between June, 1949 and September, 1950 when 49,000 people, virtually the entire Jewish population of Yemen, walked into the British Port of Aden seeking help to repatriate. The subsequent airlift by British and American planes was officially called Operation On Wings of Eagles (from Ex.19:4) but popularly known as Operation Magic Carpet.

(iii) <u>Iraqi Olim</u>: An airlift of 119,000 Jewish immigrants from Iraq, called Operation Ali Baba, took place in 1950 and 1951.

(iv) <u>Ethiopian Jews</u>: In 1975, the Ethopian Jews, whose Judaism is of a very ancient type, were accepted as the lost tribe of Dan. They immigrated to Israel in various waves between 1934 and 1990. In Operation Moses, in Novemer, 1984, 8,000 people made aliyah in 45 days, but Operation Solomon was even larger and quicker. In May 1991, 34 El-Al planes evacuated 14,200 people in a non-stop shuttle. Five babies were born in-flight (Skolnik, in Avi-Yonah (ed.), 1987/2005, 352). For humanitarian and family reunion reasons the Falash Mura are also being accepted; but more slowly. These are Jews whose forebears were forced or coerced into converting to Christianity and they are now expected to convert to normative Judaism. Genetic testing has now demonstrated that Ethiopian Jews were, in fact, descended from converts to ancient Judaism ('Origins of Falasha Jews', online). Although they are devout Jews, their genetics do not accord closely with other Jewish populations.

(v) <u>Russian and other Soviet Jews</u>: Before the fall of Communism in 1989, Israel and the democratic world waged a long campaign under the slogan "let my people go" to persuade the Soviet system to permit Jews to make aliyah. Many Jews suffered in prisons and in Siberia for their protests and dissent.

(vi) <u>Cochin/Kochi Jews, Kerela State</u>: These South-Indian Jews are a separate genetic group which numbered c.2,400 in 1954. Records show 1,000 years of residence in Kerela. Genetic testing has revealed that they have a 21% Jewish heritage but that 750 years ago Turkish, Yemenite, Iberian and Middle-Eastern Jews occasionally arrived in Kerala. These 'foreigners' (Paradesi) were only 10% of the total and were permitted to intermarry with local Jews. Virtually all of Cochin's Jews made aliyah in the 1970s.

(vii) **Bene Israel:** Before their aliyah this unique Jewish group from N-W India numbered c.60,000. They have some Mongul heritage and were 'lost' until 300 years ago. After being 'found' they were taught Jewish traditions by Cochin Jews and there has been some intermarriage between the two (Waldman et el., 'Cochin Jews', online). Genetically they are closer to Jewish populations than any other Indian sub-group (although

Pakistani-sub-groups are closer). Bene Israel originated from a small number of ancestors with more male members in one foundation event, c. 970 years ago, with a second event between 270 and 360 years ago. At one period there was some intermarriage with Indians (more with India women than men). Thus 'white' and 'black' sub-groups were formed, which previously avoided intermarriage. This further limited the small gene-pool so that certain recessive genetic disorders are more common among these groups than is usual, although no genetic difference has so far been found between 'black' and 'white' Bene Israel (Waldman, 'On The Genetic Trail of the Bene Israel', online).

(viii) <u>Pakistani Jews</u>: The Balouchi, Brahui, Makrani and Hazara tribes in Pakistan have a strong Jewish ancestry but they do not practise Judaism and have not requested immigration (Waldman, 'Bene

Israel', online).

(ix) <u>Bedouin, Palestinian Christian Minorities and Others</u>: Genetic testing of 'non-Jewish' residents of rural Israel, by Professor Ariella Oppenheim, Prof. Antonio Arnee Vilna and Tel Aviv University in 2002, indicate that actually about 90% of such residents have Jewish ancestry. The Bedouin admit to it but in recent years Palestinians keep their Jewish heritage a well-guarded secret (Bedouin Seikh, Israel National News, October 15, 2009; Misinai, 2009).

.39. <u>The Evangelical Sisters of Mary and Mother Basilea Schlink</u>

During and just after World War II a young German woman, Klara Schlink, gathered a group of teenage girls for Bible teaching. Gradually a Lutheran Sisterhood was founded at Darmstadt, led by Klara Schlink as Mother Basilea (1904-2001) and her colleague, Erika Madus, as Mother Martyria. Today over 200 Sisters (and now also Franciscan Brothers) work in

many nations. Mother Basilea was a scholarly theologian, a prolific writer of devotional works and a gifted composer of hymns. Her work is still valued. Her particular teachings on

piety included the concepts of 'repentance as the joy filled life' and 'bridal love for Jesus' – not just a metaphor but an actual calling.

.40. <u>Billy Graham (1918-2018)</u>

In 1947, soon after WW II, Billy Graham, an American Southern Baptist evangelist, began his crusades.

He modelled his crusading work on Dwight L. Moody and his soloist, Ira D. Sankey (as previously noted). He had learnt from previous revivalists, even the unsuccessful ones, so that his formula ran smoothly and was effective. For example he used prayer teams, trained counsellors and assistant evangelists, he collected decision cards so that statistics could be kept and responders followed up and he made excellent use of massed choirs and professional musicians. A key to Billy Graham's success, apart from his good looks, speaking voice, media know-how, charismatic personality and courage, was his conversational prayer with the Lord, no matter what else he might be doing. "I'll walk with God from this day on" was his reality.

From 1954, Dr Graham extended his work internationally: first in London. While he was 'Down Under', in 1959, Dr Graham preached in Auckland, Wellington and Christchurch in New Zealand and in five Australian states and in the national capital, Canberra. Crusade meetings were relayed by landline to country towns everywhere to reach three million Australians. The Australian crusades were so successful that Dr Graham was astonished at the spiritual hunger he found.[46] One hundred and fifty thousand people attended his final meeting in Sydney (Christian Today AU, online). Dr Graham's sonin-law, Leighton Ford, returned in 1968 to preach in Sydney, Brisbane and New Zealand but by the late 60s society was quite different, as will be shown later in this chapter.

.41. <u>The Five Missionary-Martyrs of Ecuador</u>

On January 8, 1956 five missionaries were speared to death in Ecuador, South America. They had gone into the jungle to preach the gospel to the Auca people. Three of them, Ed McCully, Jim Elliot and Peter Fleming were Plymouth

Brethren who worked with C.M.M.L. and Nate Saint, a WW II pilot, worked for M.A.F. These four, along with Rachel Saint (Nate's sister) worked amongst the Quechua people, in Ecuador. They invited a fifth man, Roger Youderian, a former paratrooper and missionary to the Jivaro people, to join them.

A native Auca girl, Dayuma, who was living with Rachel, was able to teach them some basics phrases in her language. When Jim Elliot located the tribe from the air the men began making contact, calling out friendly messages through a loud hailer and lowering gifts in a bucket. Soon their bucket was brought up with gifts in return: a woven headband; carved wooden combs; two live parrots; cooked fish; peanuts and a piece of smoked monkey tail (Kiefer, 'Nate Saint', online).

Five days after they landed and made camp the missionaries were speared to death: a shocking event which reverberated around the world. As a direct result more than twenty pilots applied to M.A.F. to take their place and 1,000 students volunteered for missionary service (Kiefer, online). Contact continued: Rachel Saint and Elizabeth Elloit (Jim's widow) and her baby daughter, Valerie, lived amonst the Auca for two years to translate the Scriptures into their language. They helped make a movie of the book, Through Gates of Splendor ('Jim Elliot: No Fool', online). In a further act of forgiveness and reconciliation two of Nate's children were baptised by Mincaye the very man who had killed their father (Jim Elliott, 'No Fool', online; M.A.F., online). Auca means 'savage' but the people are now called Waodani as they are no longer savage. This tragic martyrdom was the beginning of a powerful message of salvation that spread across the world (M.A.F., online).

Rachel Saint lived and died among the people: she was a translator with Wycliffe, an organisation set up by a young American missionary to Guatemale, Cameron Townsend. He had copies of the Bible in Spanish but he was asked by a tribal man, "if your God is so smart why can't he speak our language?" (Winter, online, 234).

22.8. The Second Vatican Council (1962-65)

Vatican II was called by Pope John XXIII in 1962 and lasted for three years. It resulted in biblical, liturgical and ecumenical changes to the Catholic Church. Lay people were encouraged to read the Bible (and not just Catholic translations). The Mass was to be said in each local language, not Latin. Both elements (bread and wine) were to be given to the people, who were encouraged to participate and partake, not just watch. Holy Tables were moved down closer to the people and priests now face them to consecrate. Nuns were expected to wear ordinary clothing or at least to modernise their habits. Many left their convents to help the poor (Robert, 2009, 71). Vatican II took up some of the challenges which Luther had presented in the 16th century.

Pope John XXIII had spent a decade in Turkey where he helped rescue Jewish refugees from the Nazis and Vatican II seriously reconsidered the ongoing relationship between the Catholic Church and the Jews (Shelley, 1982/1996, 452). The long-standing adversus Judaeos tradition was reversed by the Council's declaration, Nostra Aetate (In Our Time) (1965). Catholic theologians abandoned Christian triumphalism, which claimed that the church had replaced the Jews in the Divine plan, which, from the first Easter onwards, no longer included the Jews (Pawliokwski, in Wiley (ed.), 2003, 108ff). Nostra Aetate (issued on October 28, 1965) confirmed that Jesus undertook his death and passion freely.

The Second Vatican Council "condemned antisemitism and all forms of discrimination and imposing the obligation of reciprocal understanding and esteem. It advocates a better knowledge on the part of Christians of the essence of Jewish religious tradition and self-identification."

It did not, however, go far enough, for example Nostra Aetate did not mention the Holocaust, much less offer any kind of apology but it left the door open for dual-covenant theology: that Jews must live by the old covenant and gentiles by the new. Yet this was not the letter of the document and is not official Catholic teaching. Even though Nostra Aetate does not suggest this, it may be a satisfactory solution for some, for example Cardinal Walter Kasper (1976) who is quoted as saying:

"if they (Jews) follow their own conscience and believe in God's promises as they understand them in their religious tradition they are in line with God's plan (for the salvation of Jewish people)."

At the same time Cardinal Kasper holds to *"some understanding of Christ's salvific mission as universal in nature"* (Pawliokswski, in Wiley (ed.), 2003, 117).

Similarly Professor Tommaso Federici announced to the sixth annual meeting of the Catholic-Jewish Consultation, in March, 1977, that the Catholic Church rejects all forms of proselytism including witnessing and preaching, both individual and communal (Colbi, 'Jewish Christian Relations', in Encyclopedia Judaica, 118). Nostra Aetate, does not necessarily mean that Christ's death is not universally applicable and that "Christians should not target Jews for conversion" (The Christian Scholars Group on Jewish-Christian Relations, A Sacred Obligation #7) as some Catholics have concluded.

As for other Christians, throughout the 19th century there was a strong Evangelical Protestant interest in Jews and their restoration to their ancestral homeland. Some denominations, however, adopted 'triumphalism', 'replacement' or

'supersessions' ideas about the Jew which are not new ideas but were expressed in the Church Fathers, for example Tertullian's Adversus Iudaeus (c.200 CE) which concerns "the rejection of the Jews and the choice of the Christianized pagans in their place as the

People of God" (Blumenkranz, 'Church Fathers', in Encyclopedia Judaica)

Replacement Theology is now called 'Fulfillment Theology' especially in those churches which abandoned Scripture as the basis of doctrine. Fulfillment Theology teaches that "all of the Old Testament promises to Israel are fulfilled in Jesus and the birth of the church, and thus they are no longer valid with regard to modern Israel," ... Fulfillment Theology, like Replacement Theology, concludes that "God is finished with Israel" (Michael, online).

Many (mainly European) churches, however, have felt the need to address the issue of their church and the Holocaust, some following the lead of Vatican II (Jacobs (ed.), 1993). See also The Theology of the Churches and the Jewish People. Statement by the World Council of Churches and its Member Churches, (Geneva, WCC Publications, 1988). German Christians have led the way in acts of

reconciliation.

Theologially speaking, St Paul taught in Romans 9, 10 and 11 that the Jews are the cultivated olive tree into which Christians, like wild olive branches, are grafted.

But he also taught the universal call for salvation through the atoning sacrifice of the Jew, Jesus of Nazareth

. Balancing these two is perhaps a mystery, which is very difficult, especially for Protestants who tend to like certainties more than mysteries. Pope John Paul II was deeply conscious of the 'Olive Tree Message': that gentiles have been grafted into Judaism which is the root. On April, 13, 1986, he told the synagogue of Rome that Jews "are our dearly beloved brothers ... our elder brothers" but without countenancing two paths to salvation (Dulles, 2005, online).

22.9. John F. Kennedy, Robert Kennedy and Martin Luther King, Jnr.

These three exceptional American leaders and visionaries were assassinated within a period of five years. Some say they were shot by lunatics but gun-violence is so prevalent in America that mental illness is more an excuse than a reason. Since 1968, more than 15 milliion Americans have died in gun related incidents. Six times more American school-age children die by gun violence than in other developed nations and more than US military personnel die in action worldwide. Children, especially black males, are vulnerable. From 1999 to 2017, 38,942 children aged 5-18 were shot dead and 41% of victims were black children, mainly boys (although black children are only 14% of that demographic (Sanchez for CNN, 2019).

America's first Roman Catholic President, John F. Kennedy, was shot dead in Dallas, Texas in 1963. The African-American leader and civil-rights activist, Rev. Dr. Martin Luther King, Jnr. was shot dead in Memphis, Tennessee, on April 4, 1968 and John F. Kennedy's brother, Bobby Kennedy (a U.S. senator [1965-1968], presidential hopeful, and U.S. Attorney General [1961 – 1964]) was shot dead in Los Angeles on June 6, 1968. Each was deeply grieved and the nation is much the poorer for their loss as they still had so much to give: the world will never know how much. Despite such losses and the shootings of so many students of all ages in their classrooms Americans resist attemps at even minor gun-reform.

22.10. The Radical Sixties

ECCLESIA A LONG JOURNEY TO TOMORROW

The post-war period until about 1964 was the high point of church membership and church attendance in Britain, American and Australia but the next decade saw something of a crisis overtake Ecclesia. 'Beetle-mania' struck young people everywhere. The 'sexual revolution', which started in the universities, spread quickly, later with severe consequences from HIV/Aids.

In Sydney, from April 1, 1963, the radical, satirical, counterculture newspaper, Oz Magazine, was circulated amongst university students. Its subjects included: the dangers of back-street abortions; police brutality; censorship; conscription for the Vietnam War; aboriginal rights and gay rights. Its 3rd edition led to the co-editors, Richard Neville, Richard Walsh and the artist, Martin

Sharp, being found guilty of publishing obscene and indecent material, and fined. In March 1964 they were again found guilty of obscenity, but won their appeal after two long years. In London, in 1967, Oz became the

colourful, flamboyant voice of counterculture. Richard Neville, James Anderson and Felix Dennis (coeditors) were charged with blasphemy and conspiring to corrupt public

morals but the (up-andcoming) Australian human-rights lawyer, Geoffrey Robinson, won their appeal for them (Neville, 1995, 23-57).

Students were generally active in opposition to the Vietnam War and in the huge public anti-war marches. Some among the resolute, conscientious objectors to military service were jailed. Television had come into most middle-class living rooms by the 60s bringing new ideas. In Australia, satirical programmes, such as 'The Mavis Bramston Show', lampooned 'sacred cows' such as the Queen, the Church, politicians, the police and the Returned Servicemen's League (the RSL) (Hilliard, 1997, 212).

For all Christian leaders a bomb was exploded in 1963 with the publication of Bishop John Robinson's book Honest to God, which expounded a 'new theology', which was heavily influenced by leading European predecessors, such as

Rudolph Bultmann, Paul Tillich and Dietrich Bonhoffer (Hilliard, 1997, 212). Sydney Anglicans believed that, when Robinson abandoned the authority of Scripture and the supernatural, he ended up with pantheism (Knox, in The Australian Church Record, 1963). The Catholic Church was also hostile to Robinson (Rumble, in The Catholic Weekly, 1963). Anti-conservative and Liberal theology made inroads amongst clergy and seminarians and those who embraced it were most likely to leave the ministry (Hilliard, 1997, 212; 222).

In the mid 60s some Catholic bishops, such as Ryan of Queensland and Guildford Young of Tasmania, became open to ecumenism, dialogue with their 'separated brethren' and to visiting each others' churches, which had previously been forbidden (Hilliard, 1997, 216; 225).

Catholics, who had experienced euphoria after Vatican II, were shocked by the encyclical Humanae Vita in July 1968, which banned the newly available contraceptive pill. News headlines screamed *"Pope Rejects the Pill"* (The Australian, July 30, 1968, 1). There was worldwide disappointment and secret rebellion against Vatican authority and many Catholics just lapsed. In Eastern Australian 150 priests immediately resigned, including the national head of the Jesuits and other leaders, and about 10% of the total priesthood left over the next decade or so (Hilliard, 1997, 222). Two years after the pill was banned, when the Pope visited Australia, 58% of Roman Catholics disagreed with the Pope's position and only 29% agreed with it (Hilliard, 1997, 219, citing The Australian, 23/11/ 1970). Similar trends were noted in North America and Europe (Hilliard, 1997, 222).

Australian Methodists tried to synthesise with liberal theology by stressing widespread struggles for justice, freedom and peace. For Methodists of the period, service and social activism became the main purpose of Ecclesia and their experiment with ecumenism (which, in 1977, resulted in the Uniting Church in Australia and the United Church in the U.K.) has led to even more small denominations than before: as well as falling numbers, overall (Hilliard, 1997, 213). Basic to their theology was the concept of Jesus: *"whether or not he was personally a victim of it (injustice), he had an unusual sensitivity to the poor and marginalised"* (Borg, in Borg and Wright, 1999, 65).

<u>22.11. Counter Culture</u>

<u>(1) The Flower Children</u>

The Flower Children was a short-lived American and European youth-movement in the 1960s associated with liberal sexualities, alternative lifestyles, new spiritualities,

Asian religions, brightly coloured flowers, psychodelic colours and the beginnings of the drug culture. A study by San Francisco State College showed that 96% of them had used marijuana, 90% said they had tried LSD but few had tried adictive drugs like heroin (Gleason, 'The Flower Children', online). Flower Children were hippies: hip and happening teenagers and young adults who opposed the American obsession with bodily perfection:

"escapists from the affluent society that produces and sustains them. They are opposed to the middle aged values of affluent America - its commercialism, mechanism and bureaucracy, its car culture, hygiene and unquestioned acceptance of the work ethic and the quick buck." (Gleason, citing Bryan Wilson an Oxford researcher, online).

If Jesus was embraced it was as a social alternative icon, a hippie spiritual leader or an antiauthoritarian political rebel. Christianity's teaching on love was often confused with liberal morality, group sex and/ or promiscuity and (at best) serial monogamy.

(2) The Jesus Movement

In the same era, the Jesus movement gained world-wide popularity among the youth (Gleason, online). The Jesus movement was an American and European phenomenon, which began in 1967 with young people and students, amid the liberal climate of the 1960s.

In California, the Jesus People embraced the counter-cultural movement of the era, itself an offshoot of the secular hippie movement. Its manifestations included communal living,

youthful 'Jesus music' with guitars and drums, informality

and dancing in the Spirit, miracles and love, peace and harmony (Eskridge, 'Jesus People', in Fahlbusch et al., (eds), Encyclopedia of Chrtistianity, 2008).

.42. Eastern Religions in the West

In the 1960s, aspects of Buddhism and Hinduism, such as transcendental meditation, yoga and Hare Krishna monks with their saffron robes and constant saying "Hare Krishna" as a mantra, permeated first America and then the West generally. They particularly targeted young people, many of whom broke with their parents and abandoned their education to live in cult-like communes.

In 1965 America's immigration policy was relaxed, permitting large numbers of Asian, Middle Eastern and East European citizens to enter and many Asians had success in improving their economic position (Geiger, online, Graph 14). In 2017, America has 3.45 million Muslim residents and, in Europe, they made up 4.9% of the population: a proportion that was bound to increase because Muslims have a high birth-rate. Germany now has almost 5 million Muslim residents (a rise of 1.7 million in six years, 2010-2016), making them 6.1% of the population. Muslims are 6.9% of the Austrian population, 11.1% of Bulgaria's and more than 7% of the populations of Belgium, France, the Netherlands and Sweden (Pew Research, November 29, 2017, online).

Hinduism and Buddhism are also growing in America: "Over 100 different Hindu denominations and 75 forms of Buddhism have come into existence since 1965 and each now claims three to five million adherents" (Vos, 1994, 148 citing Melton (ed.), Encyopedia of American Religion, XLIV).

.43. The Charismatic Renewal

The 'Charismatic Renewal' made a dramatic worldwide impact from c.1969. By-and-large it was a development of
Pentecostalism but 'charismatics' usually remained within the
older denominations. From the 1970s the Catholic Church accepted the movement but relegated it mainly to mid-week meetings for prayer and praise, which did not compete with the Mass. These meetings were kept within the fold: led by religious, including nuns, whereas Protestant groups could be led by laity (mainly male). Charismatic music, fostered by a New Zealand couple, Dave and Dale Garrett, became so popular that it became mainstream and was relabled 'youth music'. The Charismatic movement

increased devotion, church membership, halted the decline in the numbers of church members and trainee clergy and penetrated every denomination.

There was no precipitating crisis nor any one great leader. If there was one it was Smith Wigglesworth, a remarkable man who began life as a child-labourer in Yorkshire. Smith was confirmed as an Anglican and as an illiterate choirboy he demonstrated a quick memory for music and lyrics. In Bradford, as a teenager, he became Wesleyan and absorbed Wesley's teaching on 'the deeper spiritual life'. Once he became a 'soul-winner' he was attracted to the Salvation Army. At work a Plymouth Brethren steamfitter taught him plumbing and about baptism by immersion but his fiancée, Polly, was a Salvation Army officer, which Smith was not, so after their marriage they could not remain in 'The Army' and became Methodists, (Hywel-Davies, 1987/89, 38ff).

British Methodism was experiencing revival because of the 1905/06 Welsh revival and the influence of early Pentecostalism coming from Los Angeles (from 1906) so that preachers who were successful soul-winners were welcome. Smith had a stammer and felt inadequate in public speaking so Polly preached while he organised and gave 'altar calls'. Polly also taught Smith to read and they opened the Bradford Street Mission.

In nearly Leeds, Smith attended healing meetings and then a meeting in Sunderland, which was led by the Anglican Vicar,

Alexander Boddy. Afterwards Smith had a vision of an empty cross with Jesus exalted at the right hand of the Father. When Smith opened his mouth to praise God he instantly spoke in tongues. Smith's story made headlines in the Sunderland Daily Echo.

Smith's preaching was transformed so that, the following Sunday Polly was astonished. Soon they were travelling widely so that Smith had no time for plumbing. His fame in England grew as he ministered throughout the country. After Polly's early death Smith was accompanied by his daughter, Alice, and her husband, Jimmy Salter. In 1914 Smith went to the United States, then to France, Switzerland and Scandinavia. In 1922-23 he went to Australia and New Zealand, and then to many other nations before returning to Australia in 1927 (Hywel-Davies, 1987/89, 97-117).

Smith had a particular gift for healing which increased people's faith as they witnessed the crippled and the ill being transformed. By the 1920s and 1930s he was regarded as the 'Apostle of Faith' and a patriarch of Pentecostalism although he had been a follower of the various moves of God, not an initiator, but signs and wonders did follow his preaching, including the dead being raised.

"William Herbert, in his book Smith Wigglesworth – The Secret of his Power states, 'I know of fourteen occasions when the dead were raised during Wigglesworth's ministry'" (Hywel-Davies, 1987/89, 89). In 1936, in South Africa, he prophesised to a young David du Plessis, a future leader in the Charismatic Renewal, that he would be involved in a great, world-wide revival in the old denominations, that would start after his own death. He died on March 12, 1947. By 1976 David du Plessis had come to be called "Mr Pentecost" (Hywel-Davies, 1987/89, 156).

Some small charismatic churches sprang up in the late 20th century but those which were totally independent rarely flourished or were absorbed into one another or into megachurches, such as into 'Hillsong' or 3C, in Australia, or

movements, such as the Vineyard Movement, in America

which is said to have had 100,000 worldwide members by 2002 (Noll, 2002, 181).

Apart from a proliferation of megachurches other long-term results has been the enrichment of mainline denominations over the decades and the conversion of numerous 'colourful characters' and prominent sportspeople (for example, tennis champion Margaret Court, whose Catholic faith was enlivened by a vision of the Madonna and Child years before she became a Pentecostal pastor).

22.14. Messianic Synagogues

Over the centuries thousands of Jews have been forced to convert to Christianity but some have done so willingly: for example, Solomon HaLevi (1451-1435) a rabbi who became Bishop of Burgos under the name Pablo de Santa Maria and whose parents, brothers, wife and four sons also converted (Goldberg (ed.), 2003, 21). Similary, Bishop Michael Solomon Alexander was a rabbi who became the first modern Anglican bishop in Jerusalem, from 1841 until his untimely death four years later (Crombie, 2006).

In 19th century Britain, because of the growth of interest in foreign countries and overseas missions, organisations such as the Hebrew Christian Alliance (1866) (now the International Messianic Jewish Alliance) and (in 1809) the Christian Mission to the Jews (now Christian Ministry

Among Jewish People) were formed. In the 20th century in America, beginning in Chicago in 1934, Jewish Jesus-believers formed their own congregations which, by 2003, numbered 300; with over 100 more congregations in Israel, many for Russian immigrants. Since 1989, when the High Court of Justice ruled in the case of Gary Beresford that only Jews who have not changed their religion are elegible to immigrate under the Law of Return, aliyah by Messianic Jews has become very difficult (Goldberg [ed.], 2003, 21).

22.15. The Rescue of Hostages in Uganda

On June 23, 1976, East German Red Arrow and Palestinian Popular Front terrorists hijacked an AirFrance plane out of

Athens, forcing it to fly to Libya (to collect more terrorists) and then to Uganda. There a selection took place: gentiles were freed but Israelis and those with Jewish sounding names were held as ransom for 53 Palestinians jailed for terrorism. The Captain, Michel Barcos, and his crew refused to abandon their passengers, staying to care for them and showing couragage, responsibily and true humanity (Aderet, in HaAretz World News, online). On July 3, Israel dispatched Phantom jet fighters and four troop-carrying planes to Entebbe. They rescued the 103 hostanges but lost four hostages, including Dora Bloch who was left behind in hospital. She was shot by the order of President Idi Amin as pay-back. The commander of the raid, Lt. Col. Yohanan

(Yoni) Netanyahu (P. M.

Benjamin Netanyahu's brother) was also killed. Eleven terorists were killed and 11 Soviet MiG fighters were destroyed on the ground (Etheredge, Entebbe Raid', in Britannica, online).

Plate 22.2.
Climbing the Berlin Wall. © Sue Ream
(CC By3.0) via Wikimedia Space Commons

22.16. The Fall of European Communism in East Germany

On the night of November 9, 1989 Germans began to attack the Berlin Wall. This secure and heavily guarded barrier was an icon of separation between communism and democracy; between East and West. It had divided Germany for almost 30 years ('A Short History of the Department of State', online). Thousands of East Germans poured through the hole that was made. A year later East Germany and West Germany was reunified.

22.17. The Fall of Communism in Russia

For 70 years atheistic communism ruled Russia and the USSR (McGrath, 2013, 305). A huge number of churches were destroyed or closed down. Jews were resettled in the Far East

and dissidents were sent to Siberia. The Cold War raged between the West and the USSR which stimulated a nuclear armsrace and a space race between Russia and America. Russia was the first to put a satelite into space (1957) and to put a person into space (Uri Gargaran) but at great cost, which eventually helped ruin the Soviet economy. Serious military conflict between the Soviets and Afghanistan virtually bankrupted Russia and contributed to the collapse of the Soviet system (1990/92).

The Soviet Union had been experiencing major economic difficulties when Mikhail Gorbachev was president. He, however, ushered in a period of 'glasnost' (openness) and 'perestroika' (restructuring). He was deposed by Boris Yeltsin and resigned on December 25, 1991. The Soviet Union was dissolved and Yeltsin accepted financial assistance of $4.5 billion from the old enemy, the USA.

22.18. Conclusions About the Early to Mid 20th Century

The first-half of the 20th century had been a very difficult time for the entire world, which tried to be optimistic about future political and economic prosperity. The two world wars and the Great Depression were traumatic, and post-war social reconstruction was difficult and painful. Soon, dark clouds enveloped the world including the Cold War, the threat of Communism and the 'Domino Theory' (that all of S. E. Asia would, in succession, fall to Communism) and especially fear of the newly developed Atom Bomb which hung over the chief protagonists and their allies.

The mid-century decades were very significant as, after WW II, the United Nations was formed out of the (weaker) League of Nations and numerous new nations were born: many of them former British colonies.

These included: Syria and Lebanon (1945); Jordan (1946); Pakistan and India (1947); Israel and Burma (1948);

Indonesia and Libya (1949); Egypt (1953) Vietnam (1954); and Morocco, Tunisia and Sudan (1956) (MacMillan, online, 5). Anti-colonialism often meant rejection of Christianity and Western values (Robert, 2009, 90) and some countries (such as Burma, China and India) expelled missionariers or, like Nepal, needed their expertise but severely restricted their activities.

Features of the period included: de-Nazification in Germany; a democratic and pacifist constitution for Japan (imposed by General Douglas MacArthur); the International Court of Justice (1946) and the Declaration of Human Rights (1948) (MacMillan, online, 4). Wars have continued, but (fortunately) on a smaller scale than earlier in the century: in Indo-China, Korea, Vietnam, Malaysia, East Pakistan/Bangladesh and Central America with many civil wars and civil unrest in numerpous African nations and former colonies.

When the dust of World War II settled and huge numbers of people had been displaced and then resettled it became obvious that materialism, consumerism, scepticism and individualism have become "the idolatories of our age" (Ringma, 2006/2014, xvii) eclipsing church-going, faith and community. Both Catholics and Protestants have been

swimming against the tide of the age, in their different ways and with equal difficulty. Catholics had always used clerical authority and fear of hell and purgatory to force parishoners to attend Mass. The use of contraception was forbidden, although huge numbers of Catholic women quietly rebelled. If they had not, millions of them would have been imprisoned in more drudgery and their families in more

poverty as many Catholic women in the West had ten or more children whereas non-catholics had three or four. Protestants clung to the belief that if they stayed true to the Bible their churches would grow. Neither approach was a

success. Everyone was seeking a better life for themselves and their own (fewer) children so consumerism,

selffulfillment and hedonistic love of pleasure prevailed. Charity and social justice work (now too extensive and difficult for declining and ageing church congregations) have been taken over by governments and NGOs, so that respect for the work of the church has declined.

The declining birth-rate among all Christian groups has meant fewer children in Sunday schools and in teens' activities. In North America and Australia, this compounded their drift towards secular attractions such as youth concerts until late on Saturday nights, Sunday sport, or even movies on Sundays (Wuthnow, ASR 41, 1976; McAllister, Sociological Analysis 49.3, 1988). It has been proposed that children's sport is the strongest reason for non-attendance at all forms of worship in America (Webster, online).

Churches have paid insufficient attention to youth work: Sunday schools were for childminding during the sermon, moreover the children of outsiders were not being evangelised. Failure to keep youth within the church has meant a dearth of babies for the future of the church (Hilliard, 1991, 226). While a church should grow by evangelising the unchurched, children trained up in the church form the backbone of future leadership. An issue of concern is that evangelism of people of other faiths is considered wrong by 47% of Americans of the age at which people generally become missionaries and church workers (those born 1984-1998) (Barna Group, online). There is also a 'deevangelising' effect when people who leave their church speak negatively about their experience or write a book about it, which is even more damaging.

In the West, wide acceptance of Eastern and alternative religions and practices such as yoga, martial arts, occult practices and body piercing has diluted Christianity and led to syncretism. Among young people (and their sports and 'pop' idols, the criminal element and virtually everyone) tattooing is

fashionable. The Church is silent, as if it is a personal matter,

neither right nor wrong, although it is forbidden by Scripture:

"Do not cut your bodies for the dead or put tattoo marks on yourselves. I am the Lord."

(Lev. 19:28)

The Church also fails to distinguish between Christian meditation and the Eastern alternative and between Christian mysticism and the Eastern alternatives (Butler, 1926/2003, 165f; 172-76; 182f; 193f). Saint John Paul

the Great was right to warn against such syncretism but the denominations have not repented of it, nor asked God for cleansing but continue to toy with Eastern religions. Occult practices are also forbidden by Scripture:

"Do not turn to mediums or seek out spiritists, for you will be defiled by them. I am the Lord your God." (Lev. 19: 31.)

Injecting toxic substances into the body must surely be wrong? Our bodies are meant to be dwelling places of God (I Cor. 19:6) with inner beauty not a glamorous, artifically perfect exterior and enlarged, sexy lips. So many beautiful young women are spending their hard-earned thousands on plastic surgery, breast enhancements that are often sub-standard and butt enlargements that are always downright dangerous.

Meanwhile emerging developing nations, such as South Korea, Solomon Islands and East Africa, made major changes to their ancient cultures in order to adjust to Christianity, which has been widely embraced. Growth in Christian numbers is now virtualy confined to the newer nations including former Soviet Union nations and Islamic nations as well as some in the southern hemisphere and Asia. Many areas now under Islam were once thriving Christian communities, even well after the Arab conquest (633-750 AD/CE).

Remnants of Christianity remained into this millennium, but under persecution (Jenkins, 2008, 19). The Church is being hotly contested by the rise of militant Islamic nationalism and Christians, western aid-workers and journalists are often martyred. Recently, however, many former Muslims, disenchanted with the wars, traumas and suffering in Islamic lands are turning to Christianity. This is particularly evidenced among refugees and displaced persons.

The Nazi Holocaust has left Christians with the necessity of knowing what happened to the Jewish people (and its effects upon their children and grandchildren) and reaching a personal conclusion about Christian-Jewish relations and whether or not Jews should be targets for conversion. Events and trends of the watershed decade, the 1960s, such as disruption, ferment, confusion, individualism, hedonism and decline determined the direction of Christian countries in the West for the remainder of the 20th century. The end result was 'post-Christianity' characterised by individual self-exploration, and self-transformation, informality, spontaneity and the search for the immediacy of experience (Martin, 1981).

In America, Australia and New Zealand the 1960's might be better understood as the era of the Vietnam War. America's participation in the war ran from 1/11/1955 to 30/4/1975. Australian's participation lasted from 1965 to 1972 amid great tumult and youthful, anti-authoritarian rebellion. (In Australia, conscription had always run counter to the national identity and its imposition was greatly resented.) Britain was not officially involved in the Vietnam War.

Science and technology were expanding and a new term has entered the vocabulary, 'technopolitan culture' (Cox, 1965) (cities where technology dominates). God has often been relegated to being an explanation for those mysteries which science could not quite account for (yet).

In the West belief in no religion (especially amongst university students) was increasing and church membership,

donations and participation in both church services and Sunday school were decreasing.

In most Western countries pro-rata donations to churches and missions has fallen since a peak in the early 1960s. In Australia, the Billy Graham Crusade of 1968 attracted fewer participants than the 1959 Crusade had. After WW II there was a spate of building war memorials, such as churches, schools and community halls but later in the 20th century fewer church buildings were built and some churches began to close, especially in remote communities.

22.19. From the 1970s until the 1990s

In the 1970s Catholics and Protestants were asking serious questions, such as 'what are the right functions of the ministry?' and 'what are the most appropriate forms of ministry for the modern secular world?' (Hilliard, 1997, 222). Into the 1970s, the dominant social forces in the lives of young adults were: women's liberation/feminism; anti-establishment protest; anti-racism; protest folk music; the counter-culture and liberation from antiquated morality (Hilliard, 1997, 221). Decades later, in the 1990s the same questions were still being asked.

By the end of the century, there was such a shortage of Catholic priests in parts of rural Australia, that nuns began to administer the reserved sacrament because a priest could only visit once a month. In other Western countries, priests began to be imported from Asia and Africa because local vocations to the priesthood fell to crisis levels while the Vatican maintained conservative policies about married priests and the ordination of women, even as deacons.

<u>22.20. Changes by denomination in Australia, from 1960-c.1987</u>

By 1981, although 76% of Australians identified as Christians, the post-war trend away for churchgoing was obvious (Miller, 2015, 19). At that time Catholicism was

able to retain

adherents better than Protestantism. In most Protestant denominations only 15%-20% of adherents went to church at least once a month whereas 42% of Catholics did so (Hughes, in Black (ed.), 1991, 93). This, plus post-war immigration from Italy, Malta, Germany, Ireland and Poland, kept the numbers of children needing a Catholic education high and constantly fed Catholic adults into the churches.

Catholics still had the largest families, despite the availability of contraception, but the difference was not great. In Australia, in 1987, Catholics had 1.63 dependent children per woman whereas Anglican women had 1.14 and Baptists had 1.27 per woman. Many Catholic secondary schools did not cater for the two senior years and even 15 year olds could work full-time: if so, they would not be identified as 'dependent'. Larger Catholic families, coupled with fees for their schooling, probably forced more Catholic teenagers into the permanent workforce than non-Catholic teens (if so, it served to slightly reduce the number of 'dependent children' among Catholic 15-17 year olds) - but kept many Catholic young people out of the professions.

By 1987 Pentecostalism had become important in the Australian landscape (often at the expense of other denominations) but in New South Wales in about 1987 36% of Pentecostals said they had grown up in unchurched families (compared with 27% of Baptists, 22% of Anglicans and only 12% of Catholics). These figures indicate that Pentecostal and other Protestant churches were attracting the unchurched and/or immigrants but Catholics retained their own (Hughes, in Black (ed.), 1991, 95).

22.21. Australian Values Study Survey, 1983 + Combined Churches Survey, 1987.

In 1983, Australia was not a secular society as 79% believed in a God. Despite falling church attendances, 58% of respondents described themselves as 'religious' and two-thirds prayed at least occasionally.

Detailed responses to the Combined Churches Survey of 1987 across five denominations were statistically analysed by the Christian Research Association. Four types of faith and belief were revealed which were allocated descriptive names: Conversionism, Devotionalism, Conventionalism and Principlism.

Conversionism: People with this type of faith have high attendance (more frequently than weekly) and tend to be Baptist and Pentecost. They stress a conversion experience, see the clergy as evangelists, and regard church as the gathering of the redeemed with the redemption of others as the primary task. They read the Bible literally and believed that its miracles did happen.

Devotionalism: Faith is identified as a warm relationship with God, the ever-present helper who is involved in their lives. They respond to God with loyalty and devotion, expressed through church attendance; about half attend more than weekly. Some see the clergy as having priestly functions.

Conventionalism: This group, mostly from rural areas and among the elderly, see church attendance as an important duty: 75% attend weekly with only 20% attending more often. The clergy have a priestly role. Christian faith provides values and rules to live by, notably the Ten Commandments. Jesus is seen as teacher, rather than as saviour, with little stress on a personal relationship.

Principlism: These tend to be Anglicans, Catholics and Uniting Church members, 25% of whom attended church less than once a month and only 5% of whom attended

more often than weekly. Nominalism is increasing in this sector.

Their religious motivations vary: they live by principles of love, caring and harmony rather than rules.

Social justice issues were significant. For them, God is a comforter, or creator, or a spiritual power or presence: Jesus is an example to follow or a teacher. A major function of the clergy is counselling.

The function of the church was identified as giving meaning purpose and direction to life, particularly in times of crisis and at the boundary points of the life cycle" (Hughes, in Black (ed), 1991, 99).

In conclusion, this study found that Conversionist Christians adhered well to their denomination and their congregation and continued to attend regularly, c.1980, but that attrition occurred amongst

Principlists.

22.22. Recent American Research Results, from December, 2018

(1) Only 31% of American Catholics think that Pope Francis is handling sex-abuse scandals well. (2) Three-quarters of Americans try to talk to God or another power, 90% believe in a higher power but only 56% believe in the God of the Bible. (3) 27% of men say they have been sexually harassed and about 59% of women. Hispanic women and other ethnic groups are less likely to report it, while educated, white women are more likely to report it (70%). (4) A majority of American teenagers (57%) fear a shooting at their school; 60% if they are Afro-American, and 73% if they are Hispanic. Most parents share these concerns. (5) Cyber-bullying has been experienced by 59% of teens (Geiger, online).

22.23. Factors That Have Worked For and Against Church Attendance

The Charismatic Renewal was strong in Australia in the 70's and 80's. This bolstered the various Pentecostal 'tribes without number' and gave birth to new ones (such as 3C, Dayspring, Hillsong and Vineyard) and para-church organizations (such as Aglow and the Full Gospel Business Men's Fellowship) (Noll, 2002, 181).

In 1966 Pentecostalism in Australia was small and didn't appear on the census form and in 1986 it was only 0.7% of the population, but in 2016 it was 1.1% and has become the fastest growing segment of the church scene (Hughes, in Black (ed.), 1991, 99).

The Combined Churches Survey (1987) identifies various factors that worked against church attendance: married women entering the workforce; television in every home; motor vehicles for Sunday outings; more families owning holiday homes (Hughes, in Black (ed.), 1991, 100-105). Add to this list: alternative recreation activities; Sunday sporting fixtures for adults and children and Sunday trading in all stores.

Surveys in other countries have found a close correlation between personal wealth and church attendance (although not an economic dependence). According to analysts of the European Social Survey 2012 (the ESS) and World Values Survey (WVS) the more wealthy the country, overall, the less its citizens attend church. This outcome does not apply to the USA where

there is great inequality of wealth but where 28% of self-styled Christians attend church at least monthly and the black population and especially Latin American

immigrants are very devout (The Economist Newspaper Ltd. 25/12/ 2015). Feelings of independence from God, by people who have everything, are not new. Writing to the church at Laodicea, St John said:
"You say, 'I am rich; I have acquired wealth and do not need a thing.' But you do not realise that you are wretched, pitiful, poor, blind and naked." .....
... *"Those whom I love I rebuke and discipline. So be earnest, and repent. Here I am! I stand at the door and knock. If anyone hears my voice and opens the door, I will go in, and eat with him, and he with me"* (Rev. 3:1ff).

22.24. Conclusions About the Later 20th Century

The later 20th Century was a period of great variety, turmoil and unrest. Instantaneous communication took the tribal and ethnic conflicts happening in remote places, such as the Balkans and Africa, into living rooms across the developed world. Globalisation of trade impacted every economy. The so-called 'tiger economies' of Asia grew rapidly through hard work and low wages more than good, stable government but millions in China were pulled out of starvation and many Asians moved into the middle classes.

In 1980 the Chernobyl nuclear power station in the Ukraine exploded. This (and a similar accident in 2011 in Fukushima, Japan) alerted the world to the potential death, disability and damage that nuclear power, previously so readily embraced by the West, could bring (Delouche, IHE, 1992, 377).

Israel signed peace treaties with both Egypt (in 1979) and Jordan (in 1994) but hostile relations remained with Iran and some other Arab nations. The Iranian Revolution in 1979 and the rise of the Islamic fundamentalism under the ayatollahs increased conflict in the Arab world, notably between Iran and Saudi Arabia, who are still fighting proxy wars against each other in Yemen and Syria. The first and second intifadas (Palestinian uprisings) seriously disrupted social life in Israel and the territories, especially in Gaza, which is administered by Hamas and, to a lesser extent in some 'West Bank' areas, under Fatah, which is officially called the Palestinian Authority.

Hints of how terrorists who were also Islamic extremists would operate in the future were provided by the following: the attack on the Israeli team at the Munich Olympics which killed eleven Israelis and one German police-officer (1972); the bombings, both of the US Marine barracks in Lebanon that killed 241 Americans and another that killed 50

French peacekeepers (1982); the hijacking of the Achile

Lauro (1985); the Lockerbee air-disaster (1988); and the virtually simultaneous bombings of the US embassies in both Nairobi, Kenya, and Dar es Salaam, Tanzania (1998).

The costs involved in preventing such attacks in every country are very high. These indicators had their climax in America on September 11, 2001, when terrorists flew planes into the Twin Towers of the World Trade Centre and into the Pentagon.

China began to subtly extend its influence in Africa, S-E Asia and the small South Pacific nations by using its new wealth for economic imperialism and North Korea tried to become a big player as a nuclear nation, creating anxiety in America, Japan, South Korea, Australia and even its fellowcommunist ally, China.

<u>Questions:</u>

(1) What political and social changes resulted from WW II?

(2) Why is church attendance in Europe declining? Do these factors also apply in America?

(3) Of the four types of faith and belief noted in this chapter, which best represents your own position: Conversionism, Devotionalism, Conventionalism or Principlism?

Chapter 23
Ecclesia in the Wider World.

<u>23.1. World Population</u>

Between 1970 and mid-2019 (a period of almost 50 years) the world's population grew from 1.619 billion people to about 7.7 billion, of whom 5.4 billion were adults (Worldometers, online). The world's population is growing by about 200,000 souls per day or 29,500,000 per year. Of the total, more than 1 billion are illiterate and almost a billion are slum-dwellers.

In Mid-2019, 2.3 billion, or one third of the world's total population were Christian, with over 2 billion being church members. Muslims numbered about 1.5 billion: fewer than the number of church members and slightly fewer than Christians who are both members and regularly church attenders. The popular idea that Muslims are over-running the world is not supported, although the world-wide adoption of sharia law, which is so disadvantageous to women, is a goal of Islam and some Muslim-majority countries (including democracies such as Turkey and Indonesia) are becoming increasingly fundamentalist.

Overall, females produce 2.2 children, but Muslims have 2.9 children per woman and Christians 2.6. In Europe, however, Christian deaths have outnumbered births by nearly 6 million over 5 years but there is some anecdotal evidence that Muslim refugees in Europe are converting to Christianity. Refugees are a young demographic and therefore will produce children in Europe. This increase for them will be aided by reduced child mortality, better health care and improved nourishment (Sherwood, The Guardian, 27/8/2018).

In 2009, a mere 15 million people were Jews, which was 0.2% of the world's population. In Israel c.80% of the population are Jews. Another sizable cohort lives in the USA

where 17% of adults are Jews. Their relative size has been declining since 2009 as they are an older demographic, but they are expected to grow by 15% p.a. as the proportion of the Ultra Orthodox grows (Sherwood, The Guardian, 27/8/2018).

In 2009, other small groups (despite their high profile in the West and its media) were atheists (148 million) and the non-religious (774 million). Most of the latter live in North Korea, China and the Czech Republic. As these have fewer children than others they will decline, proportionally. In the 2011 US census 390,000 people (0.7%) called themselves Jedi Knights but they failed to be recognised as a religion in 2016 and the numbers have fallen to c.176,000 (Sherwood, The Guardian, 27/8/2018).

<u>23.2. Christians in Various Lands</u>

<u>(i) North America and Europe Compared</u>

Europe is becoming increasingly secular and the role of the churches in social welfare has been taken over by the state so that "the church had lost its role in society" (Sterling, 'Rethinking Christianity in the 21st Century', online).

In all of North America in mid-2017 there were 230,277,000 church members with another 554,198,000 in Europe, including Russia; 59,1094,000 in Latin America and 582,372,000 in Africa. Church membership in North America is growing by 4,000 souls per day but in Europe the growth is only 2,000 souls per day (Pew Research Centre, 'Global Christianity', 2011). This reflects both immigration trends and birth rates. Compared with North America, there is currently a lower birth rate in Europe moreover immigrants tend to be Muslims.

<u>(ii) United States</u>

Compared with Europeans U.S. Christians have larger-than-average families and stronger adherence to church

membership and America's immigrants tend to be Hispanic, which is the most religiously observant ethnic group in America. In 2007 there were 12.7 million illegal immigrants living in America (most of them Hispanic) although this number fell to 10.7 million by 2016. The number of legally settled refugees to America is critically low. In 2017 it was only 33,000, the lowest per year since the terrorist attack of 9/11/2001 (Geiger, online, graph 8). Only 51% of all Americans (and 32% of Republicans) think that the country has a responsibility to take in refugees (Geiger, online).

(iii) Australia

In the year to 30/6/2017 Australia's total migrant intake was about 163,000 (the lowest since 2007-08) (Singh, online) of which 24,162 were refugees; Australia's highest intake of refugees (as distinct from immigrants) on record (Doherty, for The Guardian, online). Recently priority has gone to persecuted minority groups.

<u>(iv) Australia and New Zealand Compared</u>

Recent surveys suggest that all religious affiliation is declining in both Australia and New Zealand, with 45.1% of New Zealanders being unaffiliated in 2016; compared with 30.1% of Australians. Immigrants tend to have a religious affiliation and, because of its immigration intake,

this results in Australia having a greater religious diversity than New Zealand. In Australia, Buddhist are 2.4%, Muslims are 2.6%, Judaism accounts for 0.4% and the Eastern Orthodox are 2.1%. The largest Christian denominations are Roman Catholics (at 22.6%) and

Anglicans (at 13.3%). A considerable number (2.6%) said they were Christians, without further definition

(Australian Bureau of Statistics 2016 Census). These may be what are now called 'nones' – those Christians who have no denominational allegiance.

<u>23.3. Catholicism in Hispanic Lands</u>

Vatican City is the world's only Christian theocratic state. Of the world's ten largest nations only Mexico could be considered a Catholic country (Worldometers, online). Of that ten, Russia and the United States are predominantly Christian and Catholicism is the largest Christian denomination in the United States.

Catholicism has made inroads into folk religions in Latin America and has grown from 24% in 1910 to 39% in 2010 (Sterling, online)

In eighteen Latin American countries and Puerto Rico, which were surveyed in 2014, 84% of adults were raised as Roman Catholics but only 69% identified as Catholics (a drop of 15%). By contrast 9% were raised as Protestants but 19% claim to be Protestants today. The number of unaligned persons doubled from 4% to 8%. Thus Latin American Catholicism lost members to both Protestantism and to non-religion. Protestants present as both more religiously enthusiastic, more likely to be somewhat pentecostal and more conservative on social issues (such as divorce, abortion and gay marriage) than Catholics (Sahgal, 27/10/2017, online). There has been some mistreatment or persecution of Protestants because of the scale of Catholic losses.

Latino immigration to the USA (both legal and illegal) has meant that Spanish speakers are the largest minority group there and will become the majority of Americans by c. 2050. Generally they are either devout Catholics or Charismatics-or-Pentecostals (McGrath, 2013, 335; 342-44). As both groups have larger than average families, this half of America will become more religiously devout and socially conservative, diverging from the mainstream trend (towards no religion).

<u>23.4. Baptists in Various Lands</u>

In Britain there are 216,000 Baptists and in Australia 375,000 (or 1.5% of the total population). In

America there are between 13 and 16 million Baptists, with 850,000 in South America and 239,000 in Central America (Australian Bureau of Statistics, 2016; Baptist Press, online). These results in Catholicmajority countries are primarily the result of missionary work from the U.S.A.

In America, Baptists are the second largest denomination, that is, members of the Southern Baptist Convention, but there are numerous other types of Baptists, all distinguishable by their avoidance of baptising infants, although many now call themselves 'community churches'.

In America, Baptist congregations face many challenges, notably the post-denominationalism of their youth who are evangelical but not strongly Baptist and the pentecostalisation of the Church, which trends towards authoritarian or charismatic leaders and away from congregational governance and the practical application of 'the priesthood of all believers'. For Baptists, trends are towards modern 'youth music'; female preachers and confusion about which, how many or how few spiritual gifts to embrace. Doctrinally, 'prosperity doctrine' and the resurgence of Calvinism are challenges (Weaver, online).

<u>23.5. Pentecostals</u>

In 2000 a quarter of all of the world's Christians were Pentecostal, or about 425 million people, and this is the fastest growing segment.

<u>23.6. Eastern Orthodoxy and Russia</u>

In 2019, Russia was rated as the ninth largest country in the world. In 1910, Orthodox Christians were 20% of global Christianity and Roman Catholics were 47%.

A century later, in 2010, the Orthodox were only 12% but Roman Catholics were 50%. (Protestants and others made up the remaining 37.7%).[47] In Russia, the Communist government suppressed religion for about 70 years and restricted family sizes.

Meanwhile contraception was forbidden to Catholics.

Perhaps these are the reasons why the Russian Orthodox Church is not expanding in Russia, despite now enjoying state approval (along with Catholics and Baptists, but unlike the newer denominations).

In marked contrast the Ethiopian Orthodox Church (which is different from Russian Orthodoxy in doctrine, liturgy, culture and language) is growing, and 98% of the Ethiopian Orthodox say that religion is 'very important' in their lives. By contrast, Christians in the former USSR had a median score of 17% for religion being 'very important' whereas other Europeans had a median score of 46%. No nationality was even close to the score for the Ethiopians (98%). Only 59% of Greeks, 53% of Armenians, 46% of Bosnians and 43% of Moldavians rated religion in their lives highly.

The lowest scores of all the former Soviets were from Russians (17%), Bulgarians (15%), Latvians (13%) and Estonians (10%). Having had to live without religion for so long, by-and-large the former Soviet Union (fSU) peoples have learnt to live without it (Numbers, Facts and Trends Shaping Your World 8/11/2017 'Orthodox Christians in the 21st Century', Table 3, online).

Now there may not be a sufficient critical mass of mature, educated Christians and clergy to re-evangelise these nations and lead the church without outside help. Russia itself is open only to the old, pre-Communist Revolution) denominations (Baptists, Catholics and the Orthodox): others are 'underground'.

23.7. German and European Protestantism

Five hundred years since Luther's revolutionary reformation 87% of the world's Protestants live outside of Europe. More Protestants live in Nigeria than Germany and only 7% of German Protestants say they attend church weekly (Sahgal, 27/10/2017, online).

Now 20% of the world's Protestants live in the USA but in declining numbers; falling 4% in the 7 years between 2007 and 2014. Evangelical Protestantism declined only 1% in that time, so the major loss was among 'mainline Protestants'. Net loss in Protestant numbers is part of the U.S. trend towards non-religion and atheism, a cohort that increased 7% between 2007 and 2014 (Sahgal, 27/10/2017, online).

Catholicism is the largest Christian denomination in America, which will increase because 46% of all immigrants are Catholics. Southern Baptists account for one third of all American Protestants and are the second largest denomination with 6.7%, while the United Methodists are 5.1%. Afro-American congregation members account for 5.9% (Baptist Press, online).

In Europe, the ideological gap between Catholics and Protestants has narrowed. Luther's main reformist principle was salvation by faith alone (sola fide). Now, in Germany, only 21% of Protestants believe that, whereas 61% believe that good deeds and faith in God are both necessary. German Catholics exhibit similar beliefs: 58% believe in both good works and faith (which is unremarkable) but more German Catholics believe in sola

fide than German Protestants (i.e., 26% as opposed to 21%). Now this is remarkable! In Protestant Sweden and Denmark only 17% and 26% respectively believe in sola fide which means that the core value of Luther's theology is almost lost among Lutherans, there and in Germany (Baptist Press, online).

23.8. Un-evangelised Fields

Back in 1800 about 75% of the world's population was un-evangelised. This percentage dropped in the following 200 years to 30% but since then evangelisation has barely kept pace with population growth so that 28.4% of the world's people are still un-evangelised in mid-2017.

Financial donations to global missions rapidly increased over the decades reaching a peak in the 1960s.

As recently as 1970 the estimated cost per baptised convert was $US128,000.

By 2025 the cost will be about $US380,000 (Barrett and Johnson, online) but Christian donations to missions (and to churches, welfare, charities and aid) will decrease as numbers of donors in wealthy countries fall. In the West, the middle classes are being squeezed, forced to work longer and longer hours, to work online at home, to be available at night on their mobiles and to take calls from overseas at odd hours, while wage-growth stagnates and companies make ever increasing profits and out-source work to contractors (Barrett and Johnson, online).

23.9. Missionaries in Other Lands

More missionaries are in foreign fields than ever before: 430,000 of them; with an increase to 550,000 expected by 2025. Every day the number of such missionaries increases by 14 (3 men to 11 women). By 2025, for the first time, there will be more women missionaries in foreign fields than men. In 1800 only a quarter of missionaries were women

and a third in 1970. This suggests that it is now easier for a woman to be a missionary or that women are increasingly caring and courageous, that singlewomanhood is no longer a social disadvantage and/or that men are not readily responding to God's call. In contrast, every day 347 new church-workers are employed in their home country, raising the current home-based total of workers to 12,900,000 (Johnson and Zurlo (eds) World Christian Database, 2016, online). As assessed by Greater Europe Mission there are a quarter of a million towns and cities in Europe without a gospel-preaching church. God does not call everyone to go overseas but it is necessary to be willing to hear, and to go if called.

23.10. The Urban Poor

The needs of the urban poor are increasing in the 21st century
as the gap between the wealthy and the poor increases and

everywhere there are serious needs among tribal and indigenous people, displaced persons and refugees. The greatest plight is, however, that of the world's homeless children, 100 million of whom live and die on the streets (including approximately 16,000 of them in New York; 70,000 in Calcutta/Kolkata, India, and 700,000 in Sao Paulo, Brazil) (Vos, 1994, 204f).

23.11. Growth Areas

The statistics bear out the growth of Christianity in the Global South and Asia. There are 447,277,000 church members in Africa; 531,393,000 in Latin America and 366,276,000 in Asia. In Africa, Christianity is growing by 32 thousand souls per day, in Latin America by 17 thousand souls and in Asia by 25 thousand souls per day (Pew Research Centre analyses, Global Christianity, online).

(i) Christianity in Asia/Asia Minor

Of the ten most populous countries half are in Asia: in order of size these are China and/or India, Indonesia, Pakistan and Bangladesh. Asia covers huge areas and many nationalities: some of which are virtually Christian nations with expanding Christian populations and openness to missions (such as South Korea and the Philippines) while some (such as North Korea) are quite closed (as of 2021) (Fukul, for ABC Radionational).

Some nations with the largest populations have both highly restrictive government policies and social hostility towards Christianity: notably India, Pakistan, Egypt, Indonesia and Bangladesh (Pew Research Centre, 'Restrictions on religion...',

online). Other Asian nations which are also difficult for Christians include Turkey and Mayanmar/Burma (Pattisson and State, for Telegraph Media Group Ltd., 2018, 21/1/2007, online). 'Tent making' employment is the only method by which missionaries can enter these countries; and then only

for quiet, informal evangelism and even that can be dangerous. Those Asian nations with the least restrictions and social hostilities are Japan and the Philippines whereas South Korea is already perhaps 50% Christian. In

Seoul alone there are twenty megachurches, with over 10,000 members each (Fukul, for ABC Radionational). China, Iran and Vietnam have high government restrictions but only moderate social hostility towards Christianity (Pew Research Centre, 'Restrictions on religion...', online). Since Mid-2018 China has cracked-down on Christianity but it has a vibrant underground church movement and, by 2030, may well have the world's largest Christian population (Fukul, for ABC Radionational, online).

(ii) Christianity in Africa

There are many Africa Instituted Churches (or Indigenous Churches) in Africa. They contrast markedly with the European-type churches. Unlike Catholicism and Anglicanism, which use liturgies and rituals similar to those in Europe and Britain (inherited from Africa's colonial past) AIU Churches embrace elements of African culture, language, rituals, music, instruments and symbols. This apparently contributes greatly to the growth of Christianity in Africa. These churches now number from 54 to 60 million people. Recently AIU churches have begun to engage in formal theological education, to be prepared to accept modern medical care (which was previously forbidden) and to reduce tensions with older forms of Christianity (World Christianity AIU, on AIC, online).

(iii) Christianity in Sub-Sahara n Africa

In 2008, 16% of the world's Catholics lived in sub-Saharan Africa but 55% of the world's Anglicans lived in sub-Saharan Africa: whereas only 33% of the world's Anglicans lived in Britain (Sterling, online).

Sub-Saharan Africa is home to the world's most observant Christians. It is also the world's fastest growing population and an area of entrenched poverty and need (The Economist Newspaper Ltd. 25/12/2015, online). Women's ministry is vital to its growth and is culturally appropriate.

(iv) African Pentecostalism

The emerging churches hold the key to the expansion of Christianity. For one thing they can evangelise at home much more economically and culturally appropriately than Westerners can. The provision of training for them and their converts, however, has posed difficulties from the beginning, and many congregations are unorthodox in doctrine, with some syncretism with folk religions.

In 2006, Pentecostals were 12% of Africa's population or 107 million Christians, out of 890 million Africans with an additional 5% (40 million) charismatics within mainline denominations ('Spirit and Power – A 10-Country survey of Pentecostals', Oct. 5, 2006, online).

(v) Christianity in Zambia

In Zambia, a British colony until 1964, 85.5% of people are Christians and more than 20% of the population is pentecostal/charismatic. Under the first president, Kenneth Kaunda, there was oneparty rule. In 1991, Zambia, held democratic elections and President Frederick Chiluba, a Pentecostal, was elected. His constitution declared Zambia to be a Christian nation and he then dedicated Zambia and its government to the Lordship of Jesus Christ ('Spirit and Power – A 10-Country survey of Pentecostals', Oct. 5, 2006, online). His democratic reforms stalled because the instutitions, such as the law courts, functioned weakly and in the old ways: subject to bribery and coercion (Kimenyl and Moyo, 2011, online).

(vi) Christianity in Egypt

Egypt has the Middle East's largest Orthodox population: c.4,000,000 which is 4% of Egypt's population. They are mainly members of the ancient Coptic Orthodox Christian Church (Johnson and

Zurlo (eds), World Christian Database - Numbers Facts and Trends Shaping Your World: 'Orthodox Christianity in the 21st Century', online). In recent years, however, their numbers are falling because

of immigration and persecution although a quiet religious revival is in progress.

(vii) Catholicism in Africa

In 1900 only 2% of Africans were Catholics and only 9% were Christians in total. To 1970 there was rapid growth of 38% in Christianity. Between 1970 and 2005, the total percentage of Christians grew from 40% to 46% and, of that, Catholicism grew from 13% of Africans to 17% of them. Nigerian Pentecostals now outnumber the combined total of Catholics and Anglicans ('Overview. Spirit and Power – A 10-Country survey of Pentecostals', Oct. 5, 2006, online, table 1).

Ethnic tensions and violence remain critical in Northern Nigeria, with little international help but when Nigeria became independent in 1960 it was soon engulfed by civil war (1967-1970) called 'the Biafran War' in which millions of children died of starvation.

Roman Catholic efforts to be part of the solution to ethnic tensions and Muslim versus Christian violence include the Roman Catholic Nigerian Missionary Society of St Paul (MSP) which was founded in 1978. Priests from various zones and regions were formed together into the MSP to unify and evangelise across tribal, ethnic and national barriers, with financial support from Pope John Paul II. Pope Paul VI, the first Pontiff to visit Africa and who visited numerous African nations, encouraged Africa to be a missionary-sending area: to evangelise locally first, and then overseas and now many MSP priests serve overseas including in such traditional missionary-sending nations as Ireland, Germany and the North Americas (Ihunnia, MSP, online).

(viii) Christianity in Nigeria Now

In Nigeria, Muslims and Christians are now about equally numerous. Although both have grown since 1970, Christianity has grown at least 12% faster, but converts have mainly come from faiths other than Islam.

Nigeria's current serious state of ethnic hostilities is based upon religion. Most Christians live in the South and most Muslims in the North but those in the centre are at risk of persecution. Farmers are being driven off their land and/or killed by the Pulani Militia who want the land for cattle, which is leading to food shortages. In Nigeria, Christians are vigorous but Boko Haram is active. It attacks schools, Christians and churches with persecutions, killings and kidnappings, especially of schoolgirls for sexual servitude and young males for forced labour. Christians are also attacked by ISIS so that Nigeria is becoming the world's biggest killing field (Crusis staff, Aug. 20, 2020). Violence is increasing and in the first half of 2020 more Christians were killed than in all of 2019 and from 2018 groups of children are continuing to be kidnapped from their schools for ransom.

(ix) Nigerian Pentecostalism

Nigeria has Africa's largest population. As noted above, its Pentecostal citizens were numerically equal to Catholics and Anglicans combined in 2006 and, with Charismatics, account for more than 20% of the total population. Pentecostals have become active in national politics ('Overview. Spirit and Power – A 10-Country survey of Pentecostals', Oct. 5, 2006, online).

Several Nigerian Pentecostal groups are growing in different
other nations.

"Nigerian churches are helping change the face of European and North American Christianity and are part of a growing global mission force" (Effa, IBMR, 37.4 (Oct., 2013, 214-18).

.44. Christian Martyrdom

Unfortunately the martyrdom of local Christians, missionaries, Christian aid workers and Western embassy staff is still a world-problem, for example on February 22, 2021, the Italian ambassador, the driver and another man were assassinated in the Democratic Republic of Congo while travelling in a UN convey delivering food for World Food Aid.

The greatest number of Christian deaths occurred in the 1970's when an average of 377,000 people were martyred each year. The average fell to c.160,000 in 2000 and to 90,000 in 2017. It is expected to rise by 2025 to 100,000 or more (perhaps because of a rise in militant Islamic activity). Missionary work, which used to be dangerous because of lack of medical care, is now more dangerous from war, terrorism and government opposition but national Christians are being targeted because foreign nationals have international protection, while locals do not.

In 2020 persecution by Muslim extremists spread beyond Nigeria's borders: to the Democratic Republic of Congo, Mozambique and Uganda (where Pastor David Omara was strangled on October 31, 2020 for preaching on radio). Murder, rape, trafficking girls for prostitution and males for forced labour in South Africa are common options. In Mozambique, albino children are trafficked for their organs and body parts (Sekulow, 2020, online)

.45. Christianity in the Muslim-majority World

Most of these countries were once Christian: notably the
Byzantine-Empire lands. Originally, the gospel had spread out
from Jerusalem along the Ancient Persian Royal Roads, which ran from S-W Iran through Babylon, into Northern Mesopotamia and into Asian regions subjugated by Alexander the Great. The Ancient Silk Road ran from Syria
into Persia, Uzbekistan, Turkmenistan, Bukhara and Samarkand and to China (Jenkins, 2008, 50ff). Even well after the Arab conquests (633-750 A.D./C.E.) the East had vibrant Christian communities and growth continued into India but these communities shrank because Islam, a more dominant and dominating faith tradition, evolved in the Middle East, which won many hearts and minds and brutally suppressed all opposition.

Persia/Iran was once a centre of Christian scholarship, culture and monasticism (Jenkins, 2008, 6; 19). In c.550 CE, Cosmas the Monk wrote:

"Throughout the whole land of Persia there is no limit to the number of churches with bishops and very large communities of Christian people, as well as many martyrs and monks living as hermits" (Cosmas Indicopleustes, J. W. McCrindle (trans.).

Iran is now a totalitarian state: a police state. There is close surveillance of every aspect of life as the state tries to protect its population from anything outside Islamic culture and to curb outside influences.

The 56 Muslim-majority countries have a combined Muslim population of 1.1 billion people: 72% of the world's Muslims live in one of these nations and 25% of delegates to the United Nations represent them. Christians are restricted, harassed and/or persecuted in them all.

Yazidis are also persecuted. Turkomen, Shabbak, Sunni Muslims and Shia Muslims are persecuted by other Muslim groups that happen to be the majority. Rohingya Muslims and tribal Christians are persecuted by the Buddhist military government in Myanmar/Burma, Sunni Muslims are persecuted by the Assad regime in Syria and Uighur Muslims are persecuted in China ('Minority Report: Christian Persecution in Muslim-Majority Countries', online).

It is a poorly kept secret that the gospel is advancing in closed and semi-closed countries in the 'Muslim-majority world' through dreams, visions and miracles. The Institute of Muslim Studies at the Billy Graham Centre in Wheaton, USA, reports that in recent years "the frequency of dreams and visions of Christ amongst Muslims has risen dramatically". In Africa 42% of new believers come to faith through dreams, visions, angelic appearances and hearing God's voice audibly (Robinson, 2004, 273). Since the Twin Towers disaster of 9/11/2001 serious military conflicts have occurred in Afghanistan, Iraq and Syria. Millions of Muslims and local Christians became (and remain) refugees or displaced persons. Islamic fundamentalism became a major world force in the Middle East and North Africa by taking advantage of the upheavals and revolutions dubbed 'the Arab Spring' to infiltrate, terrorise and kill. Europe has not been immune from this. Islam is stridently proselytising, especially by electronic communications and through intermarriage with non-Muslims.

23.14. <u>Some reasons for the growth of Christianity</u>

In South Korea and China, education, gender equality and Christianity are seen as part of modernity. The 'Protestant work ethic' is associated with the market economy, which has a modern appeal. Christianity is associated with both social and political reform (Fukul for ABC Radionational, online).

Refugees from the Middle East are flocking into churches, notably in Germany, and the gospel is reaching people in closed and semi-closed countries via electronic media.

In Nigeria, and nations with a similar demographic, community identity becomes doubly significant and Christians have to be staunch in their identity because of persecution.

<u>23.15. Conclusions</u>

Christianity is expanding in the developing nations and in some it is competing with Islam, with violent consequences. The old ideological battle between Communism and Christianity continues but is being overshadowed. Islam has already become Britain's second religion and it will overtake Judaism as the second religion of America (Robinson, 2004, 312).

Future Church growth at present resides in the non-European world. As non-Europeans adopt Christianity in increasing numbers they are shedding the European baggage inherited from the missionaries and becoming inculturated. This means that Ecclesia will be less European and will present herself in a much greater diversity of styles, praxis and beliefs across the nations. This has so far resulted in some concerning theological differences. The need for sound teaching is a pressing problem as some of the ancient heresies are re-emerging.

Meanwhile, in Western nations a new faith tradition is evolving, which may swamp Christianity. It is a mixture of postmodern, individualist relativism mixed with a God-free humanism, by which each person decides their own relative truth, so long as others are not hurt by it. This ideology may leave only 'a remnant of faith' in Christian countries.

<u>Questions:</u>

(1) Why is Christianity expanding in Africa and how can their need for theological education be met?

(2) What do you think "European baggage inherited from the missionaries" entails in Africa?

Chapter 24
What of the 21st Century?

<u>24.1. Obvious Results of Spiritual Decline</u>

In the West, including in America, the earliest post-war signs of secularization were reduced church attendance and the prevalence of marriage break-downs. As the divorce of their parents has serious consequences for children, juvenile mental health issues, vandalism, crime and youth suicides have emerged early and with increasing frequency. Parents whose own lives have been shattered and/or whose family lives include a series of partners may be unable to provide clear moral guidance, leaving schools struggling to be the most stable institution in children's lives. In an age of poor social cohesion schools are under pressure, attempting to provide consistent, stable support for the increasing numbers of needy youth.

Anonymous and impersonal communications via social media has resulted in an epidemic of criticism, bad language and abuse, including by and of quite young children, with detrimental consequences, especially for young people, women, racial minorities and high-profile personalities. The breakdown of social cohesion and of Judeo-Christian morality amongst adults are symptoms of an emerging neo-paganism. New technologies are associated with (if not directly causing) trolling, increasing disrespect, gun violence, street violence, domestic violence and the murder of women and their children. The loss of belief that women should be respected is associated with vulgar language, blatantly sexualised behaviour, the objectification of girls and women and the wide dissemination of lewd videos.

"The astonishingly abusiveness of Twitter is dehumanising. While everybody who ventures into that sewer faces some foul level of abuse, it is worse for women because so often the abuse is sexualised

and violent in its imagery" (Sheridan, 'Society will pay for loss of its Christian ideals',

Weekend Australian, March 27-28, 2021, 15).

Most societies now fall into one of two categories: highly sexualised societies (which are mostly postChristian and Western) and repressive societies. In the latter, women are controlled, confined, completely covered and/or cloistered in case they tempt men. Homosexual men are beaten, imprisoned or even killed. Those in each type of society believe the other to be wicked. In the 21st century a balanced and/or Biblical view of sexuality can hardly be found and daily the gap between it and the neo-pagan world widens.

<u>24.2. Anti-semitism is replaced by Anti-Zionism</u>

As has been shown, since Vatican II the Catholic Church has been forging a new relationship with Jews and Judaism. Furthermore some Protestants are enthusiastic and positive 'lovers of Zion' who seek to comfort Jews and Israel. In the opposite direction certain Protestant denominations are returning to outdated attitudes. After WWII, anti-semitism was made illegal in much of Europe but the spirit behind it has not died so that another way to express the old sentiments has been found. This 'solution' is 'anti-Israel' (not 'anti-Jew') and it attempts to delegitamise the nation of Israel and to ruin it.

"Since a Jewish nation-state is antithetical to the ruling philosophies of our age, globalism and secularism, this modern form of political anti-semitism is finding large-scale

acceptance today. It is dircted not at individual Jews but

against the Jewish state and is called anti-Zionism" (Michael, online). The new millennium began with a new idea designed

to cripple Israel so effectively that (somehow) the Palestinians could gain what they want (politically, economically and socially). In 2001/2002 both the Presbyterians and the United Methodists of the U.S. passed resolutions against certain companies in what was called 'phase-selective divestment' a name which (because of a strong backlash) the Presbyterians watered down, renaming it (and claiming the moral high-ground) 'morally responsible investment'. This updated form of anti-semitism grew on college campuses by 2005 and was accepted by American denominations such as the United Church of Christ and the U.S. Mennonite Church (Farah and Wildman, online).

In about 2005, the title BDS, which stands for Boycott, Divestment and Sanctions, appeared. 'Boycott' means a boycott of all sporting, cultural and academic groups and contacts as well as of international and Israeli compnies, who are viewed as (by definition) anti-Palestinian. 'Divestment' means that banks, churches, pension funds and universities must withdrawn funds from any such companies. Governments should 'Sanction' Israel by cutting off military and trade ties and by expelling Israel from FIFA and the United Nations (which had voted to establish Israel in the first place, in November, 1947) (Palestinian BDS National Committee, online).

Britain's main contribution to BDS was a boycott of cultural and academic contacts and of the sharing of research results (shades of Medieval book burning?). This has disadvantaged the whole world because Israel does scientific and medical research so successfully.

The main rhetoric behind the BDS movement is that Israel has stolen Palestinian land, but every Australian lives on land that the British stole from the aboriginal people in 1788,

and that is accepted, worldwide, as the status quo. (North Americans and Kiwis can make up their own minds about what applies to them.) In 1066 the French (Normans) stole England from the Britons and Celts, and the Turks stole Constantinople from the Byzantine Greeks in 1453, and so on throughout history. David Wildman calls these "deeply unjust, immoral actions" (Farah and Wildman, online) but virtually the whole world is guilty; but has forgotten. China has occupied Tibet and Indonesia controls West Papua and severely punishes Papuan nationalists, but few outside voices complain. As to any right of residency for foreigners, for the sake of security no country permits entry unless it can be sure of the total loyalty of the applicant; which may not be guaranteed in the case of Palestinian 'refugees'. (But this is straying too far into politics, which is unwise.)

Pro-BDS groups appeal to the Bible for justification, but read it with a Middle Eastern minds-set. Ezekiel 18 is interpreted to mean 'boycott and divest'; Revelation 18:11 means 'boycott and divest'; and a music boycott means a total cultural boycott (18:22) (Farah and Wildman, online). By contrast no notice is taken (neither literal nor allegorical) of any clear Bible passages that would encourage Israelis, such as:

"I will build you up again and you will be rebuilt, O Virgin Israel. Again you will take up your tamourines and go out to dance with the joyful. Again you will plant vineyards on the hills of Samaria: the farmers will plant and enjoy their fruit" (Jer. 31:4-5.)

Nor is notice taken of assurances that Israel's God keeps promises, such as Jer. 33:14: "The days are coming when I will fulfil the gracious promises I made to the house of Israel and to the house of Judah" and "I will not violate my covenant or alter what my lips have uttered" (Ps. 89:34).

Economic activity and trade are two-way processes and every country which damages the process, damages itself,

which is why 'free-trade-agreements' are becoming so sought-after. BDS is, by its own admission, a small movement (Farah and Wildman, online). Recently, it has been countered by increased action by the millions of Christian-Zionists, by Jews in the Diaspora, by other supporters of Israel and, in America, by state legislation so that by May 1918, 28 states had outlawed BDS (Jerusalem Post, October 24, 2017).

Those who will suffer most from BDS are the Palestinians themselves. Take, for example, the case of the SodaStream factory in the 'disputed territories' which employed over 500 Palestinians at standard wage rates. It was forced by BDS activity to relocate to the Negev. Consequence, despite the company's efforts to obtain permanent work permits for its former workers, those Palestinians workers have lost their jobs to Israelis.

The sad thing is that certain denominations are ultimately damaging themselves also, because the Creator has said to the Jewish people, in Gen. 12:3: "I will bless those who bless you and whoever curses you I will curse and all peoples on earth will be blessed through you."

The BDS movement is widespread in Europe but, as noted, American legislators are pushing back.

24.3. The Ongoing Role of Ecclesia

The Great Commission

Ecclesia has the same purpose as God has, a big task: to restore and redeem all creation (Maddix and Akkerman (eds.), 2013, Ch 1; par 7-12). Jesus calls his followers to partner with him in mission to transform the world, as he put it, to be Salt and Light, to the world. Ecclesia must partner with God in this task, bringing forth the Father's Kingdom.

"God has one purpose and interest in humanity since the "fall". That has been to bring man (humanity) back to God.... Jesus Christ had but one interest in coming to earth.... (that) the curse (punishment for sin) be lifted" (Bartleman, 1925/1980, 112).

The means by which this is achieved is given in Mat. 22:37; 28:18-20; Deut. 6:5; Mk. 12:31; Lk. 10:27.

Jesus said:

"all authority in heaven and on earth has been given to me. Therefore go and make disciples of all nations, baptising them in the name of the Father and of the Son and of the Holy Spirit and teaching them to obey everything I have commanded you. And surely I will be with you always, to the very end of the age" (Mt. 28:18ff).

This pericope is the key to understanding God's plan and is the climax of Matthew's gospel (Otto, in Stanton (ed.), 1995, 45). The church is called to act, 'making disciples' (of every nation), to 'go' ('baptise') and to 'teach' these disciples (Wilkins, 2004, 951). To 'go' is the role of the Ecclesia: if we are to see 'all nations' come to Christ then the church must go to every nation, town and village across the earth. Mission is the centrepiece of Ecclesia's calling. There are then two objectives: 'to baptise' and 'to teach'.

Ecclesia is called to go (to all peoples), to baptise and to teach. As noted in Chapter 17, there are still peoples and language groups who have had no gospel witness so the task is incomplete but the task requires three things: people to go; people to pray and people to give (Bartleman, 1925/1980, 112). The Great Commission means bringing people into a right relationship with Creator God through the sacrificial death of Jesus. After this, people must be baptised and taught everything that Jesus taught his disciples.

The sacrament of baptism is an outward expression of recognising the reign of God in a person's life – the seal of their conversion, their new relationship with God. Those baptised people who are now living this new life, one that brings glory to the Lord, are to be taught everything that

Jesus has commanded of his followers, making teaching a most important aspect of Ecclesia's life. Educating usually

means imparting information, the dissemination of knowledge to, for example, small Roman, Greek or American children:

but when Jesus used it in a Hebrew context it was radically different from today's education; although the method was known elsewhere in the Ancient Near East (Collinson, 2004). Jesus was a Rabbi and his followers were his talmidim (pupils). Jesus and his disciples illustrate how Rabbis and tamidim related to each other within a teaching paradigm. It is said that a student would be covered in his master's dust and Jesus' students followed him everywhere They saw his public ministry and his private life, the way he conducted himself in one-on-one conversations but also in his spiritual formation and devotion (Bell, 2005, 130). This same method had been effectively practised by the Greek philosophers Socrates, Plato and Aristotle hundreds of years previously and by it both the master's philosophy of life and his behaviour was communicated (Collinson, 2014).

"Our greastest challenge is to recover Jesus the teacher.... Over the last 200 years, Jesus as teacher has simply disappeared. Whether Liberal of Conservative it doesn't make any difference" (Willard, Subversie Interview, Part 1, online).

<u>24.4. Methods for Ecclesia</u>

The problem of arresting the decline of church membership in the democratic West is presenting a challenge to the radical pastors and leaders of the 21st century. They have similar ideas but different emphases, many are simplifying their rhetoric and turning back to 'the Jesus period' for answers. Frost describes one of the most important out-workings of discipleship, "elbow learning" (Frost, 2014,

87). Jesus called his disciples to follow him, as their Rabbi. To follow one's Rabbi was to live life with him and to follow him in everything. In rabbinic tradition: "acolytes sat at the feet of their rabbi and were instructed not only with ideas but practices, liturgies and new experiences"

(Frost, 2014, 141). Apprenticeship involves not just watching but entering the arena, the contest.

The disciples would have seen Jesus performing miracles and heard his teaching. They would have seen his private life, how he treated others, how he prayed, what he did in the synagogues (Peace, 1999, 254). They would have seen him living out how he loved his Father with all that he had and his love for His neighbour... all the way to the cross. New Christians need to be discipled by living and ministering alongside mature Christians. They need to see how others are growing in spiritual maturity, how they connect with community and how they participate in spiritual practices. In Jesus' society the teacher was a rabbi whose talmidim followed him everywhere, every day, hearing him speak on every subject: mundane or academic, practical or spiritual. This was their spiritual formation; meaning, the process by which they grew to spiritual maturity, becoming like Jesus. Saul of Tarsus (Paul) was a talmid of a great Rabbi Gamaliel I, the grandson of the great Rabbi Hillel ('Gamaliel', in ODCC). Paul told the early believers: "Follow my example as I follow the example of Christ" (I Cor 11:1). Following a follower (or copying a copy of a copy) cannot continue for long. One must return to the original for a good copy (Frost and Hirsh, 2009, 188f). This is much easier for today's Christians than for St Paul's converts because the complete Bible is now readily available.

For Jesus, teaching was a holistic life-on-life approach to spiritual formation. Sunday services are important but weekly services were not the method that Jesus used to bring the twelve to spiritual maturity (nor are these services designed for evangelism, unless they are specifically 'seeker services'). Jesus taught the twelve face-to-face for about three years, which suggests a prolonged, in-depth process. After this time the twelve became the fledgling leaders, dependent upon the Holy Spirit once Jesus had departed from them.

St Aidan of Lindisfarne chose this method of education when he selected twelve English boys to be future Bishops of England: teaching them Latin literacy (first the Psalms and then the gospels) as well as how to live the monastic life.

'Elbow earning' is the context of teaching and evangelism, the call to baptise is a call to bring the lost home to the Lord, teaching is a holistic life-on-life approach. Acts 2:42-47 is a key passage on this issue:

"Therefore go (out into the wider world) to make disciples of all nations (that means Mission) baptising them in the name of the Father, Son and Holy Spirit (Trinitarian baptism) teaching them to obey (that means spiritual maturity and formation)".

This is exactly what the early saints did. They devoted themselves to the apostles teaching and to fellowship and the breaking of bread (the Holy Communion) and to prayer (Acts 2:42). *"Everything I have commanded you"* (that means that baptism is only the first step).

Teaching was to be step-by-step, incremental: first the milk then the meat of the Word (I Cor. 3:1-2). Centred in the Scriptures not in human imagination and speculation and avoiding the perpetual temptation to exchange knowledge about Jesus and faith for personal encounters with him. Christianity is not about following Jesus' teachings and religious code: it is about relationship.

"Discipleship requires a direct and unmediated relationship with the Lord" (Frost and Hirsch, 2009, 51).

<u>24.5. Spiritual Formation</u>

As noted, the process by which Christians grow to spiritual maturity is called 'spiritual formation' (learning the way of Jesus and becoming like him). The on-going process of spiritual formation is a critical concept that needs to be

understood if churches are to foster spiritual maturity. Spiritual maturity is important for each Christian and is imperative for each Christian leader.

Dallas Willard regards spiritual formation as being,

"the Spirit-driven process of forming the inner world of the human self in such a way that it becomes like the inner being of Christ himself ...the outer life of the individual becomes a natural expression or outflow of the character and teachings of Jesus" (Willard, 2002, 15). The good news is that spiritual formation (and so maturity) can be achieved.

"(It) is simultaneously a profound manifestation of God's gracious action through his Word and Spirit, it is also something we are responsible for before

God and can set about achieving in a sensible, systematic manner" (Willard, 2002, 15).

But how many leaders and pastors know what those sensible, systematic ways are? Spiritual formation and biblical understanding lead to spiritual maturity and can be attained through creating Christ centred narratives for one's-self, being cemented in a faith community and implementing spiritual practices, while recognizing that all of these need to be empowered through the Holy Spirit. Churches can promote change by creating an environment of discipleship and utilizing spiritual practices to help cement transformation. Pastors themselves must lead from a healthy spiritual maturity.

The apostle Paul calls it having a mature relationship with Christ but, in all honesty, John Stott admits that:

"Maturity is rather hard to pin down. Most of us suffer from lingering immaturities. Even in grown adults the little child is still hiding somewhere" [48]

and:

"To be in Christ is to be personally, vitally, organically related to him. In this sense, to be mature is to have a mature relationship with Christ in which we worship, trust, love and obey him"

(Stott, 2010, 41f). Jesus, however, does not mind the hidden child but he wants the mature adult, rather than the child, to be in control.

<u>24.6. Spiritual Maturity</u>

The word most commonly translated 'mature' is teleios (τέλειος), which means 'a state of full development.' Teleios, for Paul has a specific meaning, combining dual ideas: the full development of one's powers; and the accomplishment of some goal or standard (the realization of the proper end of one's existence). Later the word 'mature' has come to mean complete or full-grown, and implies maturity in character and knowledge. It is used to describe the full development of adulthood, contrasting with the immaturity of childhood (Sanders, 1986, 19-25).

Paul teaches us in Colossians 1:28: *"We proclaim him, teaching everyone with all wisdom, so that we may present everyone mature [teleios] in Christ."*

God's desire is that Christians reflect the perfect humanity of His Son, people who are able to respond to the challenges of adult life with adult responses, producing people who fulfil their humanity in conformity to Christ. Patently, only Jesus was ever completely mature but all can grow in maturity. One may view spiritual maturity as simply 'Christ-likeness'. The more like Christ we are the more mature we are. His character was complete, well balanced, and perfectly integrated. All His qualities and capacities were completely attuned to the will of His Father. As his followers, we need to seek Him and maturity will follow (Sanders, Knowing and Doing, 2005). Ephesians 4:13, develops this:

"...in the knowledge of the Son of God and become [teleios] mature, attaining to the whole measure of the fullness of Christ".

To be spiritually teleios [mature] one will seek to attain the fullness of Christ. 'Spiritual maturity' comes as a result of the ongoing process of 'spiritual formation'. McLaren explains three vital aspects to this concept: the experience of God; the formation of character; and being alert to what God is doing (McLaren, 2008, 18).

The definitions by both Willard and McLaren reveal some relevant similarities. Regarding spiritual formation, both see that relating to God enables Christians to be more Christ-like, which galvanizes believers into action, through love for one's neighbour and that healthy spiritual formation creates spiritual maturity in the Christian. As such it is the outworking of the inner-self being transformed to be like the inner workings of Christ.

One key Scriptural passage for understanding Christian maturity is found in Jesus' reply when asked, what the most important Law is. In Mark 12:28-31, citing Deuteronomy 6:5 and Leviticus 19:18, Jesus said:

"Love the Lord your God with all your heart and with all your soul and with all your mind and with all your strength...

The second is this: 'Love your neighbour as yourself.'"

24.7. The Two Great Commandments (including the Golden Rule)

Clearly, the first and greatest commandment is to love the Lord your God with all of your heart, your soul, your mind and your strength. The second is similar to it, but secondary: "you shall love your neighbour as (you love) yourself." "The first Great Commandment makes it possible to fulfil the second: Love your neighbour as oneself" (Willard, 2002, 99).

The Golden Rule is a well-accepted way to express love for others: do to and for others what you want them to do to and for you.

With the importance of these two requirements before the Christian's eyes he or she must undertake a prayerful

examination of the conscience: is this perfectly in order? How much is God loved? How is that love shown? Be warned: this love cannot be manufactured by trying harder: it is a gift of the Holy Spirit, a gift which God is willing to give, indeed is waiting to give.

First, we are to love God. This incorporates knowing Him and His character; which involves a deep connection with our Heavenly Father. Secondly we are to Love God with all that we are, which enhances a sense of 'self'. We will love God with our heart, soul, mind, and strength. This relationship transforms us from the inside out. Thirdly, we are to love our neighbours, out of our love for God. Thus the change that happens within us drives us to love our neighbour.

The Anabaptist movement illustrated this concept (of internal change from connecting with God that engenders the believer into mission). Augsburger suggests that the Anabaptists had these three components to their spirituality as each person was 'upwardly compliant' (the experience of divine encounter with God), which then led him or her to be 'inwardly directed' (the personal journey of the person being transformed) which then led to being 'outwardly committed' (the relation of integrity and solidarity with our neighbour) (Augsburger, 2006, 13).

<u>24.8. Heart, soul, mind and strength</u>

Helland and Hjalmarson believe that Mark 12:28-31 (also Mat. 22:34ff and Luke 10:25ff) provoke the Christian to have holistic love towards God and others. Holistic love encompasses every aspect of life: *"The word 'heart' in scripture is the seat of the will, mind and emotions: the individual's command center (sic). The word soul in scripture means the person or living being. We must love God from* our minds, the faculty of intelligence, thought, perception and judgment (Helland and Hjalmarson, 2011, 70, f/ n. 35; citing John Piper, 2005, 80).

Love is awakened in the Christian:

*"The first Great Commandment, to Love God with all our being,
can be fulfilled because of the beauty of God given in Christ ... ...
We love because He first loved us"* (Willard, 2002).

This has a flow-on effect. Love of God enables someone to love their neighbours: love for God moves through the believer, to others. The 'will' is at the core the individual,

without an intact 'will' one is just a shadow of themselves (Peterson, 1989, 105). Without an act of the will no purposeful action can take place. In summary:

"Spiritual formation in Christ is the process leading to this ideal end of spiritual maturity, and its result is love of God, with all of the heart, soul, mind, and strength, and of the neighbour as oneself" (Willard, 2002, 37).

<u>24.9. Spiritual Practices</u>

Throughout church history spiritual renewal movements have existed. These have taken numerous shapes and varieties but all have utilized spiritual practices to help shape their spiritual formation: although today they are virtually forgotten in Protestantism.

Utilising spiritual practises helps cement transformation and they are an important aspect of discipleship. They are patterns of cooperative human activity in and through which life together takes shape over time, in response to God (Bass and Volf, 2001, 3).

As noted above, in Chapter 16.2, the leader of Pietism, Spener (16351705), in his book Pia Desideria (Earnest Desire) concentrated on spiritual practices such as mid-week Bible studies called 'colleges of piety' and lay ministry, with a strong emphasis on morality and works of love and charity.

He encouraged the priesthood of all believers (Helland and Hjalmarson, 2011, 80). Similarly, the early Methodists

emphasized hospitality, music, Bible study, confession and discipline in inward and outward holiness for mission.

Our Christian forebears significantly utilised spiritual practices because they understood their power in building spiritual maturity, unlike the current church, which uses education as the primary tool of spiritual formation. Alan Hirsch and Dave Ferguson opine that, rather than simply listening to more sermons on how to be more spiritually mature, "the vast majority of people in the church will be changed by acting their way into a new way of thinking" (Hirsch and Ferguson, 2011, 175). If church leaders create and encourage practices that engender spiritual maturity and imbed these in a culture of discipleship, we will see people living according to their beliefs and values and lives will change. St Paul's desire is to "present everyone teleios [mature] in Christ" (Col. 1:28). True discipleship is a vital component to creating mature followers of Jesus who love God with all that they are and love their neighbour as themselves, while in a faith community.

Spiritual practices can be powerful tools in individual Christian lives but they are even more influential when entire congregations engage in these intentional patterns. Practices are important for discipleship as they direct us and keep us focused on God, each other, and the rest of the world as we spur each other on in mission (Norris, 2012, 6).

Through intentionally created practices such as prayer, eating together and blessing others the church will embody its discipleship (Norris, 2012, 25). Each church needs to tailor culturally appropriate practices to uniquely reflect their vision's heart. Acts 2:42-47 gives a list of spiritual practices, which were incorporated by the Early Church and can be grouped into three clusters.

First, the church had practices around 'connecting with God', (devoting themselves to the apostles teaching and to prayer and praising God), secondly, they had

practices around 'connecting with the faith community' (fellowship, breaking bread and spending time in each other's homes) and finally they 'connected with the wider community' (signs and wonders, charitable distribution of goods to the poor, proselytising).

McLaren defines three categories of spiritual practices: the 'contemplative way', the 'communal way', and the 'missional way' (looking inwards, looking to other Christians and looking to those outside of the church). These three groupings are logical and helpful for the church and individuals. Spiritual practices that connect us with the Father will benefit the individual, moulding the inner-self to be more Christ-like. Secondly, if we have practices that encourage us to connect with our faith community, we will benefit from their wisdom and be encouraged to progress with a healthy accountability in our spiritual formation. Finally we are being shaped for His mission. If we are more Christ-like we will care about His agenda and will become involved in our wider community. The modern church could benefit from the same spiritual practices that were used in previous eras to help people connect with God, including: fixed hours of prayer; spiritual reading and study; listening to the Spirit; singing Psalms and songs of worship; solitude; silence; fasting; Sabbath keeping; practising the presence of God and even self-imposed poverty (McLaren, 2008, 95f). Such practices will help connect us with Jesus, and help us love God with our whole self. It is important to disrupt our normal rhythms to deliberately connect with God but it is also important to find God in the everyday moments.

Mike Frost describes a group who pray five times a day. Upon rising they pray Mary's prayer of consecration (Luke1:38); in the morning, the Magnificat (Luke 1:46-55); at noon they pray

Zechariah's Benedictus (Luke 1:68-75); in the afternoon, a short Doxology (Luke 2:14) and in the evening, the aged Simeon's Nunc Dimittis (Luke 2:29-32). Does this sound too formal? No, it's Biblical and very helpful (Frost, 2014, 115-18). Too demanding? Most Muslims achieve it.

At the core of all these spiritual practices is the idea of putting others first. Two brothers once came to see a hermit whose custom it was not to eat every day. When he welcomed them cheerfully he said:

"A fast has its own reward, but whoever eats because of love, obeys two commandments, he loses his self-will and he refreshes his brothers" (Ward, 2003, 136).

Followers of Christ, who wish to live out the second commandment in Mark 12, should embrace spiritual practices that will shape spiritual formation towards evangelism, for example, forgiveness, hospitality, praying for the sick, showing mercy, service, listening, speaking truth, throwing parties, confronting evil, working for justice and evangelism (McLaren, 2008, 119).

Spiritual maturity results from a merging of Divine and human cooperation within both believers and congregations. The Holy Spirit is the final and ultimate contributing factor in the Christian's journey to spiritual maturity. As St Paul teaches (I Cor. 3:16), we are the temple of the Holy Spirit and He lives in us: *"Don't you know that you yourselves are God's temple and that God's Spirit dwells in your midst?"*

As I John 4:4 expresses it, "he who is in you (the Christian) is greater than he who is in the world". A Christian's spiritual maturity can only be fully seen with the empowerment of the Holy Spirit, but the great thing is that God gives the Spirit to all who love Him. Leaders and congregations cannot see a Spirit empowered, fully mature spirituality unless they live out the two great commandments of loving God with all that we are and loving our neighbour as ourselves.

Love of others will result in helping others. Approximately two thousand Bible passages state that issues of justice are important to God.

One difficulty with many 'missional' churches is how to maintain a balanced approach to both evangelism and social justice. In order to embrace both one must accept that both are biblical and should first inform the way that we live, secondly structure our churches and, thirdly, govern the way in which our leaders guide us in mission.

Social justice is not new to the evangelical movement (Frost, 2016, 88; Stott, 2007, 50f). As noted in Chapter 17.2, it was the Clapham Sect in England in the early 1800's that became the backbone of the abolition of the slave trade movement and set the moral compass for the society (Shelley, 1982/1996, 364-369). Yet some people struggle to see this as a Biblical concept. In discussing social justice Kevin Deyoung and Greg Gilbert opine: "we've offered no definition of the term (social justice). That's because there really isn't one..." Some see the term as "something ambiguously connected with poverty and oppression" (Deyong and Gilbert, 2011, 178f). Jesus embodied social justice in himself.

Tim Keller provides a biblical understanding by utilising two Hebrew words, 'mishpat' and 'tzadeqah'. Mishpat is translated 'justice'. It describes the action of taking up the care and cause of widows, orphans, immigrants and the poor, those who are vulnerable and marginalized such as refugees, homeless people, single parents and the aged.

Ultimately mishpat is about rectifying the wrongs against people and punishing accordingly (Keller, 2010, 4f). Tzadeqah can be translated as *'being just'* or *'being righteous'*

as it bears both meanings and brings them together. Tzadeqah refers to a life of right relationship with God that flows into right relationship with others and the community, so that all relationships are conducted with fairness, generosity and equity. Instead of rectifying wrongs like mishpat does, tzadeqah is behaviour that, if it were prevalent in the world, would render mishpat irrelevant (Keller, 2010, 10f; 4f).

The Bible links mishpat and tzadeqah many times and when used together they correspond to the English phrase 'social justice' (Wright, 2004, 257) as in Psalm 33:5: "The Lord loves righteousness (tzadeqah) and justice (mishpat); the earth is full of his unfailing love." That means that God loves social justice, which, as noted, Jesus embodied.

Further to this, the New Testament uses the Greek word dikaiosyne (translated 'righteousness' in the A.V. as in Mat. 3:15; 5:6; 5:10; 5:20; 6:33; 21:34; Rom. 3:26 and Acts 17:31, which, according to Eldin Villafane, bears the duel meaning of both mishpat and tzadeqah (Villafane, 2006, 55ff). The Bible presents justice as being grounded in the righteousness of God. God Himself is righteous and filled with justice and, as followers of Jesus, we to should endeavour to have our character shaped by Him and exhibit these traits, which overflow into action (Villafane, 2006, 55ff). Social justice is not an optional extra.

24.10. The Real Problem With Decline

John Stott celebrates the growth of the majority world church, yet he laments the lack of Christian maturity within the church in that world (Stott, 2010, 38f). Clearly, this is not the only problem in the majority world church

nor is it exclusive to that section of Ecclesia; although a lack of spiritual maturity is widespread in the western church. Immaturity is perhaps the greatest reason for lack of church growth in the West. Willow Creek Community Community

Church, near Chicago, was one of the first American congregations to offer church for the unchurched and to cater for the needs of sub-groups from the fringes of society. In twenty years (by 1995) 15,000 people attended weekly: but bringing such a large group to Christian maturity proved an enormous challenge (Noll, 2012, 183). It may be counter-intuitive but change is not achieved through programs!! Willow Creek Church, although seemingly successful, reflected upon its thirty years of ministry and found that spiritual maturity was lacking and that the structures of their programs and ministries had not been assisting. Their longstanding philosophy of ministry was that, if the church created programs and activities and that the people participated, the outcome would be spiritual maturity. Yet, after conducting major research into the church they concluded that: "increasing levels of participation in these sets of activities does not predict whether someone's becoming more of a disciple of Christ. It does not predict whether they Love God more or they love people more" ('Willow Creek Repents?' for Christianity Today, online).

In 2009 the Barna Group verified the problem with 'programism'. Nine out of ten clergy of Protestant churches asserted that spiritual immaturity is one of the most serious problems facing the church. Few pastors have clearly

articulated (written) statement to define spiritual maturity, how it's measured, the strategy for facilitating maturity, or what scriptures will help foster maturity

(Barna Group, online). Few know how to foster maturity. This generation is the most educated in history but the Christian faith in the West is in steep decline and Christians do not seem to be living out their faith like previous generations. More education is not the answer. This might appear to contradict what Willard said (in 24.4 above) about the importance of Jesus as teacher but the difference lies in the type of teacher he was and the type of teaching: 'whole of life as lived' teaching, rather than a curriculum, a program.

24.11. Churches will achieve change through discipleship

The evangelical church aims to achieve Christ-like change. It therefore emphasises Paul's statement in Romans 12:2 about the "renewing of our mind". Willard believes that to see true change in a person one must change any thoughts that are based on unhealthy worldviews into ones that are based on the idea-system that was embodied and taught by Jesus Christ (Willard, dwillard.org, online). "Have the same mindset as Christ Jesus." (Phil 2:5.). Having healthy thoughts is important, along with the need for prayer, as one Desert Father reminds us: "*Ceaseless prayer soon heals the mind*" (Ward, 2003, 131). Therefore, we cannot simply see mental exercises alone changing and shaping our ideasystems: they also require a spiritual change, as evidenced by the power of prayer. Richard Foster reminds us that, "*Prayer is learning to think God's thoughts after him*" (Foster, 1978, 42).

A key word in that sentence is 'learning'. It is rarely mentioned, except in books, that new Christians must learn to pray. But are there classes in the subject? Yet the disciples asked Jesus "*Lord, teach us to pray, as John also taught his disciples*" (Luke 11:1, K.J.V.) (Foster, 1978, 54). Saying the Lord's Prayer (the Our Father) is step one but for advanced classes one must turn to the old masters, such

as Charles Spurgeon, Ruben Torrey, Dwight L. Moody, Rees Howell and John Hyde (Praying Hyde) and the even older masters such as Brother Lawrence. God has not changed so neither has two-way communication with him, but prayer is not instinctive, it is learned behaviour. Willard says: "*Prayer is God's powersharing device for a fallen people.*" He sees the importance of God in the transforming of a believer but he also stresses the importance of individual believers themselves participating in that change (Willard, 2002).

James Bryan Smith lists three steps to real change beginning with changing the narratives in a person's mind

(Smith, 2009, 24-28). It is swapping the false narratives

that have come from culture, family or self for a narrative imbedded in Christ (his view of us, his family and his beloved). Secondly, one must engage in new practices. This is necessary because practices deepen the right narratives in the mind. "*They are wise practices that train and transform our hearts*" (Smith, 2009, 26f). Thirdly, these practices must be done in community. We are made in God's image and God lives in community (Father, the Son and the Holy Spirit). The Christian journey was always intended to be done in a faith community, which encourages us (Smith, 2009, 27) and correspondingly gives us accountability. Poeman, a Desert

Father, was once asked: *"what am I to do about my soul? I have become incapable of feeling and I do not fear God."* Poeman replied: "Go and live with someone who does fear God, and by being there, you too will learn to fear God" (Ward, 2003, 122). Similarly, when we spend time with people who are spiritually mature, we learn how to do likewise. Each of the three steps to change is furthered by the Holy Spirit working in and through us. The Holy Spirit shapes us and changes us as He sanctifies the believer to live more like Jesus (Willard, Renovation, 2002).

It is an interesting partnership between God moving in us, and each individual having a responsibility to change to be more like Christ. Believers: "make a conscious effort to respond to the grace of God and, with the help of the Holy Spirit cultivate the gift they received" (Shigematsu, 2013, 22) in sanctification.

Foster contends that: "inner righteousness is a gift from God to be graciously received. The needed change within us is God's work, not ours" (Foster, 1978, 6), yet each individual needs to be able to bring themselves to a place where God can move in their lives, a submission to the Holy Spirit. To flourish in spiritual maturity, we are to change the narratives that we have about ourselves into Jesus-centred narratives. This will come primarily from studying the Jesus narratives in

Scripture and by a commitment to spiritual practices

that will embed the new narratives into our lives.

Doing this within community encourages believers but we must let the Holy Spirit move in each aspect of these categories as without the Holy Spirit a Christian cannot find true spiritual maturity.

Some brothers went to the monk 'John the Short' and said to him: *"Thanks be to God, it has rained hard this year, and the palm trees have had enough water to begin to grow, the brothers who are the harvesters will find fruit from their hard work."* John the Short said to them, "So it is when the Holy Spirit comes down into the hearts of good men. They grow green and fresh" (Ward, 2003, 120). It is vitally important for all followers of Christ to find spiritual maturity but it is imperative for leaders, as James' instructions to teachers is that they will be judged more strictly than others. James 3:1: "Not many of you should become teachers, my fellow believers, because you know that we who teach will be judged more strictly".

It is very easy for pastoral leaders to get caught up in the 'work' of ministry and to lose sight of their own spiritual formation, which is perilous. "Pastors need to have a vision of success rooted in Spiritual terms, determined by the vitality of a pastors own spiritual life and their capacity to pass that onto others" (Willard, in Leadership Journal, 31.2, 2010, 29 (1). When pastors lack a rich spiritual life in Christ, they tend to concentrate on managing ministry activities and count success by numbers engaging in those activities and not upon a congregation's spiritual health. The trap of simply seeing ministry as issues of programs and 'human resources' has its inherent problems. A pastor's responsibility is not to solve people's problems or make them happy, but "to help them see the grace operating in their lives" (Peterson, 1989, 5). If pastors need to respond to every need in their faith community they will have little time for their own relationship with God.

"How can pastors lead people beside the still waters if they are in perpetual motion? How can they persuade a person to live by faith and not by works if they have to juggle their schedule constantly to make everything fit into place" (Peterson, 1989, 17).

There will always be spot fires that need to be extinguished, but the congregational leader can't keep running from issue to issue. A healthier approach is to assume that God is always doing something before we recognise it. The task is not to get God to do 'my thing' but instead to respond to what He is doing (Peterson, 1989, 4). Thus pastors will seek God in their lives rather than busily solving problems because of pressures and expectations. It is important for leaders to provide a warm, non-judgmental atmosphere within the congregation so that individuals will feel accepted, free to experiment with spirituality and free to be honest. This will then create an atmosphere where Christians can grow in maturity together and spur one another on in Christ.

Spiritual maturity is best reproduced in a congregational setting. While it is necessary to have a true Biblical framework in order to create a healthy church culture, more must be done to promote spiritual maturity. Leaders must be also able to create an environment of discipleship that will help believers live their life to the full by loving God with all that they are and loving their neighbour. Discipleship is essential to a church having a healthy understanding of spiritual maturity. The Great Commission passage is central to the Christian's calling and relevant to all, yet many people struggle to articulate or envisage it. Matthew 28:18-20: "Then Jesus came to them and said, 'All authority in heaven and on earth has been given to me. v.19 Therefore go and make disciples of all nations, baptizing them in the name of the Father and of the Son and of the Holy Spirit, v. 20 and teaching them to obey everything I have commanded you. And surely I am with you always, to the very end of the age.'"

In the passage Jesus instructs his followers to go into the entire world and make disciples. The Hebrew word talmid (pl. talmidim) has been considered but the Greek word translated 'disciple' comes from 'mathetes' - a student or a learner in the more traditional sense (McCallum and Lowery, 2006, K738). Hence discipleship is creating followers of the life and teaching of Jesus: one could call it, being yoked to Jesus.

As in the Mk. 12:28-31 passage, being a disciple has a duality: loving God and loving our neighbour. Given this reality it is essential for churches to refocus on embedding the Gospel into the individual. This is an outworking of the missio Dei, because we are to love God with all that we are, just as Jesus did, so that we become yoked to Jesus and are sent out in the same way Jesus was sent (John 20:21: 'Jesus said to them again, *"Peace be with you. As the Father has sent me, so I send you"'*) to perform mission, as He did: "*The Spirit of the Lord is on me, because he has anointed me to proclaim good news to the poor. He has sent me to proclaim freedom for the prisoners and recovery of sight for the blind, to set the oppressed free* (Lk. 4:18)."

We are to participate in the redemptive mission of God, engaging in missional practices that expand the Kingdom of God. Without this embodiment of the Gospel we can't truly be disciples of Jesus and our spiritual maturity is incomplete.

Discipleship involves having our life imbedded in the very character of Christ and as such "discipleship shows itself as crucial to our witness and mission." (Hirsch and Ferguson, 2011, 129). When a Christian lives yoked to Christ, living a life in submission to His will, that reflects His character, the believer's life will be very different.

They will be changed at a heart level and their behaviour, morals, attitudes and worldview will start to be transformed. This will have a flow-on effect: as they seek Christ, they will find it easier to continue to follow him in all that they do as the Holy Spirit continues to work within them. Faith community leaders need to engage in true discipleship to see healthy spiritual maturity lived out in lives.

<u>24.12. Remember the Five Fold Ministry?</u>

When members of a congregation have been taught the path to spiritual maturity various spiritual fruit, leadership potentials and ministry gifts will emerge and can be used for the benefit of the whole community, the Ecclesia. Congregations need the Biblical five-fold ministry (Eph. 4:11) of APEST (apostles, prophets, evangelists, shepherds and teachers) as the single pastor-teacher does not have all of the gifts and cannot bear the full load and variety of tasks to which the church is called. "*The system of church leadership we inherited from Christendom heavily favours maintenance and pastoral care, thus neglecting the church's larger mission and ministry.*" (Hirsch, for Christianity Today, 'Three Overlooked Leadership Roles', online). Many clergy who are good teachers are 'facts orientated' rather than 'people orientated' and find the shepherding role difficult, which would leave only one of the leadership roles out of the five filled: that of teacher. Thus believers have head knowledge without experience. When saying Mass was all that mattered one person could do that, but the Early Church did much more and, as this heritage is being rediscovered, there is a need to return to the five-fold ministry.

Alan Hirsch believes that the church in the West is failing to grow because it is unable to utilise five-fold leadership although congregations are not aware of the need and just accept the status-quo. Each congregation needs the insights of the prophet.

If broken people come into a congregation they will need the shepherding ministry (which is often unconsciously done by women or couples from a congregation). Because the congregation should reach out into society they need the leadership of an evangelist.

Plans for the future are needed, thus the apostles will have to develop leaders, extend plans and initiate new ideas. Seekers and new converts need teaching - 'no problem': this is the one area which the western church does best (Hirsch, for Christianity Today, 'Three Overlooked Leadership Roles', online).

<u>24.13. Decline Caused by Growing Biblical Illiteracy</u>

Church leaders are increasingly concerned about the lack of simple Biblical knowledge in the West (Laing, 2017, 9). (This is daily evidenced in quiz shows on television). Where once schools taught a few basics, these days even Santa Claus is under attack as being 'too religious'. It is not just terminology and concepts that are not being taught but basic historical facts relevant to Judaism and Christianity. "Biblical illiteracy is contributing to the societal and moral breakdown which is engulfing the families in their churches" (Michael, online).

Until recently when everyone read and learnt the King James Bible children were taught verses and whole chapters by heart and young people had a good grasp of it. Now, with so many different translations, each giving a slightly different slant on concepts, and because rote learning has been forsaken, this skill has been lost. Pastors

must encourage the use of one translation and preach from that consistently. Entire passages should be read in church every Sunday, preferably in sequence, not haphazardly. Sunday Schools should return to their original purpose as 'schools' rather than for childminding and children's entertainment. The, once-popular, All-Age Sunday Schools should be revived and basic lists of Biblical people and events compiled and taught.

Susan Michael opines that understanding the biblical significance of Israel and the Jewish people is the greatest antidote to biblical illiteracy.

"Understanding God's dealings with the Jewish people throughout the ages puts the whole Bible into perspective, and underscores its relevance and immediacy to all of us today. It is, in many ways, the 'answer key' that helps the rest of Scripture make sense in its proper context" (Michael, online).

For this reason it is important to read the prequel to this book:

to follow the full story of God's dealing with humanity in the

correct sequence. Preferably, volume 1, 'Synagoga's Heritage: Tabernacle,

Temple, Synagogue and Church' should be read first, or as soon as possible after reading this volume.

24.14. Conclusions

This chapter has outlined many new ideas and suggestions for stimulating church growth. These should attract interest and discussion, especially among pastors and young leaders. None is a 'silver bullet'. They should be implemented systematically and gradually and crafted and/or blended to each congregation's needs.

Here is a brief summary of options for individuals: people to go, pray and give; elbow learning; learning by living and ministering alongside mature Christians; devotion to the apostles' teaching, to fellowship, to Holy Communion, and to prayer and intercession; uphold morality; practise hospitality, works of love and charity, of priesthood, music, praise, worship and dancing; compose poems and psalms; private Bible study; confession; self-discipline; trust, love and obey Christ; be 'upwardly compliant', 'inwardly directed' and 'outwardly committed'; be alert to what God is doing; be quick to forgive; pray for the sick; show mercy and serve; listen, speak truth; enjoy small things; throw parties; confront evil and work for justice; evangelise; enjoy nature; keep silence; discard worldly thought patterns and replace them with biblical truths; be Holy Spirit led; rote-learn Scripture and proclaim Scripture before people and to the Lord. Implementing some of these will require change for any Christian and embracing doing different things or the same things differently.

Changes for congregation to implement include: adopt a five-fold model of leadership; apply principles of discipleship; seek sensible, systematic, deep, Scripture-centred teaching; value all Scripture equally as God's word;

teach the biblical significance of Israel and continuity between the two Testaments; encourage and implement spiritual practices; teach about the Holy Spirit and spiritual fruit and gifts and apply that teaching wherever possible in congregational life.

Questions:

(1) Why is discipleship difficult in the West?

(2) What changes do you intend to make in your personal and/or in your congregational life?

Chapter 25
Postscript

<u>25.1. Fifty Years After Nostra Aetate</u>

Jewish-Christian dialogue has been a work-in-progress for over five dacades, for example, the Lutheran Church renounced Luther's later views about Jews in 1983, as did the Evangelical Lutheran Church in America, in 1994 (Britannica, 'Anti-Semitism in Medieval Europe, online).

Plate 20.1.

Joshua Koffman's sculpture, 'Synagoga and Ecclesia in our time'

St Joseph's University, Philadelphia. Photograph by Calimeronte. Public domain.

Since Vatican II, more harmonious Catholic-Jewish relations have been evidenced than at any previous time and more positive steps taken to bridge the divide. Each strives to learn from the other for the common good. In 2015, St Joseph's University, Philadelphia, USA, unveiled a bronze sculpture by Joshua Koffman entitled 'Synagoga and Ecclesia in Our Time'.

It symbolises the new relationship by depicting the two crowned female figures amicably sharing their Biblical studies from a scroll and a codex.

On 30/6/2015 Pope Francis celebrated the 50th anniversary of Nostra Aetate in the Vatican with the International Council of Christians and Jews.

He said: *"We hold the Jewish people in special regard because their covenant with God has never been revoked, for 'the gifts and the call of God are irrevocable.'"* (Rom.11:29). Dialogue and friendship with the children of Israel are part of the life of Jesus' disciples. There is a complementarity between the Church and the Jewish people that allows us to help one another mine the richness of God's word" (Wallace, 'Synagogue and Ecclesia in Our Time', The Catholic Star Herald, October 1, 2015; Joseph A. Cunningham, 2015).

25.2. The Post-Pandemic World and the Church

It is difficult to know what the short-term future holds for the Ecclesia worldwide. The Church in most countries was quickly and easily robbed of its functions, at least temporarily: its ability to meet, to worship; to baptise people of all/any ages; to receive the Sacraments; to be ministered to at the time of death. The humanity of the aged was disregarded as they were forced to die alone. Many see all this as a portent of things to come.

There are embryonic but worrying movements afoot: a new distrust of governments and potential for anarchy; a rise of extremist groups on the right and the left; new concerns about Russia, North Korea, Iran and China and totalitarian and tyrannical governments in general; the dark web; conspiracies and wild conspiracy theories. The Internet is becoming more dangerous for children and more difficult to negotiate. Basically crime and criminals have been busy while the world was in lockdown, especially the drug trade and pornography. Families must provided more support and protection than before and communities must close ranks to help the most vulnerable - church communities included.

In societies in general, in the short-term, poverty, homelessness and hunger will be greater than they had been in 2018. Governments will carry high debt levels, to the detriment of welfare services and debt reduction: probably for a generation.

The long-term results of the disruption to education at all levels will be felt for a generation: education is sequential and when the sequence is disturbed or interrupted good outcomes are jeopardized. Some students have missed a whole year of school-attendance. Some students' university courses will never be completed and high school grades may suffer. Both will result in reduced job prospects and lower salaries, for life, which will impact whole economies as well as many individuals and their families, and perhaps for generations. There will be a reduction of enrolments at university of both foreign students and nationals, due to travel restrictions and reduced affluence, worldwide. Children of refugees and in nations with major civil unrest and natural disasters as well as the pandemic may have years without schooling, leading to poor income prospects.

There may be major international shifts in the balance of power. Nations which have been least affected will forge ahead economically and those who have lost mainly the elderly will fare better than those who have lost young, educated people and front-line workers.

There will be some shortage of human resources, especially of professionals and salaried workers (as distinct from wage earners). Simultaneously, there will be high unemployment in the short-term: notably in hospitality, travel and tourism, in some service sectors, and in the trading in luxury goods and imported goods, generally. Some 'essential' goods such as medicines, medical supplies, food and fuel wll be in short supply, as happened after World War II. If there are shortages of fuel and power, industries will be effected which will result in higher prices and lower consumer expectations so that local manufacturing will increase, notably of essential commodities: a degree of withdrawal from internationalism.

In developing countries, once children are no longer in school they will become workers and girls will be married earlier, reversing the gains made for both genders during the last few decades and reducing professional workforces there.

In virtually every country church members will have died, resulting in widespread grieving so the need for counsellors will be unusually high.

Many congregations may have been so decimated that support is in short supply. Many members will not have attended their church for one or more years and will stop attending, permanently. Gathering the scattered sheep will be a challenge for pastors. Other Christians, accustomed to watching religious broadcasts on television, will continue to do so rather than returning to their old attendance patterns. Some congregations will close down.

Viewing religious broadcasts will have a positive outcome for many of the unchurched, including in closed and semi-closed nations: bringing many to faith. The need for personal shepherding, discipleship, teaching and nurturing will be greater than ever, even if the supply of resources, personnel and money has decreased. The challenges for Christians will be great. At the same time there is a widespread stirring in both Catholic and non-Catholic Christianity about natural disasters as coming from Heaven upon the Earth: but these are interpreted more as increasingly severe warnings than as judgements.

Questions:

(1) What do you think that Ecclesia will look like in 2030 and 2050?

(2) Can you suggest any innovative ways to meet the post-pandemic challenges.

Appendix 1

<u>The Crusades</u>

The eight Crusades, which are described in Appendix 1, were mounted until 1270. They resulted in the early deaths of thousands of Europe's fighting elite, children and people of other faiths. The aim of the Crusades was to take back the Holy Land from the Muslims, which was briefly achieved, making pilgrimage to holy places easier. Pilgrimage to Jerusalem, Rome and other shrines was undertaken to earn time out of Purgatory and was an essential part of Medieval spirituality. The matter was urgent because of the belief that, by preventing pilgrimage to Jerusalem, Muslims were forcing Christians to spend more time in Purgatory, before reaching Heaven.

The First Crusade (1096-99). When the Byzantine emperor, Alexios I Komnenos, who had been defeated by the Seljakian Turks, appealed to the West for help to wrest Jerusalem from the Mohammedans Pope Urban II eventually agreed to help, in November 1095 (Lowden, 1997, 349). Peter the Hermit and others travelled widely in Europe to promote the cause. The First Crusaders were mainly Franks (French) led by Raymond of Toulouse, Godfrey of Bouillon, Bohemund of Otranto, his nephew Tancred, and Robert of Normandy. In 1098 Antioch was taken, and then Jerusalem in 1099.

Appendix 1 Plate 1.

Tomb of Queens Morphia and Melisende (through right archway) within 'Mary's Tomb', Jerusalem.

Public domain.

Godfrey of Bouillon ruled as King of Jerusalem, followed by his brother Baldwin I, and then their cousin, Baldwin II whose Greek Orthodox wife was the Princess Morphia of Militene. This couple had four daughters, the oldest of whom, Melisende, was trained to rule and became her father's coruler and heir. A marriage to the Crusader knight, Fulk of Anjou, was arranged and she elevated him to the throne.

Melisende ruled as queen from 1131-1153, first as consort to husband, King Fulk, and then as regent for her thirteen year old son, Baldwin III, and finally as his co-ruler in an uneasy partnership after he had defeated forces loyal to her in battle.

Queen Melisene, who was noted for her able rule, patronage of religion, culture and the arts, died in 1161 at age 55/56. She was buried beside her Armenian mother, Queen Morphia, in the chapel now dedicated to the Virgin's parents,

Joachim and Anna, in the Kidron Valley of Jerusalem. Queen Melisende's beautifully illustrated and luxurious psalter, which was probably a gift from her husband, has survived. After Melisende and

Baldwin III's deaths, her second son, Amalric I, succeeded his older brother.

The Second Crusade (1147-49). Although the Latin Kingdom initially did well, Edessa was seized by Moslem forces. Pope Eugenius III arranged for another crusade but, even though prominent rulers, French King Louis VII of France and the German, Conrad III, led this Crusade, it terminated without fighting.

The Third Crusade (1188-92). Saladin consolidate his power and captured Jerusalem in 1187, which shocked Europe. Frederick Barbarossa, Philip Augustus of France and Henry II of England combined together but Barbarossa was drowned and the other two leaders disagreed. Henry II died and his son, Richard I (called the Lionheart) and Philip II established the 2nd Kingdom of Jerusalem in a reduced area, with Acre/Acco as its capital: but they did not reconquer Jerusalem. Montfort Castle became the headquarters of the Teutonic Knights after a disagreement with the Knights Templar and the Hospitaliers. Richard made peace with Saladin in 1192.

Appendix 1 Plate 2.

Crusader remains, Acre/Acco. Photo: D. Campbell, 2010.

The Fourth Crusade (1202-04). This Crusade, under Pope Innocent III was side-tracked into meddling into Byzantine affairs so that, in 1204, European troops stormed the city of Constantinople, looting it for three days and attacking women, including nuns and matrons. This was regarded as unforgivable by the Greeks and sealed the 'Great Schism'. Westerners ruled Constantinople for nearly sixty years, Baldwin of Flanders becoming the first Latin Emperor of Constantinople, which further embittered East-West relations. The Europeans were driven out in 1261 and the Greek Byzantines regained Constantinople.

The Children's Crusade (1212). After the disaster of the Fourth Crusade, groups of enthusiastic children from France and Germany gathered to capture Jerusalem. Few survived to set

sail in Italy and none arrived in the Middle East. Legend and

fact are intermingled in this matter, including the poem, 'the

Pied Piper of Hamelin' in which children followed the piper and disappeared forever ('Children's Crusade', in ODCC).

The Fifth Crusade (1217-21). Innocent III proclaimed a new crusade at the Fourth Lateran Council in 1215. In 1221 the Crusaders captured the Holy Cross back from the Moslems. Most of the fighting occurred in Egypt.

The Sixth Crusade (1228-29). This Crusade was led by Frederick II, who had been excommunicated. He crowned himself King of Jerusalem in 1229, having gained the Holy City, Bethlehem and Nazareth by treaty. In 1244, however, he lost Jerusalem.

The Seventh Crusade (1248-54). In 1245 Pope Innocent IV preached a Crusade against both the heathen and Frederick II. The army, led by St Louis of France, was routed in Egypt and Louis was captured. He returned home in 1254 having achieved nothing.

The Eighth Crusade (1270). St Louis and his brother Charles of Anjou, joined the fray, attacking Tunisia. St Louis died there and Charles negotiated a peace.

The End of the Latin Kingdom of Jerusalem.

The fortified underground city of Acre/Acco was lost in 1291, marking the end of the Crusader period. The Latin Kingdom of Jerusalem soon passed into history ('Crusades', in ODCC) but the Levant was left dotted with their ruined fortresses, castles and a few churches (e.g., Plates 9.2, 9.3 and Appendix Plate 1.2).

It is estimated that thirty to fifty percent of European Jewry was killed during the two centuries of the Crusades (Blech, 2004, 133f).

Appendix 2
Medieval Disputations

The formal disputations between Catholic prelates and Jewish sages were part of "a broad pattern of conversionary activity" that changed the old Augustineian policy which may be regarded as "limited toleration of Jews" (Maccoby [ed.], 2006, 5). It was also part of the Dominican and other friars' campaigns to convert Jews and to demonstrate the superiority of Christianity to wavering or lukewarm Catholics.

Records are extant for the three disputations discussed below but there were also minor disputations during the period: Pamplona (1375), Burgos (1375), Avila (1375) and Granada (1430) (Maccoby [ed.], 2006, 216, Intro. 1).

Paris (1240)

The French Dominicans thought that they had enough evidence to put the Talmud on trial before the Inquisition for blasphemies against Jesus, Mary and Christians. Rabbi Jehiel/Yehiel ben Joseph (assisted by three other French rabbis) represented the Jews but Yehiel was no match for the virulent attacks and threats and the unevenness of the dispute. It was not a debate but a trial, flexing the muscles of the newly formed Franciscan Order and the even newer Inquisition.

The attack was launched by converts from Judaism led by Nicholas Donin. He perhaps was a former Karaite and he had been excommunicated from Judaism before he converted to Christianity. He divorced his wife in 1279 and, in 1287, the Franciscans condemned him for disobedience to the church. Invention of the 'blood libel' against the Jews was also attributed to him: so altogether he was 'a colourful character' or a 'rogue'. Perhaps he was also a rationalist who was never a true Christian (Rosenthal, JQR 47.1, 1956, 70, citing the Spanish scholar, Jacob ben Eli).

In Paris, Rabbi Yehiel was interrogated for two days and Rabbi Judah ben David for one. Brief records of the event in Latin and Hebrew are extant but they are not eyewitness accounts.

The five judges (high dignitaries of the French Church) took eight years to make a decision but, meanwhile, the French king ordered that twenty-four cartloads of Talmuds and Jewish books be burnt at the stake. Eventually the Jews managed to have the condemnation of the whole Talmud modified to censure and the culling of anti-Christian passages (Rosenthal, JQR 47.1, 1956, 72).

For a century, confiscation and burning of the Talmud occurred in France (Carr, in Neusner and AveryPeck, 2000, 158). Rabbi Yehiel left Europe and emigrated to Acco/Acre in Northern Israel.

Barcelona (1263)

This disputation took place between the main protagonists, Moses ben Nachmanides and some Preaching Friars, especially Fray Paul, Raymond Martini and a convert from Judaism, Pablo Christiani. The disputation was convened by King James of Aragon, Majorica, and Valencia, count of Barcelona and Urgello, and Don of Montispessulanum who had elevated some educated and capable Jewish administrators (Maccoby [ed.], 2006, 40). It began when Dominicans challenged the foremost Jewish scholar, Moses ben Nachmanides (Ramban) to a disputation, but with a friendlier attitude than had prevailed in Paris. The aim was to win over, not to convict (Maccoby [ed.], 2006, 39).

Both short Christian and detailed Jewish accounts of the Barcelona Disputation exist. The chief Jewish participant, Nachmanides, provided the latter record, which is called the Vikuah of Nachmanides. It was written for Bishop Peter of Genoa, in Spanish or Latin, but the te xt has survived only in Hebrew (Maccoby [ed.], 2006, 39). It demonstrates Nachmanides intellect and debating skills (For English translations of both disputes see Maccoby [ed.], 2006, 97-153).

Appendix 2, Plate 1.
Disputation of Barcelona.
Public domain.

The aforesaid King James culled the Talmud in 1263 and it was always a forbidden book. Because he had published his unauthorised account of the Disputation in 1265 Nachmanides was brought to trial by the Dominican Order (which had been founded in c.1220 and which was the backbone of the Spanish Inquisition) ('Dominican Order', in ODCC). The friars accused him of secretly fleeing away and departing but King James gave him a light sentence because Nachmanides had once been his advisor (Maccoby [ed.], 2006, 79; 150).

At this key point of European history the 'Golden Age' of inter-faith coexistence in Spain was drawing to a close. Following the 'Reconquest' of Spain from the Moors, Islam was no longer the threat that it had been and the Jews were no longer necessary to Spanish economic life and education.

<u>Tortosa (1413-14).</u>

This was the greatest of the Disputations in scale and splendour but it lacked the drama and nobility of Barcelona. It was sponsored by King Ferdinand of Aragon, and was heard before pseudo-Pope

Benedict XIII (Maccoby [ed.], 2006, 82f). Peter Alfonsi, Herman of Cologne and a learned convert from

Judaism, Jeronimo de Santa Fe, argued for Christianity (Carr, in Avery-Peck, 2000, 158).

The Jewish communities of Spain had been decimated in 1391 by popular massacres so the Jewish delegates feared for their lives. An appeal by Rabbi Astruk Halevi, quoted below, shows that the Jews were dispirited, hungry and afraid.

Meanwhile a Dominican, Vincent Ferrer, was visiting their families with wild bands of men to bully them into conversion. He was later made a saint because miracles were attributed to him, as well as being a supporter of Benedict XIII's claims to the Papacy (Vincent Ferrer, St, in ODCC). He had previously converted Joshua Halorki (the above-mentioned Jeronimo de Santa Fe) (Maccoby [ed.], 2006, 82ff) Some recent converts were brought to the Tortosa assembly to testify to their conversion, a painful experience for their rabbis. Rabbi Halevi pleaded:

"We are away from our homes, our resources have diminished and we are almost entirely destroyed - huge damage is resulting in our communities from our absence; we do not know the fate of our wives and children" (Rabbi Halevi in the Latin text of the Disputation, Maccoby [ed.], 2006, 84/ 94). The Jews' plea was for toleration based on the principle of religious autonomy, which the Church argued was irrational, leaving the Jews to champion blind faith against the rationality of the Church. Tortosa was intended to combine the aims of both Paris and Barecelona: to exploit the Talmud for Christian purposes and to condemn it as blasphemous, obscene and anti-Christian. Eventually the rabbis, who longed to go home, were silent. They had used every argument. More would be superfluous: but this was interpreted as defeat (Maccoby [ed.], 2006, 91) The church and state (Christendom) had conspired together and jointly condemned the Talmud and Jews, who were harassed and then expelled from Spain, in 1492.

Glossary Anabaptists : Rebaptisers, from the Greek ana, 'again'.

Blood libel : accusation that Jews killed Christians for their blood

Encomium: exaggerated praise, laudations

Exegesis : a method of analysing a Biblical pericope

Friars : monks who wandered about and begged for food

Genizah : repository for texts containing the Sacred Name

Hagiography : biography of a saint with legends and lavish praise

Hanukkah : festival of lights and of the purification of the Temple

Hedonism: pleasure-seeking, self-indulgence

Inquisition : organ of Catholicism to torture and kill heretics and unbelievers

Kabbalah : a mystical, theosophical system recorded in the Zohar

Karaite : Jews who accepted only the written Torah, not the Oral Law

Levant : geographical area to the East of the Mediterranean Sea

Mass : Roman Catholic Eucharist or Holy Communion

Mendicants : friars who begged or worked for a living and moved about

Mithraeum : a cult centre for the rites of Mithras, the Persian sun god

Nepotism : giving preferment and 'a living' to a prelate's nephew(s)

Pericope : a section or piece of text

Schism : a rupture in communion between Christian groups

Synagōgē : gathering of people, or local assembly

Talmuds : 5th-century commentaries on the Mishnah

Theocracy : political rule by God or by a religious authority

Tonsure : partly shaven head (a corona or a shaven front)

Tonsured : to be ordained a monk, to enter a monastic order

Transubstantiation : doctrine that the bread and wine become Christ's body and blood Vita : life, biography (especially of a holy person)

List of Abbreviations

AB: Art Bulletin

ADB: Australian Dictionary of Biography

AJAH: American Journal of Ancient History

Ant.: Josephus, Antiquities of the Jews

ANZAC: Australia New Zealand Army Corp

ASR: American Sociological Review

AUSS: Andrews University Seminary Studies

BA: Biblical Archaeologist

BAR: Biblical Archaeology Review

BDCM: Biographical Dictionary of Christian Missions

BDS: Boycott Disengage Sanction

BAS: Biblical Archaeological Society

BHD: Bible History Daily

BR: Bible Review

CBQ: Catholic Biblical Quarterly

CBR: Catholic Bible Review

CDDS: Complete Dead Sea Scrolls (in English)

CH: Catholic Historian

CLC: Christian Literature Crusade

CMML: Christian Missions in Many Lands

CMS: Church Missionary Society

CT: Christianity Today

CUP: Cambridge University Press

DCC: Documents of the Christian Church

DO: Dumbarton Oaks

ECW: Early Christian Writings

Eus. H.E.: Eusebius, Historia Ecclesiastica

HJ: Heythrop Journal

HTR: Harvard Theological Review

IAA: Israel Antiquities Authority

IBMR: International Bulletin of Missionary Research

IEJ: Israel Exploration Journal

IHE: Illustrated History of Europe

IVP: Inter Varsity Press

IBMR: International Bulletin of Missionary Research

JA: Jewish Art

JECS: Journal of Early Christian Studies

JEH: Journal of Ecclesiastical History

JETS: Journal of the Evangelical Theological Society jt.: Jerusalem Talmud

JBL: Journal of Biblical Literature

JJS: Journal of Jewish Studies

JNES: Journal of Near Eastern Studies

JPhil: Journal of Philology

JQR: Jewish Quarterly Review

JRH: Journal of Religious History

JSJPHRP: Journal for the Study of Judaism in the Persian, Hellenistic and Roman Period

JSNT: Journal for the Study of the New Testament

JTS: Journal of Theological Studies

L.A.: Los Angeles

m.: Mishnah

MAF: Missionasry Aviation Fellowship

NGO: Non-government agency

NT: Novum Testamentum

NTS: New Testament Studies

N.Y.: New York

ODCC: Oxford Dictionary of the Christian Church

ODS: Oxford Dictionary of Saints

OIHC: Oxford Illustrated History of Christianity

OUP: Oxford University Press

PEF: Palestine Exploration Fund

RHD: Revue dHistoire du Droit

SCM: Student Christian Movement

SJT: Southwestern Journal of Theology

Scottish JT: Scottish Journal of Theology

SS: Seminary Studies

SSEM: South Sea Evangelical Mission
SPCK: Society for the Propagation of Christian Knowledge
tb.: Babylonian Talmud TB: Tyndale Bulletin
TET: The Expository Times
U: University
UCal.P: University of California Press
UNESCO: United Nations Educational, Scientific and Cultural Organisation
USCH: United States Church History
War.: Josephus, Wars of the Jews
WWI: World War I
WWII: World War II

BIBLIOGRAPHY
Primary Sources

Holy Bible, New International Version (London: Hodder and Stoughton, 1978).

Annals of Ulster

Arad, Yitzhak, Yisrael Gutman and Abraham Margaliot (eds), Documents of the Holocaust (Jerusalem: Yad Vashem and Pergamon Press: Oxford, N.Y. and others, 1988).

Augustine, Confessions of Saint (Chadwick, trans.), (Oxford: OUP, 1991).

Cosmas Indicopleustes, McCrindle, J. W. (trans.), Christian Topography of Cosmas Indicopleustes (Dumbarton Oaks and Harvard U., Translated in 1897).

'Declaration on the Relation of the Church to Non-Christian Religions Nostra Aetate Proclaimed by His Holiness Pope Paul VI on October 28, 1965.' http://w2.vatican.va/archive/hist_councils/ii_vatican_council/documents/vatii_decl_19651028_nost

Epiphanius, On Weights and Measures

Eusebius, Ecclesiastical History/History of the Church from Christ to Constantine, Andrew Louth (ed.), G. A. Williamson (trans.) (Harmondsworth: Penguin, 1965).

Guyon, Madam, The Life of Madam Guyon (Christian Classics Ethereal Library).

Irenaeus of Lyon, Fragments from the Lost Writings of Irenaeus XIII www.earlychristianwritings.com/ireneus.fragments.htm.

Irish Ecclesiastical Record, Vol. 13 (1892).

Josephus, Antiquities of the Jews In The Works of Josephus, Complete and Unabridged in One Volume William Wiston (trans.), (Peabody, MA: Hendricksion Publisher, 1987).

Lactantius, On the Deaths of the Persecutors, II.

http://people.ucalgary.ca/~vandersp/Courses/texts/lactant/lactpers.html

Louth, A. (ed.), (M. Staniforth, trans.) Early Christian Writings (London: Penguin, 1968/1987).

Nostra Aetate (In Our Times) October 28, 1965.

Spender, Philip Jacob, Pia Desideria (Theodore G. Tappert, trans.) (Philadelphia: Fortress, 1964).

Synaxarium CP 848-852.

Life of St Anthousa of Mantineon in Bithynia.

Testament of Saint Clare

http://www.liturgies.net/saints/clare/testament.htm

The Christian Scholars Group on Jewish-Christian Relations, A Sacred Obligation #7

The Diary of Anne Frank

(Pan Books: London, 1989).

The Diary of Eva Hayman (trans. Moshe M. Kohn)

(Jerusalem and N. Y.: Yad Vashem and Shapolsky, 1988).

The Theology of the Churches and the Jewish People. Statement by the World Council of Churches and its Member Churches, (Geneva, WCC Publications, 1988).

Waddell, H (trans.), The Desert Fathers (Vintage Spiritual Classics) (N.Y.: Vintage Books, 1998).

Media Articles

Newspaper and Print Media

ABC Radionational, Masako Fukul, 'The Rise of Christianity in Asia.'

http://www.abc.netau/radionational/programs/encounter/the-rise-of-christianity-in-as/5934564

Anglican Communion News Service (ACNS), January 12, 2015. Arthur Matsiko,

'The Uganda Martyrs of Namugongo – the full

truth behind this historic event' https://www.google.com.au/search?q-the+uganda+martyrs+of+thamugongo

Baptist Press,

www.bpnews.net/27574

Christian Direct Uganda Ltd., 'List of Uganda's Christian Martyrs and how each was killed,' http://ugcchristiannews.com/editorial@ug.nationalmedia.com

CNN, March 22, 2019 by Ray Sanchez, 'More US School-age children die from guns than on-duty police or global military fatalities study finds',

https://edition.cnn.com/2019/03/22/health/gun-deaths-school-age-children-tmd/index/html

Daily Mail (Australia),'Mary Queen of Scots' half-brother killed her husband in bid to seize powser- as letter by Elizabeth I may have solved 450-year murder mystery,' by Amie Gordon,

https://www.dailymail.co.uk/news/article-6589111/Mary-Queen-Scots-husband-killed-half-brotherbid-seize-power-html

Guardian News and Media Limited,

'Richard Neville Obituary',

https://www.theguardian.com/media/2016/sep/04/richard-neville-obituary

Guardian News and Media Limited, 24/10/2004 by Jason Burke,

'Khmer Rouge embraces Jesus',

https://www.theguardian.com/world/2004/oct/24/religion.uk

Ha Aretz Aug.19, 2005, by Tamara Traubmann,

Study by the Abarbanel Health Centre and Tel Aviv University.

https://www.haaretz.com/news/study-holocaust-survivors-3-times-more-likelyto-attempt-suicide1.166386

Ha Aretz World News, by Oder Aderet, "'A Great Hero', Pilot of Air France Flight Hijacked to Entebbe, Michel Bacos, Dead at 95',

https://www.haaretz.com/world-news/europe/.premium-a-great-hero-pilot-of-air-france-hijackedto-entebbe-dead-at-95

International Bulletin of Missionary Research, January 2009, by David B. Barrett and Todd M. Johnson, https://mail.yahoo.com/?.intl=au.partner=none&.src=fpx#3616288658& [1]

International Bulletin of Missionary Research 37.4 (Oct, 2013) by Allen L. Effa 'Releasing the Tiger: The Nigerian Factor in Global Christianity'.

Israel National News, October 15, 2009, by Bedouin Seikh, 'My People are of Jewish Descent'.

Phnom Penh Post, 'Cambodians Turning to Christianity', https://www.phnompenhpost.com/lift/

Sydney Anglicans, June 4, 2009,

John Sandleman, 'Tribute to revival preacher,' https://sydneyanglicans.net/blogs/churchlife/ tribute_to_a_revival_preacher

Sydney Gazette, Feb. 4, 1814 and 4/1/1817, Letter of Rev. Samuel Marsden https://northlandhistory,blogspot.com/2014/02/letter-from-samuel-marsden-to-editor.html

Sydney Journal 2 (1) 6/2009, 5,

Geoffrey Sherington and Craig Campbell, 'Education',. http://www.lepress.lib.uts.au/ojs/index.php/sydney_journal/index

Sydney Morning Herald June 17, 2009, Lesley Hicks with John Sandleman, 'His ministry was wider than one church, Geoffrey Bingham, 1919-2009,' www.smh.com.au/comment/obituaries/his-ministrywas-wider-than-one-hurch-200906-16-ogh3.html

Telegraph Media Group Ltd., 2018. 21/1/2007.

Peter Pattisson and Kayin State, 'Burma "orders Christians to be wiped out."'

The Age, 14/3/2008, by Pullella, Philip, Rome, and Aseel Kami, Baghdad,

'Global Outcry at death of Iraqi archbishop'

---

1.   https://mail.yahoo.com/?.intl=au.partner=none&.src=fpx#a5c02393e59c943d6a75a9241140f aca33616288658_6cff047854f19ac2aa52aac51bf3af4a_

www.theage.com.au/news/world/global-outcry-at-death-of-Iraqiarchbishop/2008/03/14/1205472082065.html

The Australian, July 30, 1968.

The Australian Church Record, 21/6/1963, by Rev. D. B. Knox

The Catholic Star Herald, October 1, 2015, by Joseph D. Wallace, 'Synagogue and Ecclesia in Our Time', http://documenta-akermariano.blogspot.com/2015/07/synagoga-et-ecclesia.htm

The Catholic Weekly, Sydney, May 30, Aug. 29, 1963,

by Rev. Dr Leslie Rumble, MSC.

The Economist Newspaper Ltd. 25/12/2015, 'Christianity and Church Attendance: The future of the world's most popular religion is Africa'.

https://www.economist.com/news/international/21684679-march-christianity-future-worlds-mostpopular-religion-africa

The Good Weekend 8/11/2008 and Sydney Morning Herald 10/10/2014. Nikki Barrowclough, 'Catherine Hamlin: Ethiopia's miracle worker'.

http://www.smh.com.au/national/catherine-hamlin-ethiopias-miracle-worker-20141010114ixe.html

The Guardian, 27/8/2018, Harriet Sherwood, 'Religion: why faith is becoming more and more popular', https://www.theguardian.com/news/2018/aug/27/religion-why-is-faith

The Guardian, February 10, 2019, Ben Doherty, 'Australia takes the most refugees since start of humanitarian program',

https:/www.theguardian.com/world/2019/feb/10/australia-takes-the-most-refugees-since-start-ofhumanitarian-program

The Guardian, 2009, Margaret MacMillan, 'Rebuilding the world after the second world war', https://www.theguardian.com>world>second>world>war

The Jerusalem Post (October 24, 2017). 'Maryland Joins Nearly Half of American States with Anti-BDS Laws.'

The New York Times 15/7/2000, by Michael T. Kaufman, 'Jan Karski Dies at 86; Warned West About Holocaust'.

https://partners.nytimes.com/library/world/europe/071500poland.karski/htm

The New York Times 28/8/1975, by Alan Whitman, 'On This Day: Haile Selassie of Ethiopia Dies at 83'.

http://www.nytimes.com/learning/general/onthisday/bday/0723.html

'This is Parramatta', Mayor and Parramatta City Council (Cumberland Press, 1965).

Weekend Australian, March 27-28, 2021, 15, by Greg Sheridan, 'Society will pay for loss of its Christian ideals',

Word From Jerusalem, March 2015, Global Edition, by Ling-Yi Chin, courtesy International Christian Embassy Jerusalem.

United Nations press release, November 2, 2012, 'Father Patrick Debois to Present New Findings on

Treatment of Roma People During World War II at Kristallnacht Event', https://www.un.org/press/2012/note.6368.doc.htm

Television and Radio

ABC Radionational, Masako Fukul, 'The Rise of Christianity in Asia.'

http://www.abc.netau/radionational/programs/encounter/the-rise-of-christianity-in-as/5934564

ABC television, "Australian Story" 3/7/2017. 'Billy Graham in 1959'.

ABC television "Regional News", April 10, 2021.

BBC 29/11/200, 'In Depth: 'Israel and the Palestinians: Key Documents'.

http://news.bbc.co.uk/2/hi/in_depth/middle_east/israel_and_the

palestinians/key

BBC 'Non of Wales',

http://bbc.co.uk/wales/history/sites/st_david/pages/life.shtml

Eternal Word Television Network, 'St Olympias, Widow - 368-410', https://www.etwn.com/catholicism/library/st-olympias-widow

Commentaries, Dictionaries, Encyclopedia and Atlases

Australian Dictionary of Biography, National Centre of Biography, Australian National University, ACT.

Biographical Dictionary of Christian Missions, Gerald H. Anderson (ed.), (N.Y.: Macmillan Reference USA, 1998).

Catholic Encyclopedia, Charles George Hebermann (ed.), (N.Y.: Robert Appleton, 1914).

Dictionary of Historical Geography , A. Hart, (ed.),

(Grand Rapids: PaterNoster, 2000).

Dictionary of Historical Theology A.Hart (ed.).

(Grand Rapids: PaterNoster, 2000)

Encyclopædia Britannica, biography (online). https://www.britannica.com/biography/

Encyclopedia Judaica.

https:/www.jewishvirtuallibrary.org/

Encyclopedia of Chrtistianity

Erwin Fahlbusch, Geoffrey William Bromiley and David B. Barrett (eds.),

(Gand Rapids: Eerdmans, 2008).

Irish Ecclesiastical Record Vol. 13 (Dublin, 1892).

The Dictionary of Famous Australians, Ann Atkinson, (Sydney: Allen & Unwin, 1992/1995).

The New Bible Commentary F. Davidson (ed.),

(London: Inter Varsity Fellowship, 1953/1959).

The Oxford Dictionary of Saints, 3rd edition, David Farmer (ed.), (N.Y., Oxford: Oxford University Press, 1992).

The Oxford Dictionary of the Christian Church (F. L. Cross and E. A. Livingstone, eds),

(London: OU P, 1958, 1961, 1973).

New Bible Dictionary 3rd edition (I. H. Marshall et al. eds.), (Leicester, England: IVP, 1996/2007).

New Dictionary of Theology

(Intervarsity Press, 1988).

New International Dictionary of New Testament Theology, C. Brown (ed.), (Grand Rapids, MI. Zondervan, 1982).

New World Encyclopedia

www.newworldencyclopedia.org

The Anchor Bible Dictionary, David Noel Freedman (ed.), (N.Y,: Doubleday, 1992).

The New Dictionary for Baptist Churches (1859/1994) Edward T. Hiscox (ed.).

www.fbinstitute.com/moore/baptistdist.html

The Oxford Dictionary of Anglicanism, Vol. IV, Global Western Anglicanism.

The Illustrated Atlas of Jewish Civilization, Josephine Bacon (ed.), (London: Quantum Books, 2003).

Zondervan Pictorial Encyclopedia of the Bible, Merrill Tenney (ed.), Vol. 1., (Zondervan Publishing House: Grand Rapids, MI, 1978).

Facts and Statistics

Barrett, David B. and Todd M. Johnson, 'International Bulletin of Missionary Research, January 2009'.

https://mail.yahoo.com/?.intl=au.partner=none&.src=fpx#3616288658&

2

Barana Group. 'Barna Studies the Research, Offers a Year-in-Review Perspectives', 2009, **https://www.barna.org/barna-**update/faith-spirituality/325-barna-studies-the-research-offers-ayear-in-review-perspective#.V2NesVd6OS0

Christian Direct Uganda Ltd., 'List of Uganda's Christian Martyrs and how each was killed,' http://ugcchristiannews.com/

Estimates of the Number Killed by the Papacy in the Middle Ages and Later (2006),

David A. Plaisted,

http://www.cs.unc.edu/~plaisted/estimates.html

Johnson, Todd M. and Gina A. Zurlo (eds), World Christian Database Centre for the Study of Global Christianity at Gordon-Conwell Theological Seminary), (Leiden/Boston: Brill, 2016).

---

2.   https://mail.yahoo.com/?.intl=au.partner=none&.src=fpx#a5c02393e59c943d6a75a9241140f aca33616288658_6cff047854f19ac2aa52aac51bf3af4a_

Johnson, Todd M. and Gina A. Zurlo (eds), World Christian Database - Numbers Facts and Trends Shaping Your World: 'Orthodox Christianity in the 21st Century.' online. http://worldchristianchurch.org/

'Minority Report: Christian Persecution in Muslim-Majority Countries.'

https://www.fulerstudio.edu/minority-report-christian-persecution-muslim-majority-countries

Numbers, Facts and Trends Shaping Your World, Over: Pentecostalism in Africa https://www.pewforum.org/2006/overview-penntecostalis,-in-africa/

Lugo, Luis and Alan Cooperman, 'Global Christianity: A Report on the Size and Distribution of the World's Christian Population, 2011.'

Pew Research Centre's Forum on Religion and Public Life (Dec.19, 2011), www.pewforum.org/2011/12/19-global-Christianity-exec/

Pew Research Centre, 'Restrictions on religion among the 25 most populous countries, 2007-2015.' http://www.pewforum.org/interactives/restrictions-on-religion-among-the-most-populouscountries-2007-2015/

Pew Research Centre, 'The Growth of Germany's Muslim Population, Nov. 29, 2017'.

https://wwwpewforum.org/essay/the-growth-of-germanys-muslim-population

'Status of Global Christianity, 2017, in the Context or 1900-2025 www.worldchristiandatabase.org

The Reformation – Facts & Summary – History.com http://www.history.com/topics/reformation

Worldometers, 'World's Population Growth' https://www.worldometres.info/world-population

Secondary Sources

Alexander, David and Pat (eds), Lion Handbook to the Bible

(Lion Publishing, Oxford, England. 1973, 1983).

Augsburger, David, Dissident Discipleship:A Spirituality of Self-Surrender,

Love of God and of Neighbour (Grand Rapids: Brazos Press, 2006).

Baeyertz, Mrs, Twelve Addresses delivered by Mrs. Baeyertz, New Edition (Varley Brothers, Melbourne and Sydney, undated).

——- Six New Addresses delivered by Mrs Baeyertz (Jewish evangelist) (Sydney and Melbourne: Varley Brothers, undated) or Perth, 1905.

Bagatti, Bellarmino, (Eugene Hoade Trans.), The Church From the Circumcision: History and Archaeology of the Judaeo-Christians (Jerusalem: Franciscan Printing Press, 1971/1984/2004).

Barnett, Paul, Jesus & the Rise of Early Christianity (Downers Grove, Ill.: IVP, 1999).

BAR Staff, 'Jewish Captives in the Imperial City', BHD 28/1/2013.

Bartleman, Frank, Azusa Street: An Eyewitness Account (Newberry, FL: Bridge-Logos, 1925/1980).

Bass, Dorothy and Miroslav Volf, Practicing Theology (Grand Rapids: Eerdmans, 2001).

Bell, Rob, Velvet Elvis: Repainting the Christian Faith (Grand Rapids, MI: Zondervan, 2005).

Bettenson, Henry, Documents of the Christian Church 2nd ed. (London: Oxford University Press, 1968).

Bingham, D. Jeffrey, Pocket History of the Church (Downers Grove: Intervarsity Press, 2002).

Black, A. W. (ed.), Religion in Australia: Sociologial perspectives (Allen and Unwin: Sydney, 1991).

Blaiklock, E. M., The Century of the New Testament (Guildford and London: Billing and Sons, 1962).

Blech, Rabbi Benjamin, Eyewitness to Jewish History (Hoboken, N.J.: John Wiley and Sons, 2004).

Boer, Harry R., A Short History of the Early Church (Grand Rapids: Eerdmans, 1976).

Bonner, Gerald, St Augustine of Hippo: Life and Controversies (3rd edition) (Canterbury Press Norwich, 2002)

Borg, Marcus J. and N. T. Wright, The Meaning of Jesus: Two Visions (London: SPCK, 1999).

Bosch, David J., Transforming Mission: Paradigm Shifts in Theology of Mission
(Maryknoll, N.Y.: Orbis Books, 1991).

Brekus, Catherine A., Strangers and Pilgrims:
Female Preaching in America, 1740-1845.
(1998).

Brooten, Bernadette, Women Leaders in the Ancient Synagogues
(Chico, CA: 1982).

Brown, Michelle P., How Christianity Came to Britain and Ireland
(Oxford: Lion, 2006).

Brown, Michelle, The Lion Companion to Christian Art
(Oxford: Lion, 2008).

Bruce, F. F., The Spreading Flame (Paternoster Press, 1958/1962).

Butler, Dom Cuthbert, Western Mysticism: Augustine, Gregory and Bernard
on Contemplation and the Contemplative Life (Mineola, NY: Dover, 1926/2003).

Burke, Todd and De Ann, Anointed for Burial
(Plainfield NJ: Logos International, 1977).

Case, John Riley, An Unpredictable Gospel
(OUP, 2012).

Cameron, Averil, The Later Roman Empire AD 284-430
(London: Fontana, 1993).

Cameron, Averil, 'The Theotokos in Sixth-Century Constantinople:
A City Finds its Symbol', JTS, N.S. 29.1 (1978), 79-90.

Cameron, Averil (ed.), History as Text, The Writing of Ancient History
(Chapel Hill, NC, 1990), p. 196/16.

Campbell, Deslee, Modern Christian Martyrs (Amazon, 2020).

Campbell, Justin and Deslee Campbell, Synagoga's Heritage: Tabernacle, Temple, Synagogue and Church (xlibris, 2019/2020 and Amazon, 2021).

Chant, Barry, Heart of Fire. The Story of Australian Pentecostalism
(Adelaide: House of Tabor, 1973/1984).
Clark, Elizabeth, 'Piety, Propaganda and Politics
in the Life of Melania the Younger,'
Patristic Studies 18. (1989), 67-182.
Clark, Elizabeth A., Jerome, Chrysostom and Friends
(N.Y,: Edwin Mellen Press, 1979).
Clark, Kenneth, Civilisation
(London, 1969/1971).
Clarke, C. P. S., Short History of the Christian Church (London: Longmans, 1961).
Cohick, Lyn H. and Amy Brown Hughes, Christian Women in the Patristic World: Their Influence, Authority and Legacy in the Second Through Fifth Centuries (Grand Rapids,MI: Baker Acadmic, 2017).
Collinson, S. W., Making Disciples:
The Significance of Jesus' Educational Methods for Today's Church (Eugene, OR: Wipf and Stock, Publishers, 2004).
Cox, Harvey, The Secular City:
Secularization and Urbanization in Theological Perspective
(N.Y., 1965).
Cunningham, Mary, Faith in the Byzantine World
(Oxford: Lion, 2002).
Cunningham, Philip A., Seeking Shalom:
The Journey to Right Relationship between Catholics and Jews (Eerdmans, 2015).
Darg, Christine, Miracles Among Muslims: The Jesus Visions (Pescara, Italy: Destiny Image Europe, 2007).
Delouche, Frederic (ed.), (Richard Mayne, trans.), Illustrated History of Europe
(Paris: Hachette, 1992).
Deyong, Kevin and Greg Gilbert, What Is The Mission of the Church?: Making sense of Social Justice, Shalom, and the Great Commission (Illinois: Crossway, 2011).

Drinkwater, John and Hugh Elton (eds), Fifth Century Gaul: a Crisis of Identity
(Cambridge and N.Y.: CUP, 1992).
Driscoll, Mark and Gerry Breshears, Vintage Church Timeless Truths and Timely Methods (Illinois: Crossways Books, 2008).
Duncan, Philip B., Pentecost in Australia
(Sydney: Assemblies of God in Australia, 1947).
Einstein, Albert, (Sonja Bargmann, trans.), Ideas and Opinions (London: Crown, 1954).
Elton, G. R., England Under the Tudors (London: Methuen, 1959).
Evans, Robert, Evangelism and Revivals in Australia 1880-1914 (Hazelbrook, N.S.W.: Research in Evangelical Revivals, 2005).
——— Emilia Baeyertz, Evangelist. Her Career in Australia and Great Britain: An Historical study and a Compilation of Sources
(Hazelbrook: Research in Popular Revivals, 2007).
Ferguson, Everett, The Church of Christ: A Biblical Ecclesiology for Today (Grand Rapids, MI.: Eerdmans, 1996).
Finegan, Jack, The Archaeology of the New Testament:
The Life of Jesus and the Beginning of the Early Church
(Princeton: Princeton UP, 1992).
Fisher, H.A.L., A History of Europe, Vols I and II,
(London, Glasgow: Collins, 1964).
Ford, David Nash, 'St. Non',
Early British Kingdoms (2001).
Foster, Richard J., Celebration of Discipline: Path to Spiritual Growth (N.Y,: Harper Collins Publishers, 1978).
Fremantle, Anne, Age of Faith,
(Time Life, Inc, 1969).
Frend, W. H. C., Martyrdom and Persecution: a study of a Conflict From the Maccabees to Donatus (N.Y. University Press, 1967).
Frost, Michael, Exiles: Living Missionally in a Post-Christian Culture
(Peabody, MAS; Erina N.S.W., Australia: Hendrickson and Strand, 2006).
——- Incarnate: The Body of Christ in an Age of Disengagement, (Downers Grove: IVP, 2014).

——- Surprise the World: The 5 Habits of Highly Missional People (Nab Press: 2016).

Frost, Michael and Alan Hirsch, Rejesus, A Wild Messiah for a Missional Church
(Erina, N.S.W.: Strand Pub., 2009).
Gabra, Gawdat, Coptic Monasteries: Egypt's Monastic Art and Architecture (Cairo and N. Y.: American Universities in Cairo Press, 2002).
Galli, Mark, Francis of Assisi and His World
(Oxford: Lion, 2002).
Gehman, Richard, 'The East Africa Revival,'
Eajet, 1986, 36-56.
Gilbert, Martin, Churchill and the Jews
(London: Simon and Schuster, 2007).
Grimm, Harald J., The Reformation Era 500-1650
(N.Y.: Macmillan, 1954/1959).
Grubb, Norman, C. T. Studd. Cricketer and Pioneer
(Fort Washington, PA: CLC, 1933).
Guder and Lois Barrett (eds), Missional Church
(1998).
Guthrie, Donald, The Pastoral Epistles, Revised ed., Tyndale N.T. Commentaries
(Leister, U.K.: IVP, 1990).
Haight, Roger, Christian Community in History, Vol. I (N.Y. and London: Continuum, 2004).
Hamilton, Jill, God, Guns and Israel
(Stroud, U.K.: Sutton Publishing, 2004).
Hamlin, Catherine with John Little, The Hospital by the River (Sydney: Pan Macmillan, 2001/2016).
Harding, Mark and Alanna Nobbs (eds.), Into All the Word:
Emergent Christianity in its Jewish and Greco-Roman Context (Grand Rapids, MI: Eerdmans, 2017).

Hardman, Keith J., Charles Grandison Finney 1792-1875
(Grand Rapids, MI: Baker, 1990).
Hattaway, Paul, Back to Jerusalem
(Carlisle, U.K., Piquant, 2003).
Helland, Roger and Leonard Hjalmarson, Missional Spirituality:
Embodying God's Love from the Inside Out (Downers Grove, Ill: IVP
Books, 2011).
Herr, Friedrich (Janet Sonderheimer, trans.), The Medieval World:
Europe 1100-1359 (London: Weidenfeld, 2000).
Hill, Jonathan, The History of Christianity
(Oxford: Lion Hudson, 2007).

Hilliard, David, 'Religious Crisis of the 1960s:
The Experience of the Australian Churches,' JRH (21.2, 1997), 209-27.
——— Popular Revivalism in South Australia:
the Gordon Rowe Memorial Lecture, 1982, (Adelaide, 1982).
Hirsch, Alan and Dave Ferguson, On the Verge:
a journey into the apostolic future of the church (Grand Rapids:
Zondervan, 2011).
Holmes, G. (ed.), Oxford Illustrated History Of Medieval Europe
(Oxford and N.Y.: OUP, 1990/1995).
Hurtardo, L. W., At the Origins of Christian Worship
(Grand Rapids, MI: Eerdmans, 1999/2000).
Hutchinson, Mark, Edmund Campion and Stuart Piggin (eds),
Reviving Australia: Essays on the History and Experience of Revival and
Revivalism in Australian Christianity
(Sydney: Centre for the Study of Australian Christianity, 1994).
Hutchinson Mark and Edmund Campion (eds), Re-visioning
Australian Colonia Christianity: New Essays in the Christian Experience
1788-1900
(Sydney: Centre for the Study of Australian Christianity, 1994).
Hywell-Davies, Jack, Baptised By Fired: The Life of Smith
Wigglesworth

(Hodder and Stoughton, 1987).

Jackson, Bernard, Places of Pilgrimage
(London, Geoffrey Chapman, 1989).

Jacobs, Louis, The Jewish Religion: A Companion
(Oxford: OUP, 1995).

Jacobs, Steven L. (ed.), Contemporary Christian Religious Responses to the Shoah
(Lanhan, MD, University Press, 1993).

Jenkins, Philip, The Lost History of Christianity: The Thousand Year Golden Age
of the Church in the Middle East, Africa and Asia (N.Y.: Lion, 2008).

Jensen, Robin M., 'Material and Documentary Evidence for the Practice of Early
Christian Baptism,' JECS 20.3 (2012), 371-405.

Judd, Stephen and Kenneth Cable, Sydney Anglicans: A History of the Diocese
(Sydney: Anglican Information Office, 1987).

Kasper, Walter (V. Green, trans.), Jesus the Christ (N.Y.: Paulist, 1976).

Katarikawe James and John Wilson, The East African Revival Movement (unpublished thesis, Fuller Theological Seminary, n.d.).

Keller, Tim, Generous Justice: How God's Grace Makes us Just (London: Hodder and Stoughton Ltd., 2010).

Kidd, Thomas S., The Great Awakening. A Brief History with Documents (Boston and N.Y.: Bedford/St Martins, 2008).

Kostof, S., Caves of God
(London and Cambridge MAS.: MIT Press, 1972).

Kotlowski, Elizabeth Rogers, Stories of Austraia's Christian Heritage (Griffin Press, 2006).

Kühnel, Bianca, 'The Personification of Church and Synagogue in Byzantine Art:
Towards a History of the Motif,' JA 1920 (1993-94), 112-23.

Lawrence, Brother, The Practice of the Presence of God:
With Spiritual Maxims (Grand Rapids: Revell, 1999).

Lee, Kwang He (ed.), The Life of Arthur T Pierson, (Pyengtack, Korea, 2007).

Linder, Amnon, The Jews in Roman Imperial Legislation
(Detroit, MI and Israel Academy of Science and Humanities, Jerusalem: Wayne State UP, 1987).
Lowden, John, Early Christian and Byzantine Art
(London: Phaidon, 1997).
Luther, Martin, 95: The Ideas That Birthed the Reformation
(New Kensington, PA.: Whitaker House, 2017).
Maccoby, Hyam (ed.), Judaism on Trial:
Jewish-Christian Disputations in the Middle Ages (Oxford and Portland, Oregon: Littman Library of
Jewish Civilization, 1982/1993, reprinted 2006).
Maddix, Mark and Jay Richard Akkerman (eds), Missional Discipleship:
Partners in God's Redemptive Mission, (Kansas City: Beacon Hill Press, 2013).
Mangel, Nissen, The Rambam: A Brief Biography
(Brooklyn, N.Y.: Merkos L'inyoni Chinuch, 1985).
Mango, Cyril, 'St Anthousa of Mantineon and the Family of Constantine V,'
AB 100 (1982), 401-09.

Marcus, Robert, The End of Ancient Christianity
(Cambridge, N.Y. and Melbourne: CUP, 1990).
Martin, Bernice, A Sociology of Contemporary Cultural Change
(Oxford and N.Y., 1981).
McAllister, Ian, 'Religious Change and Secularization:
The Transmission of Religious Values in Australia,' Sociological Analysis 49.3, 1988.
McCallum, Dennis, and Jessica Lowery, Organic Discipleship:
Mentoring Others into Spiritual Maturity and Leadership.
(Houston: New Paradigm Publishing, 2006).
MacCulloch, Dairmaid, The Reformation
(London: Viking, 2003).

Maccoby, Hyam (ed.), Judaism on Trial:
Jewish-Christian Disputations in the Middle Ages (Oxford and Portland, Oregon: Littman, 1982/2006).

McGrath, Alister E., Christian History
(Chichester: Wiley-Blackwell, 2013).

McGuckin, John, Saint Gregory of Nazianzus: An Intellectual Biography
(N.Y., 2001).

McLaren, Brian P., Finding Our Way Again.
(Nashville, TN: Thomas Nelson, 2008).

McCallum, Dennis, and Jessica Lowery, Organic Discipleship: Mentoring Others into Spiritual Maturity and Leadership (Houston, TX: New Paradigm Publishing, 2006).

McLaren, Brian, Finding Our Way Again: The Return of the Ancient Practices
(Nashville: Thomas Nelson, 2008).

McManners, John (ed.), The Oxford Illustrated History of Christianity
(Oxford University Press, N.Y. and Oxford, 1990/1995).

Miller, Elizabeth, 'A Planting of the Lord: Contemporary Pentecostal and Charismatic Christianity in Australia', Ph.D. thesis, University of Sydney, 2015.

Miller, Patricia Cox, Women in Early Christianity:
Translations of the Greek Texts
(Washington, D.C. Catholic University of America), 2005).

Misinai, Tsvi Jekhorin, The Engagement:
The Roots and Solution to the Problem in the Holy Land (Lind, 2009), in English.

Murphy, F. X. 'Melania the Elder: A biographical Note', Traditio 5, 1947, 59-77.

Mursell, Gordon (ed.), The Story of Christian Spirituality
(Oxford: Lion, 2003).

Neusner, Jacob and Alan J. Avery-Peck (eds), Judaism
(Blackwell, 2000).

Neville, Richard, Hippie, Hippie Shake: The Dreams, the Trips, the Ttrials, the Love-Ins, the Screw-Ups... the Sixties (Melbourne: 1995).

Noll, Mark A., The Old Religion in a New World:
A History of North American Christianity (Grand Rapids, MI and Cambridge, U.K.: Eerdmans, 2002).
Norris, Kristophers, Pilgrim Practices: Discipleship for a Missional Church,
(Eugene: Cascade Books, 2012).
Oden, Thomas C., How Africa Shaped the Christian Mind : Rediscovering the African Seedbed of Western Christianity (Downers Grove, Ill.: IVP Books, 2007).
Okholm, D., Monk Habits for Everyday People: Benedictine Spirituality for Protestants (Grand Rapids: Brazo Press, 2007).
Orr, Edwin J., Evangelical Awakenings in the South Seas (Minnesota: Bethany Fellowship, 1976).
Oyer, John S., Lutheran Reformers Against Anabaptists (The Hague: Martinus Nijhoff, 1964).
Payton, James R. Jr., Getting the Reformation Wrong
(Downers Grove, IL: IVP Academic, 2010).
Peace, Richard V., Conversion in the New Testament
(Grand Rapids, Eerdmans, 1999).
Perreault, Jacques (ed.), Women and Byzantine Monasticism,
Proceedings of the Athens Symposium 28-29 March, 1988 (Athens: Canadian Archaeological Institute at Athens, 1991).
Peterson, Eugene H., The Contemplative Pastor:
Returning to the Art of Spiritual Direction (Dallas: Word Publishing, 1989).
Phillips, Thomas, The Welsh Revival: Its origin and development
(Edinburgh and Carlisle, Penn:
Banner of Truth Trust, 1989/2002).
Lee, Kwang He (ed.), The Life of Arthur T Pierson,
(Pyengtack, Korea, 2007).
Piggin, Stuart, Faith of Steel:
A History of the Christian Churches in Illawarra, Australia (Wollongong: University of Wollongong, 1984).
——— Evangelical Christianity in Australia: Spirit, Word and World
(Melbourne: Oxford University Press, 1996),

——- Spirit of a Nation: The Story of Australia's Christian Heritage (Sydney: Strand Publishing, 2004).

Pollock, John Charles with Ian Randall, The Keswick Story:

the Authorised History of the Keswick Convention – updated (Fort Washington, PA: CLC, 1964/2006/2013).

Quient, Nicholas Rudolph, 'Was Apphia an Early Christian Leader?' Priscilla Papers 31.2, Spring 2017, 9-14.

Qureshi, Nebeel, Seeking Allah Finding Jesus

(Grand Rapids: Zondervan, 2016).

Rack, Henry D., Reasonable Enthusiasts:

John Wesley and the Rise of Methodism (3rd edition) (London: Epworth Press, 1989/2002),

Reed, Colin, Walking in the Light

(Brunswick East, Vic.: Acorn Press, 2007).

Rees, Elizabeth, An Essential Guide to Celtic Sites and their Saints (Burns and Oates, 2003).

Ringma, Charles, 'Drinking from Many Fountains: A Missional Spirituality for Radical Evangelicals,' Phronésis 14.1 & 2 (2007), 67-84.

Ringma, Charles R., Hear the Heartbeat with Henri Nouwen

(London, 2006; Vancouver, BC Canada, 2014).

Rittner, Carol, Stephen D. Smith and Irena Steinfeldt (eds), The Holocaust and the Christian World (NewYork: Continuum, 2000).

Robert, Dana L., Christian Mission: How Christianity Became a World Religion (Chichester, U.K., Wiley-Blackwell, 2009).

Robinson, Stuart, Mosques and Miracles: Revealing Islam and God's Grace

(Mt Gravatt, Queensland: City Harvest, 1973/1978/1984/2004).

Raboteau, Albert J., 'Down at the Cross: Afro-American Spirituality,' U.S. C H 8 (1989).

Rodley, Lyn, Cave Monasteries of Byzantine Cappadocia

(Cambridge, CUP, 1985).

Rosenthal, Judah M., 'The Talmud on Trial:

The Disputation at Paris in the Year 1240', JQR 47.1 (July 1956).

Samuel, Raphael and Gareth Stedman Jones (eds), Culture, Ideology and Politics:

Essays for Eric Hobsbawm
(London: Routledge and Kegan Pauil:1982).
Sanders, J. Oswald, In Pursuit of Maturity
(Grand Rapids: Lamplighter Books, Zondervan Publishing, 1986).
Schlink, Basilea, Israel: My Chosen People
(1987).
Scott, J. Julius, Jr. 'Parties in the Church of Jerusalem as seen in the Book of Acts',
JETS 18 (1975), 217-27.
Segal, A. F., Rebecca's Children: Judaism and Christianity in the Roman World
(Cambridge, MAS., 1983).

Seiferth, Wolfgang S., (L. Chadeayne and P. Gottwald, trans.), Synagogue and
Church in the Middle Ages: Two Symbols in Art and Literature
(N. Y.: Frederick Ungar, 1970).
Shelley, Bruce L., Church History in Plain Language, 2nd ed.
(Dallas, London, Vancouver, Melbourne: Word Publishing, 1982/ 1996).
Shigematsu, Ken, God in my Everything:
How an Ancient Rhythm Helps Busy People Enjoy God (Grand Rapids: Zondervan, 2013).
Silver, Carly, 'Women of the Ancient Near East: Beturia Paulina.
A Roman Convert to Judaism', BHD April 17, 2019; 55-68.
Simpson, Ray and Brent Lyons-Lee, Celtic Spirituality in an Australian Landscape,
(2015).
Smith, James Bryan, The Good and Beautiful God:
Falling in love with the God Jesus knows (Downer Grove: IVP Books, 2009).
Spender, Philip Jacob, (Theodore G. Tappert, trans.) Pia Desideria (in English), (Philadelphia: Fortress, 1964).

Stanton, Graham N. (ed.), The Interpretation of Matthew, 2nd edition (Edinburgh: T. & T. Clark, 1995).

Starr, J., The Jews in the Byzantine Empire 514-1204 (Athens, 1939).

Stayer, James, Anabaptists and the Sword (Lawrence: Coroado Press, 1972).

Stevenson, J (ed.), A New Eusebius
(London: SPCK, 1965).

Stone, Barry, Secret Army
(Crows Nest, Australia: Allen & Unwin, 2017).

Stott, John, The Living Church: Convictions of a life long pastor (Nottingham: IVP, 2007).

——- The Radical Disciple: Wholehearted Christian Living, (Nottingham: IVP, 2010).

Swan, Laura, The Forgotten Desert Mothers:
Sayings, Lives and Storeys of Early Christian Women (Mahwah: Paulinist Press, 2000).

Talbot, Alice-Mary, Byzantine Defenders of Images
(Washington, D.C.: Dumbarton Oaks Library & Research Collection, 1998).

Testa, Emmanuel, Paul Rotondi (trans.), The Faith of Mother Church: An Essay on the Theology of the Judeo-Christians (Jerusalem: Franciscan P:rinting Press, 1992).

Thomas, Charles, Britain and Ireland in Early Christian Times (London: Thames and Hudson, 1971).

Tomkins, Stephen, A Short History of Christianity
(Oxford: Lion, 2003).

Tomlin, Graham, Luther and His World
(Oxford: Lion Publishing: 2012).

Torjesen, Karen Jo, When Women Were Priests: Leadership in the Early Church
and the Scandal of their Subordination in the Rise of Christianity (San Francisco, 1993).

Tucker, Ruth A., Jerusalem to Irian Jaya:
A Biographical History of Christian Missions (Harper Collins, 2004).

—— Extraordinary Women of Christian History (Grand Rapids: Baker Books, 2016).

Turner, John Munsey, Wesleyan Methodism
(Peterborough: Epworth Press, 2005).

Verzone, Paolo, From Theodoric To Charlemagne: A History of the Dark Ages (Methuen, 1968).

Villafane, Eldin, Beyond Cheap Grace:
A Call to Radical Discipleship, Incarnation, and Justice
(Grand Rapids: Eerdmans, 2006).

Vos, Howard F., Exploring Church History
(Nashville, Atlanta, London, Vancouver: Thomas Nelson, 1994).

Walker, Williston, A History of the Christian Church (Edinburgh: T & T Clark, 1959).

Wand, J. W. C., A History of the Early Church (London: Methuen, 1961).

Ward, Benedicta, The Desert Fathers:
Sayings of the Early Christian Monks (London: Penguin Books, 2003).

Watson, Sydney, From Darkness to Light: The Life and Work of Mrs Baeyertz
(Cork: Guy and Co, 1894).

Whitehouse, David, Renaissance Genius:
Galileo Galilei and His Legacy to Modern Science (Sterling Publishing, 2009).

Whittow, Mark, The Making of Orthodox Byzantium 600-1025
(London: Macmillam 1996).

Wilberforce, William, Real Christianity
(Ventura, CA: Regal Books, 1797/2006).

Wiley, Tatha (ed.), Thinking of Christ: Proclamation, Explanation, Meaning (N. Y. and London: Continuum, 2003).

Wilken, Robert E., John Chrysostom and the Jews: Rhetoric in the Fourth Century, (Berkeley: UCal Press:1983).

Wilkins, M. J. , Matthew (Grand Rapids, MI: Zondervan, 2004).

Wilkinson, John, Egeria's Travels
(London: SPCK, 1991).

Willard, Dallas, Renovation of the Heart: Putting on the Character of Christ (Downer Grove: IVP, 2002).

——- 'How Do We Assess Spiritual Growth?' Leadership Journal, 31.2 (May, 2010).

Wilson, Mark, 'Alternative Facts: Domitian's Persecution of Christians' BHD 24/7/2017.

Wilson-Kastner, Patricia et al., Women Writers of the Early Church (University Press of America, 1981).

Winter, Ralph and Steven C. Hawthorne (eds), Perspectives on the World

Christian Movement: A Reader (3rd ed.)

(Pasadena and Carlisle: William Carey Library and Paternoster Press, 1981/1992/1999).

Wood, John, Hannah Hurnard: The Authorised Biography
(St Albans, Hertz: Olive Press, 1996).

Wright, Christopher, Old Testament Ethics for the People of God
(Downers Grove, Ill: Inter Varsity Press, 2004).

Wright, N. T., The New Testament and the People of God
(Minneapolis MN: Fortress, 1992).

Wuthnow, Robert, 'Recent Pattern of Secularization: A Problem of Generations?'

American Sociological Review 41, 1976.

Electronic Sources

Aish. com, 'Napoleon and the Jews.'
https://www.aish.com/st/h/h/48945221.html

'A Short History of the Department of State: The Berlin Wall Falls and USSR Dissolves.'

https://history.state.gov/departmenthistory/short-history/berlinwall/

Armstrong, Chris, 'Amazingly Graced Life of John Newton' in Christianity Today. www:christianitytoday.com/history/issues/issue-81/amazingly-

graced-life-of-john-newton.html

'Albert Schweitzer', Editors of Encyclopædia Britannica,. **https://www.britannica.com/biography/Albert**

Schweitzer

Aldridge, James, 'Was there a standard method of persecuting Christians in the cities of the Roman

East from 303-324 A.D.?'

https://www.tremr.com/james-aldridge/was-thgere-a-standardised-method-of-persecutingchristians

Amber, Jasmine, 'The Queen's Mother: Marie de Guise'

https://venerablevixens.wordpress.com/2015/09/08/the-queens-mother-marie-de-guise

Ashby, Roland, 'Call from God leads to global Celtic fellowship',

www.melbourneanglican.org.au/NewsandViews/Pages/call-from-God-leads-to-global-Celticfellowship-000677.aspx

'A Short History of the Department of State. The Berlin Wall Falls and USSR Dissolves.'

https://history.state.gov/departmenthistory/short-history/berlinwall/

Ballantyne, Tony and Anna Blackman, 'Reverend Samuel Marsden (1765-1838)',

marsdenarchive. otago.ac.nz/about/marsden

'Barna Studies the Research, Offers a Year-in-Review Perspectives,' 2009, Barana Group.

https://www.barna.org/barna-update/faith-spirituality/325-barna-studies-the-research-offers-ayear-in-review-perspective#.V2NesVd6OS0

Barrett, David B. and Todd M. Johnson, 'International Bulletin of Missionary Research, January 2009'.

https://mail.yahoo.com/?.intl=au.partner=none&.src=fpx#3616288658&

3

---

3.   https://mail.yahoo.com/?.intl=au.partner=none&.src=fpx#a5c02393e59c943d6a75a9241140f

aca33616288658_6cff047854f19ac2aa52aac51bf3af4a_

Bible History Online, 'Paul's Third Missionary Journey', http://www.bible-history.com/new-testament/pauls-third-missionary-journey.html

Brown, Richard, 'How did Methodism develop under Jabez Bunting?' richardjohnbr.blogspot.com/2011/10/how-did-methodism-develop-under-jabez.html

Butler, Alban, for Eternal Word Television Network, 'St Olympias, Widow', https://www.etwn.com/catgholicism/library/st-olympias-widow

'Camp Meetings', New World Encyclopedia, www.newworldencyclopedia.org/entry/Special:cite7page=camp_meeting

Castellano, Daniel J., (Part I-II, 2009, Part III 2013, Part IV 2019), Origen and Origenism, I.1, www.arcaneknowledge.org/catholic.origen.htm.

Catholic Ireland.net: 'St. Finnian', www:monasticireland.com/storiesofsaints/finnian.htm

'Cause and Effect The First Great American Awakening.' http://www.piney.com/ColAwkEffect.html

'Celtic Monasteries'. www.orthodoxchurch.co.uk/Celtic_Monasteries.html

Charles Dickens Info, 'Charles Dickens Biography', https://www.charlesdickensinfo.com/life/biography/ Chen, Alison, 'The First Great Awakening', https://www.citelighter.com/history/history/knowledgecards/the-first-great-awakening

Christian Today AU, 'The Effects of Billy Graham Crusades in 1959 Still Being Felt Today'. Christianitytoday.com.au/news/the-effects-of-billy-graham-crusades-in-1959-still-being-felttoday.html

Christianity Today News and Reporting, Jan. 12, 2021, 'The 50 Countries Where It's Most Dangerous to Follow Jesus in 2021', https://www.christianitytoday.com/news/2021/january/christian-persecution-2021-countries-opendoors-watch-list-html

Christianity.com, 'Arthur T. Pierson, Illustrious Heritage', https://www.christianity.com/church/church-history/timeline/1801-1900/arthur-t-piersonillustrious-heritage-11630444.html

Cockburn, Patrick, 'The Vikings were feared for a reason',
https://www.independent.co.uk/voices/comment/vikings-were-feared-reason-9241032.html
Coggan, Philip, 'Christianity in Cambodia', 21/1/2016 https://www.newmandala.org/christianity-in-cambodia
Crawford, Janet, '"Valuable Helpers":
Women in the Melanesian Mission in the Nineteenth Century.'
The Canterbury Project
anglicanhistory.org/oceania/selwyn_lectures1999.pdf
Crusis Staff, 'Nigeria is becoming the world's biggest killing ground for Christians' August 20, 2020. https://cruxnow.com/church-in-africa/2020/08/nigeria-is-becoming-worlds-biggest-killing-groundof-christians/
'C. T. Studd'.
www.thetravellingteam.org/articles/ct-studd
Curtis, Ken (ed.), 'William Carey (1701-1800)'
www.christianity.com/church/church-history/timeline/wcarey1701-1800/william-careys-amazingmission-1630319
Dahlburg, Andy, 'The Celtic Monk'
The celticmonk.blogspot.com.au/2009/10/celtic-rule-of-life-htm
Davidson, Allan, 'An Interesting Experiment: the Founding of the Melanesian Mission', 1999 Selwyn Lectures at the College of St John the Evangelist, Auckland N.Z.
anglicanhistory.org/oceania/selwyn_lectures1999.pdf
Dr Majd by Khamenei.ir
http://english.khamenei,ir/news/2197/8-10-million-Irtanians-died-over-Great-Famine-caused-bythe-British
Doherty, Ben, for The Guardian, 'Australia takes the most refugees since start of humanitarian program',
https:/www. theguardian.com/world/2019/feb/10/australia-takes-the-most-refugees-since-start-ofhumanitarian-program
Dulles, Avery Cardinal, 'The Covenant With Israel, November 2005' https://www.firstthings.com/articler/2005/11/the-covenant-with-israel
Dunstan, Gregg, 'The Beginning of the Church in Australia
(and Early Hints At Apostasy)',
http://geocities.com/spenserion/dunstan.html?20087

Editors of Encyclopædia Britannica, 'Albert Schweitzer', https://www.britannica.com/biography/Albert Schweitzert

Editors of Encyclopædia Britannica, 'Anti-Semitism in Medieval Europe', https://www.britannica.com/topic/Anti-Semitism

Editors of Encyclopædia Britannica, 'Anabaptists', https://www.britannica.com/topic/Anabaptists

Editors of Encyclopædia Britannica, 'Charles Dickens: British Novelist', https://www.britannica.com/biography/Charles-Dickens-British-Novelist

The Editors of Encyclopaedia Britannica, "Entebbe Raid', by Laura Etheredge, https://www.britannica.com/event/Entebbe-raid

Editors of Encyclopaedia Britannica, 'Evangeline Cory Booth', https://www.britannica.com/biography/Evangeline-Cory-Booth

Editors of Encyclopædia Britannica, 'Hannah Whitall Smith', https://www.britannica.com/biography/Hannah-Whitall-Smith

Editors of Encyclopedia Britannica, 'Henry Barnard', https://www.britannica.com/biography/Henry-Barnard

Editors of Encyclopaedia Britannica, 'Henry Grey, Duke of Suffolk', https://www.Britannica.com/biography/Hentuy-Grey-Duke-of-Suffolk

Editors of Encyclopedia Britannica, 'Horace Mann', https://www.britannica.com/biography/Horace-Mann

Editors of Encyclopedia Britannica, 'Saint Justyin Martyr', https://www.britannica.com/biography/Saint-Justin-Martyr

Editors of Encyclopædia Britannica, 'The Church of North India', https//www.britannica.com/topic/church-of-North-India

Editors of Encyclopædia Britannica, 'Therapeutae', https://www.britannica.com/topic/Therapeutae

Encyclopedia Judaica, Bernhard Blumenkranz, 'Church Fathers', https://www.jewishvirtuallibrary.org/church-fathers

Encyclopedia Judaica, Colbi, 'Jewish-Christian Relations', https://www.jewishvirtualllibray.org/jewish-christian-relations-encyclopedia-judaica

Eternal Word Television Network, 'St Olympias, Widow - 368-410', https://www.ewtn.com/caholicism/library/st-olympias-widow-5711

Farah, Philip and David Wildman, 'The Role of the U.S. Church in the BDS Movement' http://www.thejerusalemfund.org/40/the-role-of-the-u-s-churches-in-the-bds-

Farrokh, Kaveh,

http://www.Kavehfarrokh.com/iranicas/milita/ar-mohammad-gholi-majd-great-crimes-andgenocide-in-iran-in-1917/-1919/

Ford, David C., 'St. Olympia the Deaconess, Confidante of St. John Chrysostom', https://saintolympiaorthodoxchurch.org/index.php/resources/9-st-olympia-the-deaconess

Gathro, Richard, 'William Wilberforce and His Circle of Friends', for Knowing and Doing, published by the C.S. Lewis Institute (2001). www.cslewisinstitute.org/webfm.send/471

Gehman, Richard, 'The East Africa Revival (1986)' https://biblicalstudies.org.uk/pdf/ajet/05-1_036.pdf

'Gladys Aylward - Missionary to China' (December 9, 2013) by mylordkatie. mylordkatie.wordpress.com12013/12/9/gladys-aylward-missionary-to-china

Gleason, Ralph J. 'The Flower Children'. https://www.britannica.com/topic/The-Flower-Children2101574

Goforth, Jonathan, 'When the Spirit's Fire Swept Korea', https://www.gospeltruth.nel/koreafire.htm

Grace Berkeley Church, 'Apostole Paul's Missionary Journeys', http://www.gracepointdevotions.org/2011/03/04/apostle-pauls-missionary-journeys/

Graves, Dan MSL, 'C.T. Studd Gave Huge Inheritance Away', www: Christianity.com/church/church-history/timeline/1801/c-t-studd

Hanson, Marilee, 'Lady Jane Grey- Facts, Biography, Information & Portraits.' https://englishhistory.net/tudor/relative/lady-jane-grey February 1, 2015

Hirsch, Alan, for Christianity Today, 'Three Overlooked Leadership Roles', www. christianitytoday.com/pastors/spring/732.html

'Historical information on Clonard' http://www.suttonclonard.com/clonard.htm

History Hit, 'Why Did the Vikings Invade Britain?' https://www.historyhit.com/why-did-the-vikings-invade-britain/

History of Monasticism. Christian hermits 3rd-4th century A.D. http://www.historyworld.net/wrldhis/PlainTextHistories.asp?Paragra...[4]

'History of the Melanesian Brotherhood.' orders.anglican.org/mbh/history.htm

Howarth, Janet, 'Fawcett, Dame Millicent Garrett [née Millicent Garrett]', www.oxforddnBCom/view/10.1093/ref:odnb/9780198614128.0001/odn

Hunter, Ryan, '40 Years ago: Communist Coup Deposed Ethiopia's Last Emperor,' The Institute on Religion and Democracy, 22/9/2014. https://juicyecumenism.com/2014/09/22/40-years-ago-communist-coup-deposedethiopias-lastemperor

'I Believe It Is Because I Am a Poor Indian': Samson Occom's Life as an Indian Minister'. http://historymatters.gmu.edu/d/5788

Iconandlight, 'Saint Nonna, Mother of Saint Gregory the Theologian', https://iconandlight.wordpress.com/2017/01/25/saint-nonna-mother-of-saint-gregory-thetheologian/

Iconandlight, 'St Olympia-Olympiada the Deaconess' https://iconandlight.wordpress.com/2014/07/24/st-olympia-olympiada-the-deaconess/

Ihunnia, Daniel O. MSP, 'How Africa is changing the face of mission' https://sedosmission.org/article/how-africa-is-changing-the-face-of-mission

'Illuminated Manuscripts, (600-1200)' http://www.visual-arts-cork.com/cultural-history-of-ireland/illuminated-manuscripts.htm

'James Hudson Taylor', by WholesomeWords www.wholesomewords.org/bibliography/biorptaylor.html

---

4.   http://www.historyworld.net/wrldhis/PlainTextHistories.asp?Paragra...

'Jan Karski', UniteD States Holocaust Memorial Museum, Washington, D.C.

https://ushmm.org/wlc/en/article.php?ModuleId=10008152

'Jim Elliot: No Fool'

http://www.christianity.com/church/church-history/church-historyfor-kids/jim-elliot-no-fool11634862.html

'John Bunyan, Church History Timeline'

www.christianity.com/church/church-history/timeline/1601-1700/john-bunyan

'John Bunyan'.

www.greatsite.com/timeline-english-bible-history/john-bunyan.html

katholisch.de, website of the Catholic Church in Germany.

Khamenei.ir

http://english.khamenei.ir/news/2197/8-10-million-iranians-died-over-Great-Famine-caused-by-theBritish

Kiefer, James E. , 'Nate Saint and Other Martyrs of the Ecuador Mission, 8 January, 1956.' http://justus.anglican.org/resources/bio/74.html

Kierfer, James E., 'James Hannington and the Martyrs of Uganda 29 October, 1885.' http://justus.anglican.org/resources/bio/278.html

Kimenyl, Mwangis and Nelipher Moyo, 'The Late Zambian President Fredrick Chiluba: A Legacy of

Failed Democratic Transition',

https://www.brookings.edu/opinions/the-late-zambian-president-fredrick-chiluba-a-legacy-offailed-democratic-transition/

Khup Za Go, 'Chin People in the World. A Bief History of Christianity in Burma' (Myanmar), https://sialki.wordpress.com/the-stories-of-zomi/a-brief-history-of-christianity-in-burma/ Knight, Kevin (ed), for New Advent, 'Jeanne-Marie Bouvier de la Motte-Guyon' (2012).

http://www.newadvent.org/cathen/07092b.htm

——— 'St Gregory of Nazianzus',

https://www.newadvent.org/cathen/070106.htm

Lane, Gary and George Thomas, 'Vicar of Baghdad Says Christianity is 'Over' in Iraq.'

http://www1.cbn.com/cbnnews/cwn/2017/march/vicar-of-baghdad-christianity-is-over-in-iraq

Lapa, Dmitry, 'Venerable Finnian, abbot of Clonard' https://www.pravoslavie.ru/english/print67125.htm

Lendering, Jona, 'Jewish Rome,' http://www.livius.com/artices/concept/diaspora/jewish-rome/

Lewis, Nicola Denzey, 'The Apostle Peter in Rome', https://www.biblicalarchaeology.org/daily/people-cultures-in-the-bible/people-in-the-bible/theapostle-peter-in-rome/

M.A.F. 'How five martyrs transformed the Waodani people of Ecuador'.

https://www.maf-uk.org/story/how-five-martyrs-transformed-the-waodani-people-of-ecuador

MacMillan, Margaret, 'Rebuilding the world after the second world war,' (2009) https://www.theguardian.com>world>second world war

'Martyrdom calls for Mau Mau Victims'

http://www.nation.co.uk/news/Martyrdom-calls-for-Mau-Mau-victims/1056-296513055885h/index.html

Masci, David, News in Numbers: 5 facts about the religious lives of African Americans https://www.pewresearch-org/fact-tank/2018/02/07/5-facts-about-the-religious-lives-of-africanamericans/

Matsiko, Arthur, 'The Uganda Martyrs of Namugongo – the full truth behind this historic event' Anglican Communion News Service (ACNS) January 12, 2015. https://www.google.com.au/search?qthe+uganda+martyrs+of+thamugongo

MacDonald, Charlotte, 'Between religion and empire: Sarah Selwyn's Aotearoa/New Zealand, Eton and Lichfield, England, c. 1840s-1900',

https://www.erudit.org/fr/review/jcha/2008_v19-h2-3329/03748ar/

McEwen, James Stevenson, 'John Knox: Scottish Religious Leader,' https://www.britannic.com/biography/John-Knox

Michael, Susan M., 'Anti-Semitism in Christianity Today' https://int-icej.org/susans-blog/anti-semitism-christianity-today

'Minority Report: Christian Persecution in Muslim-Majority Countries.'

https://www.fulerstudio.edu/minority-report-christian-persecution-muslim-majority-countries Mirus, Jeff, 'St. Ambrose's impact on St. Augustine: Excerpts from The Confessions', https://www.catholicculture.org/commentary/articles.cfm?id=703

Missler, Nancy, 'Who is Jeanne Guyon?' http://www.the last days.net/whoguyon.htm_

Moon, Ruth, 'Founder of World's Largest Megachurch Convicted of Embezzling $12 Million

(24/2/2014)'

http://www.christianitytoday.com/news/2014february/founder-of-worlds-largest-megachurchconvicted-cho-yido.htm

Moore, Adrian, 'Baptist Distinctive - Fundamental Baptist Institute', www.fbinstitute.com/moore/baptistdist.html

'Mothercraft: Melanesia: The Solomon Islands and New Hebrides', (London, 1949) transcribed by the Rt Rev. Dr Terry Brown, (2006).

http://anglicanhistory.org/ocenaia/sx_booklet8.html

Mowczko, Marg, 'Apphia of Colossae: Philemon's Wife or

Another Phoebe?' https://margmowczko.com/apphia/

Murre-van den Berg, Heleen, 'A brief history of Christianity in Iran.'

https://www.hlmvandenberg.me/2017/01/20-a-brief-history-of-christianity-in-iran/

mylordkatie, 'Gladys Aylward - Missionary to China' (December 9, 2013).   mylordkatie.wordpress.com12013/12/9/gladys-aylward-missionary-to-china

National Museums Liverpool, 'Abolition of slavery in the Americas',

http://www.liverpoolmuseums.org.uk/ism/slavery/americas/abolition_americas_asps

Nazret, 'Dr Catherine Hamlin of Ethiopia'

nazret.com/blog/index.php/2009/10/14/
dr.catherine_hamlin_of_ethiopia

New Lanark Trust, 'Robert Owen' www.robert-owen.com

New Advent, 'Letters to Olympias',

https://www.newadvent.org/fathers/1916.htm

Norman, Heidi, 'Parramatta and Black Town Native Institutions, 2015,

https://dictionaryofsydney.org/entry/

parramatta_and_black_town_native_institutions

'Origins of Falasha Jews studied by haphliotypes of the Y chromosome,'

https://www.ncbi.nih.gov/pubmed/1592599

Palestinian BDS National Committee, 'What is BDS?'
https://bdsmovement.net/what-is-bds

Pew Research Centre, 'Restrictions on religion among the 25 most
populous countries, 2007-2015.' http://www.pewforum.org/interactives/
restrictions-on-religion-among-the-most-populouscountries-2007-2015/

Piper, John, 'The Ministry of Hudson Taylor as Life in Christ':
Desiring God 2014 Conference for Pastors (5/2/2014).

www.desiringgod.org/messages/the-ministry-of-hudson-taylor-as-life-
in-christ

Plaisted, David A., 'Estimates of the Number Killed by the Papacy in
the Middle Ages and Later' (2006).

https://www.cs.unc.edu/~plaisted/estimates.html

Pullella, Philip, Rome, and Aseel Kami, Baghdad, 'Global Outcry at
death of Iraqi archbishop'

www.theage.com.au/news/world/global-outcry-at-death-of-
Iraqiarchbishop/2008/03/14/1205472082065.html

Quakers in the world, 'Chocolate Makers'

http://www.quakersintheworld.org/quakers-in-action/263/
Chocolate-Makers

'Religion in Colonial America: Trends, Regulations, and Beliefs'.

https://www.facinghistory.org/nobigotry/religion-colonial-america-
trends-refulations-and-beliefs

'Religion in the 13 Original Colonies.'

Eddiestonnard.blogspot.com.au/2010/10/religion-in-original-13-
colonies

Ringma, Charles, 'Drinking from Many Fountains: A Missional Spirituality for Radical
Evangelicals,'
www://servantsasia.org/drinking-many-fountains-spirituality-radical-evangelicals
Ringma, Charles, 'Contemplation and Action: Towards a Missional Spirituality.'
https://www.fortomorrow.org.au/stories/story/contemplation-and-action-part-1-towards-amissional-spirituality
Rode, Marcus of Open Doors in 'What it's like to be a Christian in Iran?' www.dw.com/en/what-its-like-to-be-a-Christian-in-Iran/a-19002952
Rosenberg, Jennifer, 'The Rwanda Genocide: A Short History of the Rwanda Genocide'.
https://www.thoughtco.com/the-rwanda-genocide-1779931
Ross, David, 'Britain Express: Altarnun Cornwall'
http://www.britainexpress.com/attractions.htm?attraction=2672
Ross, Stephen, 'Missionary Biographies, Charles (C.T.) Studd'
http://www.wholesomewords.org/missions/biostudd.html
Sahgal, Neha, '500 years after the Reformation, 5 facts about Protestants around the world', 27/10/2117.
www.pewresearch.org/fact-tank/2017/10/27/500-years-after-the-reformation-5-facts-aboutprotestants-around-the-world/
Sanders, J. Oswald, 'Knowing and Doing: A Teaching Quarterly for Discipleship of Heart and Mind',
published by the C.S. Lewis Institute (Summer 2005.)
https://www.cslewisinstitute,org/webfm_send/424
Sandleman, John, 'Tribute to revival preacher,' June 4, 2009.
https://sydneyanglicans.net/blogs/churchlife/tribute_to_a_revival_preacher
Sauvage, Pierre, 'Does "Village of Secrets" Falsify French Rescue During the Holocaust?' https://www.tabletmag.com/jewish-arts-and-culture/books/186652/m

Sekulow, Jordan, 'Horror in Africa: ACLJ Delivers Critical Universal Periodic Review to UN as Deadly Violence Against Christians Spreads Across Africa',

https://adj.org/persecuted-church/horror-in-africa-adj-delivers-official-periodic-review-to-un-asdeadly-violence-against-christians-spreads-across-africa

S-cool Youth Marketing Limited,'The Religious Settlement'.

Schafer, Thomas A., 'Jonathan Edwards', Encyclopedia Britannica. https//www.britannica.com/biography/Jonathan-Edwards

Scott, Elizabeth, 'Anabaptists: Separate by Choice. Marginal by Force.' (1995) https://www.anabaptists.org/history/sepamarg.html

Sherwood, Harriet, 'Religion: why faith is becoming more and more popular', The Guardian, 27/8/2018.

https://www.theguardian.com/news/2018/aug/27/religion-why-is-faith

Shenk, Wilbert R., 'The Contribution of Henry Venn to Missional Thought', https://biblicalstudies.org.uk/pdf/anvil/02-1_025.pdf

'04Significance of the Great Awakening: Roots of Revolution' © 2017 Great-Awakening.com   http://www.great-awakening.com/roots-of-revolution/

Singh, MP Shamsher Kainth, 'Australia's immigration intake to remain at last year's level: PM Scott

Morrison',

https://www.sbs.com.au/yourlanguage/punjabi/n/article/2018/10/10/cuts

'Spirit and Power – A 10-Country survey of Pentecostals', Oct. 5, 2006', https://www.pewforum.org/2006/overview-pentecostslism-in-africa/

State archives, 'Randwick Asylum for Destitute Children: Historical Background, Archives and Records' records.nsw.gov.au/archives/collections-and-research/guides-and-indexes/randwick-asylumdestitute-children

Sterling, George E., 'Rethinking Christianity in the 21st Century', https://reflections.yale.edu/article/new-voyages-today-and-tomorrow/rethinking-Christianity-21stcentury

Studd-Charles-Thomas

www.bu.edu/missiology-biography/c.t. studd-charles-thomas

Study by the Abarbanel Health Centre and Tel Aviv University. Tamara Traubmann in Ha Aretz (Aug.19, 2005). https://www.haaretz.com/news/study-holocaust-survivors-3-times-more-likely-to-attempt-suicide-1.166386

Taylor, James Hudson,

www.wholesomewords.org/bibliography/biorptaylor.html

The Independence Hall Association, '7b.The Great Awakening.' http://www.ushistory.org/us/7b.asp

'The Life of Our Holy Mother Saint Mary of Egypt' http://www.abbamoses.com/stmarylife.html

Uganda National Media, 'The valley that witnessesd Bishop Hannington's death', editorial@ug.nationalmedia.com

http://www.monitor.co.ug/artsculture/Reviews/The-valley-that-witnessed-Bishop-Hannington-sdeath/691232-1411440-f5po0iz/indix.html

'The Venerable Finnian, Founder of the Monastery of Clonard, Teacher of the Saints of Ireland'

www.oodegr.com/english/biographies/arxaio/Finnian_Clonard.htm

The Attempted Coronation,

https://www.ladyjanegrey.org/queen/index.html

The Reformation – Facts & Summary – History.com http://www.history.com/topics/reformation

Thorpe, Osmund, 'MacKillop, Mary Helen (1842-1909),' http://adb.anu.au/biography/mackillop-mary-helen-4112/text6575

Trueman, C. N., 'The Religious Settlement of 1559'. Historylearningsite.co.uk

Tucker, Ruth A., 'William Carey's Less-Than-Perfect Family Life', in Christianity Today (July/August 2017).

www.christianitytoday.com/history/issue-261william-careys-less-than-

Unites States Holocaust Memorial Museum, Washington, D.C. (on Jan Karski) https://ushmm.org/wlc/en/article.php?ModuleId=10008152

Van Dyck, Anthony, 'A Brief History of the Jesuits'. http://facukty.fairfield.edu/jmac/sj/briefsjhistory.htm

Waldman, Yedael, 'On The Genetic Trail of the Bene Israel',
https://jewishweek.timesofisrael.com/on-the-genetic-trail-of-the-bene-israel/

Waldman et el., 'The genetic history of Cochin Jews from India',
https://pubmed.ncbi.nlm.nih.gov/27377974/

Wallace, Joseph D., 'Synagogue and Ecclesia in Our Time' in The Catholic Star Herald, October 1, 2015.
http://documenta-akermariano.blogspot.com/2015/07/synagoga-et-ecclesia.htm

Walsh, G. P. 'Vickery, Ebenezer (1827-1906)',
Australian Dictionary of Biography, Vol. 6 (MUP), 1967.
ad.anu.edu.au/biography/vickery-ebenezer-

Weaver, Doug, 'What are the top challenges facing Baptists today?'
https://www.baptistnews.com/article/what-are-the-top-challenges-facing-baptist-churches-today

Webster, Jeremy, 'Pew: Why Americans
Go to Church or Stay Home',
**https://www.christianitytoday.com/news/2018/ju
ly/ch**urch-attendance-top-reasons-go-or-stay
home-pew.html

White, Lisa Beth, 'Carmichael, Amy Beatrice (1867-1951). Founder of the Dohnavur Fellowship', https://www.bu.edu/missiology/missionary-biography/c-d/carmichael-amy-beatrice-1867-1951/

Wigington, Patti, for ThoughtCo. 4/12/2018, 'Biography of Robert Smalls, Civil War Hero and Congressman',
https://www.thoughtco.com/robert-smalls-biography-4178440

Willard, Dallas, 'Subversive Interview Part 1',
https://dwillard.org/articles/subversive-interview-part-1

Willard, Dallas, 'The Disappearance of Moral Knowlegdge,'
http://www.dwillard.org/articles/artview.asp?artID=120

Wilson, Mark, 'Alternative Facts: Domitian's Persecution of Christians',
https://biblicalarchaeology.org/daily/biblical-topics/post-biblical-period/domitian-persecution-ofchristians/

"Willow Creek Repents?" Christianity Today: Leadership Journal, October 18, 2007.

http://www.christianitytoday.com/le/2007/october-online-only/willow-creek-repents.html

Winter, Ralph D., 'Four Men, Three Eras, Two Transitions: Modern Missions'

www.foundationscourse.org/uploads/documents/reader/31_four_men_three_eras_pdf

World Christianity AIU, 'Africa Instituted Churches in the 21st Century'.

https://worldchristianityaiu.wordpress.com/2013/12/05/africa-instituted-churches-in-21st-century/

Worldwide Evangelization Crusade (WEC).

uwww.bu.edu/missiology-biography/c.t. studd-charles-thomas

Yarwood, A. T., 'Marsden, Samuel (1765-1838)',

Australian Dictionary of Biography, Vol. 2 (MUP), 1967. http://ad.anu.edu.au/biography/marsden-samuel-2433 **End**

Notes

1 Both of the Strasbourg illustrations are licensed under the Creative Commons Attribution-Share Alike 3.0 Unported license. By Sodabottle.

2 In some examples Synagoga even carries the instrument of circumcision, for example in a 9thcentury ivory now in the Bibliotheque Nazionale, Paris. Codex Latin 9383, see G. Holmes (ed.), Oxford Illustrated History Of Medieval Europe (hereafter OIHME) (Oxford and N.Y.: Oxford University Press, 1990/1995) opposite p. 113.

3 Author: Jean Pierre Dalbéra. Title: L'eglise et la synagogue (Cathedrale de Metz). Used un creative commons license 2.0 Ceneric (CC By 20),

https://www.flickr.com/photos/dalbera/8010236397

4 From the mid-6th century, virtually all Christian churches in the Muslim world became mosques, including at least fourteen great churches in Constantinople (now Istanbul). Hagia Sophia and Chora became museums for tourists although the former, recently restored by money from overseas, is again being used for Muslim worship. Hagia Irene is used as a concert hall. In the villages church bells were removed and replaced by loud-speakers for the Islamic call to prayer.

5 Rabbinic Judaism was said to be Christianity's sister, e.g., in A. F. Segal, Rebecca's Children: Judaism and Christianity in the Roman World (Cambridge, MA., 1983), p. 181. This fascinating allegory warrants investigation.

6 Some scholars discount Peter's period in Rome, e.g., Nicola Denzey Lewis. See her 'The Apostle Peter in Rome', in BHD March 6, 2021.

7 Patricia Cox Miller (2005, 117f) provides English translations of this term, which indicate that the practice was considered illicit.

8 Reproduction of a stone tablet engraved with a Nestorian Christian cross and inscribed with Syriac writing. Found at the site of a Christian church or monastery at Fangsfhan District (◇ ◇◇) in Beijing (then called Dadu, or Khanbaliq). Dated to the Yuan Dynasty (1271-1368 AD) of medieval China. Photo by Prof. Gary Lee Todd. In Beijing Capital Museum. Use licensed under the Creative Commons Attribution-Share Alike 4.0 International 3.0 Unported.

9 Lyn H. Cohick and Amy Brown Hughes record the 5th century BCE story of Lucretia who, to demonstrate her dedication to these virtues, suicided after being raped, in Christian Women in the Patristic World: Their Influence, Authority and Legacy in the Second Through Fifth Centuries (Grand Rapids, MI: Baker Academic, 2017), p. 12.

10 Her husband of a twenty days was Nebrius, ex-prefect of Constantinople, and her father was

Seleucus, the ex-count. Palladius,
www.tertullian.org/fathers/palladius_lausiac_02_text_htm#C46
Dr David C. Ford, 'St. Olympia the Deaconess, Confidante of St. John Chrysostom', https://saintolympiaorthodoxchurch.org/index.php/resources/9-st-olympia-the-deaconess

11 Another Paladius is also a source of information about Olympias, in his Life of Chrysostom, written c.408.

12 This church was rebuilt by the Emperor Justinian in the 6th century.

13 This was a mixture of ideas which rejected the Old Testament and God and incorporated dualism, asceticism, and determinism. Its founder, Mani, had been martyred in Persia c. 267. Religionfacts, 'Augustine of Hippo', online. Bruce Shelley, Church History in Plain Language, (Dallas, London, Vancouver, Melbourne: Word Publishing, 1982/1996), pp. 125ff.

14 Jeff Mirus, 'St. Ambrose's impact on St. Augustine: Excerpts from The Confessions',

https://www.catholicculture.org/commentary/articles.cfm?id=703
A modern translation of The Confessions of St Augustine by Henry Chadwick is available (Oxford:
Oxford UP, 1991).

15 Internet Encyclopedia of Philosophy, 'Augustine (354-430 CE), Part 3.

https://www.iep.utm.edu/Augustine/

16 For excerpts from Gregory of Nazanzus the Younger's funeral orations on members of his family see Miller (ed.), 2005, 276-284.

17 At this time in Constantinople deaconesses had to be dedicated to celibacy.

Eternal Word Television Network, 'St Olympias, Widow - 368-410', online and Patricia Cox Miller, Women in Early Christianity, 62.

18 Gregory the Younger was not actually Bishop of Nazianzus but suffragan to his father and upon his death administered the diocese until a replacement could be found. His friend, St Basil, had coerced him into becoming Bishop of Sasima but he did not take up the position. He became Archbishop in Constantinople

(380-381) but soon retired to the family estate in Azianzus with ill-health. New Advent, Kevin Knight (ed.) 'St Gregory of Nazianzus', online.

19 New Advent, Kevin Knight (ed.) 'St Gregory of Nazianzus', online.

20 The most reliable text of the Vulgate, the Codex Amiatinus, was produced in England in one of the great Benedictine monasteries of Wearmouth or Jarrow, under Abbott Ceolfrid, c.716, Bruce, Spreading Flame, 1958/1962, 414f.

21 Although it is not the usual definition, according to Kaveh Farrokh genocide means "the deliberate and wilful killing of large numbers of non-combatants", in a review of Dr Mohammad-Gholi Majd: The Great Famine and Genocide in Iran in 1917-19 (University Press of America, 2003). This is a thorough treatment on the topic, but notably subjective. http://Kavehfarrokh.com/iranica/militia/ar-mohammad-gholi-majd-great-crimes-and-genocide-in-

Iran-in-1917/-1919/

22 In particular the accusations based on Dr Majd by Khamenei.ir

http://english.khamenei,ir/news/2197/8-10-million-Irtanians-died-over-Great-Famine-caused-bythe-British

24 Altarnun is our maternal ancestral home but our ancestors were Wesleyan. In 1818, a local sculptor, Neville Burnard, carved a head of John Wesley which remains over the door of the former Wesleyan Chapel, see Britain Express: Altarnun Cornwall by David Ross.

http://www.britainexpress.com/attractions.htm?attraction=2672

25 According to the Annals of Ulster, Gildas wrote De Excidio Britannia. See 'The Venerable Finnian, Founder of the Monastery of Clonard, Teacher of the Saints of Ireland' (✝551). www.oodegr.com/english/biographies/arxaio/ Finnian_Clonard.htm

26 In about 740 St Anthousa of Mantineon financed, established and ran both a large nunnery on an island in the middle of a lake and a male monastery on the nearby shore, which her nephew oversaw, Life of St Anthousa of Mantineon in Bithynia; Synaxarium CP 848-852. See C. Mango, 'St Anthousa of Mantineon and the Family of Constantine V', AB 100 (1982), pp. 401-09 and George Huxley, 'Women and Iconoclasm', in Jacques Perreault (ed.), Women and Byzantine Monasticism, Proceedings of the

Athens Symposium 28-29 March, 1988 (Athens: Canadian Archaeological Institute at Athens, 1991), p. 13.

27 Hanson, 'Lady Jane Grey - Facts, Biography, Information & Portraits,' online.

28 Osmund Thorpe, s.v. MacKillop, Mary Helen (1842-1909), Australian Dictionary of Biography, National Centre of Biography, Australian National University.

http://adb.anu.au/biography/mackillop-mary-helen-4112/text6575

29 Intriguing History, 'Elizabeth Fry Quaker Reformer',

http://www.intriguing-history.com/elizabeth-fry-reformer-quaker History's Heroes? 'Elizabeth Fry, 1780-1845', excerpted from Elizabeth Fry - Quaker Heroine 27/8/1842. historyheroes.22bn.org/othersources/108/1

30 Betsy's companion Anna Buxton, was the sister of Thomas Fowell Buxton. He married Hannah Gurney, becoming Betsy's brother-in-law, and, in 1815, he became a Member of Parliament where he advocated for her work.

31 His son with Hannah Gurney, Sir Thomas Fowell Buxton, became Governor of South Australia. 32 Quotation from Elizabeth Fry is from Mursell (ed.), Christian Spirituality, p. 185.

33 See Catherine Mumford Booth, Female Ministry: Or , Women's Right to Preach the Gospel, The

Voice, http://wwwcrivoice.org/WF-booth.html and http://webapp.dlib.indiana,edu/vwwp/ view?docld=VAB7105&doc.view=print

34 Florence S. Boos, 'The Education Act of 1870: Before and After.' BRANCH: Britain, Representation and Nineteenth-Century History. Ed. Dino Franco Felluga. Extension of Romanticism and Victorianism on the Net

www.branchcollective.org/ 7ps_aricles_florence_e_boos_the_education_act_of_1870

35 John Ramsland, Children's Institutions in nineteenth century Sydney. [Accessed 1/1/2019], citing Ramsland, Children of the Backlanes (Kensington, N.S.W.: U.N.S.W. Press, 1986),1.

https://www.dictionaryofsydney.org/entry/ childrens_institutions_in_nineteenth_century

36 Juniper Hall was restored by the National Trust for the nation's bi-centenary in 1988 and sold to the Moran family in 2012. Like us, they are descendants of the original owners.

37 The Benevolent Society also established the Royal Hospital for Women, Paddington. The asylum became both Prince of Wales Hospital and Sydney Children's Hospital. See 'Randwick Asylum for Destitute Children: Historical Background, Archives and Records.'

records.nsw.gov.au/archives/collections-and-research/guides-and-indexes/randwick-asylumdestitute-children

38 Governor King to Johnson and Others, 7th August, 1800, see A. F. Austen (ed.), Select Documents in Australian Education (Melbourne: Pitman, 1972), pp. 2-3, cited by Sherington and Campbell, 'Education,' online.

39 Eight of the ten children of Thomas and Jane Kendall survived. The famous Australian poet, Henry Kendall, was their grandson.

40 Bishop Heber wrote many hymns, including: Holy, Holy, Holy, Lord God Almighty; The Son of God Goes Forth to War and the missionary hymn, From Greenland's Icy Mountains.

41 S. H. Selwyn, Reminiscences by Mrs S. H. Selwyn, 1809-1867, with an introduction by Enid A. Evans

[Auckland], Auckland War Memorial Museum Library, 1961, Typescript, p. 44, cited in Janet Crawford, '"Valuable Helpers": Women in the Melanesian Mission in the Nineteenth Century', anglicanhistory.org/oceania/selwyn_lectures1999.pdf

42 For example that having sexual intercourse with a virgin will cure Aids.

43 The Jesuits were expelled from Paraguay in 1767. They were suppressed by Pope Clement XIV in 1773 and lost their property. Their 23,000 members scattered, but Jesuits remained

active in Africa and Russia (outside of papal control). They were restored by Pope Sixtus V in 1841.

Anthony Van Dyck, 'A Brief History of the Jesuits'. http://faculty.fairfield.edu/jmac/sj/briefsjhistory.htm

44 Copyright Plate 22.2: Sue Ream (CC By3.0)

https://creativecommons.aug/licenses/by/3.0 via Wikimedia Space Commons

45 Israel Ministry of Foreign Affairs, 'Israel's War of Independence'

https://mfa.gov.il/MFA/AboutIsrael/History/Pages

46 Billy Graham, himself, said this on an old piece of news footage from 1959 that was shown on 3/7/2017 on the television program "Australian Story" by ABC Australia, during a program about 'Uncle Ossie'. This respected aboriginal elder, who (with his late wife) was converted at the 1959 crusade, is still pastoring a church at over 80 years of age.

47 Numbers, Facts and Trends Shaping Your World 8/11/2017, 'Orthodox Christians in the 21st Century'. Table 1. Figures for 1910 are based on Johnson, Todd and Zurlo (eds), World Christian Database (Centre for the Study of Global Christianity at Gordon-Conwell Theological Seminary), f/n. 1. Figures for 2010 are based on Pew Research Centre analyses, "Global Christianity: A Report on the

Size and Distribution of the World's Christian Population, 2011", https://www.pewforum.org/2011/12/19/gobal-christianity-exec/

Also by Deslee Campbell

The Topkapi Beggar
Voices From The Silence
Why a Roman Emperor Rebuilt Jerusalem and Jerash
Stones, Walls and Watchmen
Mothers in Israel
Ecclesia a Long Journey to Tomorrow

Watch for more at www.synagogueandchurch.com.

About the Author

Deslee Campbell, a former teacher of modern history, who worked in the field of educational psychology andcounselling.She has a Bachelor of Arts degree from the University of New South Wales, a Diploma in Education from the University of Sydney, and a Graduate Diploma in School Counselling from U.W.S/Nepean.She was has a Masters degree fromMacquarie University in early Christian Studies and a Phd from Sydney University.Deslee has visited Israel nine times, the first being in January 1970. During Passover 1990 Deslee was one of threeAustralians to visit the U.S.S.R. Since 1988 Deslee, and her late husband John, .they lived with their three sons and their adopted daughter in Sydney and attend a local Anglican Church in Sydney, Now widowed, Deslee has four children and three grandchildren.Her published works include the sequel novel, Love is a Journey, which follows Karen Evan's career as a nurse.With her son, Rev. Justin Campbell, she has co-authored a major 2-volume work in the mini-series Synagogue andChurch and her YouTube presentations can be viewed via the web addresshttp://www.synagogueandchurch.com

Read more at www.synagogueandchurch.com.